D1562177

Sex Radicals and the Quest for
Women's Equality

WOMEN IN AMERICAN HISTORY

Series Editors
Anne Firor Scott
Nancy A. Hewitt
Stephanie Shaw

A list of books in the series appears at the end of this book.

Sex Radicals and the Quest for Women's Equality

JOANNE E. PASSET

University of Illinois Press

URBANA AND CHICAGO

Library of Congress Cataloging-in-Publication Data
Passet, Joanne Ellen, 1954–
Sex radicals and the quest for women's equality / Joanne E. Passet.
p.   cm. — (Women in American history)
Includes bibliographical references and index.
ISBN 0-252-02804-x (cloth : alk. paper)
1. Free love—United States—History—19th century.
2. Sex customs—United States—History—19th century.
3. Sexual ethics—United States—History—19th century.
4. Feminism—United States—History—19th century.
5. Radicalism—United States—History—19th century.
I. Title. II. Series.
HQ967.U6P37   2003
306.7'0973'09034—dc21   2002009368

Contents

Illustrations follow page 90

Acknowledgments

FOR YEARS I HAVE struggled with the title of this book. Eyebrows raise when people learn about my research on free love and sex radicals, confirming that the terms remain as misunderstood today as they were in the past. I hope this work will shed some much-needed light on sex radicalism and its relationship to the nineteenth-century movement for women's rights.

Although the historian often feels as if she or he is laboring in isolation, works such as this are the products of many hands. Able archivists and librarians have eased the way by sharing their knowledge of collections, locating elusive documents, and arranging for countless photocopies and microfilm. I would like to extend my deepest appreciation to the staffs of the American Antiquarian Society, the Antiochiana Collection of Antioch College, Center for Archival Collections at Bowling Green State University, the Chicago Historical Society Library, the Cincinnati Historical Society, the Clinton County (Iowa) Historical Society, the Edward J. Miner Library at the University of Rochester, the Indiana Historical Society Library, the Indiana University Libraries, the Irvin L. Young Memorial Library (Whitewater, Wis.), the Kansas State Historical Society Library, the Kinsey Institute for Research in Sex, Gender, and Reproduction, the Labadie Collection at the University of Michigan, the Library Company of Philadelphia, the Manuscript Division of the Library of Congress, the Milwaukee Public Library, the Musselman Library at Bluffton College, the National Museum of American History, the Newberry Library, the Northwood (Iowa) Public Library, the Ohio Historical Society Library, the Rutherford B. Hayes Presidential Center, the Syracuse University Department of Special Collections, the University of Illinois Library, the Vermont Historical Society, the Western Reserve Historical Society Library, the Willard Public Library in Battle Creek, Mich., and the Wisconsin Historical Society Library and Archives. I would specifically like to acknowledge Ann Bowers, Nan J. Card, Joanne D. Chaison, Steve Charter, James Danky, Julie Herrada, Cornelia S. King, Harry Miller, Nina Myatt, Frank Quinn, and Edward C. Webber for so generously sharing their expertise and so patiently responding to my numerous questions.

Several institutions provided grants that enabled me to complete research travel to archives, manuscript repositories, and libraries throughout the nation. I am indebted to the American Antiquarian Society for a Kate B. and Hall J. Peterson Fellowship, to the Smithsonian Institution for a Short-Term Fellowship at the National Museum of American History, to the Kansas State Historical Society for an Alfred M. Landon Historical Research Grant, and to the History Department of the University of Wisconsin at Madison for a Departmental Research Grant and a Gerda Lerner Fellowship in Women's History. The Gladys Krieble Delmas Foundation provided a grant that enabled me to present research results at an annual meeting of the Society for the History of Authorship, Reading, and Publishing, and funding from Indiana University East covered the costs of photograph reproduction and permissions.

A number of colleagues have given generously of their time by reading and commenting on the dissertation, conference papers, and portions of the manuscript that evolved into this book. They include Linda Gordon, Jeanne Boydston, Paul Boyer, William J. Reese, Wayne A. Wiegand, Martin S. Blatt, Ellen DuBois, Rob Kennedy, and anonymous reviewers for the University of Illinois Press. Their critiques have been invaluable, however, I alone am responsible for any errors of fact or interpretation that remain in the text. My thanks also go to Rima D. Apple, Saundra Altman, Jesse Battan, Robert S. Fogarty, Wendy Gamber, Thomas Hamm, Charles LeWarne, John McClymer, James H. Madison, Laverne Nishihara, David Nordloh, Ronald Numbers, Barbara Clark Smith, Katherine Tomasek, and William Trollinger for helpful conversations about my research. Additionally, I appreciate the feedback given by audiences and commentators who heard portions of my work read before the American Literature Association, the Boydston/Gordon Dissertator Group at the University of Wisconsin at Madison (especially Ellen Baker, Tracey Deutsch, Laura McEnaney, Cindy Poe, Nancy Taylor, Lisa Tetrault, and Susan M. Wirka), the Center for Archival Collections Local History Conference, the Communal Studies Association, the Ohio Academy of History, the Organization of American Historians, the Popular Culture Association, the Rural Women's Studies Association, and the Society for the History of Authorship, Reading, and Publishing. A special note of thanks is extended to Susan O. Haswell and Dale E. Treleven for research assistance, and to my graduate assistant, Holly Ann Burt, for her extraordinary ability in mining the manuscript population census records for elusive individuals. I also wish to recognize Jeanette Hubbard Steinbeck, James B. Hardin, and Bill Stillman, for sharing information about and photographs of their relatives, and Richard P. Reece, for sharing information about the Berlin Heights Free Lovers. Finally, this book would not be possible without the capable editorial, production, and marketing staff at the University of Illinois Press.

Throughout this long process, family members and good friends—who seem like family—have encouraged my interest in U.S. women's history. I am especially thankful to Carole Bailey, Damiana Chavez, Mary Fell, Susan O. Haswell, Rob Kennedy, Mary Leech, Tom Munson, Barbara Orbach Natanson, and Judith Serebnick for their sympathetic ears, sage advice, housing and food during research trips, emotional support, attempts to help me lead a balanced life, and most importantly, their constant friendship. Thank you all!

Introduction

Whoever carries out the woman's rights movement, if successful,
must destroy some of the most cherished institutions of
civilization.
—Thomas L. Nichols and Mary Gove Nichols, *Nichols' Journal,*
1 October 1853

BETWEEN 1853 AND 1910, hundreds of American women and men embraced sex radical ideas despite the negative stigma often associated with "free love." As a sex radical dimension of the nineteenth-century movement for women's rights, they represent a bridge connecting ideas articulated by antebellum advocates of women's rights with twentieth-century feminists. At a time when many advocates of women's rights sought to build a broad coalition by avoiding controversial topics, sex radicals remained steadfast in their insistence upon a woman's right to control her body and to freely discuss such critical issues as contraception, marital sexual abuse (which they defined as emotional as well as physical maltreatment), and sex education. The open discussion of female sexuality, they believed, constituted the most effective strategy for the empowerment of women. To achieve this goal, geographically dispersed and often socially alienated sex radicals relied on print culture—books, pamphlets, and especially periodicals. Sustaining the movement for over five decades, sex radical publications spread their feminist agenda from coast to coast.

At its core a feminist movement, nineteenth-century sex radicalism is distinguished by its commitment to women's social and economic equality and right to reproductive choice. Arguing that marriage does not automatically mean having babies and that conception is not the sole object of sexual intercourse, sex radicals defended female sexual desire as a healthy phenomenon. They also fought to free women from the drudgery of household labor by advocating plans for cooperative kitchens and communal child care. Woman suffrage remained a lower priority primarily because sex radicals saw a

woman's right to control her body as a fundamental change that must pre-
cede political reforms.

This study examines the diffusion of feminist ideas among sex radical
women and men and their responses to those ideas between 1853 and 1910. It
does so from the perspective of sex radicals themselves, based primarily on
letters and articles they wrote for publication in twenty periodicals (see the
appendix). From the early 1850s, when advocates of free love first coalesced
into an identifiable social movement, until 1910, when many of the movement's pioneers had died, sex radicals relied on weekly and monthly periodicals to create and sustain their shared sense of identity. Emboldened by editors' dual commitment to women's sexual emancipation and free speech,
hundreds of women discussed their private experiences in this public setting.
Some women also served in editorial capacities, but a far larger number sustained the movement with their subscriptions, purchases of pamphlets, donations of money, and printed communications. In addition to finding their
voices, they discovered a supportive community of people who shared their
vision of a new social order based on equality.

In this work I use the term "sex radical" (except when those who took part
in this social movement purposely referred to themselves as "free lovers")
to describe the broad range of nineteenth-century women and men who did
not always call themselves free lovers but who nonetheless challenged customary beliefs about sexual relationships, the institution of marriage, and
women's lack of economic, legal, and social rights. "Free love" is a problematic term because of its contradictory meanings. Mainstream newspaper
editors and clergy, free love's most vocal critics, called anyone who deviated from customary ideals of proper behavior a "free lover."[1] Nineteenth-
century sex radicals further confused matters because they could not agree
on the term's application in daily life: for some it meant a lifelong and monogamous commitment to a member of the opposite sex, others envisioned
it as serial monogamy, a few advocated chaste heterosexual relationships except when children were mutually desired, and a smaller number defined it
as variety (multiple partners, simultaneously) in sexual relationships. Many
who called themselves free lovers were married yet denounced marriage as
an institution requiring women's subordination to men. Yet no matter what
their practical interpretation of free love, they shared two core convictions:
opposition to the idea of coercion in sexual relationships and advocacy of a
woman's right to determine the uses of her body.

Sex radicals did not stand alone in their critique of marriage and sexual
relations, but other nineteenth-century Americans who perceived marriage

as a flawed institution remained reluctant to call for its abolition. Some groups, like the Shakers, the Oneida Community, and the Latter-day Saints experimented with its form, while others campaigned for the liberalization of divorce laws.[2] As purists, sex radicals insisted that the governmental and ecclesiastical bodies responsible for the regulation of marriage had corrupted it beyond repair. True equality between the sexes could never exist, they asserted, so long as the church and state continued to prescribe the subordination of wives to their husbands.

This study joins a growing body of scholarship on nineteenth-century sex radicalism, but it is the first to explore women's active participation in the movement. Earlier scholars have approached sex radicalism from the perspective of its male leaders, most of whom were periodical editors who were repeatedly prosecuted for violating antiobscenity laws. Three of these studies, John C. Spurlock's *Free Love: Marriage and Middle-Class Radicalism in America, 1825–1860,* Hal D. Sears's *The Sex Radicals: Free Love in High Victorian America,* and Martin Blatt's *Free Love and Anarchism: The Biography of Ezra Heywood,* provide valuable insights into free love's core ideologies and the men who advanced them.[3] Spurlock, reconstructing the movement's leaders, ideas, and activities prior to 1860, portrays free lovers as an "ante-bellum bourgeoisie" who offered "some of the most uncompromising expressions of middle-class beliefs." Although his study does not include the Civil War years, he nonetheless posits that this movement and related expressions of social radicalism "became largely a matter of working-class organization and left behind the cultural concerns that had been central to the free love ideology."[4] Focusing on the postbellum era, Sears thoroughly documents the Kansas sex radicals responsible for making *Lucifer, the Light-Bearer* the most widely read of nineteenth-century sex radical periodicals. He tends, however, to minimize the reach and impact of its feminist message by arguing that "Victoria Woodhull's free-love agitation in the early seventies marked the end of the serious and widespread discussion of sexual alternatives in nineteenth-century America."[5] Blatt's carefully crafted biography of Ezra Heywood (1829–93) documents the role of one of the free love movement's leading individuals and illustrates how his life came to embody a core sex radical tenet—the rights of the individual.

Several of sex radicalism's most visible women—Mary Gove Nichols, Angela Heywood, and Victoria Woodhull—are discussed in these works, but they appear as aberrants who ultimately recanted their radical views, as victims of circumstance who faded from view, or as pawns of lovers, husbands, brothers, and fathers. For the most part, the hundreds of other women—grassroots feminists—who participated in this movement have remained hidden from view. By grassroots, I mean non-elites—members of the urban working class as well as those living on farms, ranches, and in small agricultural communities—whose voices seldom are heard in national-level debates. They are the individuals who comprised and sustained this loosely structured social movement for over five decades.

Like scholars of sex radicalism, historians of the nineteenth-century movement for women's rights also have overlooked all but the most well-known sex radical women. Focusing instead on women's activism on behalf of such important causes as woman suffrage, social purity reform, charity work, and racial equality, they have conveyed to readers an impression of sex radicalism as a marginalized movement championed by a few outspoken individuals whose ideas had little resonance with women nationwide.[6] Thus, the numerous historical works in which the 1850s sex radical Mary Gove Nichols makes a requisite appearance usually present her as a single-minded albeit colorful figure whose multifaceted reform career can be dismissed in a sentence or two.[7] Until we analyze the motives behind her embrace of sex radicalism, however, we cannot begin to grasp her role in creating and building a feminist consciousness in the women she reached through her medical practice and writings. The same is true for Victoria Woodhull. Historians have examined her brief role in the campaign for woman suffrage, her leadership among Spiritualists, her campaign for president of the United States in 1872, and sensational aspects of her personal life.[8] Dismissing Woodhull as a liability to the causes for which she worked, especially woman suffrage, they generally have not considered her role in disseminating feminist ideas to grassroots women.

This study is the first to provide a gendered analysis of the nineteenth-century sex radical movement. Previous works have portrayed sex radicals as unified in support of relatively static beliefs. But when gender is taken into account a more complex and nuanced understanding of the movement emerges. For several decades, sex radical men and women did share a commitment to women's reproductive autonomy, but, as chapter 7 reveals, significant gender and generational differences developed by the 1890s. Men, supporting Moses Harman's efforts to give *Lucifer* a scholarly appearance, attempted to shift sex radical discourse from an experiential to a philosophical and theoretical plane. Evoking eugenic logic, they defended the theory of variety in sexual partners and attempted to convince women that motherhood represented their primary responsibility. As more men wrote of breeding a better race, however, longtime sex radical women challenged the vision of a genetically based new world order in which patriarchy remained intact. Asserting their right to choose when and with whom they became mothers, female correspondents continued sending missives to *Lucifer* in which they decried the consequences of sexual abuse and excessive childbearing.

Historians have explored readers' correspondence with a variety of nineteenth-century periodicals, but this is the first work to examine the role of print culture in the circulation of sex radical ideas to and among geographically dispersed women.[9] Discouraged from attending lectures in which men discussed free love, they could nonetheless consume similar content through the numerous reform periodicals that entered their homes. Moreover, sex radical editors, committed to free speech and eager to fill their pages with reader contributions, invited female readers to write freely for publication. Promising to refrain from editorial censorship or condemnation, such editors as John Patterson, Victoria Woodhull, Lois Waisbrooker, and Moses Harman encouraged women to share their perspectives on such controversial questions as abortion, birth control, monogamy versus promiscuity, and female sexual desire—subjects that few others would broach so openly and freely. While such discussions may have appealed to a few men as a form of pornography, the seriousness with which most male correspondents discussed sexual topics suggests that the primary goal of uncensored communication was self-education and reform.

Many of the women who accepted, promulgated, and acted upon sex radical beliefs were rural and by no means economically privileged. Earlier accounts, in which such female sex radicals as Mary Gove Nichols and Victoria Woodhull appear as members of an urban avant-garde, obscure the fact that similar discussions about sexuality, marriage, and women's freedom occurred among non-elite women—midwestern and western women whose families struggled to make farm mortgage payments during years of drought and economic depression. Their letters provide numerous clues that make it possible to categorize them as non-elite, including references to their daily work, level of education (or lack thereof), financial struggles, and social interactions. In this context, "rural" includes people who lived in small farming communities and those who lived in the country and practiced agriculture, logging, or mining. Beginning in 1870, the federal population census defined rural as incorporated agricultural centers of less than twenty-five hundred residents. By that definition, the nation remained predominantly rural until 1920.[10] Many sex radicals had transient lifestyles, and when they moved from rural areas to cities they remained informed by the idea of agrarian individualism.

Other historians have explored efforts to contain nineteenth-century rural women's sexuality, but few manuscript materials survive to document the perspectives of the women themselves.[11] This study recovers some of their voices, preserved on the pages of a sex radical press that enjoyed its greatest popularity in predominantly agricultural states of the Midwest and Great Plains. In rural enclaves the belief in individual sovereignty remained a core value even during a postbellum era characterized by increasing government and corporate regulation. Rural residents accepted government intervention when it was to their benefit (for example, leveling the playing field in the market place by regulating railroads), but they consistently disdained government intrusion into their private lives.

Residents of rural communities ranged on a spectrum from well-to-do landowners and merchants to tenant farmers struggling to subsist on drought-stricken lands. But economic depressions in 1857, between 1873 and 1877, in the late-1880s, and between 1893 and 1897 made it difficult for many to sustain their sense of well-being. Feeling powerless and alienated culturally, economically, and geographically, rural women and men constituted a receptive audience for organizations (such as the Patrons of Husbandry [Grange], farmers' alliances, and the People's party) dedicated to addressing their economic, legal, and social dependence and for social movements that promised to alleviate the plight of the oppressed. Appealing to economically marginalized women and men, sex radicalism offered a strategy by which they could challenge the root of their legal and economic oppression: free women from sexual slavery and they would give birth to healthy and wanted children who would in turn redeem the race.

This book also expands our understanding of the religious traditions informing nineteenth-century sex radicalism. Scholars tend to classify sex radicals as freethinkers, seldom taking into account the millennialistic and Spiritualistic ideas they embraced.[12] As chapter 1 and chapter 3 reveal, a number of antebellum sex radicals believed that the Second Coming of Christ would occur when humans had advanced to a state of perfection individually and in their relationships with one another. A few openly denied the existence of God, but many others rejected the authoritarianism and ritual associated with organized expressions of Christianity. The church in conjunction with the state, they believed, had corrupted marriage by granting men patriarchal power and implicitly sanctioning the undisciplined indulgence of their sexual desires within marriage. Thus, sex radicals reasoned, the long-awaited millennium could never occur so long as that institution resulted in sexually abused wives unfit to bear healthy children.

Antebellum Roots of Sex Radicalism

Sex radical beliefs had their origins in antebellum economic currents and around several strands of religious thought. Born in the early nineteenth century, pioneers in the sex radical movement grew to adulthood in the aftermath of the War of 1812, a time when many American men and women believed they possessed a unique and brief opportunity to shape the young nation's institutions and hence its destiny.[13] Religious revivals, advances in transportation, increased geographic mobility, and the transition to a market economy encouraged this conviction. The latter fostered faith in individualism, but the need to conduct business transactions with distant creditors and to participate in remote markets also heightened awareness of the artificiality of relationships and contributed to the dissolution of established patterns of behavior in urban and rural environments. Even as Jacksonian-era politics reinforced the ideal of individual sovereignty and, in turn, agrarian individualism, economic realities increasingly meant that very few Americans could attain these ideals.[14]

An inability to control their personal economic circumstances left many feeling anxious, isolated, and insecure and led them to focus instead on attaining salvation. Thousands of Americans found inspiration in the powerful preaching of Charles Grandison Finney and other revivalists during the 1820s and 1830s.[15] Their portrayal of a loving God who made each sinner responsible for his or her own salvation convinced many women and men that they not only possessed the power but also had a mandate to eradicate the individual sins that manifested themselves in the form of disease and social disorder. Revivals had a democratizing message that affected not only those in an emerging middle class but also those "whom the market revolution had either bypassed or hurt." Presenting sin as a problem to be resolved, not as a permanent condition, revivalists encouraged millennialism (belief that the kingdom of God on earth was imminent) and perfectionism (belief that people could achieve sanctification while on earth).[16]

A severe economic depression, beginning in 1837 and persisting into the 1840s, an apparent powerlessness on the part of politicians in either major party to turn the economy around, and an increased awareness of social and political inequalities further fostered desire for immediate solutions and increased men's and women's susceptibility to schemes that promised relief, be they secular or religious, individual or corporate, immediate or in anticipation of the "Good Time Coming." As antebellum reformers and social philosophers attempted to construct solutions, they were guided by two seemingly opposite social visions—one centered on individual freedom, the other on cooperation. Those who placed their trust in the redeeming value of individual liberty directed their efforts toward freeing and perfecting the body through a variety of health reforms that focused on diet, dress, and temperance, while those who blamed external factors for human suffering focused their energies on the reform of social order and looked with great interest to such communal-living experiments as the French-inspired Fourierist phalanxes, the Oneida Community's settlement in New York, and to numerous other smaller ventures scattered throughout the nation. The boundaries between the two impulses remained fluid prior to the Civil War, and people moved back and forth with ease, propelled by their yearning for perfection and their belief in the millennium.[17]

Several core ideas of the nineteenth-century sex radical movement coalesced in this environment: women's inherent equality with men, the necessity to emancipate women from flawed institutions that robbed them of that equality, and their right to determine when and with whom they had children. The first—women's inherent equality with men—drew strength from several religious traditions.[18] Revivalists, with their messages about individual sanctification and spiritual equality before God, prompted women to question the social, legal, and economic inequalities they experienced in marriage. Wives, comparing themselves with unmarried women, became keenly aware that no matter how autonomous a single woman might be, marriage required the complete surrender of her independence. The Quaker belief in the Inner Light—the idea that a divine presence enlightened and guided each soul—encouraged the idea of women's equality. And although it did not gain widespread acceptance until the late 1840s, Spiritualism—a movement based on a belief in the ability of the living to communicate with the dead—empowered women to speak and provided a forum in which they, as mediums between the two worlds, could offer critiques of marriage.[19]

Several antebellum currents provided support for a second sex radical conviction—that marriage was a flawed institution because it perpetuated women's unequal status by rendering them a form of property and destroying their health through sexual abuse and repeated childbirth. Beginning in the 1830s, Garrisonian abolitionism helped awaken women's feminist consciousness by increasing their awareness of the theoretical similarities between chattel slavery and marital slavery.[20] And as chapter 3 illustrates, some sex radicals—influenced by Garrisonian abolitionism—regarded as inseparable the intertwined issues of slave emancipation and self-emancipation. At the same time, several health reformers linked sexuality with disease and embarked on a crusade to help both women and men overcome this problem. The minister-turned-health reformer Sylvester Graham (1794–1851) had a significant influence on antebellum Americans who yearned to improve their health.[21] Pointing to such stimulants as coffee, tea, meat, and spices as factors promoting sin and lust, Graham regarded sexual excitement—mental as well as physical—as a source of debilitation and something even married couples would be wise to avoid. Stopping short of condemning marital sexual intercourse, Graham urged men and women to adopt a stimulant-free vegetable diet, which he believed would facilitate self-control. Combined with the routineness of seeing each other's naked bodies, he espoused, this would dampen ardor, decrease instances of sexual abuse, and result in fewer and healthier children.

Many of those who regarded church- and state-sanctioned marriage as flawed nonetheless nurtured an idealized vision of relations between the sexes and endowed alternative forms of marriage with an almost redemptive power. The ideas of the Scandinavian mystic, philosopher, scientist, and theologian Emanuel Swedenborg (1688–1772) gained currency in New England during the 1830s and 1840s and encouraged this conviction.[22] Sex radicals found Swedenborg's theories about spiritual affinities (articulated in *Conjugal Love and Its Chaste Delights*) especially compelling because they offered an elevated notion of sexual love, one in which souls, not only bodies, united in harmony.

Swedenborg's emphasis on communication with the spirit world also helped prepare antebellum Americans for Fourierism and Spiritualism in the 1840s and 1850s. Claiming to be a revelator, he wrote that "the purpose of the spiritual and natural creation was to form a heaven from the human race."[23] The author Henry James Sr. and others who later offered critiques of marriage embraced Swedenborg's theory of regeneration—the concept that the human race would be restored to a higher, more perfect state through the birth of children to divinely sanctioned couples. Swedenborg, along with the Spiritualists, heightened receptiveness to the concept of spiritual affinities (the idea that each man and woman had a divinely intended mate) and thus a highly idealized vision of what marriage could be. But, they pragmatically realized, people sometimes erred in choosing husbands and wives, and indissoluble marriage prevented them from rectifying their mistakes and moving on toward a higher stage of progress—and thus the millennium. Such conditions, antebellum sex radicals concluded, warranted an aggressive challenge to the institution of marriage.

Reinforced by such convictions, some antebellum women and men attempted to perfect marriage by altering its form. In New York City during the 1830s, for instance, the self-styled Prophet Matthias successfully recruited a small following of men and women "caught in bewildering times" who believed that altering sexual and family norms would remedy problems wrought by economic and social turmoil.[24] That experiment ended with a sensational murder trial and accusations of sexual crime. Nonetheless, antebellum Americans remained receptive to the possibilities of cooperative life. In the 1840s they could choose from a profusion of communal experiments inspired by either charismatic religious figures or philosophical concepts.

Virtually all utopian reformers struggled to resolve two critical issues—ownership of property and the inequalities inherent in the institution of marriage.[25] The Shaker belief in celibacy, the Latter-day Saints' practice of polygyny (having two or more wives or concubines simultaneously), and the Oneida Community's system of complex marriage (in which each male was considered married to each female) represent three alternatives to lifelong monogamous marriage sanctioned by church and state.[26] The Shakers, concluding that humans had not yet developed the ability to control sexual passion, dissolved the nuclear family and created in its place an egalitarian community in which residents were monitored to guard against masturbation, bestiality, and other forms of sexual expression deemed undesirable. The Mormons, often regarded as promiscuous because of their practice of polygyny, in fact regarded procreation as the primary objective of sexual relations. And under the leadership of John Humphrey Noyes, the Oneida Community (1847–81) placed sexuality and reproduction under communal control.[27]

In contrast to Noyes, sex radicals embraced a third conviction: a woman, as birth giver, should have the right to determine when and with whom she had children. Challenging the notion that a wife must submit to her husband's sexual demands, they asserted that the decision to engage in sexual relations must be mutual. Until such a time, they reasoned, women would continue to suffer from gynecological ailments related to repeated childbirth, their poor health would render them ineffective as mothers, and their children, bearing a legacy of disease and defects, would negate any possibility of regenerating society and inaugurating the millennium.

The Emergence of the "Free Love" Movement at Mid-Century

Many of the American followers of the French socialist Charles Fourier (1772–1837) focused on his promise of a new economic structure, some valued his scientific theories, and others responded to the communitarian order and symmetry of his plan.[28] But until the late 1840s few knew of his ideas for the sexual reorganization of society. Fourier's American publicist, Albert Brisbane, intentionally omitted Fourier's critique of marriage from his *Social Destiny of Man; or, Association and Reorganization of Industry* (1840), which became "the founding text of the American movement," and from his subsequent lectures, translations of Fourier's works, and journal, *The Phalanx*, because he knew it would detract from Fourierism's economic message.[29]

After prosperity returned to the nation in the mid-1840s, many of those who had looked to Fourierism as a model for economic reform began losing interest; however, a group of Swedenborgian-influenced Fourierists shifted their attention from Fourier's economic schemes to his plans for the sexual reform of society.[30] Several—among them Henry James Sr.; the attorney, abolitionist, and anarchist Stephen Pearl Andrews (1812–86); Albert Brisbane; the author and hydropathist Mary Gove Nichols; her husband, the author and editor Thomas Low Nichols; and a physician named Marx Edgeworth Lazarus—gathered in New York City, where they became instrumental in publicizing reformist theories that quickly became identified as free love.

Fourier, who died before his ideas circulated widely in the United States, blamed "civilization" for separating people's physical natures from their moral beings. False institutions, he reasoned, imposed restraints that prevented people from pursuing their attractions, whether in occupational choice or in the selection of a marriage partner.[31] In an attempt to bring this critique to light, James translated Victor Hennequin's Fourierist-inspired tract, *Love in the Phalanstery*, in 1849, thereby introducing thousands of American readers to Fourier's sexual theories. Resulting in polarized opinions about marriage, this work initiated a heated debate that dominated much of the early 1850s.

In 1852, one of James's associates, Marx Edgeworth Lazarus, published a tract entitled *Love vs. Marriage, Pt. 1*, in which he portrayed marriage as incompatible with social harmony and the root cause of mental and physical impairments. Like others in his circle, Lazarus (born in 1822 to a prominent North Carolina family) sought improved health through myriad channels, including vegetarianism, water cure, Spiritualism, and mesmerism (a belief that magnetic forces passing between two people had the power to heal). Indulging his penchant for mystical theories and social philosophies, he also immersed himself in Transcendentalism and Fourierism. Despite having rejected his own Christian and Jewish heritage, Lazarus laced his writings with the religious rhetoric of his youth, a factor that rendered his radical ideas all the more comprehensible and tolerable to a population steeped in evangelical Christianity.[32]

Love vs. Marriage triggered great concern among newspaper editors and members of the clergy because they feared it represented a plot to transmit Fourier's allegedly aberrant sexual theories to unsuspecting men and women. Fourier believed that everyone (whether married or single) had the right to a "sexual minimum" and endorsed the idea of variety in sexual partners. Additionally, he did not limit his theories to heterosexual relations but advocated the universal gratification of desire regardless of the sexual object (so long as the parties involved participated willingly and without becoming abusive).[33]

Horace Greeley, the editor of the *New York Tribune* and an early supporter of Fourier's economic theories, denounced *Love vs. Marriage* as part of a systematic plan to abolish the institution of marriage. Greeley had cause for alarm. The appearance of Lazarus's work unleashed restraints that had inhibited the open discussion of Fourier's ideas about sexual reform. Even more important, its publication provided nascent sex radicals with an economic critique of marriage that highlighted gender inequalities and with a vocabulary for critiquing the sexual dimension of marriage. It also offered communitarianism as a potential space within which sex radical theories could be perfected and paved the way for the melding of Fourierism with the anarchism of Josiah Warren.[34]

Considered by many as the father of American anarchism, Warren (1798–1874) had resided for a short time at Robert Owen's utopian community of New Harmony in southern Indiana during the 1820s. Disillusioned, he developed several of his own theories, among them "individual sovereignty," in which he held the individual to be "'at liberty to dispose of his or her person, and time, and property in any manner in which his or her feelings or judgment may dictate, without involving the persons or interests of others.'"[35] Warren first attempted to implement his ideas at Equity, a utopian community established near Cincinnati, Ohio, but by mid-century he had relocated to the community of Modern Times on Long Island, New York. Warren adopted a cautious stance toward free love, arguing that it was unwise to make sudden changes to the institution of marriage.[36] But while he refrained from applying his theories of laissez faire to marriage, his disciples did not.

Responses to *Love vs. Marriage* sparked a several-months-long debate in the *New York Tribune* by three participants—James, Andrews, and Greeley—all of whom had been active in Fourierist circles during the 1840s.[37] Greeley defended indissoluble marriage with reiterations of conventional religious and moral teachings, Andrews advocated the abolition of marriage, and James sought a middle ground that recommended monogamous and lifelong marriages yet acknowledged the need for more liberalized divorce laws until such time as people could exercise greater wisdom in choosing mates. Building on the momentum created by Lazarus, the three men drew public attention to such heady questions as the definition of marriage, the role of the church and state in its governance, and the rights of women and children. The crux of the debate, however, was the question of whether the family or the individual constituted the nucleus of society. Such ideas resonated with many men and women who eagerly followed the Andrews-Greeley-James debate because they concurred that marriage suffered from an absence of love, compounded by the institution's indissoluble nature, women's economic, political, and social inequality, and the adultery, marital rape, and prostitution that all too frequently contaminated it. Those who willingly embraced the label "free lover" agitated for these issues and more for the remainder of the century.

Periodization: Sex Radicalism across Six Decades

Nineteenth-century reform movements progressed through several stages of development, including the creation of a collective consciousness, the clarification of a vision and goals, education and recruitment, and finally politicization.[38] Each is tempered by opposition that, if strong enough, may inhibit or even squelch a movement's further development. Because participants in a social movement often coalesce around a charismatic leader, it also may splinter or flounder if a leader suddenly disappears or is challenged and consequently loses charisma. Yet movements can withstand even this, remaining dormant until another leader emerges. Such was the case with nineteenth-century sex radicalism.

Between 1853 and 1910, the sex radical movement evolved through four stages, some of which blended into the next. During the first stage, which extended from 1853 until 1870, sex radicals coalesced as a social movement and print culture enabled them to develop a collective consciousness. Several events in the late 1840s helped spur this development: the establishment of an organized movement for women's rights (marked by the Seneca Falls Women's Rights convention), the popularization of Spiritualism, and the American publication of Hennequin's *Love in the Phalanstery*. Steeped in abolitionism and sympathetic to the plight of chattel slaves, many antebellum sex radicals nonetheless regarded the abolition of women's slavery in marriage as a higher priority than the elimination of African American slavery because they believed that the former encouraged men's tendency to dominate others. Revolutions in Europe and subsequent emigration further contributed to the coalescence of sex radicalism as a social movement, but it was the emergence of a sex radical press in the 1850s that gave form to the movement. Through this forum, sex radicals articulated, clarified, debated, and promoted their ideas.

During the second stage, which spanned the 1870s and 1880s, sex radicals found their movement tempered by opposition. Periodical editors risked prosecution and imprisonment for publishing frank discussions about sexual topics and, as a consequence, found themselves the frequent targets of the social purity reformer and censor Anthony Comstock. This stage was peopled by such vivid personalities as Victoria Woodhull, Tennessee Claflin, Ezra Heywood, and Moses Harman, each of whom defied Comstock and his lieutenants on numerous occasions by publishing materials deemed obscene. In consequence, leaders of the organized movement for woman suffrage distanced themselves from sex radicalism during the 1870s. Its controversial reputation, they feared, might hinder their efforts to cultivate perceptions of woman suffrage as a respectable cause. As chapter 4 illustrates, lectures by the charismatic Woodhull and the widespread dissemination of sex radical periodicals consequently became all the more critical in dispelling myths constructed about sex radicalism and in recruiting women and men throughout the nation to the movement.

Politicized during the 1880s and 1890s, sex radicals in the movement's third stage challenged government's power to regulate their private lives and to circumscribe their freedom of expression. In the process, readers came to regard such sex radical editors as Moses Harman, Ezra Heywood, and Lois Waisbrooker as martyrs to the cause of sex radicalism and therefore eagerly consumed their words and accounts of their activities on the pages of the sex radical press. As chapter 6 reveals, their prosecution transformed one regional paper, *Lucifer, the Light-Bearer,* into the national voice of sex reform. During this phase, some sex radicals also turned to alternative political parties in the hope that their platforms would lead to women's social and economic equality. Often, such activities instead heightened their anarchistic sympathies.

The nineteenth-century sex radical movement began to fracture and lose momentum during its fourth phase, which extended from the 1890s to 1910. Beginning in the 1890s, men increasingly touted eugenics as a higher priority than women's sexual emancipation. As chapter 7 portrays, gender and generational tensions developed among veteran female sex radicals, men, and the "New Women" who embraced the movement in the 1890s. Shaped by different cultural milieus, the latter had more in common with male sex radicals who embraced eugenics than they did with women whose sex radicalism had antebellum roots. By 1910, the movement's ranks were decimated by infirmity and death, making it impossible for those who survived to sustain it or its press.

Sex Radical Periodicals and Their Readers

Several characteristics define a sex radical periodical. Most championed a number of libertarian and reform causes but also were recognized by nineteenth-century Americans as sites that not only tolerated but also encouraged discussions of free love. As with many nineteenth-century reform publications, those devoted to sex radicalism had a precarious existence, and editors often struggled to find enough money to purchase type, ink, and paper. Moreover, the necessity of moving a press from one community to another or the legal battles and subsequent jailing of an editor for violating obscenity laws meant occasional gaps in the appearance of these weeklies and monthlies. No single publication spanned the entire period, yet the extant issues of the twenty titles I have studied cumulatively provide a window into the lives and ideas of sex radicals across six decades.

The periodicals examined in this study hold the key to understanding the extent of sex radicalism's reach in nineteenth-century America. Unlike such movements as woman suffrage and temperance (with their state and national suffrage societies and Woman's Christian Temperance Union), sex radicalism's inherent anarchism inhibited the formation of national or even long-lived regional organizations, and therefore there are no institutional records to document membership.[39] Many who held sex radical beliefs kept their convictions secret and often resided in a community for years without knowledge of neighbors who shared their convictions. Editors of sex radical periodicals, however, helped foster a sense of community by publishing reader communications ranging in length from a few lines to several columns. Most required authors to identify themselves and their places of residence.

Preserving in print the conversations among sex radicals, the periodicals examined in this study represent unique sources for exploring women's and men's participation in this movement. Beginning with *Nichols' Journal of Health, Water-Cure, and Human Progress* in 1853, the only time period not represented extends from 1860 to 1864, when sex radical editors ceased publishing out of increased fear over wartime censorship of subversive publications. As the longest-lived paper circulating to the largest number of states, *Lucifer, the Light-Bearer* featured letters from readers living in more states (thirty-six) and nations (nine) than did any of the other publications (see the appendix). Because of the large volume of letters submitted to these periodicals over a fifty-eight-year period (1853–1910), I took "snapshots" of 3,439 letters written by 1,751 readers, a sample from each decade under consideration (see the appendix).

Writing from the privacy of their homes, yet for public consumption, sex radical women spoke freely about such issues as marital sexual abuse, infanticide, and abortion because they regarded these periodicals as "safe" spaces.[40] For many of these women, the act of writing to sex radical periodicals represents a form of confession that, according to the French social philosopher Michel Foucault, is a ritual Western culture relies on for the "production of truth."[41] The graphic revelations of sexual experiences shared on the pages of these publications helped shatter the predominant myth of marital and domestic tranquility. Over time these women's exchanges with one another through print encouraged them to question their rights as married women, helped to alleviate their sense of isolation, and fostered the construction of new social worlds with other readers of the same periodicals.

Overview of Chapters

Chapter 1 illustrates how the literary and reform career of Mary Gove Nichols uniquely prepared her to introduce sex radical theories to antebellum women. Her work as a water-cure practitioner and health reformer helped construct her sex radical identity even as it uniquely positioned her to disseminate sex radical ideas to women.

Chapter 2 surveys the history of the sex radical press and the demographics of its readership across six decades. Exploring the printed texts through which mid-century women encountered sex radical concepts, it documents the extent to which they participated in the sex radical movement and reveals how sex radical periodicals raised women's consciousness about their rights and encouraged a sense of unity and purpose among the movement's geographically dispersed constituents.

Chapter 3 reveals the challenges utopian socialists faced when they attempted to implement an alternative social order in Berlin Heights, Ohio. An egalitarian society, theirs entailed women governing the uses of their bodies, owning property, keeping their names, having custody of their children, and having opportunities to achieve economic self-sufficiency. Female free lovers also challenged efforts by the dominant culture and male free lovers to define white American women's sexuality by boldly sharing accounts of marital rape and emotional abuse in a monthly entitled *Social Revolutionist.*

When opponents target a radical movement's charismatic leaders, constituents often rally to their support. This is exemplified in chapter 4. Beginning with an examination of the controversial and complex life of Victoria

Woodhull, it portrays her as outspoken and willing to sacrifice social standing for the cause of women's rights. Such actions prompted hundreds of women—many of whom lived in rural communities in the north-central United States—to view her as a martyr.

Further underscoring the significance of Spiritualism, anarchism, hydropathy, and third-party politics to the sex radical movement, chapter 5 illustrates paths leading two nineteenth-century women to sex radical feminism. Opposed to the monopolistic powers of organized religion, politics, and medicine, this amalgam of nineteenth-century reform movements provided such women as Lois Waisbrooker and Juliet Stillman Severance with opportunities for geographic mobility, economic self-sufficiency, and access to a network of reform-minded women and men.

Chapter 6 examines sex radical constructions of freedom by focusing on responses to the highly publicized free marriage of the *Lucifer* staff members Lillian Harman and Edwin Walker in 1886. As individualist anarchists, they believed women could never be free so long as the state-licensed and church-sanctioned institution of marriage perpetuated sexual inequality. Recurring drought and economic depression in the 1880s and 1890s not only heightened rural interest in individualist anarchism but also influenced the development of sex radical theories about the role of the state in regulating private life. With its predominantly midwestern and western readership in the 1880s and 1890s, *Lucifer*'s columns thus shed important light on rural sex radical women's involvement in nineteenth-century individualist anarchism.

As chapter 7 reveals, urban and rural individualist anarchists had different priorities when it came to the subject of freedom for women. Gender and generational differences also began to permeate sex radical discourse by the turn of the nineteenth century, as sex radical men and a new generation of sex radical women co-opted the movement. Disappointing veteran sex radical women, they abandoned their call for women's emancipation and instead embraced eugenics as a solution to the nation's social and economic woes. As their decades-long debate about a woman's right to control her body illustrates, nothing is more political than the personal.

1. Revelations from a Life

The first most earnest advocates of individuality and affectional
freedom—Dr. Nichols and Mary S. Gove Nichols—have done a
work in the field of agitation and real Social Science, which can
never be lost.

—*Age of Freedom*, 11 March 1858

IN SEPTEMBER 1855, Henry B. Blackwell spent a Sunday afternoon reading
the recently published novel *Mary Lyndon; or, Revelations of a Life*.[1] Touted
as the *Uncle Tom's Cabin* for women, this fictionalized autobiography recounts the tragic life of a "victim to customs which time, and reason and
religion, have unitedly served to sanctify."[2] Its heroine, whom Blackwell and
many other readers immediately recognized as the multifaceted reformer
Mary Gove Nichols, struggles throughout her life to overcome the disabili-
ties she associates with being female and married—sexual abuse, repeated
pregnancies, ill health, and the absence of legal rights to children, earnings,
and property. Through hard work and determination, by 1850 she gains both
entrée into New York City reform and literary circles and a well-deserved
reputation as a physician for women. Nonetheless, Blackwell and his wife,
Lucy Stone, who ranked among the leading advocates of women's rights, saw
in *Mary Lyndon* proof that an impressionable Mary Gove Nichols had suc-
cumbed to free love and feared that she would in turn infect her predominantly female and unsuspecting readers.

Blackwell and Stone saw free love as the antithesis of women's rights, yet
Mary Gove Nichols and other antebellum women and men who adopted free
love in theory, if not in practice, saw its primary plank—a woman's right to
control her body—as the key to women's full equality. The feminist pioneer
Elizabeth Cady Stanton concurred that the "whole question of women's
rights turns on the pivot of the marriage relation," yet most advocates of
women's rights generally avoided the topic.[3] Undeterred, free lovers advanced
their feminist agenda at a variety of meetings and in publications. The con-
troversies their actions generated ensured that sex radical ideas ultimately

circulated to an audience well beyond the northeastern, middle-class, urban intellectuals with whom they originated. The life of Mary Gove Nichols, an important pioneer in the dissemination of those ideas to antebellum women, illustrates one woman's evolution as a sex radical. As an author, health reformer, and Spiritualist, her quest for self-knowledge, individual empowerment, and health led her into the center of New York City's reform-minded free love community. Once in their midst, she quickly became a symbol of the movement's most potent threat: its potential appeal to women had the power to destabilize society's gendered order. Demonized by free love's critics, she ultimately abandoned cause and country, yet the ideas she circulated lived on in the minds of her readers—many of them female.

Revelations from a Life

Born to an economically marginal New Hampshire family in 1810, Mary Sargeant Neal grew to womanhood in the aftermath of the War of 1812.[4] There was, according to the historian Arthur Bestor, "something extraordinary about the moment then present, that the opportunity of influencing the future which it proffered was a unique opportunity, never to be repeated so fully again."[5] Like many others who came of age during that era, Mary Neal's spiritual beliefs evolved as she encountered several religious traditions, each of which reinforced the notion of an individual empowered to act by virtue of her or his direct relationship to a divine being. Restiveness, compounded by a variety of physical maladies, led the intellectually hungry young woman to embark on a highly individualized quest for spiritual light and physical health. Neither the beliefs of her freethinking father nor her strict Calvinistic mother suited Mary Neal's inquisitive and creative mind. Even conversion at a Finneyite-inspired revival in the mid-1820s did not allay the loneliness and sense of isolation she felt in the rural New Hampshire and Vermont communities of her youth. Turning to books for solace and inspiration, Mary Neal encountered a Quaker schoolbook entitled *The Monitor*. Captivated by the history and description of the Society of Friends, the imaginative young girl adopted Quaker habits of dress and speech long before her first encounter with a Friend. Quaker theology, with its emphasis on the Inner Light, reinforced Mary Neal's nascent interest in individual autonomy. It also provided consolation to a young woman who frequently regarded herself as an outsider.[6] Drawing strength from the sense of belonging to a larger community—the Quakers—she became even more interested in becoming one after she encountered a strong-minded Quaker wife who spoke freely, intelligently, and equally to her husband.[7]

An 1831 marriage to a conservative Quaker hatter named Hiram Gove led to Mary Gove's disillusionment with both the Quaker lifestyle and marriage and reinforced the urgency of her quest for physical salvation and personal autonomy. Suffering from tuberculosis (known in the nineteenth-century United States as consumption), Mary Gove endured five pregnancies—with only one live birth—during the first ten years of marriage.[8] Her resentment and frustration grew when her possessive and jealous husband (many years her senior) attempted to stifle her intellectual curiosity and literary aspirations by restricting her access to books and thinking people.[9] Those experiences, enhanced by the reading of medical and legal texts that she borrowed secretly from sympathetic lawyers and physicians in her community, contributed to Mary Gove's development into an advocate for women's rights.[10] Seeking to exercise some control over her life, she persisted in medical study and experimentation, treating herself and her daughter Elma (born in 1832) as the need arose.

At the onset of a devastating economic depression that began in 1837 and spanned five years, the Gove family attempted to improve their financial condition by moving from Weare, New Hampshire, to Lynn, Massachusetts. Prosperity eluding him, Hiram Gove joined other faltering heads of households by increasingly depending on his wife's ability to supplement his declining income with her earnings from sewing, selling stories, and conducting a school for young girls. In addition to using her money to pay the family's living expenses, he applied it toward payment of debts he had accrued prior to their marriage.[11] As her ability to earn money grew, Mary Gove gained a greater understanding of the limits of a wife's power: no matter how successful a woman became, her husband retained the legal right to control her earnings and her body.

Unable to alter the economic currents that buffeted them, the Goves joined thousands of antebellum Americans in seeking to rid their bodies of imperfections. In the fall of 1837 an attentive Mary Gove listened to the minister-turned-health reformer Sylvester Graham (1794–1851) lecture in Lynn about the effect of diet on health.[12] Enthusiastically embracing his recommended prohibitions on alcohol, meat, and sexual indulgence, she became one of his most ardent disciples: within a few months of his visit to Lynn she had converted the students in her school to a Graham diet and had begun offering them lessons in anatomy and physiology. Dr. Harriot K. Hunt, who visited the school in 1838, considered Mary Gove fanatical: "This is frequently the case with the downright ultras; they ruin their own health, and then prescribe rules for everybody."[13]

In Grahamism, with its emphasis on the conservation of energy, Mary

Gove believed she had discovered a key to restoring women's health. So long as women and men regarded marriage as a fully sanctioned site for men's physical demands, she reasoned, women would suffer the consequences— sexual abuse, physical illnesses, and stillborn or sickly offspring. Freed from an obsession with the act of coition, however, they could realize the reformatory and redemptive potential of their sexual natures.[14] Men alone, she contended, were powerless to effect this change because they lacked woman's greater ability to control sexual urges. Defying convention, she insisted upon a woman's right to refuse a man's sexual demands—even if he was her husband. Thus, her earliest vision of women's rights, while labeled "free love," in reality was based on chastity, not promiscuous indulgence.

Male reformers like Sylvester Graham risked being accused of improprieties when they spoke about health-related topics to female audiences, a factor that led to the inauguration of Gove's career as an itinerant lecturer. Aware of the anatomy lessons she offered in Lynn, the health reformer William Alcott invited her to deliver a ten-week course of lectures on health to the Boston Ladies Physiological Society in the fall of 1838. Gove accepted, insisting that she had "no theory of women's rights to promote," but she nonetheless heightened audience awareness of "the wrongs of women . . . destroyed health, wrecked constitution, and shortened lives." Exploring "all manner of reforms" and social philosophies, she began to construct her critique of the institution of marriage.[15]

With her first series of engagements in Boston pronounced a success and her anxiety about lecturing alleviated, Gove embarked on a tour throughout New England and the mid-Atlantic states. As the women's rights lecturer Lucy Stone had discovered, lecturing could be a profitable occupation for a woman: in 1854 she made more money in one week than her husband, Henry Blackwell, had in the previous four years.[16] Lured by the prospect of a lucrative source of income, Hiram Gove withdrew objections to his wife's new venture and accompanied her as a guardian and collector of gate receipts. Motivated by her childhood experiences and a strong sense of mission, the plainly attired woman commenced a campaign against tight lacing. A competent speaker, Gove thrived on the lecture circuit: "fluent and correct in expression," speaking "with enthusiasm and power." Defying social conventions, she demonstrated the harmful consequences of tight corsets by lacing herself into one—albeit over her clothing—before a large audience of women and men. To Gove, the use of corsets represented far more than an ill-advised attempt to appear fashionable: even as a teenaged girl she had comprehended that the use of corsets stifled a female's mind *and* body, or in her words, they "crowded my soul." Criticisms of Gove's frank lectures fueled her determination to save other young girls from a similar fate. They also fed her sense of martyrdom: "the world misunderstands and abuses me but I shall yet have a *name* and a *place* among the benefactors of our race."[17]

Because of her success as a lecturer, 1839 began rather grimly with Mary Gove's expulsion from the conservative Weare Monthly Meeting of the Society of Friends. Publicity about her expulsion, however, resulted in her friendship with a progressive Quaker editor named Joseph S. Wall, and by year's end she had earned a regional reputation as a medical authority, lecturer, editor, and author.[18] In addition to defending Gove in editorials he published in *The Reformer,* Wall made her coeditor of a new publication, the *Health Journal and Advocate of Physiological Reform* (sent to subscribers of the recently defunct *Graham Journal and Advocate of Physiology*). As had Sylvester Graham, Gove published an antimasturbation tract (albeit anonymously) entitled *Solitary Vice: An Address to Parents and Those Who Have Care of Children.* Gaining confidence in her medical knowledge, she also published four pseudonymously attributed articles in the prestigious *Boston Medical and Surgical Journal.*[19]

Travels as an itinerant lecturer provided Mary Gove with additional glimpses of women's health concerns and problems. Encountering wives who suffered from numerous gynecological problems—frequent miscarriages, prolapsed uteruses, venereal diseases, and complications from abortions—she concluded that those ailments clearly represented the unnecessary by-products of male-dominated marriage. The solution, she reasoned, was for sexual relations to be consensual. On a personal level, she yearned for freedom from her sexually demanding husband. Empowered by the knowledge that she could earn a satisfactory income on the lecture circuit and through the sale of her written work, Mary Gove left him. Taking Elma, she returned to her parents' home on August 1841 and promptly began making confidential inquiries about married women's legal rights and options.[20]

Aware that divorce would compromise her growing professional reputation, Mary Gove sought alternative solutions to her marital unhappiness. Like Elizabeth Cady Stanton and Margaret Fuller, she explored the social theories of the French philosopher Charles Fourier because they addressed such issues as the abuse of power within monopolies (of which, he believed, marriage was one), economic independence, and property rights.[21] Encouraged by Fourierism's popularity in New England, Mary Gove anticipated that Fourierist phalanxes would become legally safe havens for married women like herself, who wished to separate from their husbands. Under the roof of a phalanx, she envisioned women commanding the fruits of their labor—be they children, property, or earnings. When she attempted to join the Brook Farm community (in West Roxbury, Massachusetts) during its phalanx phase, however, Gove discovered that the residents did not wish to jeopardize their economic agenda by associating with a sexually suspect woman.[22] Rejected, she recognized that the path to women's freedom was littered with social as well as economic and political obstacles.

With the phalanx no longer an option, Mary Gove continued to support herself through writing. In 1842 she published *Lectures to Ladies on Anatomy and Physiology* (retitled *Lectures to Women on Anatomy and Physiology* in a subsequent edition), a text that emphasized women's strength without overtly threatening masculine power. "I am not one of those who charge man with injustice to woman," she assured readers. "Man is no more unjust to woman than he is to himself."[23] Convinced that women's misery stemmed from ignorance, she encouraged them to seek education, adopt healthful diets, partake in exercise, and cast off their corsets. The latter action had symbolic as well as health value—it suggested that women had it within their power to break free from restraints of all kinds.

Mary Gove had experimented with the use of cold-water treatments, as had many healers through the ages, before they gained widespread acceptance in the United States in the 1840s. She learned about European water-cure techniques from Henry Gardiner Wright, a British reformer and former patient of Vincent Priessnitz, the founder of water cure, when Wright visited Massachusetts in the fall of 1842. When Wright was in the United States to join the reformer Bronson Alcott in an experimental farm (Fruitlands), his interest in Alcott's venture waned as circumstances delayed its inauguration. Drawn to Gove because of their mutual interest in vegetarianism and communitarianism, he sought lodging in the Neal household, and by January 1843 the couple had embarked on a cooperative venture, a publication entitled *The Health Journal and Independent Magazine*. Unfortunately, Wright's incurable lung cancer cut their editorial career short, and in July 1843 he returned to England and his wife and died soon after.

Saddened by the loss of her friend and wearied by her estranged and embittered husband's accusations of adultery, Mary Gove suffered yet another loss the following January with the death of her father, William Neal. Taking advantage of the situation, Hiram Gove removed Elma from the Neal family home while Mary was on a lecture tour in Pennsylvania and Ohio. Although Elma was reunited with her mother after several agonizing months, years passed before Mary Gove recovered from the emotional and financial strain of this incident (which involved the rekidnapping of Elma and a lengthy legal battle).

Wright's knowledge of water cure lived on in his student and friend. After two short hydropathic apprenticeships—one at the Brattleboro (Vermont) Hydropathic Establishment and a second at the Lebanon Springs (New York) Water Cure—in late 1845 Mary Gove moved with her daughter to New York City and established herself as a water-cure physician.[24] As a system of cleansing, hydropathy appealed to women because it provided practical relief from gynecological problems, furnished spaces—water-cure resorts and boarding houses—in which they could develop supportive networks of female friends, and offered them a means to assert control over their lives and the health of their families. Hydropaths, in accord with Grahamism, attributed disease to a waste of vital energy that resulted when people ate meat, drank such stimulants as tea and coffee, or allowed themselves to become sexually excited. In addition to cold-water treatments—in the form of wet sheets, vigorous rubbings, and a variety of baths, some so powerful they could knock a patient down—hydropaths taught their patients the value of diet, dress reform, and exercise.[25]

Boarding with Fourierist friends, among them the southern-born philosopher Marx Edgeworth Lazarus, Mary Gove embarked on her career as a water-cure practitioner.[26] In contrast to the many other hydropathists who treated a relatively privileged clientele in their rural water-cure resorts, Gove treated a few patients in her home but also traveled throughout the city providing medical services to domestic servants, immigrants, and prostitutes.[27] Encountering women who had committed infanticide or who had attempted self-induced abortions because they wished not to bear the children of "brutish husbands" who had infected them with venereal disease, Gove grew even more adamant that women must be able to refuse a man's sexual advances. Women, she acknowledged, were not yet strong enough to claim this right: "Many a wretched wife have I strengthened by Water-cure to return to her bonds, or to remain in them, or to be more a victim."[28]

Meanwhile, a still-married Mary Gove struggled with legal bonds as she continued to support herself and Elma and to send payments to her estranged husband. Short stories and novels, published in the popular *Godey's Magazine and Lady's Book,* and several didactic novels supplemented the income she earned from practicing water cure. Recognizing that reformers could use women's preference for fiction to advantage, she frequently addressed the themes of courtship, love, and marriage.[29] Applying her pen to virtually every cause she embraced, Gove also wrote numerous essays on such topics as diet, dress reform, gynecology and obstetrics, water cure, and women's rights for medical and reform publications. She intended for her didactic stories and novels to awaken women's minds and for her treatises on health to empower them to care for their bodies. Readers, many of them women, thus came to know and trust Gove *before* her name became identified with free love.

Mary Gove's developing reputation as an author not only brought her financial stability but also provided her with entrée to such influential and literary-minded people as the authors and editors Horace Greeley, Nathaniel Parker Willis, Edgar Allan Poe, Catharine Sedgwick, Ann Stephens, Bayard Taylor, and her future husband, Thomas Low Nichols.[30] Like Gove, Nichols had been born in an isolated New Hampshire village and evinced an early interest in the study of medicine. After only one term at the Dartmouth (New Hampshire) Medical School, however, he recognized that his talent lay elsewhere. Influenced by a vegetarian professor and exposure to the ideas of Sylvester Graham, he became a convert to health reform and began delivering lectures on phrenology and physiology to audiences throughout New England. Life on the lecture circuit, however, provided many temptations, and he became a "backslider."[31] Turning to journalism, Nichols produced travel narratives, edited a weekly anti-Catholic newspaper (from Boston) entitled the *Standard* during the mid-1830s, wrote for the *Buffalo (New York) Commercial Advertiser* beginning in 1837, and edited a sensational tabloid entitled the *Buffalonian*. Casting caution to the wind, Nichols dedicated himself to exposing the Buffalo community's scandals and soon found himself charged, tried, and convicted of libel.[32]

Young, witty, and egotistical, Nichols boasted that women found him attractive and proudly referred to himself as "an accomplished rake."[33] After a brief sojourn in Rochester (where he found the women far more interesting than the community), Nichols moved to New York City, where he worked as an editor, published racy novels, and wrote for political journals. Although he continued to travel with some frequency, by 1847 he had—by virtue of his journalistic contributions—become part of the New York City literary salon to which Gove belonged.

When Mary Gove met Nichols at a social gathering in December 1847, she dismissed him as a dandy and determined to resist his advances: she knew an affair would compromise her reputation as a lecturer and water-cure physician and her ability to support herself and Elma. Applying his powers of persuasion, Nichols's personality nonetheless triumphed during a several-months courtship. When Hiram Gove finally petitioned for a divorce (because he wished to remarry), Nichols proposed marriage, and Mary Gove yielded. On 29 July 1848, only seven months after they had met, the two reformers wed in a Swedenborgian ceremony.

Thomas and Mary Gove Nichols spent the ensuing four years productively, immersing themselves in writing, journalism, and the study and practice of medicine.[34] In addition to returning to medical school for an M.D. degree, which he earned in 1850, Nichols published a treatise entitled *Woman in All Ages and Nations*. Mary Gove Nichols also remained active. After a visit to the Nichols residence in 1849, Mrs. R. B. Gleason expressed her admiration for Mary's "talent, and extraordinary energy of character."[35] In addition to treating patients in their homes and boarding others in hers, Gove Nichols offered lectures, supervised water-cure students, wrote regular essays for the *Water-Cure Journal,* and gave birth to a second daughter, Mary Wilhelmina, on 5 November 1850.[36] She also enjoyed a cordial relationship with the women's rights pioneer Elizabeth Cady Stanton, with whom she intermittently exchanged correspondence about dress reform and women's rights meetings.[37] Capitalizing on their momentum, the Nicholses opened the American Hydropathic Institute, one of the nation's first water-cure colleges, in New York City in September 1851. Expanding their operation the following May, the couple relocated to Port Chester, an hour's distance from New York City. By 1853, however, the couple began suffering a reversal of fortune, when their sex radicalism became more visible.

Several events in 1852 and 1853 propelled the Nicholses into the center of a free love controversy. In 1852, when Marx Edgeworth Lazarus published his Fourierist critique of marriage (*Love vs. Marriage*), it became the focus of the debate among the editor Horace Greeley, the author Henry James, and the social reformer Stephen Pearl Andrews in the pages of the *New York Tribune.* After Andrews invited Gove Nichols to contribute the perspective of a woman and physician on the subject, however, Greeley abruptly curtailed the discussion.[38] Matters worsened in the spring of 1853 when Thomas Nichols published *Esoteric Anthropology.* With sexually explicit content, the 482-page illustrated physiological manual, advocating that women determine when they would have sexual relations, offended the sensibilities of the hydropathic leader Russell Trall.[39] As the editor of the profession's leading journal, the *Water-Cure Journal* (which by 1849 reported a readership of fifty thousand), Trall had the power to silence Nichols by refusing to advertise the work or to publish any more contributions from him and Mary Gove Nichols.

Responding immediately, the Nicholses inaugurated their own publication, *Nichols' Journal of Health, Water-Cure, and Human Progress.* Beginning with the first issue, dated April 1853, it served as a mouthpiece for their ideas and a vehicle for advertising and distributing their publications. Meanwhile, Andrews, a noted free lover, joined the Nicholses at Port Chester and began sharing his vision of sexual equality with their predominantly female students. By July, an anonymous letter published in the *New York Tribune* alleged that Nichols and Andrews had "plied" female students at the American Hydropathic Institute with "the doctrines respecting woman, and her sexual functions, and duties." The correspondent continued: "Whether the practical application was taught among the pupils, I cannot say. . . . there is, however, every reason to believe that it was." Unable to withstand the devastating rumors of sexual misconduct (which they believed originated with Trall), the Nicholses closed the school's doors.[40] The couple's downward spiral continued when Charles Wilkins Webber, a disgruntled former patient who wanted to marry Elma Gove against her mother's wishes, published a novel portraying Mary Gove Nichols as a spiritual vampire.[41] Capitalizing on an antebellum fascination with vampires, Webber employed this imagery in an attempt to further weaken her power to influence people.

After the closure of the American Hydropathic Institute, the Nicholses disposed of their Port Chester property, removed to the communitarian experiment of Modern Times on Long Island, New York, and announced plans for the construction of a new school, to be known as the Institute of Desarrollo. In March 1851, the anarchist reformers Josiah Warren and Stephen Pearl Andrews had founded Modern Times on two principles: equitable commerce and individual sovereignty. The idea that labor, regardless of sex, could be treated equitably appealed to the Nicholses because they expected the venture to raise compensation for women's labor to a level comparable to that received by men.[42] A tense relationship, however, developed between the Nicholses and other residents at Modern Times: the latter acquired a reputation as a free love colony because of the Nicholses' presence. Warren, who refused to address the subject of free love, wanted to distance Modern Times from any specter of promiscuity, but because he also respected the individual sovereignty of each resident, he could not turn the couple away.

Mary Lyndon

When the Nicholses defaulted on the mortgage for their Modern Times property in the fall of 1855, the Institute of Desarrollo had not yet materialized, yet they had found other ways to spread their message of health and freedom.[43] Inveterate communicators, they focused on publishing: issuing *Nichols' Journal,* marketing *Esoteric Anthropology,* and collaborating on a new work, *Marriage: Its History, Character, and Results* (1854). *Marriage,* which called for the abolition of marriage as a form of slavery, along with the *Journal,* placed the Nicholses in the center of New York City's free love movement. With her youngest daughter cared for in the Modern Times common nursery, Gove Nichols also found time to write a novel based on her life. Entitled *Mary Lyndon,* it appeared in serialized form in *Nichols' Journal* during 1854 and was published in the summer of 1855 as a book. Critics immediately condemned the novel as a work of free love propaganda. Expressing dismay that a woman with "a great deal of talent & a little genius" had been "so de-

ceived by a person" like Nichols, the women's rights advocate Henry Blackwell assumed that "his views" dominated the couple's writings, teachings, and
medical practice. Blackwell feared for more than Gove Nichols's reputation:
with her help, he projected, Thomas Nichols's free love theories would now
assume a "Woman's Rights disguise" and travel to thousands of unsuspecting readers.[44] Women's responses to *Mary Lyndon* confirmed his fears.

According to the literary historian Nina Baym, *Mary Lyndon* represents
the "most extreme" fictionalized critique of marriage written by a woman
during the first six decades of the nineteenth century.[45] In the compelling yet
thinly veiled autobiographical novel, Gove Nichols blends her extensive explorations of philosophy, science, and theology with personal experiences.
The result, which male reviewers found so alarming, simultaneously indicted the institution of marriage and advocated a woman's right to determine
the fate of her body.

Other antebellum novelists also challenged the institution of marriage and
repressive attitudes toward sexuality, yet they continued to observe certain
conventions that preserved their reputations. Gove Nichols's novel, for instance, is not unique for its depiction of a divorced heroine or its discussion
of female sexuality. The very popular Sara Payson Willis Parton, writing as
Fanny Fern, strongly repudiated marriage in her novel *Ruth Hall,* also published in 1855. Likewise, slightly more than half of the stories Lydia Maria
Child published in *Fact and Fiction* (1846) had explored such themes as failed
marriage and forbidden love.[46] In such works, fictional widows find happiness in a second marriage, but divorced women cannot. Mary Gove Nichols, however, defied customary practice by featuring a heroine who not only
falls in love with another man while still married but also remarries happily
and finds sexual fulfillment. Using her life story as the narrative thread, she
heightened public awareness of troubled marriages and introduced readers
to such seldom-discussed social problems as abortion, infanticide, and marital sexual abuse, topics of great concern to many literate women at mid-century.

Prior to *Mary Lyndon*'s appearance, members of the clergy, newspaper
editors, and women's rights advocates like Blackwell believed it possible to
protect women from the contamination of free love. Few, they speculated,
would choose to spend their leisure time reading such turgid free love tomes
as Lazarus's *Love vs. Marriage* or Andrews's *Love, Marriage, and Divorce,* filled
with mystical philosophies and scientific theories.[47] Moreover, they doubt-
ed that many women would voluntarily associate themselves with known free
lovers who were, as published accounts of Modern Times inferred, sexually
deviant and eccentric in their dress and diet. True, some women there did

adopt the reform dress, which, as Mary Gove Nichols and other female lecturers discovered, made them the targets of ridicule. Embracing the bloomer
costume for health reasons, Gove Nichols encouraged like-minded reformers to decorate it with lace and ruffles in order to distinguish themselves from
"bold masculine women" whom men regarded as threats to the nation's
social order.[48]

The publication of *Mary Lyndon,* encapsulating as it did Mary Gove
Nichols's life and ideas in fiction, signals her formal emergence as a sex radical feminist and marks the zenith of her influence on women. Envisioning her novel as an *Uncle Tom's Cabin* for women, she portrays the title character as a woman unable to remain "content with bonds" after knowledge
shatters her ignorance.[49] In a twofold message to readers, *Mary Lyndon* first
demonstrates that a woman need not remain a passive victim to a sexual
double standard or to marriage customs and laws that destroy her identity
and integrity. Second, it portrays a woman who lives independently and
finds sexual fulfillment during her earthly life. Defying social and moral
conventions by initiating the dissolution of her marriage and asserting her
own emotional needs (experiencing romantic, albeit chaste, love while still
married), the heroine of *Mary Lyndon* finds true happiness in a second marriage to a spiritual affinity with whom she enjoys sexual passion. The story appealed to women who yearned for the "Good Time Coming" because
it offered a vision of an ideal world in which an autonomous woman—free
because she is healthy and economically independent—can live lovingly yet
chastely with her spiritual affinity until she chooses to become pregnant.
The healthy children born to those love matches, they expected, would regenerate society and inaugurate the much-anticipated millennium.

Mary Lyndon's feminist message—that a woman could challenge existing
gender and moral systems and still find happiness in this life—alarmed newspaper editors and clergy who feared that literate middle-class women lacked
an ability to discriminate between moral and immoral fiction. Women who
knew Gove Nichols as a physiological lecturer, dress and health reformer,
water-cure physician, and author of medical works, they predicted, would
want to read her latest work. Highly animated and full of powerful description, it would captivate those women who normally found such theories
distasteful. Moreover, anticipated a *New York Times* reviewer, thousands of
unhappily married women would read *Mary Lyndon* and naively act upon
its message because they identified with the author's life trajectory, which
included a marriage of necessity, unwanted pregnancies, poor health, and
economic dependency.[50] The sensationalism surrounding the novel's publication, another reviewer speculated, would guarantee its popularity among

members of New York City's "fashionable circles" and, because of their social prestige and influence, well beyond.[51]

The depth of reviewers' concern about the anticipated popularity of *Mary Lyndon* is evident in the fact that they lambasted this novel at a time when newspaper reviews of books tended to be brief, bland, and interspersed with long extracts of the work in question. Under the heading "A Bad Book Gibbeted," Henry J. Raymond devoted nearly four full columns in the *New York Times* to a devastating critique that was reprinted in papers as far away as Chicago.[52] Labeling Gove Nichols as "coarse, sensual, and shamelessly immoral," he pronounced her novel "a deliberate attempt to teach the art of adultery."[53] Other reviewers reminded readers of the author's earlier interest in Fourier's ideas and her endorsement of communal living, unitary (communal) kitchens, and collective child care. Devotees of socialism, warned a writer for *Littell's Living Age,* had ceased to openly advocate their cause and now relied on such "kindred covert modes of advocacy" as this novel. People could, he observed, protect themselves against lectures and dry tracts written by Fourierists, but novels could convey Fourier's doctrines in a highly popular format, "one calculated to enlist far more popular interest."[54]

Reviewers' objections to *Mary Lyndon* confirm their recognition of a book's power to reach and influence people. The author of a three-page critique in *Norton's Literary Gazette* reluctantly acknowledged the volume as a "powerful production" but cautioned potential readers that "the book may become the channel of a widely extending evil influence, by reason of the extreme and loose positions assumed and maintained by the writer." A more sympathetic reviewer for the *New York Daily Tribune* also concurred: "staunch defenders of things as they are cannot fail to be scandalized at her ill-concealed hostility to most of the fixtures which they consider essential to the preservation of the existing social fabric."[55] Even editors of a free love monthly entitled the *Social Revolutionist* found some flaws in Gove Nichols's work: despite being an "excellent autobiography," it had "too strong an infusion of romance."[56]

In all, *Mary Lyndon*'s portrayal of a sexually autonomous woman provoked the patriarchal ire of reviewers who believed that sexual anarchy would result if unhappily married women read the tome, identified with the heroine's life trajectory, and attempted to follow a similar course. Demonizing both the novel and its creator, they branded the fictional heroine Mary Lyndon as the epitome of "completely a sensual woman—the slave of the coarsest lust" and accused her of delighting in her "soiled morality."[57] Convinced that Gove Nichols's aim was the subversion of male authority, reviewers ignored the author's assertion that individual freedom could only be attained through strict physical discipline that included rigid rules governing diet and health.

They also overlooked the fact that she actually possessed a hyperidealized vision of marriage as a monogamous, lifelong union of two souls, albeit one that men could not legislate. Protesting the negative treatment given her novel by the *New York Times,* Gove Nichols complained that it and its "echoes all over the land" had overlooked her efforts to elevate women and men "out of a preponderant sensuality" and to consecrate "the whole love nature . . . to a wise paternity."[58]

While every woman who read *Mary Lyndon* would not necessarily become a free lover, the novel's critics clearly believed that its free love ideas could unsettle minds already shaken by reform movements of the 1840s and 1850s. Public awareness of the flawed nature of marriage had spread during the 1840s as reformers sought to alleviate the plight of drunkards' wives, inequities in married women's property rights, and artificiality in all kinds of relationships. Novelists highlighted disastrous examples of marriage contracted out of economic necessity or for social advantage, and health reformers exposed married women's gynecological and obstetrical ailments. Agitation from several quarters for liberalized divorce legislation in tandem with an increasingly vocal women's rights movement created a context in which, critics believed, Gove Nichols's novel could undermine respect for marriage, the legal and ecclesiastical authorities that enforced it, and the patriarchal authority it conferred upon men. They had good reason to be concerned. The practical utility of her message, the multiple channels in which she circulated, her determination to share her ideas with an ever wider audience, and her literary talent enabled her to cultivate a devoted constituency, one recognizing the many meanings conveyed by two simple words—free love.

Mary Gove Nichols and Her Readers

In October 1855, the *New York Times* attempted to destroy the city's free love menace by publishing an exposé of a popular "Free Love Club." A social group, it had begun as a series of conversations held in the home of Stephen Pearl Andrews before moving to rented rooms on Broadway. In addition to studying foreign languages, economics, philosophy, and related topics, its male and female members read and discussed *Mary Lyndon.* Although critics of Gove Nichols's novel predicted that its primary audience would consist of highly impressionable and easily misled women, newspaper accounts contradict themselves by portraying female club members as intelligent, well educated, "strong-minded," and able to converse easily on such subjects as art, economics, literature, and philosophy. Labeling the women who participated in the club promiscuous, journalists nonetheless described them as modest, neat, and sensibly attired.[59]

Limited extant manuscript sources make a thorough analysis of the socio-economic class of readers who consumed *Mary Lyndon* impossible, but textual evidence suggests that many married women devoured it enthusiastically despite reviewers' warnings. An Illinois reader who first encountered the novel in serialized format in *Nichols' Journal* during 1854 declared: "I am so much interested in the story of *Mary Lyndon,* alias Mrs. Nichols, that I cannot miss a chapter and can hardly wait till the numbers come."[60] Reading the book despite the objections of her husband, another correspondent offered an explanation for the novel's appeal: "The free, loving, sensitive, impulsive, enthusiastic nature of Mrs. Nichols is so like my own, that I feel drawn toward her with more than a sister's love."[61] And an Iowa reader of several of Gove Nichols's publications praised her for giving "full and entire expression of thoughts which have struggled within me for some years."[62] Yet even as those women praised *Mary Lyndon* for illustrating principles leading "to purity, chastity, uprightness, honor, integrity, and a restraining of the passions," at least one other recognized that "low-minded sensualists" could read into the same text "authority for the gratification of every passion." One had to be pure in mind, this reader reasoned, to comprehend the purity of the author's message.[63]

Several factors explain Mary Gove Nichols's success in cultivating such devoted readers. First, literary ability and access to multiple periodicals and publishers enabled her to construct, through the printed word, a persona with whom readers could identify and bond. The very appearance of her name in print implied acceptance and a measure of credibility, which was further reinforced by newspaper accounts of her involvement in New York City's reform circles and literary salons and her interactions with well-known abolitionists, Fourierists, health reformers, authors, and editors. Few readers knew that she struggled to sustain connections with people who admired her work as a medical practitioner yet felt repulsed by some of her sex radical theories. The dress reformer and temperance advocate Amelia Bloomer (also editor of *The Lily*), for instance, shared some of Gove Nichols's reform agenda and praised her hydropathic contributions yet denounced the author of *Mary Lyndon* as "insidious" and "dangerous."[64]

Second, Gove Nichols seldom used the phrase "free love" in her essays, and she objected vociferously when newspapers linked her name with adultery and licentiousness. Instead, she preferred to speak of "spiritual affinities," "true marriage," and "purity in love relations," concepts that did not threaten her readership but instead resonated with them. Love in freedom, Gove Nichols assured them, was "an elevation out of a preponderant sensuality."[65] Third, she clearly regarded herself as a martyr for the cause of women's rights, one willing to suffer and sacrifice for those lacking strength to defy social conventions. She reinforced that image by interspersing in her writings vivid descriptions of the mobs who hissed at her when she boldly demonstrated the evils of tight lacing or when she wore her reform costume (a knee-length dress worn with trousers) in public.[66] Readers of *Nichols' Journal* and its successor, *Nichols' Monthly,* responded favorably to such tactics. One, who regarded her trials as necessary, wrote that a "loving shield" protected Gove Nichols from harm. A clergyman who acknowledged that Gove Nichols had adopted far more "radical" positions than his own nonetheless endorsed her work, concluding: "A *timid* Reformer is about as good as no Reformer at all."[67]

Fourth, gendered understandings of what was and was not appropriate in print also enhanced Gove Nichols's rapport with her female readers. Male editors of reform periodicals often shied away from in-depth discussions of women's physical or emotional concerns, while female counterparts monitored their publications' content to preserve its reputation for respectability. Consequently, both remained reluctant to include ultraist critiques of marriage. Bloomer's temperance journal *The Lily,* for example, published articles about moral and legislative relief for drunkards' wives but avoided such controversial topics as the medical consequences of sexual abuse within marriage. Even Paulina Wright Davis's *Una,* which she began as a women's rights periodical in 1853, focused on such topics as dress reform and the legal reconstitution of marriage rather than on its interpersonal dimensions. Consequently, antebellum women who hungered to know more looked to Mary Gove Nichols's works.

Fifth, *Mary Lyndon*'s author cultivated an enduring bond with readers by fostering a sense of intimacy in her writings. Her contributions to the *Water-Cure Journal* often appeared in the form of letters to "her sisters," and the inclusion of excerpts from readers' letters in *Nichols' Journal* and *Nichols' Monthly* reinforced her image as confidante and trusted advisor. She further invited their trust by making public some of the most private aspects of her own health and marital history. Gove Nichols also appealed to their egos by informing them that she wrote not for the "mass of women" but only for those with enough strength to bear her criticism. They, in response, described the "spiritual kinship" they felt with her and the joy with which they received her periodicals as welcome visitors in their homes.[68]

Sixth, Gove Nichols emphasized her spirituality because she recognized that anyone who challenged existing customs and beliefs would be denounced as an "Infidel, though he may have a better religion than those who condemn him."[69] In an attempt to defuse such criticism, she frequently interspersed her publications with religious rhetoric that suggested her sense of "duty to God and the race." She even offered to pray for women who lacked the courage to speak out as she did.[70] In the face of protagonists who regarded her criticism of the patriarchal institution of marriage as a direct attack on Christianity, she remained steadfast in her insistence that it was sacrilege for human laws to make a couple live together as husband and wife once the "Divinity" of their marriage had been destroyed. "We believe that Love alone," she wrote in 1853, "sanctions the union of the sexes."[71] Invoking a spiritual justification for women's autonomy, she argued that a wife could not obey divine laws until she was free from "the lustful despotism of one man" and "the selfish or unwise legislation of many."[72] Because of Gove Nichols's emphasis on a higher moral order, the deeply spiritual women who read her work found it easier to discount and dismiss reviewers' comments.

Finally, Gove Nichols reached privileged as well as working-class readers living in both urban and rural settings with her message of female equality and sexual autonomy. As a woman of humble origins who had overcome economic and social obstacles to gain economic independence and prominence within New York City's intellectual circles, she drew upon her own life experiences to craft a message relevant to women in various socioeconomic environments. Filling her works with examples of women at all points across the spectrum, she described the lives of New York City's cultural elite as well as female factory workers, domestic servants, prostitutes, African Americans, and recently arrived Irish immigrants. Even if the latter groups did not read her works, they nonetheless had firsthand encounters with the inveterate reformer when she treated their maladies. Thus, educated white women who could afford to purchase Gove Nichols's books and who had enough leisure time to read them consumed her ideas, as did the urban working women she healed and the wives of struggling farmers and mechanics who shared copies of *Nichols' Journal* with one another because they could not afford individual subscriptions.[73]

Spiritualism and a Move West

Like many other Americans at mid-century, Thomas and Mary Gove Nichols became converts to Spiritualism, a belief in the ability to communicate with the dead. Although she claimed to have had a tendency to "second sight," Gove Nichols remained skeptical about Spiritualistic communication until 1850, when she encountered a sailor who practiced as a physical and writing medium.[74] Holding séances at their school in Port Chester, the Nicholses developed a network of Spiritualist friends sympathetic to the couple's reform ideas. By 1855, as her opponents increasingly branded Gove Nichols a free lover, she began attributing her actions to the influence of a spirit guide. That fall he directed the Nicholses to move from Modern Times to Cincinnati, Ohio, a city well served by land, rail, and water transportation routes. By mid-century, it had become the fourth largest publishing center in the United States and, as such, a logical place for the author-editor team to settle.

Prior to their move to Ohio, the Nicholses attempted to solidify their support by announcing the establishment of the Progressive Union, a "Society for Mutual Protection in Right." Asserting women's and men's right to healthy bodies, the Progressive Union represents an attempt by the Nicholses to unify the disparate band of women and men who endorsed their ideas. Members, the prospectus announced, were encouraged to break "old bondages" and to form "harmonial" relationships that would foster their progress to perfection.[75] Women living "in the bondage of unhappy domestic relations" would benefit from learning the names of members: instead of suffering alone they could reach out to like-minded individuals for words of support, money, and even housing.[76] The Progressive Union also provided the Nicholses with opportunities to generate some income (from donations and through the sale of publications) and helped them remain connected to subscribers during their transition from the East Coast to the Midwest.

As the site of earlier utopian experiments, southwestern Ohio contained numerous reformers and Spiritualists who welcomed the Nicholses into their midst.[77] Unsettled by the spread of slavery and unmoored by periodic economic downturns, Ohioans eagerly sought solutions to their individual and collective struggles. Itinerant lecturers regularly traversed the state, sowing the seeds of radicalism as they spoke about the abolition of slavery, free love, phrenology, Spiritualism, women's rights, and other issues and concerns of the day.[78] Restive midwesterners also turned to the printed word for guidance. Thus, by year's end, Thomas Nichols had found an outlet for both his lectures and publications: in December 1855 he had delivered a discourse on free love and Spiritualism at Cincinnati's Foster Hall, and only a month later he gave an address at Cincinnati's anniversary observance of Thomas Paine's birth date.[79]

A collegial yet pragmatic relationship developed between the reform-minded Cincinnati publisher Valentine Nicholson (1809–1904) and the Nicholses when he visited Modern Times in early 1855. Like Mary Gove Nichols, Nicholson once had been a member of the Society of Friends, had become interested in Spiritualism, and believed equitable relationships could be attained in communal settings.[80] To the chagrin of his family and friends, Nicholson not only loaned money to Gove Nichols but also offered to publish *Nichols' Monthly* and other works by the couple from his office. An associate who had found the *Monthly*'s predecessor, *Nichols' Journal,* to be repugnant complained to Jane Nicholson about her husband's friends. The couple's "egotism of style" and the "unhappy influences," he wrote, had "a negative effect upon the minds of some of my acquaintances, both in respect to the domestic relations, and the management of the sick." Another friend attempted, also unsuccessfully, to persuade Nicholson to refrain from promoting the Nichols's "false issues."[81] Yet disparaging comments did not discourage Nicholson and others who regarded the Nicholses as martyrs to a higher cause.

Inveterate teachers as well as authors, the Nicholses waited only a few months before announcing the establishment of yet another institute, to be known as Memnonia. They had, supporters learned, leased a water-cure resort in the small Greene County community of Yellow Springs, Ohio. More than a utopian experiment, it was to be a place of preparation where members of the Progressive Union, invalids, and water-cure students could progress to a "Purer and Truer Life." If all lived according to the institute's motto—"Freedom, Fraternity, Chastity"—Memnonia residents would, the Nicholses believed, avert undue criticism.[82] Unfortunately, their reputation as free lovers preceded them, prompting an alarmed Antioch College President Horace Mann to dedicate himself to ridding the community of "that hideous sect of Free lovers" and protecting the college from "an awful demoralization."[83] In addition to dismissing a student from the college who lived with the Nicholses, he pressured the Adelphian Union Literary Society to withdraw the couples' books from their library and insisted that the bookstore cease selling their works.[84]

Contrary to Mann's expectations, residents of Memnonia led a progressively ascetic lifestyle that included labor, study, and daily confession. Instead of advocating promiscuity, they advised couples to avoid "material union" except on those occasions when they mutually desired to conceive.[85] The editor of the nearby *Daily Springfield Nonpareil,* describing Dr. Nichols as "a good deal worse in theory than in practice," dismissed him as a harmless fanatic and ignored Mary Gove Nichols altogether. By early spring, the bane of Mann's existence had faded. On 29 March 1857, the Nicholses, their daughter Wilhelmina, and one other member of Memnonia—following the advice of a spirit guide—recanted their earlier beliefs and converted to Roman Catholicism.[86] Valentine Nicholson struggled to explain the action to *Nichols' Monthly* readers when it abruptly ceased publication, while Progressive Union members and other devoted supporters pondered the abrupt change. Sophronia Powers, a resident of a colony of free lovers in Berlin Heights, Ohio, later reflected that there was nothing so hard to bear as "suppressed ambition (or frustrated ambition)" and concluded that this force had driven the Nicholses into the Catholic church. Some, less forgiving, pronounced many of the couple's endeavors "ill conceived," "badly carried out," and "injudicious." Focused on their own progress, such critics reasoned, the Nicholses abandoned the cause because other reformers did not respond appreciatively enough to "their services as leaders to the extent anticipated."[87] Such observers failed to recognize the consistency in Mary Gove Nichols's transition from free love to chastity: using her definitions, both ensured a woman's right to her body, mind, and soul.

Throughout her years of agitation, Mary Gove Nichols emphasized the need for individual empowerment and action. Positively influenced by early exposure to Fourierist phalanxes, she nonetheless regarded them as temporary measures—a place where women and men could prepare themselves to live as self-controlled sovereigns. This early interest in Fourierism provided her with access to New York City's free love community, not the women's rights movement. While such advocates of women's rights as Elizabeth Cady Stanton, Amelia Bloomer, and Henry Blackwell kept the sexually suspect woman at a distance, avant-garde social philosophers like Stephen Pearl Andrews and Marx Edgeworth Lazarus welcomed her as an intellectual equal.

From each vantage point—as an author, health reformer, physician, utopian, and Spiritualist—Mary Gove Nichols offered herself as a model for women, describing her arduous path to economic self-sufficiency. Many of her earlier works included subtle sex radical themes, including the right of a woman to govern her mind and body. With marriage to Thomas Low Nichols, however, her identity as a free lover began to overshadow her reputation as an advocate for women. Convinced that they knew the best way for women and men to inaugurate the "Good Time Coming," the couple focused more on self-control and less on individual freedom and thus lost their base of support. Nonetheless, they had made important contributions to the free love movement during its formative years through their publications, their institutes, and the Progressive Union, offering a vocabulary for the discussion of male and female sexuality, drawing women into conversation about "the social question," and fostering a sense of community among geographically dispersed and socially isolated sex radicals.

2. The Power of Print

*. . . our movement must be carried on, by means of books and
magazines, rather than by public meetings [and] discussions.*
—Anonymous, *Social Revolutionist*, December 1856

"ONE OF THE BEST MEDIUMS for extending the principles of liberty," wrote
Julia C. Coon in 1908, "lies in the local press." But, Coon acknowledged, "articles to these papers must be short and not too strong, or they will not appear."[1] Mary Gove Nichols and her husband Thomas had learned a similar
lesson more than a half-century earlier when editors refused to publish or
advertise works in which the couple discussed sexuality or challenged such
deeply entrenched social and legal institutions as marriage. Consequently, the
sex radical press was born. Between 1853, when the first issue of *Nichols' Journal of Health, Water-Cure, and Human Progress* appeared, and 1910, when the
American Journal of Eugenics ceased publication, over a dozen periodicals
circulated sex radical ideas to hundreds of readers living from Maine to California and in ten locations outside the United States. Some titles lasted less
than a year, others for over two decades.

In many ways the nineteenth-century sex radical movement consisted of
its press. Lacking formal organizations, dues, and regular meetings, sex radical women and men relied on periodicals to create a sense of connection to
each other. According to a sex radical residing in Boston, the true meaning
of free love could not be comprehended until one had carefully read and
digested key texts.[2] Sex radicals actively participated in the movement by
recruiting new subscribers and contributing to defense funds when editors
had legal battles. They further invested in the cause by ordering books and
pamphlets and sending cash donations (albeit often small) or gifts in kind.[3]
Editors encouraged readers' active involvement in other ways. *Nichols' Journal, Woodhull and Claflin's Weekly,* and *Lucifer, the Light-Bearer* encouraged
them to form clubs, *The Word* hired female agents to canvas for new subscrip-

tions, *Vanguard* and *Lucifer* often published the names of subscribers, and *Lucifer* solicited contributions to a defense fund to support editors in their legal battles. But most importantly of all, sex radical periodicals encouraged the development among readers of a collective consciousness of themselves as a social movement. Contributors' numerous letters—in which they shared their ideas and experiences and engaged others in debate—gave sex radical periodicals the appearance of an ongoing conversation among many participants. Those periodicals and the people who edited and read them are the subject of this chapter.

Nineteenth-century women had few outlets in which they could openly explore and share their ideas about sexual topics. Those who attended lectures given by itinerant free lovers, for instance, risked social ostracism. Yet women could consume radical critiques of marriage that transcended domestic spaces by means of the printed page. Through patient and thoughtful study of these texts, hundreds not only came to accept the controversial ideas known to nineteenth-century Americans as free love but also found an active means by which they could participate in a movement they believed would advance the cause of women's rights.

A Revolution in Reading

A revolution in reading, beginning in the late eighteenth century and continuing until the mid-nineteenth century, resulted in the United States when rising levels of education and literacy converged with improved access to books and periodicals.[4] Earlier in the nineteenth century, winter weather conditions—especially frozen, snow-laden rivers—had prevented periodicals from circulating nationwide except between late spring and late fall. The rapid extension of railway lines, reduction in postal rates, improved printing technology, and growing affordability of print culture, however, meant that by the 1850s women and men's access to books and periodicals had expanded dramatically.[5] Additionally, the advent of local lyceums, the spread of public education, and a growing desire for self-improvement further fed men and women's hunger for reading matter.

Unmoored by changes associated with the transition to a market economy, antebellum Americans turned increasingly to books and periodicals for information and guidance. Many sought counsel in behavior and marriage manuals. Often written by clergymen, these tended to elevate women's spiritual rather than their sexual nature.[6] Members of the medical profession further encouraged the desexualization of women's bodies, and over time the range of female sexual conduct that was deemed socially acceptable narrowed. Yet debate over the "marriage question" (as nineteenth-century Americans came to call their obsession with this institution's flaws) continued in numerous sites, including such widely circulated titles as *Harper's Weekly,* the *Liberator,* the Oneida Community *Circular,* and the *Water-Cure Journal.* A growing body of periodicals edited by and for women reflected similar concerns, but few openly addressed the subject of female sexuality.[7]

Reading had profound significance for nineteenth-century women because it conferred on them a degree of independence.[8] Members of the clergy became alarmed when women displayed a penchant for reading novels in which heroines not only challenged conventional notions of female sexuality but also questioned the patriarchal institution of marriage. But until recently, historians have underestimated the power of periodicals as agents of radicalism in the lives of nineteenth-century women. In *The Radical Women's Press of the 1850s,* Ann Russo and Cheris Kramarae document the growth of periodical readership among nineteenth-century women. Their study, however, focuses primarily on periodicals devoted to such concerns as dress reform, temperance, and women's rights.[9] We cannot fully understand the diffusion of radical theories to women without an examination of the sex radical press.

The Sex Radical Press in Nineteenth-Century America

As shown in the previous chapter, Russell Trall, the editor of the *Water-Cure Journal,* in early 1853 refused to publish advertising copy for Thomas L. Nichols's *Esoteric Anthropology,* because of its explicit sexual content. Yet many ordinary women and men reported reading the health and water-cure manual to family members, friends, and neighbors. Widely denounced by medical practitioners and members of the clergy because it equated physical relations in loveless marriages with prostitution and argued that "every child should be a love child," the work nonetheless sold thousands of copies. Many of them became dog-eared when devoured by multiple readers.[10]

Shortly after the Nicholses established *Nichols' Journal* as a weekly forum for the discussion of their ideas about marriage and sexuality, other sex radical editors followed suit. John Patterson of Ohio began the *Social Revolutionist* in 1856 when editors of other publications rejected his essays on social reform, and a year later Alfred and Anne Denton Cridge commenced publishing *Vanguard.* The titles of those papers, and their immediate successors— *Age of Freedom, Good Time Coming,* and the *New Republic*—vividly capture their editors' zeal and messianic spirit.[11] And in them idealistic, impecunious editors urged the immediate abolition of all forms of slavery, especially a woman's slavery in marriage.

By publicly stating their positions, those editors served as standard bearers for sex radicalism, and their publications thus became primary sites for the exchange of ideas and the sale of sex radical books and pamphlets. Such early sex radical periodicals as *Social Revolutionist* and *Vanguard* attracted a core list of several hundred dedicated subscribers and drew an even larger readership because subscribers shared their copies with friends and families. Setbacks nonetheless occurred. The *Social Revolutionist* ceased publication in late 1857 after a group of angry women, disturbed by its contents, seized and burned the November issue before it could be delivered to the post office.[12] Such actions proved futile. In that instance, a determined editorial staff published one more issue and then inaugurated a new publication (*Age of Freedom*), increased its frequency to weekly, and adopted an even bolder stance on the social question. In the spirit of free inquiry, the editors denounced such artificial social constraints as marriage and called for women's immediate emancipation. Somewhat surprisingly, given their limited resources and the opposition they faced in the form of local mobs, they sustained this endeavor for nearly a year.

The Civil War destroyed the momentum of most antebellum reform movements, including sex radicalism, and by 1870 several leading antebellum sex radical leaders and the periodicals they published had vanished.[13] Pointing to the government's suspension of the writ of habeas corpus in September 1861, editors voiced concern that imprecisely worded directives would be used to mute their publications and their critiques of the nation's socioeconomic structure. In reality, government suppression of radical papers was unnecessary because patriotic women and men used social pressure and, at times, the threat of violence to silence unpopular editors. Thomas Nichols, reflecting on this era, recalled: "It was useless then, in America, to write anything but war; and somewhat dangerous for a Northern man to write what did not suit the Government. The freedom of the press was, for a time, suspended."[14]

Although sex radical papers ceased publication during the Civil War years, other groups continued to discuss key sex radical concepts and to provide venues in which antebellum free lovers could air their ideas. They found, for instance, common ground with such movements as American nonresistants who opposed all forms of coercion (the reason they refused to take up arms) and who also embraced "the New Testament ethic of love without regard to consequences."[15] Not all sex radicals professed pacifism, as is evident in Berlin Heights Free Lovers' willingness to take up arms for self-defense (see chapter 3), but they nonetheless yearned for the day when women and men could free themselves from the bonds of coercive institutions. Like sex radicals, nonresistants also believed in the necessity of overturning the existing socioeconomic order and establishing a society of regenerated persons motivated to obey God because of internal convictions, not external restraints.

Spiritualism provided another arena in which sex radicals could continue to articulate their ideas. Women, according to the historian Ann Braude, found Spiritualism especially conducive to active participation. In their role as seemingly passive trance mediums they could acceptably utter radical pronouncements about their rights, including the right to sexual autonomy.[16] Moreover, Spiritualism, with its belief in the existence of divinely chosen spiritual affinities, reinforced sex radicals' hyperidealized view of marriage. Even though the noted Spiritualist Andrew Jackson Davis in 1864 warned those who attended a meeting of New York Spiritualists to exercise restraint in their critiques of marriage, many women remained steadfast in their belief that "true love will harm no one" and continued to speak out against the evils of marital slavery and false social restraints that impeded their attainment of an idealized state of sexual freedom.[17]

Both nonresistants and Spiritualists responded positively to the appearance of a small monthly periodical entitled *Kingdom of Heaven,* first issued in January 1864. Its editor, a financially struggling Indiana Spiritualist and nonresistant named Thomas Cook, sustained the paper for at least five years and in so doing reached women and men in the northeastern and midwestern United States. Presenting himself as the Second Coming of Christ, Cook advocated what he called the "love principle."[18] He distinguished between his principle and free love by defining the latter as promiscuous sexual indulgence and the former as monogamy. Yet his advocacy of a woman's right to choose when and with whom she bore children defines him as a sex radical. Cook also believed that women and men—as fallible beings—required extensive experimentation in order to find their divinely intended mates. Regarding the practice of variety (simultaneous and sequential sexual relationships) as a temporary phase through which imperfect individuals must pass before they progressed to a higher phase of development, he held fast to his ultimate goal, monogamy. Putting theory into practice, Cook in 1860 renounced his marriage vows but did not seek a divorce from the state because he denied its authority to govern his private life. "Giving" his wife her freedom and responsibility for their children, he set out in search of his spiritual affinity.[19] Never finding her, despite an extensive search, in the process he served as a conduit for sex radical ideas. During the course of his travels, which ranged from Indiana to Boston, New Jersey, and New York, Cook periodically returned to Huntsville, Indiana, where he boarded with the mother of his children, but by the late 1860s he had settled in Berlin Heights, Ohio. Many of his subscribers came from areas he visited.

Both male and female correspondents to the *Kingdom of Heaven* praised Cook's freedom of thought, advocacy of such biblical maxims as "love one another," and defense of their right "to secede and be free from all human authority," and they strived to live according to the Golden Rule (the basis of his love principle).[20] Even Cook's call for the abolition of marriage did not deter female readers. Instead, they responded enthusiastically to his description of a new social order in which women determined when a couple would indulge in "food of the soul" (a euphemism for sexual relations). Thus, while most of Cook's subscribers never considered themselves free lovers, they nonetheless joined him in accepting sex radical ideas "as a power in the land, like war, to disintegrate, to break down and destroy the slavery of marriage."[21]

In the 1870s, the sex radical periodicals *Woodhull and Claflin's Weekly, The Word,* and *Hull's Crucible* emerged to rekindle the embers of sex radicalism. Published in the eastern United States, their pages contained the familiar names of antebellum free lovers as well as those new to the movement. From its first issue on 14 May 1870 through its final number on 10 June 1876, *Woodhull and Claflin's Weekly* featured articles designed to challenge, provoke, and excite those who consumed them. Its editors, the New York City stockbrokers Victoria Claflin Woodhull and her sister Tennessee (also known as Tennie C.) Claflin, began the *Weekly* as a multifaceted reform paper reflecting a combination of Spiritualist, reform, and political interests. On 30 December 1871, for example, it published an English translation of the *Communist Manifesto,* the first to appear in the United States. The paper's sixteen pages, produced with the assistance of the financier Cornelius Vanderbilt and replete with the intellectual contributions of such men as Stephen Pearl Andrews and Woodhull's second husband "Colonel" James Harvey Blood, appeared each week for nearly seven years with a few exceptions.[22]

The editors' highly publicized and unconventional lifestyles and the *Weekly*'s reputation for carrying articles on such issues as free love, marriage, divorce, and prostitution immediately made it a mouthpiece for the free love movement. Woodhull is best known for declaring that she had a right to change lovers daily if she chose and for accusing the nation's most popular clergyman, Henry Ward Beecher, of adultery with a married parishioner, Elizabeth Tilton, in 1872. The following year, the American News Company, whose agents distributed periodicals throughout the nation, announced that it would no longer carry the *Weekly.* By that time, however, Woodhull and Claflin had cultivated a dedicated body of readers who formed clubs to ensure its continued circulation throughout the nation. Endorsing the *Week-ly*'s power for good, one subscriber declared: "Where its influence is felt for a single twelve-month . . . freedom is surely born."[23]

Ezra Heywood (1829–93), an early supporter of Woodhull's right to free speech, began editing another sex radical paper, *The Word* (a monthly dedicated to economic reform and individual freedom) from his Princeton, Massachusetts, home in May 1872 and continued as editor until his death in 1893.[24] Beginning with the first issue, in which he announced that the paper favored such causes as "the abolition of speculative income, of woman's slavery and war government," he routinely published discussions of free love and sexual ethics. His wife, Angela Fiducia Tilton, wrote many of the articles in her distinctively effusive and frank prose.[25] Committed to his belief in the freedom of speech, Heywood was convicted for violating the Comstock Law (1873), which prohibited the distribution of obscene material through the U.S. mail. After his first arrest in 1877 for publishing and distributing an antimarriage tract entitled *Cupid's Yokes,* hundreds of sex radicals, anarchists, and freethinkers rallied to his support, successfully petitioning President Rutherford B. Hayes for his pardon, granted in 1878. As an outward sign of Heywood's rejection of Christianity, that same year he replaced the Christian dating system (A.D.) with Y.L. (Year of Love) on *The Word*'s masthead. Making the change retroactive to 1873, the date he founded the New England Free Love League, the year 1878 became Y.L. 6. Convicted again on federal obscenity charges, Heywood paid dearly for his adherence to sex radicalism. Sentenced to two years, he emerged from Charlestown State Prison in 1892 a worn and weak man and died a year later in Boston at the age of sixty-three. Angela Heywood, left on her own with four children, virtually disappeared from the sex radical scene as she dealt with the realities of day-to-day existence, outliving her husband by nearly forty-three years.

Ohio-born Moses Hull (1835–1906) edited *Hull's Crucible* (1871–77) in Boston with the assistance of his brother D. W. Hull and companion Mattie Sawyer. Reform-minded Spiritualists, their weekly appealed to *Social Revolutionist* regulars, *Woodhull and Claflin Weekly* supporters, and women and men who read *The Word* and later *Lucifer, the Light-Bearer.* A religious conversion at sixteen and his subsequent embrace of Adventism led Moses Hull to discover his calling as a preacher and skill as a charismatic public speaker. After 1862, when he became a Spiritualistic medium, his belief in Spiritualism gradually took precedence over his earlier religious beliefs. Hull had witnessed the rigors of marriage for women as a young man, when his mother gave birth to sixteen children, only nine of whom lived to adulthood. His attitude toward church-sanctioned and state-licensed marriage further eroded after his first marriage, to Cynthia Ann Conde in the mid-1850s, ended with her death eight weeks later. A second marriage to Elvira Lightner lasted eighteen years and produced four daughters, but time and Hull's long absences from home (due to lecturing) resulted in marital dissatisfaction. In 1872, still married, Hull became companion to Mattie Sawyer, the wife of a Civil War veteran. The couple aired their defense of free love, their criticisms of institutionalized marriage, and the persecution they received in the pages of *Hull's Crucible*.[26]

Struggling financially during the Panic of 1873 and its aftermath, the Hull brothers and Sawyer supported the *Crucible* with fees earned from lecturing, the sale of their publications, advertising, job printing, and donations, supplemented by earnings from "doctoring" and lodging boarders. Sawyer, who by 1877 had assumed full responsibility for producing the paper, suffered poisoning from the type she set and ultimately a physical breakdown. With over five hundred subscribers "in debt for one or more past volumes of the *Crucible*," the team suspended publication in late 1877.[27]

Sex radicals who wanted a paper that made sex reform its highest priority could, in the 1880s, turn to *Lucifer, the Light-Bearer*. Published between 1883 and 1907, it represents the longest-lived nineteenth-century periodical dedicated to sex radicalism, surpassing Ezra Heywood's *The Word* by several years. Its editor, a former abolitionist, Methodist Episcopal circuit rider preacher, and teacher named Moses Harman, moved from Missouri to the rural community of Valley Falls, Kansas, in 1879 and became active in the local chapter of the National Liberal League, an organization devoted to the unequivocal separation of church and state. Within a year, he became coeditor of the league's paper, the *Valley Falls Liberal*, and in 1881, as sole editor, he broadened its scope and renamed it the *Kansas Liberal*. Aggressively anticlerical, his paper stood apart from other National Liberal League publications because of its advocacy of anarchism and oppressed groups. Like many other radical editors, he adopted an alternative calendar. Harman's "Era of Man" dated from 1600 (the year the astronomer Giordano Bruno was executed as a heretic); hence, the first issue of *Lucifer* is dated E.M. 283.[28]

Christian residents of Valley Falls, disturbed by the presence of the *Kansas Liberal* in their community, became even more alarmed in 1883 when Harman rechristened his paper *Lucifer, the Light-Bearer*, a title it retained until 1907. Subscribers periodically debated the merits of the paper's title, but Harman remained steadfast in his assertion that *Lucifer* meant "Light-bringing or Light-bearing" and that his paper stood "For Light against Darkness— for Reason against Superstition; For Science against Tradition . . . For Liberty against Slavery—For Justice against Privilege." It taught, he explained to those who accused him of free love, "Libertarianism, *not* Libertinism."[29] Despite those distinctions, some subscribers worried that their neighbors and local postal officials would not understand the paper's higher purpose. "Do not send anything in those envelopes with advertisement of the purposes of your paper printed on them," wrote Mrs. Susie P. of Pennsylvania. "The last you sent caused a great deal of ignorant comment."[30]

As *Lucifer*'s masthead indicated, Harman dedicated himself and his paper to "The Emancipation of Woman from Sex Slavery" and, like Victoria Woodhull, Tennessee Claflin, Ezra Heywood, and the Hulls, to "An Untrammeled Press." Acting on his convictions, Harman gave his many correspondents complete freedom of expression, publishing frank language and graphic discussions of such topics as venereal disease and oral sex.[31] In consequence, he and several members of his family endured arrest, conviction, and incarceration for periodic violations of the Comstock Law. His ongoing legal battles and his search for a more tolerant environment led Harman to move *Lucifer*'s editorial offices from Valley Falls to Topeka, Kansas, in 1890, and to Chicago in 1896.[32]

Sex radicals of the mid-1880s and early 1890s also could look to several smaller publications for discussions of sex reform and libertarian views of women's rights. When a small periodical entitled *Foundation Principles* appeared in the mid-1880s, readers recognized editor Lois Waisbrooker's name from her earlier contributions to the *Kingdom of Heaven, Woodhull and Claflin's Weekly, Hull's Crucible, The Word,* and to such Spiritualist papers as *Banner of Light* (Boston) and the *Religio-Philosophical Journal* (Chicago). Issuing early numbers from Clinton, Iowa, in the mid-1880s, she moved the paper with her to the Antioch, California, home of her son and by 1886 had suspended publication. Resurrecting *Foundation Principles* in Topeka, Kansas, in 1893 and 1894, Waisbrooker discovered that she had retained a loyal following but had to again discontinue the publication before a year had passed. Obscenity charges compounded by poverty made it impossible for her to maintain a regular publication schedule. Six years later she announced plans to again publish *Foundation Principles,* but when it did appear from her San Francisco residence (and later from Home, Washington), it bore the title *Clothed with the Sun.* This new publication appeared intermittently until its demise circa 1902. Waisbrooker, whose ideas and prose dominated the pages of her periodicals, believed that women, by virtue of motherhood, possessed a unique opportunity to redeem the world. "Foundation Principles," she enunciated in the first publication's masthead, "are the rock upon which Motherhood Must Rest. Search for Them." Women, many of them living in the Midwest and Great Plains states, did just that, responding enthusiastically to Waisbrooker's ideas and making *Foundation Principles* the only sex radical periodical in which female correspondents outnumbered men.

In 1888, the anarchist Edwin C. Walker and his free love companion Lillian Harman began editing a publication entitled *Fair Play*. Emphasizing the importance of individual sovereignty, the editors proclaimed their intent to cooperate "with *Lucifer* in the defensive warfare against Comstockism." In contrast to Benjamin R. Tucker's avoidance of such topics as sexual slavery in his anarchistic weekly, *Liberty*, Walker and Harman filled their publication with philosophical discussions of sexual slavery, love, and marriage. Unlike *Lucifer, Fair Play* minimized the role of reader contributions and instead featured Walker's views and carefully selected excerpts from such publications as the British *Westminster Review*, Waisbrooker's *Foundation Principles*, and an Iowa publication entitled *New Thought*. Although the couple began *Fair Play* in Valley Falls, Kansas, they had relocated to Sioux City, Iowa, by 1891. The paper ceased in January 1908.[33]

In December 1895, Moses Harman commenced a new endeavor, entitled *Our New Humanity*. Its goal, he announced in the first issue, was to unite land, marriage, and divorce reformers. With a smaller format and monthly frequency, it resembled a scholarly journal. In addition to poems by Charlotte Perkins Stetson and excerpts from the prose of Olive Schreiner, it contained essays by such sex radical regulars as Rachel Campbell, Lucinda B. Chandler, Lizzie M. Holmes, and Edwin C. Walker. Unable to sustain both *Lucifer* and *Our New Humanity* during the economic depression of the 1890s, Harman suspended the latter title in 1897.

The West Coast anarchists Henry Addis, Abner J. Pope, and Abe Isaak created a forum for print-based discussions of anarchism, free love, and Comstockery when they began editing the *Firebrand* in January 1895 from Portland, Oregon. Dedicated to the "Burning Away of the Cobwebs of Ignorance and Superstition," this weekly featured such women as the Chicago anarchist Lucy E. Parsons, the Missouri farm wife Kate Austin, and *Foundation Principles* editor Lois Waisbrooker arguing about the causes of sex slavery.[34] In September 1897, however, the paper suspended publication when the three members of the editorial team were arrested for sending allegedly obscene matter through the mail—Walt Whitman's poem, "A Woman Waits for Me." In an effort to fill the void, Isaak (a Mennonite who had immigrated to the U.S. from Russia) moved to San Francisco and in November 1897 inaugurated *Firebrand*'s successor, *Free Society*, with the help of his wife Mary and the couple's three children (who set type and addressed wrappers). *Free Society*'s editorial offices quickly became a focal point for San Francisco anarchists. A weekly, it had moved to Chicago by 1900, and publication had ceased by 1905. Like *Lucifer, Free Society*'s pages contained women and men's thoughts on such subjects as the sexual slavery of marriage, the flaws of institutionalized marriage, and attacks against "God and Grundy."

A number of *Free Society* and *Lucifer* contributors also sent letters to the tabloid-sized *Discontent: Mother of Progress,* a weekly published in Lake Bay, Washington, between 1898 and 1902. The anarchists who published it, residents of a community known as the Home Colony, were committed to battling "for the freedom of the human race from tyranny and superstition of all kinds and sorts." Striving to attain this idealistic goal, contributors freely and enthusiastically discussed such topics as economics, politics, religion, and sexuality. Committed to using print as a form of propaganda for anarchism, *Firebrand* editors Addis and Pope moved to Home Colony and helped produce *Discontent*. Readers recognized the power of this periodical and the anarchist pamphlets its editors sold. "This means of propaganda is a very important auxiliary in our campaign," wrote one subscriber, Thomas Sheedy, in 1899 after listening to Emma Goldman lecture in Tacoma, Washington. "When the voice is stilled by exhaustion those silent missionaries are ever active after the excitement has subsided." Another, E. J. Schellhous, concurred. "Your paper is a sort of auditorium whose audience is the readers, your contributors the speakers, your printer the recording secretary, and yourself the presiding genius."[35]

In an attempt to dignify and professionalize the subject of sex reform, Moses Harman in 1907 gave *Lucifer, the Light-Bearer* a new format and name—*American Journal of Eugenics*—and changed its frequency from weekly to monthly. As a scholarly appearing journal containing such essays as "The Science of Stirpiculture" and "Our Drift toward Imperialism," it no longer reprinted wordy correspondence but instead included brief excerpts of letters in a column entitled "Various Voices." As the journal shifted in tone and format, its growing numbers of male supporters directed discussions away from women's emancipation to the study of eugenics. Harman, who outlived most of his nineteenth-century sex radical colleagues, died in Los Angeles in July 1910, and the journal ceased soon after.[36] As had been the case with other nineteenth-century sex radical periodicals, longevity depended upon the dedication of a charismatic editor.

Sustaining a Movement

"I am alone in my study of the reform questions," confided a female reader of *Foundation Principles* in the fall of 1893, and have "very few lady friends who are not astonished and mortified when I approach such a subject as sex slavery."[37] For this woman and many like her, periodicals served as the primary means by which they could sustain their sex radicalism. Unlike advocates of such other nineteenth-century reform movements as antislavery, dietary reform, and temperance, few nineteenth-century Americans could openly embrace the cause of sex radicalism nor could sex radicals call upon the support of prominent businessmen, politicians, and civic leaders. They established a few loosely organized and short-lived associations, including the New England Free Love League and the Western Woman's Emancipation Society, but they seldom did more than hold a few meetings and publish sets of resolutions.

Under those circumstances, sex radical periodicals sustained geographically dispersed women and men's commitment to this unpopular cause by serving as a channel of communication among advocates. Subscribers who lived on the "sparsely settled frontier" of Iowa or in the "wilderness" of Wisconsin wrote about their sense of intellectual alienation from neighbors.[38] Those living in more populous areas also looked to sex radical periodicals as a means by which they could communicate with like-minded women and men. "Free lovers," wrote a Quaker living in Worcester, Massachusetts, "are as scarce here as snow in mid-summer. . . . I welcome it [*Social Revolutionist*] at every recurring visit as the returning of a friend from afar."[39] In addition to providing contact with distant women and men who shared their values and viewpoints, free love periodicals like the *Social Revolutionist* (which published the names of subscribers and correspondents) enabled sex radicals who had lived undercover within a community to find others in their area who shared the same convictions. They had, observed the editor William Denton, "been living alone for years, passing each other in the streets and even transacting business with each other, without knowing that they had a reformatory thought in common."[40]

On several occasions editors attempted to compile lists of women and men who embraced sex radical tenets, but none of the lists appear to have survived. Such lists were problematic because some people wished to preserve their privacy, while others at times played pranks on their neighbors by submitting their names for inclusion. According to John Humphrey Noyes, Thomas and Mary Gove Nichols compiled at least four lists of members of their Progressive Union in the mid-1850s, and these lists contained 324, 527, 506, and 155 names, respectively, but with some duplication.[41] In the spring of 1857, the *Social Revolutionist* collected names for a list of individuals who believed in varietism. "It is in the interest of all who desire such freedom," editor Patterson wrote, "to become acquainted with each other." No copies of the list, which he promised to mail in a plain wrapper to anyone who sent nine or ten cents, are extant.[42]

Periodicals became an especially important channel for transmitting sex radical ideas to women because they provided opportunities to study and reflect upon their content in private. Due to the potential for social ostracism, antebellum women seldom attended lectures given by known free lovers. In an account of his career as an itinerant lecturer, Warren Chase recalled speaking to small groups of men: before arriving in town, political and religious leaders had spread rumors linking him to sexual misconduct in order to discourage women from attending.[43] Chase and others like him nonetheless played a vital role in transporting sex radical ideas from community to community. Holding discussions in the private homes in which they lodged, such traveling lecturers also sold books, pamphlets, and subscriptions to sex radical periodicals. Thus, readership of sex radical literature increased in areas the lecturers visited. The *Kingdom of Heaven,* for example, attracted its largest number of subscribers from New York, where its editor, Thomas Cook, had spent time searching for his spiritual affinity. Lecturing extensively in the Midwest for several years beginning in 1873, the charismatic Victoria Woodhull gained significant numbers of subscribers to the *Weekly* in Michigan, Ohio, Illinois, and Iowa. After hearing her speak, women often felt compelled to subscribe immediately. Mrs. J. M. S. of Bay City, Michigan, writing in 1874, declared: "I cannot go to bed till I have told you how glad I am that it was my privilege to hear both your lectures."[44] *Lucifer's* junior editor Edwin C. Walker's 1887 lecture tour to Iowa evoked similar responses, resulting in numerous subscriptions from that state.

Before the advent of home mail delivery in 1862 and the earliest efforts to provide rural free delivery in 1896, it would have been intimidating for women to visit their local post offices—an environment dominated by men—to pick up issues of sex radical periodicals.[45] Still, some would have read sex radical periodicals to which their fathers, husbands, and brothers subscribed. Once in the home, those texts became powerful tools for stimulating communication among family members. Mrs. Malachi Ellis of Westmoreland, New York, for instance, told other readers of *Woodhull and Claflin's Weekly:* "I could not make myself understood with my husband until reading your blessed paper. Now we can reason together rightly."[46]

In addition to circulating sex radical ideas, sex radical periodicals provided opportunities for women to play active roles in the movement. Women served as editors, coeditors, and acting editors of several monthlies and weeklies, and on occasion both male and female editors made a point of hiring female compositors as a sign of their commitment to woman's economic independence.[47] Several women served as coeditors with men: Mary Gove Nichols (*Nichols' Journal* and *Nichols' Monthly*), Anne Denton Cridge (*Vanguard*), and Cordelia Barry (*Age of Freedom*), while Victoria Woodhull and Tennessee Claflin jointly produced *Woodhull and Claflin's Weekly*. Mattie Sawyer assumed full responsibility for *Hull's Crucible* in 1877 while its namesake devoted his time to the lecture circuit. In Kansas, Lois Waisbrooker edited *Foundation Principles* and served as an acting editor for *Lucifer, the Light-Bearer* along with Lillie D. White and Lizzie Holmes. In addition to serving in editorial capacities, "sister contributors" sent frequent letters for publication and also recruited new subscribers. A Utah woman wrote of sharing copies of *Nichols' Monthly* with her "Mormon sisters," and another managed to obtain twenty-four new subscribers for *Nichols' Journal* while she awaited the arrival of a stagecoach in Griggsville, Illinois, in 1853. Finally, others linked their names to the cause, signing calls for "free conventions," sending donations, and submitting their names for inclusion in published lists of free lovers.[48]

It is difficult to determine precisely how many women and men subscribed to or read sex radical periodicals because they typically shared issues with one another. Editors of two antebellum Ohio titles, the *Social Revolutionist* and *Vanguard*, reported that they had between 350 and 400 reliable subscribers. Such numbers are considerably smaller than circulation records for other reform periodicals of the era, for instance, *The Lily* (devoted to temperance) with a circulation of four thousand.[49] The Nicholses boasted that they had thousands of subscribers for *Nichols' Journal* and its successor *Nichols' Monthly*, but in all likelihood they blurred the distinction between subscribers and readers. Between August and November 1853, for example, they claimed to have a readership ranging from eighteen to fifty thousand, at times citing conflicting numbers on different pages of the same issue. One explanation for this is that their readers sometimes formed "clubs" in which members may have shared issues. One Ohio club, for example, reportedly had a membership of 150 women and men.[50] Although the Nicholses undoubtedly inflated their numbers, it is likely that their journal—with its broader appeal to health reformers and devotees of water cure—had more subscribers than did the *Social Revolutionist* and *Vanguard*.

Antebellum sex radical periodicals may have had small subscription lists, but it is wrong to assume they had equally limited readership and influence. Readers of the *Social Revolutionist*, wrote editor John Patterson, were "thinkers, many of whom are lecturers, writers, and others who are qualifying themselves for agitation and propagandism."[51] Possessing a strong desire to proselytize, they routinely shared their copies with friends and neighbors. A reader writing from Worcester, Massachusetts, described receiving a copy from a friend: "I doubt not that it was read by hundreds, for it passed from hand to hand, and from town to town, till it was pretty well read."[52] Because readers so frequently circulated issues within communities as well as mailed them to friends in distant locations, few copies are extant today.

Reflecting on the power of print to convert people to sex radical beliefs, a *Woodhull and Claflin's Weekly* correspondent named Jane A. Simpson observed in 1875: "If people would only read they would believe the truth, and the truth would make them free." As proof, she cited the example of a seventy-year-old unmarried woman who "never dared read Woodhull's paper, as she thought Mrs. Woodhull a very bad woman." But after reading one issue she became "thoroughly converted."[53] Inspired by such convictions, subscribers shared their precious copies of sex radical periodicals far and wide.

Readers did express some concern that potential converts might have closed minds influenced by the controversial reputation associated with most sex radical periodicals and their editors. As a strategy, John Patterson suggested that subscribers to *Social Revolutionist* who feared its content might be too strong for the uninitiated should first give people copies of *The Sibyl*, a dress reform periodical. It would, he believed, serve as an introduction to topics discussed more extensively in his publication and would "plant seed that would in time produce many fold."[54] Others proposed that women and men who refused to accept issues of sex radical periodicals would read them if they found the papers inserted inside issues of other, more acceptable, titles. Albina Washburn of Colorado adopted another tactic in the 1890s as she attempted to introduce *Lucifer* to suffragists and members of the Woman's Christian Temperance Union (WCTU) in that state. Declaring that she never traveled anywhere without a bundle of *Lucifers* in her bag, she expressed great delight in 1893 when a WCTU woman asked to borrow a copy so she could finish the article Washburn had been reading to her.[55]

Albina Washburn represents just one of the 130 women and men whose letters appeared in two or more sex radical periodicals.[56] Fully one-third of these were women, and the percentage may be even higher because readers contributors often used pseudonyms or initials during the early years of their correspondence. Their persistence across time indicates that many who wrote to those periodicals took the subject of sex reform seriously. Because the sex radical movement would have perished without the support of such women and men, it is useful to delve more deeply into their backgrounds. Few left diaries and correspondence for historians to analyze, thus the only surviving insights to their lives often are found in the letters they submitted to the editors of sex radical periodicals.

Who Were the Sex Radicals?

Far more has been written about the editors of sex radical periodicals than about their readers. Yet readers' letters on the pages of sex radical periodicals contain numerous clues about their geographic distribution, the degree to which they lived in urban or rural environments, and their sex, age, race or ethnicity, socioeconomic status, levels of education, and political beliefs and activities. Given the lengthy period this study covers and the scant numbers of some sex radical periodical titles extant, it was difficult to draw a systematic sample of readership for each year. Instead, generalizations about sex radicals are based on "snapshots" of the readership taken at intervals between 1853 and 1908. In order to develop a fuller picture of the women and men who composed this print-based network of sex radicals, I gathered additional data about readers from such sources as manuscript federal population census records, city directories, and county histories (see the appendix).

Although Thomas and Mary Gove Nichols only infrequently provided the full names or places of residence of the correspondents whose letters they excerpted in *Nichols' Journal* and *Nichols' Monthly* during the mid-1850s, many of their successors in the sex radical press asked readers to provide more complete information.[57] The practice of including reader names and places of residence had numerous advantages. The visibility of other contributors' or subscribers' names lent an air of authenticity and credibility to a periodical's content. It reinforced the notion that editors did not stand alone in their endorsement of sex radical beliefs but in fact had the support of others. Seeing the names of people they knew encouraged some readers to become subscribers, and women in particular found it reassuring to discover the presence of feminine voices. Finally, publishing excerpts of letters or lists of subscribers served a more practical function: it enabled editors to answer readers' questions and to acknowledge receipt of payment for subscriptions or for books and pamphlets.[58]

Men more frequently provided their full names than did women. Despite a policy requiring authors of letters to provide names and places of residence, many female contributors wished to preserve their privacy and continued to send letters signed with pseudonyms or initials. G. P. from Vineland, New Jersey, sheds light on this practice in her request to Moses Harman: "Please don't quote me with name; it brings too many supplicating letters." Women, Lois Waisbrooker elaborated in 1894, hesitated to give their names for publication because some men, hoping to find sexual partners, wrote to women whose names appeared in liberal papers.[59] Describing her disgust with a few of the men who wrote to her, Mary W. Conway in 1895 complained that they demanded a "detailed history of your innermost, or most private life, especially all of your sexual experience." Her revelation suggests that some men may have regarded the content of sex radical periodicals and their resulting correspondence with women as a form of pornography. Conway further observed that few of *Lucifer*'s female readers could afford the cost of postage to reply to such letters and that they also feared "being entrapped by a Comstockian decoy" (a ploy on the part of the postal censor to trick them into sending sexually explicit material through the mail).[60] Given these circumstances, editors sometimes published letters anonymously when they knew the author. In such instances, they typically noted the sex of and community in which a contributor resided (i.e. "a woman from Peru, Indiana, writes . . ."). As correspondents gained confidence in speaking about their ideas and experiences, some who initially protected their identities began giving their full names.

Between 1853 and 1908 by far the largest number of correspondents to sex radical periodicals resided in the Midwest, which I define as the states located in the Old Northwest Territory (Illinois, Indiana, Iowa, Michigan, Ohio, and Wisconsin), followed by women and men who lived in the Central Atlantic states, the Great Plains, and the West.[61] As table 1 illustrates, nearly two-

Table 1. Readers by Geographical Region and Sex

Region of Residence	Males	Females	Initials and Pseudonyms	Subtotals
New England[a]	56	30	47	133
Central Atlantic[b]	87	47	87	221
South[c]	50	31	46	127
Midwest[d]	178	129	201	508
Great Plains[e]	71	40	98	209
West[f]	48	53	109	210
Non-United States[g]	22	5	23	50
	512	335	611	1,458

a. Connecticut, Massachusetts, Maine, New Hampshire, Rhode Island, and Vermont.

b. Washington, D.C., Delaware, Maryland, New Jersey, New York, and Pennsylvania.

c. Alabama, Florida, Georgia, Kentucky, Louisiana, Missouri, South Carolina, Tennessee, Texas, Virginia, and West Virginia.

d. Iowa, Illinois, Indiana, Michigan, Ohio, and Wisconsin.

e. Dakota Territory, Kansas, Minnesota, North Dakota, Nebraska, Oklahoma, and South Dakota.

f. Alaska, Arizona, California, Colorado, Hawaii, Montana, New Mexico, Nevada, Oregon, Utah, Washington, and Wyoming.

g. Australia, Canada, Denmark, England, Italy, Mexico, New Zealand, Scotland, South America, and the South Pacific.

thirds of the 1,458 contributors for whom residence is known lived between Ohio and California. A title usually (but not always, in the case of *Kingdom of Heaven* in 1865 and the *American Journal of Eugenics* in 1907–8) attracted its greatest readership from the state in which it was published. Yet the expanse of sex radical periodical readership spread over time: the *Social Revolutionist* circulated to women and men in nine states in 1857, *Woodhull and Claflin's Weekly* subscribers spanned the continent from Maine to California in 1873 and 1874, and by 1897 *Lucifer, the Lightbearer* reached readers in at least thirty-seven states and territories plus the District of Columbia and more than eight nations beyond the United States. The most notable void in 1873–74 appears in the former states of the Confederacy: it is unlikely that readers struggling to rebound from the Civil War and chafing over the impact of Reconstruction would have subscribed to a sex radical paper published in New York City or Boston or to one known for its advocacy of free love. Of the sex radical periodicals under consideration, only *Lucifer* succeeded in attracting correspondents from southern states, experiencing its widest appeal in that region during the snapshot year of 1887.[62]

Published correspondence also sheds light on the geographic mobility of readers within a region. Railroad connections between Sandusky, Zanesville, Springfield, and Cincinnati, Ohio, for example, facilitated the diffusion of sex radical ideas within that state, and in the 1850s residents living in the Lake Erie community of Berlin Heights traveled with some frequency between northern Ohio and New York's Oneida Community.[63] Itinerants announced their availability to lecture in communities located near railroad lines.[64]

We often think of sex radicals as urban, and yet until the early twentieth century correspondents often resided on farms, ranches, and in rural communities. Urban individualist anarchists tended to prefer the Boston-based *Liberty* to the agrarian, individualized anarchism expressed in Moses Harman's Kansas-based publication. The anarchist Emma Goldman provided a glimpse into the life of one regular correspondent to *Lucifer* and *Free Society*, a Caplinger Mills, Missouri, farm wife named Kate Austin. In 1898 Goldman traveled to meet the woman whose letters to *Lucifer* and *Free Society* had caught her attention. The ride from the railroad station over a twenty-two-mile stretch of road, so rough and rutted that the wagon in which she rode landed in a ditch, reinforced Goldman's understanding of the hardship and isolation farm women endured: an endless struggle against a variety of enemies, including bankers, railroads, and drought. When Goldman inquired how a woman living in "such a dull and limited sphere" could have gained so much knowledge and such a broad perspective, her hostess simply replied: "From reading." Raised by a father who constantly devoured texts, Austin (whose formal education had been limited to two years in a district school, in part because her mother died when she was eleven) read voraciously and widely and encountered the ideas of such freethinkers as Robert G. Ingersoll, Moses Harman, and Lois Waisbrooker. As Goldman looked about Austin's home, she observed "works on philosophy, on social and economic questions, and on sex . . . side by side with the best in poetry and fiction."[65] Austin represents just one of many nineteenth-century rural women who participated in an ongoing print-based discussion about sexuality during the second half of the nineteenth century.

Women's social and intellectual isolation led them to develop a special affinity for the editors of sex radical periodicals. Of the correspondents for whom sex can be determined, the 40 percent who were female demonstrated a strong sense of allegiance to the female editors Mary Gove Nichols, Victoria Woodhull, and Lois Waisbrooker and to *Lucifer*'s Moses Harman. Those who supported Woodhull saw her willingness to discuss sexual topics as serving a higher purpose, one that ultimately promised to strike at the gendered roots of their marginalized status as women. "I wish," wrote one *Woodhull and Claflin's Weekly* reader, Mrs. Eliza Cooper from Eureka, California, in 1875, "all the world could feel as I do the importance and truthfulness of your teachings." Lois Waisbrooker evoked a similar response in her readers. "Every fiber of my soul," confided a Madrid, Iowa, woman in 1894, "vibrates in sympathy with your efforts to inform women and elevate the standard of social purity." Indeed, many of Waisbrooker's readers came to regard her as a trusted friend and confidante: "You seem nearer and dearer to me than many of my blood relations, because I think our ideas are more in accord," wrote one from Junction City, Washington. "I never write what I feel to any of them."[66]

Contrary to a popular notion that associated sex radicalism with youth, correspondents to *Lucifer* included many veteran reformers in their seventies and eighties. An Iowa contributor urged all to give their ages "so we know whether they have had any experiences in life to make their opinions of value." Not everyone complied, but often those who did had been active in reform movements since the 1830s and 1840s. "I have been 'hot' in reform from the age of fifteen to this moment," wrote seventy-three year old E. F. Curtis from Farmington, Ohio, in 1894. Another septuagenarian *Lucifer* correspondent residing in Michigan described himself as "one of those horrid antislavery infidels we used to hear so much about." Committed to the ideal of individual freedom for all, reformers who came to sex radicalism by way of abolitionism refused to rest so long as any form of slavery—wage or women's—persisted. Occasionally, however, octogenarians did cancel their subscriptions, citing as reasons their diminished eyesight or that they expected to expire before their subscriptions.[67]

Contributors seldom revealed their race or ethnicity, but it is evident from contextual cues that most who expressed interest in or support of this cause were of Anglo-Saxon and Protestant backgrounds. Surnames like Adams, Chandler, Davis, Luce, Stewart, and Wilcox fill the pages of sex radical periodicals, with only a smattering of such identifiable ethnic names as Neidermeier, Rollwage, and Ruedebusch. Instances of African American contributors are rare. In 1873 an African American man wrote *Woodhull and Claflin's Weekly* to announce that he had formed a club of forty readers in Providence, Rhode Island. His interest stemmed, it appears, from an appreciation for the *Weekly*'s advocacy of individual freedom more than it did an interest in the reform of sexual relations. "I am," he recorded, "one of the unfortunate race who for more than a century was denied ownership of our own bodies . . . the colored people of this country can never consent to see the freedom of the press . . . put down. The power that can crush that, may enslave us again."[68]

For the most part, nineteenth-century sex radicals lacked formal educations but instead pursued their quest for knowledge through extensive reading and correspondence with one another—in person and through the pages of sex radical periodicals.[69] The grammar, spelling, sentence structure, and references to authors and particular works contained in their letters suggest that many had read widely. Like the youthful Mary Gove Nichols, who devoured a wide array of texts—medical, legal, and theological—which she borrowed from neighboring professional men, many geographically isolated sex radical women turned to books and periodicals because they hungered for knowledge they could use to improve their condition and that of the world around them. Many women purchased liberal or radical books and pamphlets from the editorial offices of sex radical periodicals and thereafter discussed their reactions to the works in the letters they submitted for publication.[70]

Correspondents to sex radical periodicals include a substantial number (40 percent) of women and men from non-elite backgrounds (see table 2). By non-elite, I mean that they belonged to the working class and often struggled financially to sustain themselves and their dependents. Making countless references to their failed crops, depressed livestock prices, or lost sources of employment, "impecunious" farmers, miners, mechanics, and domestics often had difficulty finding enough money to renew or subscribe to the radical papers they so dearly treasured. "The class of people that think along *Lucifer*'s lines are," concluded a reader from Ohio, "most of them I take it, involved deeply in the struggle for 'bread and butter.'"[71] Upon closer examination, it becomes clear that even those among the nearly 60 percent of readers who

Table 2. Sex Radicals by Occupational Category

Occupational Category	Males	Females	Initials and Pseudonyms	Number (Percentage)
Professional[a]	10	3	—	13 (6.1)
Business/government[b]	18	2	1	21 (9.9)
Education/culture[c]	12	9	3	24 (11.3)
Communications[d]	13	6	—	19 (8.9)
Medical[e]	22	7	20	49 (23.0)
Agricultural[f]	26	3	—	29 (13.6)
Skilled labor[g]	25	1	4	30 (14.1)
Unskilled labor[h]	6	19	—	25 (11.7)
Other[i]	2	—	1	3 (1.4)
				213

a. Attorneys, bankers (1), lawyers, and ministers.

b. Cashiers/clerks, clothing retailers, grocers, hotel keepers, manufacturers, merchants, postal carriers, secretaries, shorthand reporters, and stenographers.

c. Artists, authors, dancing teachers, law reporters, lecturers, students, and teachers.

d. Editors, law reporters, printers, proofreaders, and publishers.

e. Clairvoyants, nurses, patent medicine manufacturers and distributors, and physicians.

f. Farmers, fruit growers, and ranchers.

g. Bakers, broom makers, carpenters, cloak makers, coal miners (2), dressmakers, edge-tool makers, firemen, mechanics, millers, shoemakers, painters, and watchmakers.

h. Domestics, homemakers, and laborers.

i. Indigents, fishermen, and hermits.

came from more privileged backgrounds considered themselves outsiders. Fully 23 percent of correspondents identified themselves as medical practitioners, but as water-cure practitioners, clairvoyant healers, and distributors of patent medicines, they found themselves at odds with credentialed "regulars." Likewise, sex radical editors, publishers, printers, and lecturers could by occupation be considered middle-class, but they struggled financially to subsist because of the controversial causes they chose to advocate.

Because so many of *Lucifer*'s subscribers were impoverished, Moses Harman carried them on his subscription list for years without payment. But when subscribers to *Foundation Principles* pleaded poverty, a disgusted Lois Waisbrooker retorted: "Do you not believe that if your soul went out to the cause . . . as earnestly as your words seem to imply, you could save that much a week toward sustaining a paper?"[72] Harman's strategy, however, succeeded, and with the support of his loyal following he kept *Lucifer* alive many years after *Foundation Principles* had faltered.

By non-elite, I also mean that sex radicals generally lacked social status in their communities, in part because of economic circumstances and partly because they embraced unpopular social and political views separating them from neighbors. United by their shared sense of oppression and widening awareness of a class divide rooted in economic conditions, those who wrote to *Lucifer* during the drought-stricken 1880s and the economically depressed 1890s filled their letters with complaints about "the monster, Monopoly," and endorsements of Jacob Coxey's army of unemployed.[73] Aligning themselves with Moses Harman's anarchistic perspective, they blamed their poverty on a few powerful men who controlled money, land, transportation, and the tools of production.

Little is known about anarchism's appeal to rural people. Classic studies of this faction-ridden movement emphasize its roots, core beliefs, and urban manifestations. The historian James J. Martin divides anarchists into two major categories: native-born (on U.S. soil) and those with European roots.[74] The former often embraced individualist anarchism, believing in individual freedom (or, as they called it, sovereignty) so long as it did not interfere with the liberty of others, and they advocated ownership of private property for the purpose of subsistence. Many individualist anarchists gravitated to *Liberty,* a weekly published in Boston by Benjamin R. Tucker (formerly an associate of Victoria Woodhull and Ezra Heywood), leaving an impression that this strand of anarchism had a predominantly eastern and urban constituency. Communist anarchists, like many of the individualist anarchists who wrote to *Liberty,* also tended to reside in cities, but their ranks included many immigrants and working-class men and women. Moreover, they rejected the notion of private property, which they believed contributed to class divisions, and instead placed their faith in collectivist solutions. Several bloody incidents, among them Chicago's Haymarket Massacre in 1886, also contributed to a reputation for violence.

Liberty occasionally printed women's correspondence about sexuality and maternity during the 1880s, but those few contributions declined markedly by the close of the decade. Benjamin R. Tucker accorded women's issues far less importance than such topics as economic reform and freedom of speech. Some of his readers concurred, arguing that if discussions of sexual relations did occur, they should be handled only by "men of science."[75]

In contrast to *Liberty,* rural midwestern and western women, many of them sympathetic to Moses Harman's presentation of individualist anarchism, aired their ideas on the pages of *Lucifer.* Yet rural women remain largely absent from the histories of American anarchism, even in those studies focusing specifically on female anarchists. The historian Margaret Marsh, for instance, divides female anarchists into three categories: educated professionals, the daughters of working-class and immigrant families, and those who reveled in sexual experimentation. The rural women who either professed or expressed sympathy for anarchist ideas and sex radicalism do not fit neatly into any of these categories. Few correspondents to the sex radical periodicals under consideration expressed delight in sexual experimentation. Instead, they focused on the promise of individual freedom for women: the right to control their bodies.[76]

Correspondents to sex radical periodicals also differed from those around them because of their heterodox ideas about religion. Often freethinkers, they had come to freethought on a path filled with a variety of religious experiences, including the Calvinism of their parents, conversion experiences, and exposure to Quaker theology, Swedenborgianism, and Spiritualism.[77] In sum, those experiences reinforced the notion of an individual empowered to act by virtue of his or her relationship to a divine being. Building on this conviction, sex radicals who professed freethought, along with a small number who boldly denied the existence of God, devoted substantial discussion to the subject of organized religion. Condemning religious bigotry and hypocrisy, they blamed the church for teaching men to treat their wives as property and for telling women they must submit to their husbands' commands, precisely because they retained their idealistic expectations and their belief in the millennium.[78]

The marginalized economic and social status of rural women and men heightened their receptiveness to protest movements that offered the possibility of individual empowerment. Thus, rural men and women could support the farmers' alliances to establish cooperatives and to work for the regulation of transportation and marketplace monopolies, Bellamy Nationalism to nationalize industry and utilities, and the People's party to make their voices heard politically.[79] Others, less trustful of the state's ability to remedy their problems, embraced anarchism, the most extreme solution because it called for the abolition of government. Viewing their world through an anarchistic lens, they protested institutions that prescribed female submissiveness and loss of identity, abhorred the state licensing of marriage, and idealistically yearned for the day in which they, as individual sovereigns, would be free to determine if, when, and with whom they had children. With its vision of an equitable society composed of free individuals governed by an internal power rather than by arbitrary and externally imposed laws, anarchism resonated with many who read sex radical periodicals.

Despite their shared belief in the value of individualism, equality, and freedom, the readership of sex radical periodicals seldom participated in such moral and political reform movements as woman suffrage societies, farmers' alliances, and the People's party. Mattie Sawyer, of *Hull's Crucible*, argued in 1876 that "rank and file" working women would never find "hope" in the "party known as the Woman Suffragists." As proof, she pointed to a recommendation that property become the basis of the elective franchise for women. "Voting covers a small part of the issue," she exclaimed. "We demand work, and pay for it."[80] A subsidiary goal, likeminded reformers concurred, should be pursued only after economic and social reform had been achieved.

Others regarded government as corrupt and saw no benefit in voting. "Balloting for a change of rulers," argued Myra Pepper in 1903, "can never benefit a people." "To me," wrote another *Lucifer* correspondent from Missouri, "political rights are secondary as compared to the right of woman to her own body."[81] Such anarchistic Luciferians believed that the abolition of wage slavery could not occur without woman's emancipation from sex slavery. "The surest and only way to successfully free the wage slave," Moses Harman reasoned, was "to free the mothers, so that no more subjects for the wage boss could or would be born." Even readers who protested the existence of wage slavery believed that the emancipation of women from "sex slavery" should be a higher priority "because it is through heredity that wage slaves [are born]."[82]

Few members of the WCTU, farmers' alliances, and state or local woman suffrage societies would have welcomed sex radical women and men to their ranks. Following their interactions with Victoria Woodhull in the 1870s, many suffrage associations distanced themselves from the stigma of free love because they did not wish to alienate religious and political leaders. In 1893, for example, Albina Washburn reported that the Colorado WCTU had appointed her to carry out suffrage work for the Colorado Woman Suffrage Association, but the organization immediately withdrew the appointment upon learning that she not only subscribed to *Lucifer* but also distributed copies to other women. Organizations like the WCTU and the alliances often assumed their members to be Christian. Members were required to be of "good moral character" and to believe in "the existence of a Supreme Being."[83]

In the Great Plains and West, the distance from population centers—both geographically and socially—also would have inhibited farm women's participation in woman suffrage, the WCTU, and women's club meetings. Farm women ventured into town less frequently than did men because they "felt particularly awkward about town ways" and were "painfully aware of the perceived deficiencies of their patched and faded dresses."[84] Aside from lacking appropriate clothing, manners, and education, few could find spare time from farm and house work for meetings or other such outside activities.

In the sex radical press, however, socially and economically alienated rural women and their urban sisters found acceptance, community, and an environment in which they could openly and freely explore and express their ideas about women's rights. Such periodicals as *Nichols' Journal, Woodhull and Claflin's Weekly, Hull's Crucible, The Word,* and *Lucifer, the Light-Bearer* propelled the sex radical movement in which they participated across time and space. Yet the power of print also resided in novels and pamphlets. Indeed, some women might never have embraced sex radical ideas had they not encountered them first in fictional form.

3. The Good Time Coming

You say that "Woman's Rights" has no connection with Free Love. I
say that they are almost wholly identical. Woman's most essential,
all-embracing right, is her *right to herself*, her right to *self-ownership*.
The recognition of this right *constitutes* the abolition of marriage.

—Francis Barry, 1871

IN 1853, A SOUTHWESTERN OHIO FARMER named John Patterson penned
a scathing fictional critique of marriage entitled *Charles Hopewell; or, Society As It Is and As It Should Be*. It features an intelligent and articulate wife
and mother of three named Amelia. "Without much property and unable
to hire help," Amelia observes, "I have had to support the drudgery of the
kitchen, and the care-taking of my children. Instead of living up to the aspirations of a human being, I have had to be a work-brute; and when one is
exhausted, body and soul, in menial service, the tendency is toward beastliness, and nothing else can be made of it."[1] Amelia does not address the subject of sexuality openly, but her comments nonetheless suggest that she views
marriage as physically degrading rather than spiritually uplifting to a woman. A plan for association (communal living), she proposes, would offer
women the prospect of relief. On the one hand, it would free them from
endless rounds of daily chores. On the other hand, it would mean that no
one, married or single, would have to worry about economic security. Hereditarianism also informs Amelia's worldview: like many other women of
the era she links unwanted children with inherited disease and defects. In her
ideal vision of society, however, personal choice rather than economic or
social necessity would govern women's decision to marry (or to prostitute
themselves). Only then, reasons Amelia, could children be conceived in love
and endowed with the potential to redeem the world. But until a plan for
cooperation is established, woman will continue to "pollute the temple of her
soul" by having unwanted sexual intercourse and to "burthen herself and the

race with inferior offspring . . . all because the moral sense of society is too gross and besotted to perceive the soul-destroying wrong."[2]

In a decade characterized by change and uncertainty, *Charles Hopewell* resonated with midwestern readers, especially those set adrift by land and railroad speculation run rampant. Like the novel's title character and his sister Amelia, hundreds of women and men explored the possibility of joining communal experiments, turning to such sites as Modern Times, New York; Ceresco, Wisconsin; Memnonia, in Yellow Springs, Ohio; or the communal family headed by James W. Towner in West Union, Iowa. Even John Patterson attempted to live the life he described in his novel when in 1853 he joined with seven other adults and five children to form the Rising Star Community in rural southwestern Ohio.[3] None of these ventures, however, generated more sensationalism and controversy than did the band of socialists who became known as the Berlin Heights Free Lovers. Attempting to make the theoretical concrete, they offered women sexual autonomy and economic opportunity and thus provoked fear in those who believed freedom and equality for women would destabilize the nation's social order.

Historical accounts of this socialistic experiment tend to portray the Berlin Heights Free Lovers as a short-lived, male-dominated band of eccentric misfits who offended local moral sensibilities.[4] A reexamination through gendered and economic lenses, however, alters this perception. Evidence drawn from contemporary periodicals, federal manuscript population censuses, county court records, manuscript collections, and newspaper articles confirms that women played a far greater role in the community than previously recognized. Additionally, it reveals that local objections to the "Free Love menace," which coincided with the aftermath of the Panic of 1857, had economic as well as moral underpinnings.

The Marriage Question

The metaphor of marriage as a form of women's slavery has its roots in several antebellum reform movements. Garrisonian abolitionism played a key role in increasing women's awareness of the similarities between chattel and marital slavery. Awakening a feminist consciousness within them, it presented the issues of slave emancipation and self-emancipation as intertwined. Consequently, antislavery newspapers became an early outlet for feminist protest, and the visibility of female abolitionist lecturers provided models of women who possessed the courage to speak in front of mixed-sex audiences.[5]

Others reinforced the parallel between slavery and marriage. In 1850, the founder of the Oneida Community, John Humphrey Noyes, published a tract entitled *Slavery and Marriage* in which he satirized the similarities embedded in the arguments southerners used to justify slavery and northerners used to defend indissoluble marriage. Both, he noted, rested on an assumption of a hierarchical order rather than an egalitarian relationship, assumed cruelty to be an exception rather than the rule, expected the law to protect dependents from abuse, and posited that women and slaves lacked the capacity to care for themselves in freedom. Drawing similar comparisons, southern newspaper editors reminded their readers of the hypocrisy of northern abolitionists who attacked chattel slavery yet denied their wives the right to vote, own property, or have custody of their children. The reform of marriage, the editor of Georgia's *Augusta Chronicle and Sentinel* claimed, undermined the customary authority of white male heads of household by threatening to deny them the private property that enhanced their patriarchal status. And in the north, a correspondent to William Lloyd Garrison's *Liberator* echoed this line of thought, pointing out to readers the irony of Massachusetts (a state that was home to numerous abolitionists) holding one-half of its population—women—in legal slavery.[6]

Temperance reformers contributed to the critique of marriage as a form of women's slavery by focusing on the victimization of wives and children by inebriated men. Because the prevailing social code labeled women who discussed sexual topics as morally suspect, advocates of temperance instead emphasized the consequences for children born to alcoholic fathers. Nonetheless, reformers could not completely ignore the existence of domestic violence when they campaigned for legislation to grant divorces to the wives of alcoholics.[7] In an 1852 address before the first convention of the New York State Woman's Temperance Society, the women's rights advocate Elizabeth Cady Stanton urged women to resist having sexual intercourse with "drunkards." Relying upon her audience's familiarity with hereditarian thought, she argued that women had a responsibility to prevent their children from inheriting paternal weaknesses.[8] Under this logic, the denial of a husband's marital rights, even though sanctioned by church and state, became the ultimate moral act.

Dress reformers, encouraging women to assert their independence from the chains of fashion, stressed the relationship between constrictive clothing, slavery, and women's rights. As a correspondent to the dress reform periodical *The Sybil* observed, a campaign for women's rights was pointless so long as women continued, in exchange for a home, to make "the silly promise to become [a] man's pet and plaything, his doll-baby and pussy-cat, his household divinity, his nurse, his drudge, his dishwasher and baby-rocker, his tool to keep his parlor and kitchen in order by day, and pander to his lusts by night." Yet many who advocated dress reform, *Social Revolutionist* editor John Patterson observed in 1857, "do not in the least suspect that this freer style of dress is a protest against the slavery of woman, and that the agitation respecting it is clearing the way for the utter abrogation of marriage slavery."[9]

While many people discussed the "marriage question" at mid-century, the most persistent voices, and the ones most likely to describe marriage as a form of women's slavery, belonged to ultraist reformers. Yearning for the millennium, ultraists attempted to eliminate impurities from their lives and the lives of others. Hence, they supported such demands as the immediate abolition of slavery, total abstinence from alcohol consumption, and the establishment of a new social order. Ultraists, according to the historian Thomas Hamm, perceived American society as "so fundamentally flawed that radical change was imperative in economic, political, gender, and other relations." The historian Nancy Hewitt concurs that ultraists often eschewed formal organization but nonetheless were "visible and vocal" as they explored unorthodox spiritual and social ideas designed to establish society on a more equal footing.[10] Located on the fringes of an emerging middle class, ultraist reformers could be found among rural families, Spiritualists, and Hicksite Quakers with a penchant for criticizing social institutions.

Spiritualists often "led so-called ultraist wings" in many of the reform movements that flourished in the Midwest at mid-century, including abolitionism, dress reform, temperance, and women's rights. As a movement that provided women with a forum in which to speak freely, Spiritualism had great appeal to women eager "to depart from the traditional social order and especially from existing gender roles." Because seemingly passive trance speakers and mediums serving as vehicles for the messages of spirits could more easily utter subversive messages, mediumship "gave women a public leadership role that allowed them to remain compliant with the complex of values of the period that have come to be known as the cult of true womanhood." Spiritualists' tendency to freethought, observed a Portage, Ohio, reformer, made them "more likely to examine free love theories than those who have not been emancipated from the thralldom of mental bondage."[11] Thus, Spiritualism provided restive women of the 1850s with an important arena in which they could begin proclaiming their freedom.

Often those who agitated for the reform of marriage also professed a belief in Spiritualism. Embracing a hyperidealized vision of heterosexual love, which they described as divinely sanctioned, they yearned for marriages of "two souls with but a single thought, two hearts that beat as one."[12] True love, they believed, could sanctify sexual intercourse, whether or not it was authorized by the state or blessed by the church. But even they did not regard divine sanction as a guarantee of love's longevity. So wedded were Spiritualists and free lovers to the conviction that force polluted love, that they urged men and women to stop living together as husband and wife if their love for one another withered and ceased altogether.[13]

Spiritualists believed that this idealized form of marriage held the key to lasting social change: only after a man or woman joined with a true love could they progress together from an animal (or sensual) plane to a highly desirable spiritual plane of existence. Based on this logic, the Spiritualists who became associated with free love looked to "true marriages" as the source of "love children—the product of design and an enlightened understanding— not of repulsion and chance."[14] Such children, they believed, would possess the power to regenerate society and inaugurate the millennium. A significant impediment to their vision, however, lay in the fact that men and women, due to worldly pressures, economic expediencies, and geographical barriers, found themselves married to the wrong person. In such cases, Spiritualist advocates of social freedom contended, legal marriage was no better than slavery, and dissolution was warranted.

Free Love's Appeal to Women

As they searched for order and improvement in their lives, hundreds of women and men eagerly read periodicals bearing such titles as *Agitator, Vanguard,* and *New Era.* Editors of many reform publications, however, refused to publish the ultraist critiques of government and marriage submitted to them by Patterson and other marriage reformers. Determined to share his viewpoint, Patterson secured a printing press and type, and in January 1856 issued the first number of his aptly named *Social Revolutionist,* a "medium for free discussion." Contributors responded enthusiastically, filling the densely packed monthly with essays in which they challenged the role of government in private life, questioned the existence of God, criticized the institution of marriage, debated the merits of free love, and explored the prospects of establishing communitarian ventures. From its inception, Patterson and corresponding editor William Denton (an itinerant lecturer and social reformer) devoted so much space to critiques of marriage and debates about sexuality that the *Social Revolutionist* soon became synonymous with the cause of free love.

Few outlets existed in which women openly could discuss marital abuse (which they defined as unwanted sexual intercourse as well as the stifling of their minds), thus many suffered in silence. Some conversations occurred at water-cure resorts, where those who could afford such treatment took refuge from the responsibilities of marriage and sought relief for what today would be known as urogenital diseases. Sharing intimate details about the physical and emotional dimensions of marital life raised their awareness of the relationship between marriage and women's health. In a course of treatment for tuberculosis, for example, one *Social Revolutionist* correspondent, Damaris Colburn Bush, made frequent visits to water-cure resorts, where she had her consciousness awakened by a series of conversations with "victims of sexual abuse."[15]

Initially, male contributors dominated the discussions of sexuality and women's rights that appeared in the *Social Revolutionist.* One of the most articulate, Francis Barry (a Garrisonian-styled abolitionist who had moved to Ohio from the East), denounced marriage as "a system of Prostitution . . . sexual intercourse without love. . . . It is the commonest thing that a woman marries for a home or for a position in society, or for some other reason." Like prostitutes, he explained, wives sold themselves for monetary compensation. "Indeed, the common prostitute has some choice, but the wife has no choice—she is a FORCED prostitute!" In freedom, Joseph Treat elaborated, people could "live together in pairs; and have and rear families." Products of such love unions, he firmly believed, "won't be born with rottenness in their bones, nor lust in their hearts,—as almost all the offspring of marriage are."[16]

After digesting such comments, thirty-one-year-old Minerva Putnam encouraged each female reader to "rise in the dignity of her nature and declare herself free." "Will you let men fight the battle for you," she admonished, "when, without your help, they can never conquer[?]"[17] Putnam, a regular reader of the *Social Revolutionist,* believed that women would never fully comprehend the necessity of political rights unless they first recognized the extent and severity of their own economic and social subordination. Only then could women appreciate the necessity of attaining and preserving the rights for which advocates of woman suffrage claimed to fight. And where better to begin, she reasoned, than by breaking the code of silence that hid the existence of "woman's slavery" in marriage?

Domestic abuse, whether openly acknowledged or not, was a significant problem at mid-century. As one indication, nineteen states had provisions for the granting of divorce on grounds of cruelty by 1850. Robert L. Griswold's study of divorce in California between 1850 and 1890 further confirms the seriousness of the problem: nearly 46 percent of the suits filed by women against their husbands included accusations of cruelty that included sexual abuse as well as "character defamation and false imputations of infidelity." Despite these indicators and the fact that a number of reformers expressed concern about marital cruelty, few addressed the subject explicitly. Instead, they channeled their energies into moral reform movements focused on eliminating the problem by curbing men's behavior.[18]

At a time when social custom prescribed that women eschew such topics as female sexuality and marital sexual abuse, the willingness of the female readers of the *Social Revolutionist* to speak openly confirms the depth of their despair and discontent. John Patterson promised that he would publish letters anonymously if *he* knew who wrote them. He and the corresponding editor, William Denton, would have known many contributors in the Ohio-Indiana-Michigan area where they regularly traveled and lectured. Thus encouraged, hundreds of female correspondents, writing from the privacy of their homes, responded to Putnam's call for testimonials. Written under the cover of pseudonyms, yet often known to each other, those missives collectively constituted a print-based form of consciousness raising. Space limitations prevented Patterson from printing all of the letters, but over a two-year period he published portions of letters from at least twenty women, some of whom wrote several times.[19]

The women who broke the code of silence shrouding their sexual subordination in marriage shared Putnam's conviction that each woman must participate in her own emancipation. "Better that our modesty be shocked a little," declared a correspondent who signed herself Lily White, "than that the whole race be ruined by unchecked licentiousness, though sanctioned by law and public opinion." A dress reformer noted that the "shackles of custom and law" prevented enslaved people—wives as well as chattel—from recognizing "what is natural and what is not." After repeated submission to husbands' legally sanctioned power, other women observed, many wives lacked the emotional and physical strength to speak out, let alone resist. Years of being told, "I have bought you, I've paid for it, and it's mine by law! Don't I own you, body and soul?" or, "You shouldn't a been a woman then; that's what you were made for" had crushed their spirits.[20]

Committed to improving the lives of married women, those who chose to share their experiences and observations with other readers of the *Social Revolutionist* focused first and foremost on men's sexual abuse of women in the context of marriage. In confessional style, they relayed accounts of physical and emotional abuse, including curses, blows, and broken bones that resulted when a woman refused her husband's sexual advances. Women dread revealing such secrets, explained a woman writing under the name Minerva Putnam, "for fear it will break up the family," but knew they must in order to free those living in isolation (who remained blinded to enslavement in marriage) and their daughters, whom they wanted to protect "from this holocaust of death."[21]

Comparing wives to slaves and prostitutes, neither of whom could exert sexual autonomy, contributors thus laid the groundwork for a wider understanding of wives' undesirable position in marriage. In letter after letter they illustrated the consequences of women's marital enslavement by relaying accounts (both real and possibly exaggerated) of selfish husbands and submissive wives. A woman named Louisa shared with readers the sad tale of her mother, who died at the age of forty-seven after enduring years with a husband who reportedly demanded sexual intercourse four and five times each night. Another, writing under the pseudonym Justicia, told of a husband who forced his fifty-year-old wife to have intercourse with him only two days after she had given birth. Contributors depicted marriage as a site where women became weary, worn down by the daily demands of an isolated home, and old before their time. But even worse, as their testimonials confirm, was the repeated subjection to unwanted sexual intercourse. Nothing, argued the physician Vivian Grey, aged a woman faster or debased her more than being treated like a piece of property. Some women, attempting to take control of their lives, terminated unwanted pregnancies by applying methods described in Thomas Nichols's health manual, *Esoteric Anthropology*. Others, wishing to avoid such drastic measures, declared: "Sleeping ALONE is the best medicine I've ever tried."[22]

Women did attempt to moderate their criticism of husbands by reminding readers that the institution of marriage also victimized men by turning them into brutes. "Marriage," wrote Lily White in the spring of 1857, "gives man power over woman and few are so perfect but that they will abuse that power, though many of them do it without evil intent."[23] Sex radicals believed that the social, legal, and economic imbalance of power created by marriage laws encouraged men to regard their wives not as equals but as sexual objects dedicated to the gratification of their legally sanctioned sexual desires. This sense of absolute power, women like Lily White reasoned, prevented the responsible practice of freedom, which they believed had limits. A person could act freely, they contended, only so long as he or she did not restrict the freedom of another. Men's current behavior in marriage, they reasoned, had larger consequences: it established a precedent for their behavior in other relationships. Because the slaveholder had his first lessons about slavery from watching his father rule his mother, it followed that marital slavery represented the root cause of all other forms of slavery. After digesting all that women had shared about their marital lives, the itinerant lecturer and abolitionist Francis Barry declared that such "sexual bondage" as occurred in marriage found "its equal only in the slave-breeding of the Slave States."[24]

Women who described marriage as a form of "dreary slavery in the free states" blamed the church as well as the state for perpetuating this deeply ingrained pattern of male power and female submission. Religious leaders, they argued, had exacerbated married women's suffering by teaching young boys to suppress their sexual desires until after their wedding day. Consequently, men learned to regard marriage as the only legitimate site for the exercise of their sexual passions. They could, of course, turn to prostitutes for sexual release, but officially the church condemned such behavior as sinful. A female physician who had treated numerous women suffering from gynecological ailments thus blamed the church for teaching men to think of women as "low and sensual" and to regard "the central idea of marriage" as sexual release rather than as a partnership between loving equals. And so long as the church fostered the development of men's "animalistic" sexuality rather than "its sanctification by the spiritual," argued another *Social Revolutionist* correspondent, neither men nor women could progress to a higher state of spiritual development.[25]

As if to counter the objection that only debased men would abuse their wives, married women provided numerous examples of men who cited biblical authority when commanding their wives to submit to selfish sexual demands. They told of hypocritical (because they were so outwardly pious) Baptists, Congregationalists, and Presbyterians who compelled their wives to submit to sexual intercourse several times nightly, during menstruation, or immediately before or after childbirth. How could any man who felt "one finger-touch of God," another correspondent demanded, believe that the marriage contract had given him "any moral right to the control of a woman's person against her wish?" Confronted with these issues, some women rejected Christianity and embraced freethought. "Don't talk to me," one younger correspondent declared, "of the holiness of the marriage relation!"[26]

Women also blamed the isolated home for enslaving them and thus preventing them from attaining their full emotional and intellectual potential. By isolated, they meant a woman who lived in a separate household with her husband and children and who had full responsibility for the household chores and child care. Earlier in the 1850s, Cordelia Barry noted, she had thought "the isolated home, with its two lovers, the sweetest spot on earth." But time and experience led her to regard it and marriage as "two wheels of Juggernut [*sic*], to crush its victims everywhere." Evoking the image of "women, isolated over their cooking stoves, with little children clinging to them," Cora Corning agreed that marriage and its accompanying household drudgery robbed women of individuality. In addition to "crushing out her life by inches," Damaris Colburn Bush added, it also rendered a woman an "imbecile in intellect, a mere apology in a physical sense, and spiritually anything but a woman." A woman could never "rise above the place she now holds," Bush continued, so long "as she remains in isolation." The solution, correspondents proposed, lay in cooperative housekeeping because it would provide women with daily periods for rest and individual pursuits.[27] Pointing to the efficiency of communal kitchens at the Oneida Community and efforts to establish unitary homes with collective child care, others remained adamant in their assertion that the isolated home prevented women's freedom by keeping them separated, subjugated, and exhausted.

Awakened to their powerlessness in marriage, female free love advocates began to ponder how they could secure "equal rights and privileges" with men. The nature of the power men exercised over women in marriage was extremely difficult to eradicate because it was not simply dual (i.e. a dominant husband and a submissive wife) but also involved a complex web of relationships that included clerical and legal structures and the social customs that reinforced them.[28] This reality inspired Lily White's desire to prevent young girls from entering marriage "blindfolded." Many had discovered too late, she reminded them, that "there is no way to get out of it respectably." Moreover, a woman who experienced cruelty in the form of physical, verbal, and emotional abuse risked economic insecurity as well as community ridicule and censure if she abandoned her accepted and expected role as dutiful wife. "Reformers tell us we must rouse ourselves, and assert our rights," one observed. But who, she asked, will give "money to feed and clothe us while we are proclaiming our freedom?"[29]

In addition to exploring such issues in print, some women delivered bold public indictments of marriage at Spiritualist meetings. In a controversial address delivered before Spiritualists, abolitionists, free lovers, and advocates of women's rights gathered in Ravenna, Ohio, in 1857, a married woman named Carrie Lewis provoked widespread condemnation by declaring the right to be "the divine monarch of myself." Evoking the Quaker belief that each person possesses a spark of the divine within, she denounced forced sexual relations as an unholy act, one with severe consequences: the birth of defective children, the perpetuation of social ills, and the delay of the "Good Time Coming." On this basis, she justified her oft quoted demand—that women have the right to choose the father of their children.[30]

Lewis, as had Elizabeth Cady Stanton before her, regarded women as more spiritual than men and thus better equipped to ensure that they would give birth to children capable of inaugurating the millennium. Farmers, contended the reformer Laura Jones at a meeting of the Friends of Progress (radical reformers who had separated from the Hicksite Friends), took greater effort to improve their livestock than they did in selecting wives to bear their children.[31] But while women defended their moral superiority, male critics believed that giving a woman the right to choose the father of her child would lead to the downfall of existing moral and social order. Assuming that women promiscuously would choose a different man to father each child, men failed to recognize that speakers like Lewis and Jones in fact sought a woman's right to refuse the sexual advances of a man she did not love, even if he was her husband.

A year later, in 1858, reformers representing a diverse array of causes gathered in Rutland, Vermont, where they heard the Spiritualist Julia Branch make a declaration not unlike that of Lewis: "You speak of her right to labor—her right to teach—her right to vote, and lastly though not least, her right to get married, but do you say anything about her right to love when she will, where she will and how she will?" For Branch, described as being a plain, "slight," and poorly dressed woman in her late twenties, a woman's ability to control access to her body represented the ultimate right, one from which all other rights would flow. Her critics, in an attempt to undermine the effect of her words, dismissed Branch as a common prostitute: "Think of a woman making such a speech as this anywhere, and especially in the presence of coarse and brutish men!" As the statement suggests, that male journalist believed Branch had transcended the prescribed "bounds of modesty" for a middle-class woman. Like many other men, he expected women to possess both greater self-control and less sexual desire.[32]

Reclaiming Female Sexual Desire

The idea of women as sexual beings ran counter to the prevailing expectations of women in antebellum America. As the rise of evangelical religion between the 1790s and the 1830s contributed to a shift from woman as carnal (Eve) to woman as moral (Mary), men increasingly entered paid employment in the public sphere. When their wives and daughters remained responsible for reproductive and household work in the domestic sphere, it became all the more evident that "women had neither the property and political rights, nor the freedom of movement enjoyed by white men." One response, on the part of the white wives of merchants, prosperous farmers, educators, and others who considered themselves part of an emerging middle class, was to emphasize the perception of themselves as inherently more moral than men. Cultivating an image for woman as sexually pure, they became "a good investment for a man who wanted to get ahead." Resourceful, respectable, and pure, a virtuous wife could help her husband cultivate the self-control necessary for advancement in an industrializing world. Yet the women who accepted this responsibility acceded to "a new sexual politics of erotic guilt and asexual love."[33]

Political and moral authorities further reinforced the idea of antebellum women as passionless by emphasizing their role as moral exemplars for their husbands and children. Whigs and then Republicans expected women to curb men's errant behaviors by cultivating in them such domestic virtues as temperance. Moreover, clergymen and others published etiquette manuals intended to convey to women the desirability of remaining pure and consequently asexual.[34] Cumulatively, such messages told women that it was unnatural for them to acknowledge—let alone act upon—their sexuality. Nonetheless, some protested those assumptions.

After having reviewed many issues of the *Social Revolutionist,* a woman writing under the name Cora Corning objected to the fact that the letters published therein left readers with an impression of women as less sexual than men. "Does not the sexual supply in woman equal the same demand in man?" she asked. If women, she continued "are not equal to the demand, there is a cause for it, not originating in nature, but acquired." Corning did not stand alone in asserting women's capacity for experiencing and enjoying sexual passion. A contributor named Mary Chilton also challenged the idea of purity as abstinence: "A fine, healthy manly man meets a lovely womanly woman. . . . He awakens her." "Call it 'sensual,' brand it 'bestial,' denounce it as 'lust,' base 'selfishness,' anything an impure imagination can suggest; but ever will nature vindicate the purity of that admiring, reverential look" with the incarnation of love "in Human Form Divine."[35]

Yet even women who openly discussed their sexual feelings and described them as natural confessed that they felt awkward and uncomfortable divulging the depth of their passion in print. It was not, they recognized, socially acceptable to admit having sexual desire during pregnancy, to say that their husbands did not "half satisfy" them, or to acknowledge that they had grown even "more amorous . . . in marriage." This may in part explain the tendency for female correspondents to portray sexual intercourse in hyperidealized terms, attributing their capacity for passion to external forces. One, after describing the "electric" sensations that occurred when a woman was attracted to a man, claimed that they occurred because of "an angel visitation."[36] Some described sexual intercourse as a form of spiritual communion expressed in a physical way; others justified sexual desire as a gift bestowed upon them by nature.

When it came to the subject of variety in sexual relations, *Social Revolutionist* correspondents could never reach an agreement. Many argued that nature intended for women and men to live in lifelong, committed monogamous relationships, and blamed variety for causing "the foulest diseases" (syphilis and gonorrhea) in women and the children they bore. The social reformer William Denton raised an issue that resonated with many others—the fate of variety free lovers' offspring. He warned that "children born in consequence of transient unions are almost certain to be left orphans in the worst possible sense." Arriving in the world "sin-stamped and cursed from their birth . . . destitute of a father's care," they would be cast on the "charity of friends and that of the public."[37]

Most of the *Social Revolutionist*'s female contributors either chose not to discuss variety or took a neutral position on the subject. Hesitant to declare herself either way, Charlotte H. Bowen confided: "Thus far I have never loved but ONE individual at the same time." As a "progressive being," however, she would not rule out the possibility of growing "into the truth of variety" by meeting with individuals she had not seen before. Others, like Cordelia Barry, believed that people were in a transitional state and therefore could not yet comprehend the full meaning of freedom until they advanced to a higher plane of development. "We grow," she wrote in 1857, "and every step upward brings a different landscape to our eyes—a different shape and shading to all objects. Growth and change are the reasons why you can't mark one 'straight and narrow way.'" Adopting a nonjudgmental position, she refused to label varietists or strict monogamists as either higher or lower. Instead, she reasoned, "the myriad voices of Nature speak to each soul differently. . . . So, on whatever plane we are, we must live out our own natures—be true to our own interior convictions."[38]

Only a few correspondents defended variety as natural. Utopian idealism led some, especially those who yearned for a harmonious existence among all men and women, to view variety in sexual relations as the epitome of selfless love. Minerva Putnam admitted feeling repulsed when her husband first introduced the idea to her, but after much study and thought she concluded that loving another person would enrich them both. It would, she reasoned, help them overcome the selfish tendency to possess one another. "When he loved another," she wrote, "I loved her too. I took to my heart as a dear sister, the one whose love had made happier the heart I prized so much." Lest others might consider her long-suffering and tolerant of her husband's other loves, however, Putnam hastened to assure readers that she too had taken a lover, and it had enriched everyone. Viewing variety as a social reform that would lead to the inauguration of heaven on earth, Putnam and others who defended this controversial concept feared that impure-minded women and men—standing on a lower developmental plan—would easily misunderstand its purpose. Variety, James W. Towner reminded *Social Revolutionist* readers, was meant to be "part of a whole social scheme, of which the unitary home and woman's pecuniary independence are essential elements." In the context of a communal setting, he assured, the question of who assumed responsibility for the children of variety free lovers would no longer be an issue.[39]

In Search of Community

Socially marginalized by their religious affiliations (or lack thereof), family background, and inability to compete in a rough and tumble market economy, ultraist reformers who wrote to the *Social Revolutionist* resided primarily in rural areas of the Midwest. Railway expansion and the availability of affordable western lands had fostered extensive speculation in that region during the early 1850s. Many farmers, caught up in the promise of prosperity, invested in railway companies because they expected the prices of agricultural commodities to continue rising as railroads made it easier to transport their crops to market. The end of the Crimean War in the spring of 1856, a bumper wheat crop, and the drying up of the foreign grain market, however, caused the land boom to collapse. As it brought many to the edge of bankruptcy, the Panic of 1857 and its aftermath simultaneously fanned the sparks of midwestern social radicalism among many who felt they had lost control of their lives. Antiauthoritarianism flourished as northern "cash-crop farmers, artisans, and commercial men" became increasingly aware of the precarious nature of their supposedly "free" status. Citing as proof the Methodist church's split over the issue of slavery and the 1846 annexation of Texas as a slave state, they pronounced both church and state corrupted by a powerful slave-owner conspiracy.[40] Rural women and men in the northern states became increasingly distrustful of external efforts to regulate their lives and thus constituted an especially receptive audience for movements that emphasized equality, self-emancipation, and individual sovereignty.

Ohio, in particular, became a seedbed for reform activism in the 1850s. An itinerant lecturer who traversed the northern part of the state during the winter of 1857 observed: "There is no territory of the same extent so reformatory as the Western Reserve." The south-central portion of the state—settled by Quakers and known as the Virginia Military District—also contained many women and men who listened attentively to ultraist lecturers when they critiqued marriage as yet another form of monopoly, denounced the isolated home as a prime example of exclusiveness applied to private life, and called for the abolition of both. Approximately two thousand women and men, for instance, turned out to hear William Denton lecture at Yellow Springs in 1856.[41] His words alleviated their sense of isolation, fueled their radicalism, and gave them cause for hope.

Some who attended ultraist lectures continued discussing the issues raised by Denton and other itinerants in the *Social Revolutionist.* Writing from Illinois, Indiana, Iowa, Ohio, Texas, and Wisconsin, readers expressed their desire to live in a world filled with mutual respect, equal rights, and ample economic opportunities. In addition to debating the merits of free love, they explored the prospects of establishing communitarian ventures. When it came to the latter topic, many had less-than-successful firsthand experience.[42]

In response to those who expressed concern about the possibility that a utopian venture would fail (as many had in the past), a charismatic and youthful itinerant lecturer named Francis Barry assured readers that earlier experiments had collapsed because their organizers had not adequately addressed the question of individual difference. Prospective communitarians, Barry reasoned, stood on different planes of development; therefore, any effort "to combine a large number of persons of independence of character, and (necessarily) diversity of habits, tastes, opinions and tendencies, in one specific experiment would assuredly fail." When it came to organizational structure, he concluded, "the less the better."[43]

An ideal community, Barry envisioned, would be flexible enough to include people who chose to live communally in households organized around shared beliefs and personal affinities as well as others—individuals who still believed in private ownership—who would live in close proximity. The composition of households would fluctuate, he anticipated, as individuals progressed from selfishness to selflessness. In time, it followed, the many small associations would evolve into one large entity. Abhorring the idea of a joint stock company, Barry proposed that individuals should retain enough private property to ensure self-sufficiency, and, like the utopian reformer Josiah Warren of Modern Times, he also endorsed the idea of equitable commerce—that people should sell and acquire goods at cost.

Barry, born in Massachusetts in 1827, began promoting Berlin Heights, a small village in north-central Ohio, as an ideal location in which to establish a communal experiment based on free love principles. It offered, he boasted, such advantages as tolerant residents, inexpensive land, fertile soil, healthful climate, and accessibility by rail. Eager to test his theories, Barry convened a meeting of socialists there in October 1856. Participants, attending from six states and Canada, included practicing communitarians as well as women and men who were intrigued by the promise of communal life. Speakers included James H. Cook, a former boatman on the Erie Canal; the "cool, reserved, philosophical" *Social Revolutionist* editor John Patterson; James W. Towner, who would later challenge John Humphrey Noyes for leadership of New York's Oneida Community; and Joseph Treat, an idealistic public speaker in his early thirties who resided at Memnonia, with Thomas and Mary Gove Nichols.[44]

Women and men in attendance vigorously debated the prospect of establishing a cooperative community and its location. Some favored Kansas or western Virginia because those regions offered more affordable land, but abolitionist-minded socialists voiced concern that they could never enjoy their freedom while living in areas torn apart by proslavery agitation. Members of the convention considered other western sites but ultimately dismissed them as being "under the thumb of the priests," "unfavorable to social and intellectual culture," or "over-run by speculation and monopoly."[45] Unable to bridge their differences of opinion by convention's end, most participants departed without reaching a consensus concerning the next step. Nonetheless, Barry had achieved two critical goals: he had brought prospective participants together, and they had seen Berlin Heights.

Berlin Heights, an Ideal Location

With approximately three hundred inhabitants at mid-century, the village of Berlin Heights had several stores and churches, a public hall, and a large hotel. It was, Barry proclaimed, an ideal site because of its beautiful scenery, good soil, affordable land, access to railroads and markets, springs of clear water, and climate conducive to fruit growing. Free lovers, he predicted, would face "no danger of physical violence" from area residents who were known for their "intelligence and liberality." They would, he asserted, "associate with us, and listen to our arguments."[46] Two additional factors heightened Barry's desire to transform Berlin Heights into what he envisioned as a grand reform center: he had fallen in love with Cordelia Benschoter, the daughter of a prosperous area farmer, and through her had met several liberal-minded men who promised to lease property, extend credit, and offer moral support to the free lovers.

After extensive reading and study of water cure, Cordelia Benschoter (born circa 1833) cut her hair short, adopted the reform dress, and began to question the sanctity of marriage and the "isolated home." Unable to "affinitize" with people in her community, she placed a matrimonial ad, which caught Barry's eye, in the *Water-Cure Journal*. A visit to Berlin Heights convinced the couple that each had found an affinity, or true love, and Barry settled there by 1854. Sharing similar views of legal marriage, they commenced housekeeping without the benefit of clergy or government license. In an effort to protect his daughter's reputation, Cordelia's father Daniel Benschoter registered a Barry-Benschoter marriage—that the couple asserted never took place—at the Erie County courthouse.[47] This action, and the fact that Cordelia began using Barry's surname, led local residents to assume the two had legally wed.

Undeterred by the inconclusive outcome of the 1856 convention of socialists, Joseph Treat and the Barrys soon moved forward with plans for a communitarian experiment. Treat purchased property that quickly became known as the "Free Love Farm," announcing that it could accommodate twenty people. By June 1857, the trio announced to readers of the *Social Revolutionist* and other reform periodicals that they had leased the community's only hotel, a defunct water-cure establishment known as the Davis House. With those elements in place, the Berlin Heights Free Lovers offered prospective communitarians land on which to sustain themselves as fruit growers and a centrally located building to house a printing press, serve as a meeting place, and accommodate all who might flock there in pursuit of a better life. As economic conditions worsened during the winter of 1857–58, and readers of the *Social Revolutionist* lost jobs and property or found their prospects of land ownership diminishing, the free love settlement attracted dozens of converts. Berlin Township observers acknowledged that women and men who joined the Free Lovers that winter were motivated by "disappointed hopes and blasted expectations."[48]

Life among the Free Lovers

"We . . . are sick," wrote Francis Barry, "of the isolation, the antagonisms, the slaveries, the frauds, the jealousies, and general selfishness and discord of . . . civilized society." Marriage, he reasoned, was the source of those problems because it rendered a woman "a petted or a tortured slave," imprisoning her in "the isolated family, with its drudgeries, its wastefulness, and its social starvation."[49] Calling for its abolition, Barry and those who joined him in this loosely structured yet highly publicized venture soon became known as the Berlin Heights Free Lovers.

Several published sources shed light on the lifestyles of the utopian-minded reformers who moved to Berlin Heights beginning in 1857. In 1862, the American humorist Artemus Ward (1834–67) made them the object of satire in a piece entitled "Among the Free Lovers." On one level, we can dismiss his description as a caricature. Yet his article provides a window into some of the socialists' beliefs and practices. According to Ward: "The men's faces was all covered with hare and they lookt half-starved to deth. . . . Their pockets was filled with tracks and pamplits and they was barefooted." The women, he added, "wore trowsis, [and] short gownds." Other contemporary sources support Ward's portrayal. Hannah F. M. Brown, the Cleveland-based editor of a reform periodical entitled *The Agitator*, noted that some Berlin Heights women had short hair and wore knee-length dresses with trousers. At least one area resident equated the reform dress with free love, as is evidenced in the comments of John Fish, a Berlin Township native serving in the Union army. In a letter written while stationed at Port Hudson, Louisiana, he described his encounter with a woman wearing the bloomer, or American, costume: "You would think her a Free Lover." Cordelia Barry and others who shared her water-cure-inspired ideas about dress and health joined other Free Lovers in abstaining from meat, practicing temperance, and reading extensively.[50]

As Francis Barry predicted, not everyone who joined the Berlin Heights movement stood prepared to dissolve their marriages, pool their resources, and form a single community. Settling near the Free Love farm, such families nonetheless played an active role in community activities. John Patterson's brother Samuel, for instance, headed a nearby communal household that included his wife and children and several other Free Lovers. Men like James A. Clay (a mechanic from Maine) maintained a single-family dwelling for his wife and children because he regarded joint-stock companies as "part of the present organized society, which true reformers ought not to carry with them to their new homes."[51]

A number of others, however, welcomed an opportunity to alter their social and economic relationships. Dissolving their families and pooling their resources, they formed several households based on shared interests, attractions, and convictions. Women—often widows or runaway wives—and children predominated in such settings. Writing in the 1890s, the reformer Alvin Warren recalled at least three households based on "affinities": the Overton group (committed to Spiritualism), the Page group, and the Barn group.[52] The 1860 federal manuscript population census provides glimpses into their composition. The Overton household consisted of seven women and four men who bore eight different surnames. All workers, the six domestics, a seamstress, a miller, two laborers, and a farmer joined together because of their shared belief in Spiritualism. Following the example of the Shakers, they sent their children to live in a separate household headed by an Irish couple. A second communal household consisted of eight women and six children. Similar to the Overton group, members of this "family" bore seven different surnames and identified themselves as domestics and laborers. Finally, a third dwelling housed ten members, including four men and two women—all with separate surnames—and four children. In addition to a farmer and a printer, the adults again identified themselves as domestics and laborers.

Unable to purchase tracts large enough to support livestock and grain farming, the Free Lovers followed Barry's advice and established themselves on smaller plots of land as fruit growers. As their orchards and vineyards began to yield bountifully, they purchased a factory for the manufacture of much-needed crates for transporting the fruit. The industrious Free Lovers also operated a grist mill, and one, James Clay, built a store that also served as a dance hall and meeting place. Free Lovers—eager to protect their children from harassment as well as orthodox religious ideas—held a school there too, conducted by Mary Hall, who reportedly also served as the hostess for the Free Lovers' weekend dances.[53]

The numerical dominance of women and the presence of many small children at Berlin Heights suggest that the Free Love experiment did harbor a few runaway wives. Newspapers publicized their experiences in an attempt to discourage other women from following suit. Such examples, however, reveal that unhappily married women did seek refuge among the Free Lovers. In a highly publicized and sensationalized case, a Skaneateles, New York, woman named Mary Lewis left her family and fled to Berlin Heights. Her irate husband, accompanied by a party of friends, traced down the "fugitive wife" and forcibly removed her from the Free Lovers. The *Detroit Free Press* reported another instance—widely reprinted in newspapers throughout the region—in which a discontented wife accompanied by a female relative traveled to the Free Love community. After several weeks, her husband reportedly consented to take back his "shame-stricken but wiser wife and mother" despite "her moral and physical contamination." Artemus Ward further reinforced the image of married women abandoning their homes when he wrote: "you wimin folks go back to your lawful husbands if you've got any."[54]

The original members of the Berlin Heights Free Love community stand apart from other antebellum social reformers because of their uncompromising insistence on women's social and economic rights. "We shall do all in our power," wrote Francis Barry in March 1857, "to establish and encourage those branches of business in which woman—poor, crushed, starved, insulted, and abused woman—may find honorable, healthful, and profitable employment." Opposed to segregating women in a few occupations, he argued that both sexes would be strengthened by working and playing together. Moreover, economic security would prevent women from entering into loveless marriages. Other communal experiments spoke of sexual equality, but as the experience of Fourieristic women illustrates, persistent gender conventions governed daily reality, even in utopian settings.[55]

Several clues indicate how the Berlin Heights Free Lovers attempted to transform their convictions into realities. First, in contrast to other women in the township, female Free Lovers consciously sought recognition for the economic worth of women's labor. When the census taker visited them in 1860, they reported working as hotel keepers, editors, printers, teachers, and typesetters. Instead of indicating that they were "Keeping House," as did most married Berlin Township women, over half of the adult women associated with the Free Love settlement identified themselves as domestics and laborers. This fact is all the more striking because it is unlikely that female Free Lovers were working as domestic servants in the township.

Second, Free Lovers believed that the prevailing socioeconomic system victimized women by denying them adequate opportunities for justly compensated employment. Acting on their conviction that social reform could not begin so long as women had to sell themselves as wives or prostitutes in exchange for economic independence, editors of free love periodicals employed female compositors in their printing offices. Some male Free Lovers further recognized the economic value of women's household labor by paying them wages for such domestic tasks as cooking, laundry, and child care. At least one correspondent reported that he had divided his assets with his wife in an attempt to equalize their relationship. As well-intentioned as Free Love men were, each of those instances nonetheless subtly reinforced their superior status: they were in a position to give, and women to receive.[56]

Moral Objections to an Economic Menace

When Francis Barry initially invited Free Lovers to settle in Berlin Heights, he praised the community for its liberal-mindedness. By the fall of 1857, however, Berlin Township residents' capacity for tolerance had begun to erode as the Free Lovers held public dances, dinners, and conventions without seeking permission from the township clerk. Refusing to observe the Sabbath, they further annoyed their neighbors by spending the day in noisy "labor, recreation, visiting and dancing" within hearing range of one of the most popular churches. The fact that Free Lovers opened their meetings to the public and freely shared their radical literature with all who expressed interest in learning more about free love triggered further concern that they would infect others in the community with their pernicious ideas.[57]

It is difficult to determine precisely how much influence Free Lovers had on their neighbors, but evidence suggests that some men as well as women left their families to join the settlement. In a widely reprinted article entitled "Letter from a Deserted Wife," an Ashtabula County, Ohio, woman named Anne Hunter described her struggles to support three children and an elderly father-in-law after her husband "roamed around in search of free love companions, and having found a number of which, he took them to Berlin." Locally, Rosetta Kline, a fifty-two-year-old mother of six, cited her husband Barnart's conversion to free love as the cause when she sued him for divorce in December 1857. After attending Free Love meetings during the summer months, she alleged, he had become physically abusive and "sour." A sympathetic judge granted Rosetta the divorce and three thousand dollars in alimony.[58]

Alarmed by the Free Lovers' position on women's rights, Berlin Township residents predicted that their community would become a haven for unhappily married women. In the 1850s, Ohio women could seek a divorce on grounds of adultery, impotency, extreme cruelty, fraudulent contract, gross neglect of duty, or habitual drunkenness for three years. Negative stigma and women's economic inability to support themselves and their children, however, inhibited the filing of divorce petitions. At least a few unhappy wives, however, looked to Berlin Heights as a refuge. Other utopian communities often protected their moral reputations by refusing to accept divorced or separated women as members, but the Free Lovers welcomed them and their children.

As a steady stream of prospective Free Lovers flowed into Berlin Township, several concerned area residents met in August 1857 to discuss the Free Lovers' impact on the community's economic health and moral reputation. Published resolutions capture the sentiment of local farmers Isaac Fowler, Zenophin Philips, Hudson Tuttle, and others who thought "that the time has arrived, if not already passed, beyond which a forbearance of this public expression would . . . cease to be a virtue in us." Motivated by economic and moral concerns, they feared that negative publicity would deter future economic growth and force "respectable" residents to sacrifice their homes and property at reduced prices. The Free Lovers' presence "at or near the centre of our township," they proclaimed, "is deeply felt to be detrimental morally and pecuniarily to us." Generously conceding that Barry and his band had settled there "under a mistaken notion as to the real views and feelings of the inhabitants," the authors of the resolutions optimistically hoped that the mere expression of their true feelings would induce the Free Lovers to leave.[59]

Accounts of the meeting reveal a divided community. Minutes taken by Job Fish, a township resident, portray the highly emotional opponents of the

Free Lovers as sources of great amusement. Describing one, Fish observed: "he clutched the end of the pew from where he stood in the aisle, and, to show that his abhorrence of the Free Lovers possessed the whole man, gesticulated for a while with the other end of his body, his motion closely resembling that of a trip hammer or kicking donkey. . . . The mass of the people were convulsed with laughter." Free Lovers also attended the meeting, Fish noted, but were not allowed to speak. Upon reading reports of the meeting in the press, residents of nearby Florence took a dim view of Berlin Heights's treatment of its communitarians. Criticizing the "spirit of passion, intolerance, insubordination, and persecution" manifested at the meeting, they noted that "a large majority of those present" exited in a display of disgust.[60]

An undaunted Francis Barry exacerbated tensions within the community by convening a second meeting of socialists in late September 1857, thus dashing local hopes that the Free Lovers would depart quietly. Women and men traveled to Berlin Heights from Illinois, Indiana, Iowa, Maine, Massachusetts, Michigan, Minnesota, New York, Ohio, Wisconsin, and Canada to discuss the prospects for a communal society based on free love principles. Fifty-five participants voted in support of proceeding, a strong majority endorsing Berlin Township as the site. By year's end, a hundred or more hopeful women, men, and their children had migrated there and built shanties on the "Free Love Farm."[61]

Overwhelmed by the Free Lovers' apparent momentum, several Berlin Township residents determined they must mount a counteroffensive. Operating in conjunction with Harlow Lewis, the New York man whose wife had sought refuge in Berlin Heights, they brought charges of fornication, adultery, and keeping a house of prostitution against nine Free Lovers. The Erie County judge who heard the case in November 1857 ordered them to sign a quit-claim deed for the Davis House (the hotel they had transformed into their headquarters) and to remove their press from its premises. Releasing most on their own recognizance, he advised the Free Lovers to leave the area. To ensure their departure, the seller of the Free Love farm, Henry Hammond, sued Joseph Treat for defaulting on his $3,206 farm mortgage.[62] The judge in that case ordered Treat to pay the amount in full within five days. When Treat could not comply, the farm sold at sheriff's auction.

Prospects looked dim, but the Free Lovers refused to abandon their cause. Departing Berlin Heights proper, they leased more land, dwellings, and grist mill privileges from sympathetic farmers in the township. Much to the chagrin of their opposition, the trial had generated a great deal of publicity, which renewed the influx of Free Lovers and curious onlookers to Berlin Heights.

Setting up their printing press on property leased from the Hill family, Free Lovers erected five or six new buildings to accommodate their ever-growing ranks and settled in for the winter.[63]

A mob of Berlin Heights women, angered by the inability of civic leaders to evict the Free Lovers legally, attempted to finish the job their husbands had begun. On a winter day in late 1857, Francis Barry loaded his wagon with baskets containing over 450 copies of the November issue of the *Social Revolutionist* and headed for the Berlin Heights post office. As he approached the hitching post, "a gang of infuriated women" managed to wrest control of his cargo and "ran off with the packages and burned them." According to a report in the *Sandusky Commercial Register*, "The ladies of the village had heard of his coming, and prepared to testify their appreciation of his 'perseverance under difficulties.'" Attempting to rescue his cargo from the flames, Barry stumbled and fell, at which point some of the stronger women held him down, seized his beard, and threatened to shear it off. Satisfied that Barry had been suitably chastised, the triumphant mob gave him a head start before chasing him out of town.[64]

Relishing their role as martyrs to their cause, Free Lovers attributed their harsh treatment to the fact that they dared "to ask for women the rights of individual sovereignty."[65] Determined to hold their ground, they issued one more number of the *Social Revolutionist* before inaugurating a new, more strident publication entitled *Age of Freedom*. Coedited by Francis Barry, Cordelia Barry, C. M. Overton, and John Patterson, the new paper made its first appearance in January 1858 with a masthead declaring: "The Martyrs of To-Day are the Heroes of Tomorrow." Overton, in an effort to highlight the hypocrisy of the Free Lovers' enemies, published a "Confession of Faith" in which he cited several sources from which the Free Lovers had constructed their worldview. In it, he drew analogies between the Free Lovers and several well-respected figures. Like Horace Greeley, he wrote, they embraced elements of Fourierism because they regarded "perfect order compatible with the most entire Individuality." Like Thomas Jefferson, they stressed "the inalienability of human rights." Like Martin Luther, they held to the "freedom of conscience, the right of each human being to choose his own God (or gods) and worship him as his conscience dictates." Drawing his argument to a close, Overton pointedly observed that unlike their Christian neighbors, Free Lovers regarded "every act of life," whether "at labor or at recreation . . . a religious act."[66]

Unconvinced by Overton's rhetoric, local residents worried that a rapidly growing population of Free Lovers would prevail at the ballot box in the spring election and seize control of the township. In reality, only three Free Lovers voted. Given the numerical dominance of women and children in their community and the fact that many opposed the idea of government, the lack of electoral participation is not surprising. Even without their vote, the "toleration ticket" triumphed, defeating candidates whose primary agenda had been the ejection of the Free Lovers from Berlin Township.[67] At last, it seemed the Free Lovers would be able to live in peace.

Members of the Free Love community, however, seemed determined to perpetuate their notoriety by continuing their bold defiance of convention. In mid 1858, a farmer, reportedly in pursuit of a lost cow, claimed to have witnessed a dozen male and female Free Lovers bathing nude together in a stream northeast of the village. This widely publicized occurrence, observed the *New York Times,* confirmed that the Free Lovers remained "fierce, loose and rampant." Angered by this continuing negative publicity, some Berlin Heights property owners again voiced concern over their community's moral reputation and economic health. Holding a new round of indignation meetings, they criticized several local men who did business with the Free Lovers for giving "aid and comfort to this enemy of good morals and good citizenship." Law and moral suasion failing, they again threatened mob action.[68]

Local unrest continued into the fall, at which time the Free Lovers, whom many assumed to be pacifists or nonresistants, declared: "If the mob attempts to break up [our] general bed and board they will do it at their peril." At this, threats of violence subsided. "Justice," reflected an increasingly sympathetic Job Fish in 1858, "hardly requires . . . that we rid ourselves of ill at the expense of others." Perhaps local critics of the Free Lovers also recognized that the tide had turned. After the *Social Revolutionist* bonfire, journalists who initially had focused on the Free Lovers' "loose" morals began to portray them as icons of free speech and a free press. On the eve of the Civil War, the specter of border ruffians and the martyred newspaper editor Elijah P. Lovejoy was all too vivid. If their opponents persisted, promised C. M. Overton, Berlin Heights would become the "Alton of Ohio."[69]

After threats to their well-being subsided, the disparate band of reformers known as the Berlin Heights Free Lovers struggled through a period of adjustment and realignment. A disillusioned Joseph Treat departed shortly after he lost the Free Love farm. Loyal to Mary Gove Nichols's definition of free love, he no longer wished to associate with Free Lovers who advocated "commerce between the sexes for something beside parentage." Nonetheless, he continued to defend them as "better and purer" than the world they attempted to reform.[70] Moving east, he became an associate of Victoria Woodhull in the 1870s, but again grew disillusioned when he recognized that her definition of free love diverged from his own. The Spiritualist C. M. Overton lingered in Berlin Township through 1860 but eventually left to join an intentional community in Bishop Hill, Illinois. Likewise, Francis and Cordelia Barry moved west to stay with friends in Lake County, Illinois, where their son was born in 1860. A year later, however, the couple returned to Ohio, and in 1862 Barry began editing a short-lived periodical entitled the *New Republic.* That failing, the Barrys sojourned in New York City where they attempted to implement an urban communitarian venture called the New Protectorate. The family next settled in Portage County, Ohio, where Barry farmed. A reformer to the end, he remained a regular contributor to numerous radical reform periodicals and spearheaded the formation of the Western Woman's Emancipation Society in the early 1870s.[71]

Other Free Love pioneers remained in Berlin Heights, dedicated to the idea of living "in community." A decade after Free Lovers first gathered there, members of affinity-based households continued to group and regroup, periodically adding new members and losing others. Some traveled to New York in 1863 and 1864 and sought membership among the Perfectionists at John Humphrey Noyes's Oneida Community. A small number eventually joined, but the lingering taint of free love prevented others from becoming members, and the disappointed utopians returned to Berlin Heights.[72] Ultimately, the north-central Ohio locale proved to be a conducive climate in which impoverished and idealistic socialists could find economic stability. As the Berlin Heights communitarians began to prosper as fruit farmers and small manufacturers, objections to their presence eventually evaporated. "They began poor," one observer noted in 1867, "but by industry, temperance, and perseverance are surely on the road, if not to wealth, at least to competence."[73]

The "Love Principle" in a Nation at War

Editors of free love periodicals abandoned their public advocacy of this contested cause as the nation moved toward war, yet strands of sex radicalism survived within Spiritualism. In 1860, an Indiana Spiritualist named Thomas Cook decided to put his theories about variety free love into practice. After he "gave" his wife her freedom, responsibility for the couple's five children, and his worldly goods, this editor of a monthly periodical entitled *Kingdom of Heaven* set out in search of his spiritual affinity. Eventually settling in Berlin Heights, where he lived communally with survivors from Francis Barry's experiment, he first traveled from Indiana to New Jersey, with many stops along the way. His acceptance of sexual variety, Cook informed readers, represented a spiritual quest: human fallibility made experimentation a necessary phase through which individuals must pass in order to progress to a higher level of existence. Nature works in pairs, he continued. "Yet all exclusiveness is selfish and unnatural. . . . When one soul can retain one of the opposite sex no longer by love, it should be permitted to depart in peace." Ultimately, he anticipated, monogamy would replace variety. But a person first must find his or her divinely sanctioned soul mate in order to progress to that higher state.[74]

Women who previously had been attracted to the ideas of Thomas and Mary Gove Nichols welcomed Cook's words because they emphasized the spiritual rather than a material bond between women and men. "I have been a believer in the principles of 'purity between the sexes,'" wrote a correspondent from Ravenna, Ohio, "ever since the Nichols movement 'went up.' Therefore I feel especially encouraged to see you so fearless and explicit upon so vital and essential a point." Those who viewed his "love principle" through the lens of Spiritualism or millennialism regarded his endorsement of variety in sexual relations as part of a holy plan. "When man and woman have gone through this purifying process . . . and stand in true relationship to each other," wrote an anonymous woman in July 1865, "the Divine elements from the celestial sphere blending with theirs, will constitute a condition which I term the Kingdom."[75]

Even Cook's call for the abolition of marriage did not deter them; instead, women enthusiastically interpreted his description of sexual relations in the new social order as a time when "food of the soul" would be indulged in only when a woman chose. Much like John Humphrey Noyes, Cook endorsed a form of male continence that offered "passionate embrace without consummation."[76] He also promoted hereditarian ideas. Citing the free lover's core tenet of individual sovereignty, he thus reasoned that if men and women refrained from sexual intercourse until a time when they experienced mutual desire, women no longer would give birth to diseased and deformed children. But so long as marriage law compelled a woman to submit to her husband, Cook continued, marriage would remain the birthplace of criminals and other socially undesirable people.

Informed by the free love theories so widely disseminated and discussed during the 1850s, correspondents to the *Kingdom of Heaven* responded enthusiastically to Cook's "love principle." Examining it through the lens of Spiritualism, they saw his defense of variety in sexual relations as a rung on the great ladder of progression, one that eventually would lead to a much-desired millennium. Cook's *Kingdom of Heaven* and other Spiritualist publications, along with lecturers, thus preserved key sex radical ideas of Thomas and Mary Gove Nichols, Francis and Cordelia Barry, and dozens of grassroots women and men through the Civil War era. Despite national focus on a war that severed the nation in half, a persistent network of radical Spiritualists continued to promote social freedom's promise to women through lectures and writings. Embers of their ideas would be rekindled by the fiery Victoria Woodhull in the 1870s.

Mary S. Gove Nichols (1810-84), a multi-faceted reformer, lecturer, and water-cure physician, struggled throughout her life to overcome the difficulties she associated with being female and married. (Courtesy of the American Antiquarian Society)

Juliet Hall Worth Stillman Severance, M.D. (1833-1919), a dress reformer, water-cure physician, itinerant lecturer, Spiritualist, and third-party activist, completed her medical training in 1857-58 at Russell Trall's Hygeio-Therapeutic College in New York City. (Courtesy of the Western Reserve Historical Society)

The Berlin Heights Free Lovers transformed the Davis House into their headquarters. Drawing of the Davis House, Berlin Heights, Ohio, from the *Combination Atlas Map of Erie County, Ohio,* 1874. (Courtesy of the Center for Archival Collections, Bowling Green State University)

Victoria C. Woodhull (1838-1927) reading a memorial resolution concerning woman suffrage before the Judiciary Committee of the House of Representatives in January 1871. (Courtesy of the Wisconsin Historical Society)

Elmina Drake Slenker (1827-1908) and her "ghostly friends." Slenker, a temperance reformer and lapsed Quaker, endorsed Alphaism and conducted a correspondence bureau for sex radical women and men. (Courtesy of the Wisconsin Historical Society)

Moses Harman (1830-1910), editor of *Lucifer, the Light-Bearer* (1883-1907) and the *American Journal of Eugenics* (1907-10), was imprisoned four times (1890, 1892, 1895, and 1906) for sending allegedly obscene materials through the mail. (Courtesy of the Moses Harman Papers, 1858-1984, Western Historical Manuscript Collection, Columbia, Missouri)

L. HARMAN
E. C. WALKER

Lillian Harman (1870-?) and Edwin C. Walker (1849-1931) defied Kansas state law when they entered into a nonstate, nonchurch marriage, popularly known as the "free marriage." The couple published *Fair Play* (1888-91) from Valley Falls, Kansas, and later Sioux City, Iowa. In 1893, Lillian became a "free mother" when she gave birth to a daughter, Virna Winifred Walker. (Courtesy of the Labadie Collection, University of Michigan)

An author, itinerant lecturer, Spiritualist, and anarchist, Lois Waisbrooker (1826-1909) edited *Our Age, Foundation Principles,* and *Clothed with the Sun* and served as acting editor of *Lucifer, the Light-Bearer.* (Courtesy of Lois Waisbrooker's great-granddaughter Helen Doris Hawkins Hardin and great-great-grandson James B. Hardin)

Mattie Sawyer Hull. In addition to editing *Hull's Crucible* while coeditors Moses and David Hull lectured throughout New England, Mattie Sawyer raised much-needed funds by selling pamphlets, doing job printing, and taking in boarders. (Courtesy of the Labadie Collection, University of Michigan)

Cornelia Boecklin of Burlington, Iowa, read and contributed to a number of "radical papers," including *Lucifer* and *Liberty*. A dress reformer, infidel, and anarchist, she observed "that in families where there was little or no government, there was the most happiness to be found." (Courtesy of the Labadie Collection, University of Michigan)

4. We Are Cowards and She Is Not

I for one am not afraid to trust myself or my sisters
with freedom.

—Laura Cuppy Smith, *Woodhull and Claflin's Weekly,*
18 October 1873

ON A MONDAY EVENING in mid-November 1871, Victoria Woodhull lectured
on "The Principles of Social Freedom" to several thousand men and wom-
en gathered in New York City's Steinway Hall. Reading from a prepared text
for nearly two hours, this modestly attired Spiritualist and advocate of wom-
en's rights declared the primary goal of sexual relations to be the production of healthy children. But when audience members demanded to know if
she professed free love, Woodhull issued her infamous and oft quoted declaration: "Yes, I am a Free Lover. I have an *inalienable, constitutional and
natural* right to love whom I may, to love as *long* or as *short* a period as I can;
to *change* that love *every day* if I please."[1] Shock waves from this statement
reverberated throughout the nation, causing mainstream advocates of woman suffrage to distance themselves from Woodhull and her controversial social agenda. Yet hundreds of women and men—non-elites, many of whom
lived on farms, ranches, and in small agricultural communities throughout
the Midwest, Great Plains, and West—nonetheless continued to read and
listen to Woodhull, convinced that the ideas she espoused would lead to freedom, purity, and a better world for all.

This chapter examines women's responses to Victoria Woodhull (1838–1927)
and the sex radical ideas she promoted through lectures and *Woodhull and
Claflin's Weekly,* which she edited with her sister between 1870 and 1876.
Woodhull served as a bridge connecting the utopian free love theories of Thomas and Mary Gove Nichols and the Berlin Heights Free Lovers with the anarchistic postbellum sex radicalism of Moses Harman, Ezra Heywood, and Lois
Waisbrooker.[2] On the one hand, Woodhull's idealistic portrayal of free love's

potential to solve social ills resonated with women and men whose formative years had been shaped by such antebellum currents of thought as abolitionism, Spiritualism, and women's rights. On the other hand, Woodhull's youth and energy, her dramatic flair, and her willingness to challenge the status quo enabled her to cultivate a new audience, one left restive by postbellum economic, political, and social change. Both groups made themselves heard through letters to the *Weekly*. As readers discussed the victimization they felt as a result of current marriage and divorce laws and social customs, they asserted themselves, demonstrating that women's private concerns about the use of their bodies for sexual pleasure and reproduction also lay within the sphere of women's rights.

Woodhull's words resonated most powerfully among economically disadvantaged rural women living in the Midwest and West. Increasingly ostracized on the East Coast, Woodhull carried her vision of social freedom westward beginning in 1873. That her popularity in farming communities and midwestern cities and that of *Woodhull and Claflin's Weekly* in the western half of the United States grew after the Panic of 1873 is no coincidence. Precipitated by a number of factors, including the collapse of Jay Cooke's investment firm, the ensuing five years of depression fostered a climate conducive to economic, political, and social radicalism. Farmers, especially hard hit by falling prices and the demonetization of silver in 1873, found themselves blamed for overproduction. Growing resentful of the force of monopolies in their lives, they turned an attentive ear to Woodhull's message of individual freedom.[3] Her popularity transcended dualistic perspectives—East versus West, urban versus rural, capitalist versus producer—because Woodhull's words appealed to the many who sought explanations for and solutions to widespread unemployment, business failures, and foreclosures. She acknowledged rural correspondents' suffering and articulated their frustrations, joining them in indicting capitalistic greed for spawning social evils.

Women who accepted and supported Woodhull's ideas represent an underexplored dimension of the nineteenth-century movement for women's rights. Such sex radicals often are excluded from historical accounts of women's rights in part because they questioned the validity of woman suffrage as a solution, but also because they so openly challenged customary notions of female sexuality as passionless.[4] The words of women who wrote to Woodhull thus serve as a counterpoint to a familiar narrative, with its emphasis on the campaign for woman suffrage. They also shed light on the politicization of women who, prompted by economic conditions and Woodhull's speeches and writings, began to question their relationship—as women—to such deeply entrenched patriarchal institutions as the church, the state, and marriage.

Love, Marriage, and Divorce in an Era of Reconstruction

Following the Civil War, criticisms of marriage and discussions of divorce and sexuality increasingly became subject to repression and censorship. Civic and moral leaders, convinced that the institution of marriage ensured social order, feared it was in jeopardy. Extraordinarily high wartime casualties, for instance, created numerous widows even as it rendered marriage an unattainable goal for scores of single women. Alarmists believed that women, alone in a world that did not offer them adequate opportunities for economic independence, would destabilize an already fragile balance by turning to prostitution or filling charity rolls. At the same time, temperance reformers (emphasizing the hereditary transmission of disease and undesirable personality traits to children) became more willing to accept divorce as a justifiable option for the wives of alcoholics. Statistics confirm that divorce became "a woman's remedy" between 1872 and 1876. Approximately 63 percent of all divorces during those years were granted to women who had charged their husbands with "cruelty, desertion, drunkenness, and neglect to provide."[5]

Public concern about sexual danger rose in the late 1860s as several legal cases illustrated that social problems not only could but did cross over from the working class to the middle and upper classes. In 1868, readers digested journalists' sensational accounts of the Hester Vaughn case. An English immigrant, deserted and alone, Vaughn secured work as a dairy maid, suffered seduction at the hands of her employer, and gave birth to an illegitimate child who died shortly after. The judge in the case chose to make an example of this young woman by sentencing her to death for infanticide. Outraged, the suffragists Elizabeth Cady Stanton and Susan B. Anthony used the case to critique the sexual double standard. Rallying to her support, they ultimately exerted enough pressure to secure Vaughn's pardon and raised money for her return to England.[6]

A year later the highly publicized McFarland-Richardson case served as another reminder that neither economic independence nor social class could protect women from male power. An aspiring actress named Abby Sage McFarland left her "alcoholic, tyrannical, and abusive husband" Daniel McFarland and moved to a boarding house in 1867. There she met and fell in love with Albert Richardson, a reporter for the *New York Tribune*. In 1868 she moved to Indiana, known for its liberal divorce laws. After divorcing McFarland on the grounds of cruelty, she returned to New York about a year later and resumed her friendship with Richardson. A jealous and irate McFarland responded by shooting Richardson in his *Tribune* office. Adding even more drama to this turn of events, the Reverend Henry Ward Beecher—who saw the couple's desire to marry as the epitome of romantic love—united Abby Sage McFarland to her lover in a deathbed wedding. McFarland's acquittal after a sensational and highly publicized murder trial sent several messages to women: it reaffirmed wives' position as property, the superiority of husbands, and the notion that even abused wives must remain faithful.[7]

Feminist responses to the McFarland-Richardson case illustrate how divisive marital and sexual issues had become for postbellum suffragists. Stanton, as she had in the Vaughn case, organized indignation meetings to protest the court's decision and the inflexible marriage and divorce laws that had produced it. In contrast, many members of the Boston-centered American Woman Suffrage Association (AWSA), led by Lucy Stone and Henry Blackwell, pointed to the case as confirmation of how distracting social issues could be to the cause of woman suffrage. In the weeks following the decision, Blackwell noted, such influential publications as *The Nation*, the *New York Times*, and the *New York Tribune* had seized the opportunity to critique woman suffrage by linking it to Abby Sage McFarland. The only way to advance women's rights, AWSA leaders concluded, was by avoiding such controversial social issues as divorce and the reform of marriage laws until after women possessed the legal power to grapple with them.[8]

Attempts to Legislate Morality

One way for advocates of woman suffrage to distance themselves from the taint of free love was by joining with social purity reformers in the fight against sexual danger. A euphemism for sexual purity, social purity reform appealed to men and women who distrusted human nature and people they viewed as their social inferiors. Advocates of social purity reform also believed that imposition of their standards of sexual behavior would solve many of society's problems. Thus, they determined "to achieve a set of controls over sexuality" that would protect women from sexual danger because they were "structured through the family" and "enforced through law and/or social morality."[9] Initially, social purity reformers and sex radicals shared some core convictions, for instance, the importance of consensual sex for women. But over time the social purity campaign's repressive tendencies "overwhelmed its liberatory aspects" for women.[10] Those who attempted to abolish prostitution by criminalizing it, for example, overlooked the fact that this work represented a source of livelihood for some, including impoverished wives. Moreover, the campaign to protect young women from sexual danger by raising the age of consent ignored the fact that such laws denied women, not men, the freedom of heterosexual expression.

Beginning in the 1870s, a dry goods clerk who had served in the Union army spearheaded a movement to eliminate the presence of social vice in print. Like many other Americans, Anthony Comstock had learned an important lesson from his wartime experience—that federal power could be invoked to regulate individual behavior. In 1872 the New York City Young Men's Christian Association (YMCA) placed Comstock in charge of its newly established offshoot, the New York Committee for the Suppression of Vice. Less than a year after his appointment, Comstock successfully lobbied to secure the passage of a federal obscenity statute. The Act for the Suppression of Trade in, and Circulation of Obscene Literature and Articles of Immoral Use (widely known as the "Comstock Law") in 1873 provided him with the means and the authority to wage a full-scale campaign against vice. Not only did it prohibit the distribution through the mail of such "obscene" materials as pamphlets on birth control and pornography, it also inspired legislators in over twenty states to pass "little Comstock laws" during the next twelve years. Some state statutes even went beyond the 1873 federal measure by prohibiting the verbal transmission of information about contraception and abortion. As a result, Comstock and an army of postal inspectors harassed and prosecuted those who persisted in publishing and distributing such literature.[11]

While men constituted the membership of the Comstock-inspired and -led anti-vice societies, postbellum women also organized on behalf of social purity reform. In 1874, only a year after Comstock achieved the legal means necessary to effect his social reform agenda, the U.S. Sanitary Commission veteran Annie Wittenmyer took up the temperance cause and formed the soon-to-be powerful Woman's Christian Temperance Union (WCTU). Following in her steps, WCTU president Frances Willard employed moral suasion to mobilize thousands, among them many who viewed suffragists' demand for equal rights as too radical a cause to support. Wittenmyer and Willard directed the WCTU's programmatic efforts to social purity reform, establishing in 1877 a Committee for Work with Fallen Women that eight years later became the Department of Social Purity. In the 1870s a few national WCTU spokeswomen may have expressed reservations about Comstock, but beginning in the mid-1880s they generally supported his agenda. By 1890, the WCTU's dues-paying membership of approximately 150,000 devoted itself in part to "saving the prostitute from her life of sin by converting her to evangelical Christianity and teetotalism."[12]

Feminist historians contend that Comstock devoted substantial energy to restricting women's access to abortion or contraceptive information because he feared such knowledge would release women from their roles as wives and mothers and thus destroy the social hierarchy that gave men their power and social status.[13] His relentless pursuit of sex radical periodical editors from the 1870s until his death in 1915 gives every indication that their conclusion is well founded. In all, Comstock devoted over forty years to his crusade against the "urban gamblers, swindlers, abortionists, birth-control advocates, lottery operators, and obscenity purveyors" who he believed "were gnawing away at the moral order."[14] Victoria Woodhull became one of his earliest targets.

"Mrs. Satan" and the Suffragists

Numerous biographers and historians have struggled to capture the complex and contradictory life and meteoric career of Victoria C. Woodhull with varying degrees of success. All too often she and her associates are marginalized as cranks or anomalies in narratives focusing on her colorful personality and on the sensationalism and controversy surrounding her sex radicalism.[15] While such accounts make compelling reading, they unfortunately gloss over the significance of Woodhull's appeal to grassroots women and men and her role in shaping their understanding of women's rights. Members of the clergy and newspaper editors branded her an advocate of promiscuity and social disorder, and Spiritualists and suffragists splintered as a result of her presence in their midst, yet thousands of women and men remained receptive to Woodhull's ideas because she addressed concerns few others did.

The seventh of ten children, Victoria Claflin Woodhull was born in Homer, Ohio, in 1838 to an impoverished itinerant carnival and medicine show operator, Reuben "Buck" Claflin, and his illiterate wife, Roxanna Hummel Claflin. As part of her father's traveling troupe, Victoria and her sister Tennessee (1845–1923) learned to enthrall audiences with fortune telling, palm reading, and their clairvoyant powers (from childhood, Victoria believed that she was protected by and could communicate with spirits). Seeking escape from this marginal existence, a teenaged Victoria married Dr. Canning Woodhull, nearly twice her age, and bore two children—a mentally retarded son, Byron, and a daughter, Zulu Maud. Those experiences informed her subsequent critique of marriage and her belief in the redemptive power of motherhood.[16]

Supporting her family by working as a needlewoman and actress in San Francisco and as a Spiritualistic healing medium in Indianapolis and Terre Haute, Indiana, she divorced her alcoholic husband after eleven difficult years of marriage. By 1868, having married a Saint Louis Spiritualist and reformer known as Colonel James Harvey Blood, Woodhull had moved to New York City. She earned much-needed income by working as a clairvoyant, magnetic healer, and Spiritualistic medium, while her sister Tennessee captivated a client, the wealthy Commodore Cornelius Vanderbilt. He ensured that the two sisters had the financial backing necessary to open their Wall Street brokerage in 1870 and to begin publishing *Woodhull and Claflin's Weekly* that same year.[17]

For a short time in the early 1870s, Woodhull captured the support of the National Woman Suffrage Association (NWSA), in part because of the memorial resolution on woman suffrage she presented before the Judiciary Committee of the U.S. House of Representatives on 11 January 1871. Pale but articulate, she argued that women already possessed the right to vote under the Fourteenth and Fifteenth Amendments to the Constitution. Recognizing the significance of her testimony, Susan B. Anthony, Elizabeth Cady Stanton, Isabella Beecher Hooker, and other suffragists attended the hearing to lend their support. Despite the logic of Woodhull's argument, her charismatic presence, and the NWSA's support, the committee's majority report refuted her interpretation.[18]

Eager to infuse life into her movement, Anthony ignored some women's discomfort with Woodhull's increasingly infamous reputation and invited her to deliver a major address four months later at the NWSA's convention at New York City's Apollo Hall. In an attempt to legitimize her presence, Anthony seated Woodhull on the platform between herself and Lucretia Mott. The sex radical's presence in their midst, however, became more difficult for suffragists to justify after her infamous "Principles of Social Freedom" speech in November of that year. Many suffragists regarded her declaration—"Yes, I am a Free Lover"—as confirmation of Woodhull's low moral condition, but a few continued to view her through an idealistic lens. Stanton, for example, interpreted Woodhull as waging a valiant battle against the double standard, while the spiritually minded Isabella Beecher Hooker contended that Woodhull, as "a divine instrument," had been sent to remove the burden of radicalism from the NWSA.[19] Both accused Woodhull's critics of being narrow-minded and biased.

The controversy surrounding Woodhull reverberated within state boundaries as well as at the national level, forcing advocates of women's rights to take a stand on the free love she professed. During the winter of 1871–72, for example, Iowa suffragists mounted a major campaign for statewide suffrage. Stanton and Anthony had lent their support to the cause earlier in the year when they lectured extensively throughout the state. But Woodhull's social freedom speech provided antisuffragists with a powerful tool: men seized the opportunity to charge that suffrage would lead women to abandon their homes, families, and socially ordained roles. Between October 1871 and January 1872 (the period just prior to and immediately following Woodhull's address) the Des Moines–based *Daily Iowa State Register*, the *Dubuque Herald*, and the *Burlington Hawkeye* published nearly seventy articles about Woodhull and free love (evidence also of the extent to which small-town dailies would go to stimulate readership). Attempting to discredit the suffrage movement by linking Woodhull to it, Iowa papers circulated such highly exaggerated descriptions of her as this one in the *Daily Iowa State Register:* "Her hair is cut close like a boy's; she can ride a horse like an Indian, climb trees like man's remote ancestor, swim, row, play billiards, dance, and walk like an Englishman. She is a free lover, of course."[20] Iowa suffragists struggled unsuccessfully to separate their cause from Woodhull's free love ideas, and in March 1872, after months of controversy, the Iowa suffrage amendment went down to defeat.

Woodhull widened the gap between herself and suffragists in the spring of 1872 when she had proof sheets made of an exposé entitled "Tit for Tat." Mailing it to a number of women's rights leaders, she threatened to publicize their sexual secrets unless each paid her five hundred dollars. When the NWSA held its annual convention in New York City in May 1872, an irate Susan B. Anthony ordered the hall closed after Woodhull announced her intent to establish a political party and to run as its candidate for president of the United States. Undaunted, Woodhull convened about six hundred supporters (among them Hooker and Stanton) of the newly formed Equal Rights party the following day at Apollo Hall.[21] Caught up in the enthusiasm of the moment, their support for Woodhull nonetheless waned almost as quickly.

Woodhull perceived a coordinated effort to suppress her ideas when the *New York Tribune* editor and presidential candidate Horace Greeley refused to cover her political campaign. Other editors adopted a similar stance. Adding to the furor, Harriet Beecher Stowe satirized Woodhull as a character named Audacia Dangyereyes in her novel *My Wife and I,* and the illustrator Thomas Nast caricatured her as "Mrs. Satan" (a winged devil with horns) in *Harper's Weekly.*[22] Thus, when Woodhull learned from Elizabeth Cady Stanton of an extramarital affair between Stowe's brother, Reverend Henry Ward Beecher (who had criticized Woodhull for being a free lover), and Elizabeth Tilton, she decided to seek vindication by disclosing his hypocrisy.

In an act of retaliation guaranteed to garner substantial publicity, Woodhull and Claflin resurrected the *Weekly* (which had ceased publication in June 1872) and exposed the Beecher-Tilton affair. As head of the New York Society for the Suppression of Vice, Anthony Comstock sought the editors' arrest for disseminating literature he deemed immoral. While the two women awaited trial in early 1873, Comstock petitioned Congress to revise the postal law of

1865 to include weeklies and prohibitions against the sale of contraceptive devices through the mail. Suffragists, still stinging from Woodhull's attempt to blackmail them, refused to come to her aid. From their Ludlow Street Jail cell, the two sisters conducted a fund-raising campaign while they awaited trial. Freed on bail in December 1872, they resumed lecturing and publishing. Woodhull determinedly continued to taunt Comstock, a fact that resulted in her repeated arrest and release during delays in the trial's prosecution. By the end of June, however, the trial concluded with the judge instructing the jury to find the defendants not guilty upon ruling that the 1872 statute under which they had been charged did not apply to newspapers. Fallout from the Beecher-Tilton scandal, however, persisted for three years and culminated in the nearly six-month-long Beecher-Tilton trial in 1875, a hung jury, and Beecher's exoneration by his congregation.[23]

The visibility of Woodhull and the issues she espoused made it difficult for suffragists to appear in public without declaring themselves either pro– or anti–free love. Consequently, leaders of the organized movement for women's rights found it politically expedient to distance themselves from Woodhull, eschew divisive social issues, reinforce their image as moral women, and to make the campaign for woman suffrage their highest priority. Forcing them to confront their social and cultural biases, Woodhull had taught them a difficult lesson: it was one thing to espouse equal rights for all and to refer to all women as sisters, but it was quite another to welcome and withstand a woman of her repute into their midst.

Taking Her Message to the People

Losing assets and clients in risky stock market transactions, Woodhull relied on the lucrative public lecture circuit as a source of much-needed income for the support of herself and an extended family that included present and former husbands, parents, and children. Her lecture career blossomed in 1871, shortly after she delivered the memorial resolution to Congress. In the tradition of a Spiritualist trance speaker, she credited her ideas to "Spirit Guides" speaking through her: her human guides, however, included men like her husband, Colonel Blood, and Stephen Pearl Andrews (known for his advocacy of free love in the 1850s). Andrews's free love philosophy provided Woodhull with the idealistic rationalization she needed to justify her unconventional sexual behavior, which (as with Mary Gove Nichols) included marriage, divorce, and remarriage with impunity.

AWSA members inadvertently helped enhance Woodhull's popularity in other parts of the nation by exerting their influence to deny her access to lecture halls in and around Boston. Mary Livermore and the women and men who composed the Boston-based AWSA forced the free love advocate to seek out other venues because they considered her "unclean" and a severe liability to the woman suffrage movement.[24] In an attempt to secure engagements, Woodhull assured lecture hall managers that she would confine her remarks to financial reform. This tactic, however, proved disastrous: the orator who earlier had attracted thousands when she spoke about social freedom struggled to draw audiences of one hundred interested in her views on finance. Coming to her aid, a supportive Ezra Heywood organized the New England Free Love League in early 1873—an outgrowth of the New England Labor Reform League—specifically to provide Woodhull a platform from which to speak freely about any topic. Heywood and other Free Love League members clearly regarded her cause as far more than a social issue: they were determined not to let the forces of capital crush the liberty of the press. Their example inspired the creation of similar leagues and women's emancipation societies across the nation.[25]

Ultimately, Spiritualism provided Woodhull with a much-needed base from which to operate and thus became the primary channel through which she connected directly with people in midwestern and western states. The prevailing image of nineteenth-century Spiritualism is one of middle-class women and men holding seances and listening to trance mediums, but as letters to *Woodhull and Claflin's Weekly* and such Spiritualist periodicals as *Banner of Light* and the *Religio-Philosophical Journal* illustrate, believers stretched from coast to coast and crossed gender, geographic, and socioeconomic lines. Accessible to any individual through direct spirit communication, Spiritualism had particular appeal to women because it provided them with a powerful resource for coping with inequality. Both a religious belief system and a reform movement, it offered nineteenth-century Americans a means by which they could navigate their disorderly world. Crime, disease, and poverty existed, they believed, among people at lower levels of development. Yet even fallible human beings could progress to a higher state of existence if they united in "true marriage" with a divinely intended mate. Such beliefs also contributed to heightened romantic expectations of marriage.[26]

Woodhull, aware of the similarities between her interpretation of free love and Spiritualistic ideas about "true marriage," positioned herself to become president of the American Association of Spiritualists (AAS) in 1871, an office she occupied for three consecutive years. With Woodhull presiding, so many women spoke at the 1873 AAS meeting in Chicago that one participant dubbed it a "woman's meeting." Indeed, women's voices dominated the sessions held in Grow's Opera House even though they constituted scarcely one-third of the total delegates in attendance. Traveling to Chicago from at least fifteen states, attendees praised Woodhull for possessing the courage to lead them across "the Red Sea of the social question."[27] The outpouring of their testimonies—about abortion, infanticide, prostitution, the sexual double standard, and women's enslavement in marriage confirmed women's eagerness to bring such issues into the open. The warm reception those in attendance gave Woodhull also fed her ego and suggested that the Midwest and West would be receptive and thus lucrative fields for future lecture engagements. During the next year she spent so much time there that rumors began to circulate about imminent plans to relocate herself and *Woodhull and Claflin's Weekly* to California.[28]

Without a doubt, Woodhull's personal interactions with people living outside the boundaries of New England and the Mid-Atlantic states helped weaken the web of myths that eastern and urban journalists had spun around her. Even though newspaper editors and clergy in midwestern and western communities visited by "The Woodhull" advised "virtuous mothers, wives, and daughters" to refrain from attending her lectures, such warnings generally had the opposite effect. "All classes everywhere," as Mrs. M. E. French of Greenville, Michigan, observed, "have a desire to see the 'elephant.'" And when they heard her, women and men often had their preconceptions challenged. The day after Woodhull spoke in Cedar Springs, Michigan, for example, the local *Clipper* recorded the "seeming disappointment of everybody that she appeared and acted for all the world like a woman . . . and that she was not a cross between the devil and an orang-outing." In many instances, observed a correspondent from Ohio, western newspapers not only gave Woodhull positive coverage but also published excerpts of speeches, extending her ideas well beyond the hundreds who listened to her lectures and read *Woodhull and Claflin's Weekly.*[29]

Wisconsin proved to be an important stop on Woodhull's lecture tour, and she addressed many audiences there in 1873, 1874, and 1875. In the spring of 1873, recently released from jail following her clash with Anthony Comstock, Woodhull chose a tantalizing title guaranteed to draw large audiences: "The Naked Truth; or, The Situation Revealed." Whether audiences expected her to relay salacious details about Henry Ward Beecher or to defend herself, they turned out in large numbers. Determined to discredit "Vic Woodhull," male reporters for the *Milwaukee Sentinel* branded her a "crazy harridan" and a "strident virago," suggesting that the paper would be shut down for obscenity if it reprinted her speech. Compelled to explain the significant presence of women at her talks, reporters castigated them, noting that the "seats of the Opera House were occupied by many . . . who would not have been attracted by a sermon, or by a decent production of any sort." Newspaper editors in Chicago also assumed a condescending tone when describing the "unusual size and susceptibility" of women present for Woodhull's lectures at the Academy of Music in that city. Females who attended such lectures, one reporter suggested, needed male protection and guidance. Otherwise, he explained, vulnerable and easily misled women would regard "with favor some of the exposures she claimed to make" despite the "coarse, gross" language she employed to discuss the sexual hypocrisy of leading religious and governmental figures.[30]

Woodhull's enemies as well as her supporters recognized her charismatic presence at the podium. Even the caustic *Milwaukee Sentinel* acknowledged her ability to connect with her audiences, noting that "the eloquence which poured from her lips . . . swept through the souls of those present," causing them "to burst every now and then into uproarious enthusiasm." Despite journalists' efforts to demonize her, Woodhull's words reached large numbers of Wisconsin women and men: some curious, some derisive, and some who shared her critique of the social order. Crisscrossing the Badger state, Woodhull's 1874 and 1875 lecture tours included stops in Berlin, Janesville, La Crosse (where she spoke opposite a temperance lecturer and drew by far the larger crowd), Madison, Menasha, Portage, and Sheboygan. Woodhull's impulsive actions kept her in the news: after a February 1874 engagement before a large "admiring" and sometimes "boisterous" audience at Madison's Opera House, she and her sister Tennessee made an unprecedented visit to the state legislature, then in session.[31]

The editor of the *Oconto County (Wis.) Register,* one of the few journalists to provide readers with balanced and full coverage of Woodhull's presentation, acknowledged her as "the smartest, most brilliant, female orator we have ever heard" and stood in accord with many of her statements about the "prevailing social evil." Spiritualists in the audience understood Woodhull's explanation for the high numbers of idiots in state asylums: "If man or wife live unhappily, they cannot have perfect children." But the writer differed with Woodhull's solution—for women to have children only with men they loved. Acknowledging the social and economic realities that led women to marry, he raised a question that plagued Woodhull and other sex radicals: what about the children? Evoking an image of chaos that must result from the dissolution of marriage, he declared: "God pity the poor, homeless, motherless, fatherless little ones, with none to care for them and no one to love them."[32] The utopian solution Woodhull (and some sex radicals who preceded her) offered—the management of children and property in common—did not satisfy ambitious middle-class men such as this editor. Intent on acquiring property and status, such class-conscious patriarchs depended on the accoutrements of marriage to establish their position in society. Woodhull's message, however, had great appeal to thousands of people who found it difficult to hold their own during the era's economic cycles.

Conscious of the need to attract large audiences in order to remain financially solvent, Woodhull adopted what she called a "New Departure" in early 1874 and focused on presenting herself as a devout Christian woman. Lacing her speeches and written works with biblical references and religious rhetoric, the outspoken freethinker carefully scripted her performances and warmed up audiences by having her daughter, Zulu Maud, deliver an earnest, poetic, and often religious reading. Woodhull then appeared on stage modestly attired in black with a trademark tea rose demurely pinned at her neck, giving every indication of respectability, and read from a prepared text. Only after her audience relaxed and she warmed to her subject did she extemporize. By then, "whatever feelings of prejudice the hearer may have" had evaporated, as each member of the audience saw "before him a woman terribly in earnest . . . an angel of beauty."[33]

Woodhull's dramatic persona captivated many of her listeners, and their response fueled her sense of mission. "She electrifies, startles, astonishes, and melts her audiences to tears," observed a correspondent who had heard Woodhull in San Jose, California, in 1874. Others told of being so overcome by emotion after hearing her speak that they could not rest until they had written to her. Aware of Woodhull's rapport with audiences, and especially the women in them, the eastern suffragist Isabella Beecher Hooker observed in a letter to Susan B. Anthony that she had "not heard one word of criticism from any who have *seen her for themselves.*"[34] Even those who attended her lectures out of curiosity could depart as converts, disarmed by her impassioned eloquence and dexterous arguments.

So effective was Woodhull's "New Departure" that some women even elevated her to martyr status. Woodhull encouraged this practice and did not hesitate to remind readers and audiences that her efforts on their behalf had taken a heavy toll. "My body has been crucified until I am almost unable to use it anymore," she informed them, and her advocacy of their needs had "made a poor woman of me."[35] Comparing her to Jesus Christ, contributors to *Woodhull and Claflin's Weekly* filled their letters with metaphorical descriptions of her "receiving the nails into her hands and feet," going "on the cross for you as well as for us," and serving her readers and listeners "the bread of life." Like Jesus, they wrote, she was of lowly birth, suffered at the hands of the authorities, and had come to fulfill her mission as the savior of Spiritualism and "the last victim sacrificed on the altar of women's suffrage." Another impassioned supporter, exemplifying the sentiments of many, praised Woodhull as a "noble woman in a noble cause—the cause of humanity." To such individuals, she was on a "holy mission," shattering the silence that kept women enslaved and awakening them to their responsibility for the regeneration of the world.[36] While it is impossible to determine the precise impact of this worshipful admiration on Woodhull beyond her use of it to financial advantage, her lecturing had a profound impact on thousands who pondered the meaning of women's rights.

Women Speaking Out

Comstock's efforts to silence Woodhull after she published the Beecher-Tilton exposé had the opposite effect: growing numbers of women and men sought opportunities to read and discuss her ideas. Some subscribers read *Woodhull and Claflin's Weekly* out of curiosity, but many others did so because they supported Woodhull's right to the freedom of expression. Without a doubt, the controversy she generated meant that many people, even if they did not subscribe to the paper, had some knowledge of her ideas. Before Comstock arrested Woodhull in November 1872, for example, only one person in Dowagiac, Michigan, subscribed to *Woodhull and Claflin's Weekly*, but half a year later twenty-six residents in the town of approximately two thousand had subscriptions. As a result, one reader there confided, "Sexuality is now discussed freely and seriously by almost all classes of thinking people."[37]

Women who lacked the courage to brave gossip or censure to attend one of Woodhull's public lectures could consume her ideas in the privacy of their homes. Many did, and avidly. When the American News Company refused to continue distributing *Woodhull and Claflin's Weekly* in early 1873 (after the sisters' arrest), readers banded together and formed clubs to ensure the paper's uninterrupted distribution nationwide. Comstock's actions and the repressive measures he inspired convinced a Fremont, Indiana, woman that the social purity reformer had ignited a war. Prior to the winter of 1872–73, another correspondent explained, women had not submitted many letters for publication because "we are cowards and she is not." Emboldened by Woodhull's example, women from coast to coast began sharing their opinions—through the venue of print—on "themes generally considered unchaste."[38] This public airing of their ideas on marriage and sexual ethics not only empowered them as individuals but also fostered the construction of an informal network of like-minded thinkers, one capable of sustaining and nourishing sex radical ideas after Woodhull departed permanently to England in 1877.

Many of the earliest contributors to *Woodhull and Claflin's Weekly* resided in the East. Fifty-two-year-old Hope Whipple, a machinist's wife residing in Worcester, Massachusetts, had in the 1850s become interested in Stephen Pearl Andrews's writings on marriage and divorce. The social reformer Laura Cuppy Smith supported the *Weekly* too, politicized by her daughter's experience as an unwed mother. A frequent contributor, she offered her ideas about the moral double standard and marriage laws. After 1872, published correspondence increasingly came from women living in such predominantly agricultural communities as Winterset, Iowa, and Whitewater, Wisconsin. Often, contributors wrote from areas Woodhull had visited during her extensive western lecture tours.

Struggling to cope with the wrenching impact of economic depression, women looked to *Woodhull and Claflin's Weekly* as a site where they could explore solutions to the domestic tensions exacerbated by financial distress. Some who addressed such concerns included the itinerant Spiritualist lecturers Lois Waisbrooker and Sada Bailey Fowler, water-cure practitioners like Wisconsin's Juliet H. Stillman Severance, the thirty-two-year-old wife of a pattern maker living in Fitchburg, Massachusetts, and the twenty-nine-year-old Kansas farm wife Jennie Tibbot, who took in boarders to ease the family finances, and the thirty-two-year-old wife of a pattern maker living in Fitchburg, Massachusetts. Such men as a farm machinery dealer from Illinois, a baker in Milwaukee, and a future chief justice of the Kansas Supreme Court also expressed their frustrations with social conditions exacerbated by economic conditions. Like their female counterparts, some of them had first encountered sex radical theories in the 1850s and viewed free love as part of a larger plan for the socioeconomic restructuring of the nation. A broom maker from Bates, Illinois, for instance, attributed his interest in Woodhull's theories to his earlier reading of the *Social Revolutionist*.[39]

Expressing boundless confidence in the potential of freedom—be it free labor, free trade, or free love—those midwestern and western correspondents attributed their sense of kinship with Woodhull to her lower-class origins. Many rural women and men who sent letters to *Woodhull and Claflin's Weekly*, for instance, expressed admiration for her ability to transcend socioeconomic limitations. She intentionally reinforced this impression through the use of frequent references to herself as "a poor, weak, unlettered woman" (although she was anything but weak) victimized by eastern editors, journalists, and clergymen.[40] Through such practices Woodhull touched a raw nerve among those who blamed eastern financial institutions for their inability to recover and prosper.

Readers' letters to *Woodhull and Claflin's Weekly* stand as confessionals and as indictments of the socioeconomic system that governed their lives. In issue after issue correspondents described themselves as "down-trodden and oppressed," "poor," and overwhelmed with the responsibilities of caring for large families. It was "hard to break away from the customs and usages of centuries," wrote Nellie L. Davis from Louisville, Kentucky, when "the path trodden has been the only thoroughfare of the human family for thousands of years and each succeeding epoch has riveted the closer the chains of earth's famishing millions."[41] But Woodhull, her female supporters believed, was striking a blow at systematic social and economic efforts to enslave them. Joining her in the fight, they stepped forward to air their own ideas on three major topics: the hypocrisy of the sexual double standard, the role of the church and state in institutionalizing woman's inequality, and the meaning of social purity.

"It Was Henry Ward Beecher That Made a Free Lover of Me"

For many readers of *Hull's Crucible, The Word,* and *Woodhull and Claflin's Weekly,* the Beecher-Tilton case served vividly as an example of how a church- and state-sanctioned sexual double standard rendered women powerless. Delegates attending a Social Freedom Convention in Boston in 1875 referred to the scandal as a contest between Elizabeth Tilton's legal owner and her lover. Neither man, they argued, recognized her natural right "to be free from the barbarous control of both." Angered by journalists who portrayed Woodhull's published allegation of Beecher's adultery as a violation of his privacy yet who simultaneously demanded a full accounting of Woodhull's own sexual history, readers vigorously denounced the customs and traditions that imposed one moral code on their sons and another on their daughters. Men, they knew all too well, could escape blameless from pre- or extramarital sexual encounters while moral authorities, insisting that women remain chaste and monogamous, labeled their female partners "fallen women" and pronounced them unfit for marriage. Contemplating the hypocrisy of this dual standard, as exemplified in the case of the popular clergyman who seemingly practiced free love while condemning it in others, Mrs. Dr. Barnes from Chicago declared: "It was Henry Ward Beecher that made a free lover of me."[42]

The women whose letters appeared in *Woodhull and Claflin's Weekly* not only attributed the sexual double standard to the church and state but also chastised both for institutionalizing woman's inequality by granting husbands full legal and religious rights to their wives' bodies. Many women shared Sarah Norton's assertion in 1870 that the object of marriage was "the entire control over the woman" and that of a Vermillion, Ohio, woman who concluded that women could love only at the expense of their liberty and rights. Men, women reasoned, had been socialized to regard marriage as the sole legitimate site for sexual expression and no longer felt compelled to exercise sexual self-control after their wedding day. Nothing, wrote a woman from Waukegan, Illinois, gave more license to sexual indulgence than marriage. And the church, an anonymous Michigan woman added, compounded the devastating effects of this sexual imbalance of power by requiring wives to be submissive. Describing the abuse she suffered at the hands of a husband who quoted scripture to justify his sexual demands, a Catholic woman indicated that she had remained in her unsatisfactory marriage because of Christian teachings about duty and self-sacrifice. Over time, however, those teachings lost their power to assuage women's sorrow, pain, and anger.[43]

The Search for Social Purity

Instead of viewing post–Civil War feminism as a tug-of-war between sex radicals on one end and suffragists, social purity reformers, and members of the WCTU on the other end, their relationship is best captured by the analogy of fluid coalitions "jostling" one another.[44] Like suffragists, the sex radicals who supported Woodhull sought equality, and like social purity reformers, they yearned for order. But in contrast to those two groups, sex radicals often eschewed participation in an existing—and, they believed, flawed—political system. Holding fast to their faith in individual freedom, they inevitably clashed with those who feared that some classes of citizens could not be trusted to live morally. Thus, while social purity reformers focused on protecting "innocent" youth and women from sexual danger, sex radicals—harkening back to their antebellum roots—reiterated their confidence in the power of self-control. Shifting their gaze from society to the individual, they observed that failed attempts to self-regulate relations between the sexes had produced several destructive by-products: prostitution, abortion and infanticide, and repressed female sexuality. Until remedied, they concluded, these social problems would remain roadblocks to the "Good Time Coming."

Prostitution, often portrayed as an urban phenomenon, resonated with Woodhull's predominantly rural readership because it provided them with a platform from which to critique the socioeconomic structure that governed their lives. They perceived it as flawed because they felt marginalized and unable to prosper. The church, observed the midwestern sex radical C. L. James, taught that men and women must marry before they had sexual intercourse. Caught in a web of financial panic and economic depression, many men consequently found it necessary to delay marriage yet lacked the self-control necessary to remain celibate. This conundrum, James argued, created a market for prostitution and a population of hypocritical men who patronized prostitutes by night and condemned them by day. Such hypocrisy, he concluded, could not help but permeate other aspects of men's lives. One *Woodhull and Claflin's Weekly* correspondent, Nellie Davis, indicted the socioeconomic system "that demands a quarter of a million prostitutes to sustain it" while reminding readers that many of them had exchanged sexual favors, through marriage vows, for security and status. A reader from Maine bluntly summed up such sentiments: "Money is the god, man possesses it, and woman sells her sexuality for it."[45] With this thought in mind, numerous correspondents pondered which was worse, to sell their bodies in prostitution or in marriage?

Woodhull, whose own life experiences had heightened her awareness of women's economic dependence on men, approached the subject of prostitution from a pragmatic perspective. The poorly paid working woman, she reasoned, often had no other choice. Men, she elaborated, turned to prostitutes because the institution of marriage confined women to their homes, kept them ignorant of public affairs, and thus rendered them less desirable to their husbands.[46] Female correspondents to *Woodhull and Claflin's Weekly*, recognizing that reality, joined Woodhull in blaming the male-established and -dominated socioeconomic system that denied them equal access to educational and employment opportunities. Laura Cuppy Smith informed readers in 1873 that she no longer tried to relieve the condition of prostitutes but instead reserved her "heaviest blows" for "the condition of society which makes prostitution possible." Because sex radical Spiritualists regarded prostitution a transitional state, they did not despair. Instead, they advocated that their movement embrace prostitutes (theoretically, if not in practice). Reiterating prostitution's similarity to chattel slavery, the veteran free lover Austin Kent likewise urged *Woodhull and Claflin's Weekly* readers to "welcome the harlots to our own ranks as the North did the Negro." Others, optimistically sharing Angela Heywood's conviction that this "matter of business" would disappear once greater employment opportunities opened to women, supported Kent's view.[47]

Woodhull's supporters in midwestern and western states thus perceived a widening gap between themselves and their privileged eastern sisters—whom they referred to as a "trim and rigid sisterhood"—when it came to the question of prostitution. They also resented what they saw as condescending sympathy offered by suffragists to their "fallen sisters." They understood all too well that economic dependency could force almost any woman to sell her sexual rights. Moreover, they condemned the cultured women who in their support for Henry Ward Beecher condoned a man who victimized vulnerable women, concluding that such individuals had in fact compromised the broader movement for women's rights.[48]

Sex radicals blamed church and state for exacerbating two other interconnected social problems—abortion and infanticide. Both occurred, correspondents asserted, because sexually submissive wives, obedient to their marriage vows, found themselves weary and worn from numerous pregnancies and even infected with venereal diseases. Unmarried women occasionally resorted to abortion to preserve their social standing, correspondents to *Woodhull and Claflin's Weekly* acknowledged, but they believed that most abortions occurred within Christian marriage.[49]

Unlike the social purity reformers who sought the criminalization of women who aborted their fetuses, Woodhull's followers viewed them as victims and the abortive act a form of resistance. Evoking images of the antebellum South, contributors to *Woodhull and Claflin's Weekly* compared those who sought abortions to enslaved women who had resorted to abortion or infanticide to prevent their children from enduring similar hardships and indignities. They further indicted the institution of marriage by sharing such accounts as that of a Pennsylvania woman whose husband forced her to undergo an abortion because he deemed her unfit for motherhood and a Toledo, Ohio, wife of a syphilitic who repeatedly committed infanticide to spare her children from suffering the consequences of their father's disease. Until women had the right to control their bodies, Woodhull's followers contended, they would continue to commit such acts.[50]

In addition to critiquing the sexual double standard and church- and state-sanctioned marriage, Woodhull's supporters challenged the prevailing idea of female passionlessness. That they did not equate purity with chastity is clear in the words of the itinerant lecturer Helen Nash, who in 1875 wrote: "There is such a thing as sexual purity, but it is not sexual deadness."[51] Much like the women who had read *Nichols' Monthly* in the 1850s, *Woodhull and Claflin's Weekly* correspondents often endowed sexual intercourse with spiritual significance. Some further believed that sexual fulfillment must occur before women could achieve purity in themselves or their children. They did not eschew physical relations with the opposite sex but instead envisioned sexual relations on a spectrum ranging from animalistic sexual passion to a hyper-romanticized spiritual communion. Believing that most people had not yet advanced beyond the animalistic stage, many correspondents blamed the institution of marriage and husbands for their lack of progress. "The laws of legal marriage," wrote Mrs. H. A. Richardson of Santa Barbara, Califor-

nia, "have robbed woman of her sexual rights and placed them in the keeping of the man."[52] Such day-to-day realities merely served to heighten their
yearning for a purer and more satisfying love, which they believed was necessary before women could bear healthy children capable of regenerating the
world.

Unlike suffragists, few *Woodhull and Claflin's Weekly* correspondents equated sexuality solely with reproduction. According to a Vermont woman, sexual expression had two benefits beyond reproduction during adulthood:
growth during youth, and "the up-building of the spiritual" during postre-
productive years. Linking female sexual desire to spirituality, she announced
in an extraordinary statement that even Jesus Christ had a sexual nature. But
like "many a lone, sensitive, starved, misunderstood woman of to-day," she
reasoned, he had not found anyone "pure enough in spirit" with whom to
blend. Other correspondents expressed similar sentiments, positing that sexual relations between a spiritually developed man and woman became "a holy
sacrament of love in which shame has no part."[53]

Women Coming Out

In 1874 Sarah S. Penoyer described her "coming out"—her ability to speak
her mind freely on sexual topics—as the first time she arose to speak in freedom.[54] Without a doubt, Woodhull, by example and through the ideas she
espoused, empowered significant numbers of women to ponder openly their
status in marriage, if not to proclaim themselves sex radicals. Focusing on
the promises of free love rather than on sensationalistic portrayals seized
upon by the popular press, grassroots consumers of Woodhull's theories
believed they embodied the epitome of social purity. Moreover, they grasped
the necessity of first reforming a social and economic system that privileged
a few and disempowered the many.

Woodhull's supporters concurred that reproductive freedom held the key
to empowering women and thus ensuring their rights. "Woman's first great,
and all embracing right, without which all talk of other rights is but mock-
ery and nonsense," affirmed delegates to the Western Woman's Emancipation Society meeting at Ravenna, Ohio, in 1874, "is the Right to Herself."
Grounding their justification in widely held hereditarian beliefs, meeting
participants envisioned a world in which women as "queens of parentage"
would bear children who no longer required regeneration.[55] More demanding than the idealistic free lovers of the 1850s, sex radicals of the 1870s looked
simultaneously backward to a utopian ideal and forward to the establishment
of a scientifically based, egalitarian social order. Once society abolished ar-

bitrarily created moral restraints, they anticipated, women and men would cease viewing freedom as a license for selfish indulgence. Freedom alone, *Woodhull and Claflin's Weekly* readers asserted, could bring about true purity and desired motherhood.

Even as Woodhull's ideas gained momentum, the controversial lecturer's interest in respectability and security grew. The death of the sisters' patron, Commodore Cornelius Vanderbilt, in 1877 led the two women to leave the United States for England. Like the Nicholses, Woodhull again flourished as a lecturer, and an 1883 marriage to the banker John Biddulph Martin brought economic security. Eventually she, like American sex radicals she left behind, became enamored with eugenic thought. From 1892 until 1901 Woodhull and her daughter published a journal dedicated to that cause, *The Humanitarian.*

Despite Woodhull's departure from the American sex radical scene, her ideas lingered. What did it matter that Woodhull and the Nicholses had "left the field?" the veteran free lover J. H. Cook queried in 1884. "Are the truths they uttered *lost* upon the world? Is not the seed they sowed now germinating in many minds?"[56] Woodhull, Cook astutely recognized, by the mid-1870s represented only one of several women willing and able to advance the cause of sexual freedom. Lesser known today, her successors built on Woodhull's foundation to set an equally large number of women on the road to freedom.

5. Roads to Freedom

> We are rebels in the fullest sense of that word. We are determined
> to overthrow the ruling power, to dethrone it.
> —Lois Waisbrooker, 1873

"Why is it," Lois Waisbrooker demanded in 1873 from the platform of a
national meeting of Spiritualists, that "when prostitution runs riot on our
streets . . . leading Spiritualists do not seem particularly distressed? When
advertisements for the cure of diseases brought on by abuse of the sexual
functions are posted upon almost every street corner. . . . When women are
forced to prostitute their bodies almost daily to the abuse of legal brutes called
husbands." Whenever the agitation of "freedom for women increases," she
noted, Spiritualists call for "freedom from side issues."[1] Freedom, a contested term in Reconstruction-era America, had many definitions, yet the audience knew how Waisbrooker defined it. Along with Victoria Woodhull, the
president of the American Association of Spiritualists, she advocated economic self-sufficiency for women and the right of all to control the uses of
their bodies.

The colorful and controversial Victoria Woodhull presided over this tenth
annual meeting of the American Association of Spiritualists, an assemblage
containing—as Waisbrooker's speech illustrates—other equally radical wom-
en. This chapter illuminates the lives, beliefs, and opinions of two leading
voices at that meeting—Lois Waisbrooker and Juliet H. Stillman Severance.
The two represent a complex amalgam of nineteenth-century reform movements. Abolitionism awakened the rebel in each, while Spiritualism challenged thinking and provided opportunities for each to find her voice. Spiritualism also provided both women with a national outlet through which they
could disseminate sex radical ideas, generate an income, and cultivate relationships with reform-minded women and men.

Active during five decades characterized by periodic economic depression, political corruption, industrialization, immigration, and spiritual turmoil, Waisbrooker and Severance joined with antebellum advocates of women's rights to condemn a legal and economic system that gave men unfair economic, political, and social advantages over women and the moral double standard that resulted. After the Civil War, however, the women's rights movement split when it became clear that Congress would grant African American men—not women—the right to vote. The NWSA, led by Elizabeth Cady Stanton and Susan B. Anthony, persisted in discussing such subjects as legislation liberalizing divorce and improved working conditions for women, but over time they acknowledged the liability of linking woman suffrage to such causes. Far greater numbers of women supported the AWSA, which carefully eschewed discussion of topics that might link, and thus retard, their campaign for woman suffrage with free love or infidelism.[2]

In contrast, Waisbrooker and Severance allied themselves with marginalized groups. Whether they looked to anarchism, sex radicalism, or political third parties for the implementation of a shared vision for women, their intent remained the same: to overthrow the "ruling power" that prevented women from achieving sexual equality. Keeping such topics as abortion, divorce, marital sexual abuse, prostitution, and the sexual double standard before the public, they also contested male-prescribed definitions of freedom and asserted their belief in the positive power of female sexuality. The controversy and hostility their activism engendered underscores the highly contested nature of the power they claimed for themselves and their sex.

Becoming Lois Waisbrooker

Lois Waisbrooker's early life—punctuated by poverty, poor health, and marital failure—provided a solid foundation for her feminism. Born Adeline Eliza Nichols in Catharine, New York, in 1826, she was the daughter of a day laborer of modest means and a consumptive mother of seven who died at the age of thirty-six. "I remember," Waisbrooker wrote in a tribute to her father, "the continuous toil, the coarse fare, the poor attire that was thine, in order that thy children might have bread." Even more significantly, she recalled that "others grew richer for thy toil."[3] As a youth living in the "Burned-over" district of New York as well as in the Western Reserve of Ohio, she learned to question the logic of religiously sanctioned, male-dominated institutions. Like many Christians who later became infidels, she admitted to a belief in Jesus and his teachings but rejected the hypocrisy embedded in "what is called the religion of Jesus."[4] Because of the family's several moves and impover-

ished condition, Waisbrooker had limited opportunities for formal education, and at seventeen she found herself pregnant and "forced" to marry
George Fuller. Referring to her husband as "a comparative stranger," she
recalled "the bitter rueing of my haste, and the blighting desolation which
bowed me to the very earth."[5] Although she married five months before giving birth to a daughter, she suffered the stigma of being a "fallen woman,"
an experience that indelibly influenced and informed her subsequent reform
work.[6]

Widowed when not yet twenty, Adeline Fuller lacked the financial means
to support her daughter and a subsequently born son. Placing the two with
other families, she became a live-in maid for a sympathetic family. "The lady
with whom I staid seemed to understand me better even than I understood
myself," Waisbrooker recalled, and she encouraged her to study to become a
teacher. Although her mistress was unable to provide financial aid toward this
goal, Waisbrooker recognized that she had received a far more valuable gift:
"the encouragement which enabled me to use my own resources."[7] Led by
her sympathy for oppressed groups, the newly prepared educator accepted
a position teaching African American children in Muskingum County, Ohio.
In 1856, however, she interrupted her teaching career for a brief, unhappy
second marriage when her father pressured her to marry Isaac Snell, a man
"for whom she had no attraction."[8]

Beginning in the late 1850s, Spiritualist meetings and periodicals became
forums for heated discussions about marriage. Spiritualists who gathered in
Rutland, Vermont, in 1858 heard Julia Branch denounce marriage as a form
of women's slavery; in 1859 the trance speaker Lizzie Doten captivated eastern audiences with her utterances about free love and affinities. Many people, she argued, married mistakenly because their "love principles" remained
undeveloped.[9] Numerous articles in the immensely popular Spiritualist periodical *Banner of Light* reinforced the desirability of finding one's spiritual
affinity, even if it meant dissolving an existing marriage to progress to higher levels of personal development. Such speeches and articles not only raised
women's expectations of marriage but also urged them, if necessary, to "stand
forth and break free." Empowered by such ideas, a number of reform-minded
readers took action, exchanging their marriage vows for spiritual affinities.
Between 1856 and 1865, Adeline Nichols Fuller Snell joined many other Americans in discovering Spiritualism. Saying goodbye to her second husband and
her tumultuous past, she changed her name to Lois Waisbrooker, became a
public speaker and author, and set out on the road to freedom.

"Spiritualism," explains the historian Ann Braude, "helped a crucial generation of American women find their voice."[10] Lois Waisbrooker belongs to

that sorority. Throughout the 1860s and early 1870s she crossed the nation attending Spiritualist meetings and lecturing on such topics as illegitimacy, free love, motherhood, and women's rights.[11] Despite regular interactions with numerous male Spiritualists and reformers, Waisbrooker held a negative opinion of their sex. Men were, she believed, inherently destructive, while women were creative. This conviction led her, like members of the NWSA, to repudiate male spokespersons and women who thought like men, maintaining that only free women like herself could authoritatively speak on woman's behalf. The survival of the human race, she argued, depended on liberating women from social and economic constraints so they could, in turn, redeem men and together conceive "a god-like race."[12]

In addition to freeing women's minds, Spiritualism gave Waisbrooker and women like her a means to achieve economic self-sufficiency and physical mobility. Such Spiritualist periodicals as Boston's *Banner of Light* and Chicago's *Religio-Philosophical Journal,* for instance, contained numerous announcements of women's availability for speaking engagements and advertisements for their services as clairvoyants, psychometric readers, and healing mediums. In the process, they developed a supportive network that sustained them during times of sickness and economic hardship. In 1869, a Missouri friend in whose home Waisbrooker recuperated during one of her periodic bouts with illness announced the availability of her modestly priced "Spiritual Tracts" (a series of ten four-page pamphlets) and urged readers to "remember the widows and fatherless in their inflictions, and, especially, such as do not wish to be numbered on the lists of 'The Indolent' or the 'Superannuated.'"[13]

Like a host of other Spiritualist women, Waisbrooker at times lectured as a trance medium, yet her fragile health made printed works the most effective means of reaching her intended audiences. Between the 1868 publication of *Suffrage for Woman: The Reasons Why* and her death in 1909, the itinerant lecturer and author wrote twelve novels and pamphlets, edited three periodicals (*Our Age, Foundation Principles,* and *Clothed with the Sun*), and served for a year as the acting editor of the sex radical weekly *Lucifer, the Light-Bearer.* Many of her works employ frank language to describe women's sexual enslavement in marriage and contain autobiographical elements portraying young women victimized by the sexual double standard.[14]

Informed by her own youthful first marriage and the experiences of women she had met on the Spiritualist lecture circuit, Waisbrooker dedicated herself to exposing the negative consequences of the moral double standard and the institution of marriage for young women. Readers found her first novel, *Alice Vale, a Story for the Times* (printed by the *Banner of Light* publishing office in 1869), "interesting," but their enthusiastic response to *Helen Harlow's Vow* (1870) ensured that it would remain in print for the remainder of the century.[15] Dedicated "to woman in general, and to the outcast in particular," Waisbrooker's novel recounts the story of a young woman's seduction and desertion and her subsequent experience in coping with the prejudices of society, raising her son, and establishing a place for herself in the world. Waisbrooker's message—that women must free themselves because no one else will—struck a responsive note with mothers like Mrs. Lavinia S. Woodard of Fruitland, Illinois, who encouraged other readers to "place it in the hands of your daughters." They would, she explained, learn from the title character's example "that if woman *respects herself,* she will always command the respect of others." "There are few families in the land," concurred a Laona, New York, reader, "that cannot apply some part of Helen Harlow's experience."[16]

In the 1870s, with the nation caught in the grip of a devastating economic depression, Waisbrooker began exploring the downturn's relationship to women's freedom. After joining a community of health reformers and Spiritualists at Battle Creek, Michigan, in the early 1870s, she inaugurated a periodical entitled *Our Age* in 1873, the same year she published *The Sex Question and the Money Power.*[17] Editors of the era's other radical reform periodicals frequently excerpted from *Our Age,* which Waisbrooker devoted "to the interests of Spiritualism in the broad sense of that term." Keenly aware of farmers and workers who struggled to cope with the monopolistic practices of railroad companies, she issued a call in *Our Age* for a nationwide economic restructuring based on a new, cooperative social order: "This present unjust, unbalanced condition of things must break in pieces of its own weight, and then we shall want something lasting upon which to reconstruct."[18] Her publication ceased in 1874 due to continuing health problems and lack of funds. When Waisbrooker persisted in agitating such topics as monetary and sexual reform in the increasingly conservative Spiritualist press, the *Banner of Light* editor joined with the editor of *Religio-Philosophical Journal* in rejecting her contributions and advertisements for her works. They refused, Waisbrooker confided to the free love Spiritualist and Greenback party supporter Moses Hull, to discuss the "bread and butter question."[19] Those editors' actions represented more than a silencing of her ideas; they hindered Waisbrooker's economic well-being by sealing off a crucial outlet for the publication, distribution, and sale of her work.

Radical social reformers like Waisbrooker still could turn to *The Word,* which Ezra Heywood had published with his wife Angela from their Princeton, Massachusetts, home since 1872. Both the Heywoods and Waisbrooker shared an avid interest in the relationship between the sex question and economic matters and a belief that the issue must be discussed in plain language.[20] After meeting Waisbrooker at an 1875 social freedom meeting in Boston, Heywood found her to be comparable to a Roman Sibyl, Margaret Fuller, and Sojourner Truth, "'all rolled into one.'"[21] Although the two shared many reform interests, Waisbrooker's sympathies increasingly lay with the needs of rural laborers in midwestern and western states, a population minimally represented in Heywood's East Coast publication.

Physically depleted after her editorship of *Our Age,* Waisbrooker sought temporary refuge with her son, Abner Fuller, who in the mid-1870s had relocated to Contra Costa County, California. With the small community of Antioch as a base, she worked to establish herself there by reconnecting with radical Spiritualist friends and supporters who invited her to lecture in their West Coast communities. In San Francisco by 1876, she issued a call (through the pages of the sex radical periodicals *Woodhull and Claflin's Weekly* and *Hull's Crucible*) for the creation of a network of correspondents—men and women—who were "free" and "ready and willing to assert their freedom." Recognizing the geographical scattering of individuals who shared her values, Waisbrooker hoped they could continue struggling for "the emancipation of sex" through correspondence.[22] She may also have expected to sell some of her publications to respondents.

By 1883 Waisbrooker had returned to the Midwest and settled among longtime friends in the small Iowa community of Clinton. Home to a number of Spiritualists as well as the location of a water-cure resort, Clinton became headquarters for her new endeavor, *Foundation Principles,* an eleven-by-seventeen-inch biweekly first issued in 1885. "Foundation Principles," she proclaimed in her masthead, "are the rock upon which Motherhood Must Rest. Search for them." Several hundred subscribers paid fifty cents annually for the four-page publication, but to make ends meet Waisbrooker herself often set the type and operated the hand press. A typical issue contained her opinions on current affairs, especially as they related to women and economics, presented portions of her works in serialized form, provided excerpts from reader correspondence, and carried advertisements for radical publications, many of them her own. *Foundation Principles* quickly became an important avenue through which Waisbrooker could preach her message about women's freedom while earning enough to provide a very modest existence. A year later, in 1886, another bout of poor health interrupted her editorial endeavors and forced her to interrupt publication and return to California. From her son's home in Antioch she attempted to resume *Foundation Principles* but lacked the resources to print more than an issue or two.

Waisbrooker, as with a number of her predominantly midwestern and western subscribers, also read an anarchistic freethought weekly published in the rural community of Valley Falls, Kansas. Edited by the freethinker and sex radical Moses Harman from 1883 until 1910, *Lucifer, the Light-Bearer* advocated woman's emancipation from sex slavery and encouraged readers to engage in vigorous and frank discussions in print on sexual and economic topics. Like his counterpart Ezra Heywood in the East, Harman often published words and subject matter deemed "obscene" by Anthony Comstock and his army of postal inspectors and periodically endured prosecution for sending *Lucifer* through the mail. Waisbrooker soon lent her support to Harman's endeavor, and "Sister Lois" became a familiar name from regular appearances in *Lucifer's* pages.[23]

The Panic of 1893 and the following years of economic depression created a receptive audience for socioeconomic critiques of society, especially in the drought-stricken heartland, and a reinvigorated Waisbrooker thrived on new opportunities to share her solutions in print. While serving as acting editor of *Lucifer* in 1892 and 1893 (during one of Moses Harman's four prison sentences), the aging radical decided that it was time for a female editor to challenge the Comstock Law. As she anticipated, postal authorities banned from the mail an issue of *Lucifer* in which she reprinted part of a government document that mentioned the horse's penis. However, she was not prosecuted. Stepping down from her temporary editorial position in 1893, Waisbrooker settled in Topeka and, with *Lucifer's* moral if not financial support, resurrected *Foundation Principles* (which had ceased seven years earlier). She also established the Independent Publishing Company, from which she issued several of her works: *The Occult Forces of Sex; The Fountain of Life; or, The Threefold Power of Sex; The Wherefore Investigating Company;* and *A Sex Revolution.* The populist lecturer Mary E. Lease endorsed *A Sex Revolution,* a small book about women, as a sex, going on strike: "I wish every woman in the land could read your book. You gave expression to my thoughts so clearly that it almost startled me."[24]

No *Foundation Principles* subscription lists survive, yet it is possible to offer several observations about the periodical's readership based on the ninety-four individuals whose letters appeared in print from mid-1893 to late 1894. First, women comprised slightly more than half (52 percent) of those who gave their names when they wrote, making Waisbrooker's paper one of the few sex radical periodicals—if not the only—in which women's voices outnumbered men's. *Foundation Principles* circulated widely, with correspondents living in at least twenty-four states. Ranging from Maine to Florida and from California to Washington, the largest number of those who sent communications resided in rural Kansas and Illinois. That Waisbrooker's readers lacked economic means is evident from their frequent references to the consequences of prolonged drought and unfair working conditions and in their difficulties accumulating enough money to renew subscriptions and to purchase the radical books and pamphlets for which they yearned. "We need so many things," wrote an anonymous correspondent in 1894, "I don't know what to get first, but it seems as if I could hardly live without some good paper. My papers are about all the *real* company I have."[25] In addition to the California reformer Caroline Severance and Mary E. Lease, correspondents included social reformers, populists, Spiritualists, freethinkers, anarchists, dress reformers, and free lovers.

As their communications illustrate, female correspondents to *Foundation Principles* often felt isolated from neighbors because of their unconventional views about women's rights, religion, and sexuality. One described herself as "alone in my study of the reform questions." "There are near me very few lady friends," confided another, "who are not astounded and mortified when I approach such a subject as sex slavery." Such readers grew to consider Waisbrooker a trusted friend and confidante. "You seem nearer and dearer to me than many of my blood relations," confessed a correspondent from Junction City, Washington. "I never write what I feel to any of them." Readers also found great comfort in the sense of community Waisbrooker's paper afforded them: "I cannot do without your paper," wrote Ellen H. Taylor in August 1894. "Its arrival is welcomed as I would receive an old friend whose thoughts are congenial with my own."[26]

Many who read Waisbrooker's periodical shared her reformist zeal and gave copies of *Foundation Principles* to their friends and relatives. "I wish," wrote a reader from Council Bluffs, Iowa, that "every mother in the land could have it to read." Mailing copies back and forth until they virtually had been read to pieces, readers also asked Waisbrooker to send sample copies to friends and relatives who they believed needed to hear her message. A reader from Golden Eagle, Illinois, for instance, requested sample copies be sent to several women, including one, "born and brought up in hell at home," who had "grown into a thinker." Some, volunteering to recruit subscribers for *Foundation Principles* in their communities, encountered objections to its content. Undeterred, George McNinch of New Basil, Kansas, promised to "keep right on distributing the papers" even though people believed they dealt "with spiritualism and immoral topics."[27]

During her seventeen-month editorship of the revived *Foundation Principles,* the "small woman with a pleasant and intellectual face" insisted on maintaining an uncompromising stand on free speech. In the 5 June 1894 issue she published a letter ostensibly written by a sexually dissatisfied husband. When its author, one of Anthony Comstock's agents, arrived to arrest her on 2 August, she declared: "[If anyone] has obscenity in his soul, it's yourself, sir." Readers rallied to support Waisbrooker, sending words of encouragement and enclosing money for her defense. In a letter to the U.S. attorney general, one supporter, E. B. Foote, admonished: "If Mrs. Waisbrooker is compelled to go on trial in this matter, we know there will be no cringing, and that she will defend to the last inch her rights as a citizen to publicly discuss matters of sexual abuse and reform . . . [and] there would be nothing which could bring it more into prominence than the pushing of this prosecution."[28]

Waisbrooker remained in Topeka during numerous delays in the prosecution of her case until a judge finally dismissed the action in the spring of 1896. California anarchists claimed some credit for her release because they had flooded the judge with letters in her support.[29] The experience heightened her hostility toward government, and she returned to California a further radicalized woman. Settling in San Francisco, home to the anarchist publishers of *Free Society,* she found herself living among supportive working-class radicals who read voraciously and engaged in vigorous debate. Even as she adopted their anarchist stance toward government intervention, Waisbrooker remained open to such proposals as the Ruskin colony, Eugene V. Debs's democracy, and Bellamy Nationalism because each made people think.[30]

In January 1900, on the eve of her seventy-fourth birthday, Waisbrooker announced plans to begin yet another small monthly, to be entitled *Clothed with the Sun.* Calling for the scientific study of women's sexual desire, she remained determined to awaken women to the consequences of their sexual and economic enslavement. "Oh, woman, WOMAN!" she wrote in 1902, "Wake up and demand your Liberty!" As she had for a number of years, Waisbrooker stressed that women could begin to empower themselves by subscribing to her publication as well as other radical titles. "Remember!!! If you do not sustain outspoken papers your utter subjection is sure!—your children and your children's children slaves!!!"[31]

From the outset, however, *Clothed with the Sun* was plagued by such obstacles as a small subscriber base and rulings that denied Waisbrooker affordable postage rates. After issuing a few numbers from San Francisco, she moved north to the small anarchist colony of Home, Washington, where she sporadically printed the monthly for several years. When the assassination of President William McKinley in 1901 by the anarchist Leon Czolgosz led to a renewed government crackdown on anarchist activity, Waisbrooker became one of its targets. Arrested for yet another violation of the Comstock Law after she published an article entitled "The Awful Fate of Fallen Women," the septuagenarian received a relatively modest one-hundred-dollar fine from the sympathetic judge who heard her case.[32]

Leaving Home Colony in 1904, Waisbrooker spent her remaining years boarding with friends and family in Colorado and California. She continued to issue books and pamphlets, but her readership had begun to wane. Mainstream periodicals, with regular publication schedules, now included articles about such topics as women's employment and independence. Moreover, few "New Women" of the 1890s and early 1900s shared Waisbrooker's uncompromising view of men as destructive, nor did they welcome her belief that contraceptive devices enslaved rather than liberated women. Some former supporters became uncomfortable with her embrace of anarchism, while others, aged like herself, struggled to remain financially solvent. Dependent upon subscriptions and sale of her books and pamphlets for a livelihood, Waisbrooker's plaintive pleas for support gradually diminished her power as an editor and left her dependent on the good will of erstwhile friends and longtime supporters. It pained them to see the woman they had called "the mother of coming generations" making personal appeals for the sale of her books so she might have bread and shelter.[33]

Penniless at the time of her death in 1909, Lois Waisbrooker had spent over forty years promoting the twin ideas of assertive womanhood and female sexuality as a positive power. Spiritualism set her on the path to sex radical reform by helping the impoverished young woman find her voice and providing access to a national network for circulating her feminist message. The venue of print enabled her to reach geographically, economically, and intellectually marginalized readers. After digesting her works in the privacy of their homes, those women and men interacted with one another through letters Waisbrooker reprinted in *Our Age, Foundation Principles, Lucifer, the Light-Bearer,* and *Clothed with the Sun.* The interpretive community those readers formed not only sustained Waisbrooker ideologically and economically but also ensured that a radical vision of what women's rights must entail would endure after her death.

The Woodhull of Wisconsin

Unlike her friend Lois Waisbrooker, Juliet Hall Worth Stillman Severance enjoyed material comfort during most of her life. Born in Madison County, New York, on 1 July 1833, she spent her formative years in a dairy farming area peopled by abolitionists, health reformers, advocates of Washingtonian temperance, mesmerists, and phrenologists. Fourierists, Millerites, Quakers, Seventh-Day Baptists, and Spiritualists contributed to the community's religious

diversity, while to the north, members of the Oneida Community experimented with sex relations. West, in Seneca Falls, the Worth family's distant cousin
Lucretia Mott addressed the first women's rights convention in July 1848.[34]

The thirteenth in a Quaker family of seventeen children, Juliet had ample
opportunity to observe the effects of marriage, motherhood, and farm life
on women. The eleven children born to Walter F. Worth and his first wife,
Abigail Macy, arrived every two years until Abigail died in 1828, as did the
seven children born to Worth and his second wife, Catherine Stillman. Despite ill health as a youth, Juliet learned to card, spin, weave wool and flax,
and to make butter and cheese. Women's uncompensated and often unac-
knowledged contributions to the farm economy made a deep impression on
the young girl, who observed that women's hard work enabled their husbands
to build reputations and to prosper. The farmer, she learned, receives reward
for his labor, while his wife, who "works more hours than he does owns nothing, not even herself, her husband, or the children."[35] A wife's economic powerlessness, she concluded, bore a striking resemblance to the chattel slavery
so vehemently opposed by Worth family members and their nearby Quaker
brethren.

The rigors of farm life not only increased Juliet Worth's awareness of wom-
en's economic limitations but also piqued her interest in the laws of heredity. Why did farmers, she pondered, devote more attention to the care of their
breeding animals than they did to their pregnant wives and the "propagation
of the species"? All around her, she saw "prematurely old, broken down, dis-
heartened" women giving birth to diseased and deformed children. At the end
of the day, farm women must continue to labor on behalf of their families
while their farmer husbands have time to cultivate their minds. An intelligent, even precocious child, Juliet chafed at the prospect of "domestic drudgery," devoid of reading, attending lectures, and partaking in other forms of
instruction and amusement.[36]

As with other Quaker households, the Worth family valued education. In
1846, thirteen-year-old Juliet Worth matriculated with her sisters at the
DeRuyter Seminary, a school conducted by Seventh-Day Baptists. Her in-
structors included Baptist elders and a graduate from the Troy Female Seminary, a school known for the rigorous curriculum Emma Willard had introduced at its inception in 1821. Like many other young women living in
New York's Burned-over district, Juliet Worth had a religious conversion experience. Abandoning her Quaker faith for that of the Seventh-Day Baptists, she sought outlets for her reformist zeal. Embracing the antislavery,
temperance, and women's rights movements, she also donned the "Turk-
ish trousers" later popularized by Amelia Bloomer. Several years of teach-

ing country children during summer months, combined with speeches given to seminary classmates, honed her powers of persuasion and oratory skills.[37]

The poor health that had delayed Juliet Worth's matriculation at the DeRuyter Seminary led her to search for explanations and cures. With the assistance of a sympathetic local physician who agreed to instruct her in "hygienic methods of treatment," she embarked on a three-year tutorial.[38] The intellectually hungry young scholar did not let the Madison County Medical Society's efforts to discredit the mesmerists and clairvoyants who circulated throughout the region in the 1840s and 1850s deter her interest in exploring alternatives to allopathic, or "regular," medicine. Hydropathy, introduced to the United States in the 1840s, appealed to the reform-minded young woman because it offered "moderate remedies utilizing water and changes in personal habits, as opposed to vigorous drug and depletion therapeutics."[39] Inherently feminist, it empowered women to exert greater control over their lives.

In 1853, twenty-year-old Juliet Hall Worth married John Dwight Stillman (a man who bore the same surname as her mother). The young couple resided in Unadilla, New York, for several years before moving to DeWitt, Iowa. With her husband's financial support, Juliet Stillman (by then the mother of two small sons) traveled to New York City in the fall of 1857 and matriculated at the nation's leading institution for training water-cure physicians, Russell Trall's Hygeio-Therapeutic College. Trall, with Joel Shew, had founded the hydropathic movement in the United States over a decade earlier. He edited the widely read *Water-Cure Journal*, established in 1844 as a primary vehicle for communication within the movement.[40] Trall's program, which taught such students as Juliet Stillman the fundamentals of hydropathy, emphasized the necessity of demystifying women's physiology, presented female sexual orgasm as natural, pleasurable, and desirable, and taught that a woman alone should decide if and when to become pregnant. Like the hydropathic physicians Thomas L. and Mary Gove Nichols, Trall issued a disclaimer in his published texts to avoid censure for providing information about contraceptives and abortifacients. In justification of such content, Trall argued that so long as "the present false habits of society exist, so long will there be a demand for relief in this direction. And if these sufferers cannot find the desired remedy in the knowledge imparted by this work, they will seek it in more desperate and dangerous measures."[41]

Hydropathy's emphasis on "personal and social advancement through health" and the redefinition of women's sphere by rejecting the notion of females as physically and mentally hampered by their physiology permeated the curriculum.[42] Trall's emphasis on water cure's hygienic laws, which included dress, diet, exercise, and bathing, prepared students to provide their patients—who were often female—with tools for empowerment. Unlike "regular" medical schools, his and other hydropathic colleges encouraged students of both sexes, including married women, to apply: Juliet Stillman's class of twenty-three students, for instance, included six married and four single females. The school also brought together reform-minded couples, and Hygeio-Therapeutic College classmates often united their "hands, hearts, fortunes and *diplomas*."[43]

During her New York City sojourn, Juliet Stillman acquired more than knowledge of water cure: that year she delivered her first speech on the subject of women's enslavement in marriage. Moreover, she encountered a spiritualistic medium "whose tests of the return of spirits were so strong and convincing as to upset her religious views."[44] Searching to understand this phenomenon, she devoured such printed texts as Thomas Paine's *Age of Reason*. Later study of Charles Darwin's *Origin of Species* (1859) and T. H. Huxley's biological treatises led her to accept the theory of evolution and abandon Christianity. Evolution, she concluded, provided scientific proof of Spiritualism. Both emphasized the notion of "eternal progress" and provided support for her evolving critique of indissoluble marriage.[45]

Students who completed one term of study at the Hygeio-Therapeutic College received a certificate of study, but those who remained for the winter and spring earned an M.D. degree. Selecting the latter course, Juliet Stillman graduated on 13 April 1858 and proudly affixed "M.D." to her name. Shortly thereafter she settled with her family in Iowa. Located on the route of numerous stage coaches and wagon trains, the village of DeWitt provided goods and services for travelers and area farmers. After the Chicago, Iowa, and Nebraska Railroad reached the community, DeWitt consolidated its position as a distribution center for grain, stock, farm produce, and lumber.[46]

In DeWitt, John Dwight Stillman flourished as a trader, but Juliet—like her classmates elsewhere in the nation—encountered the hostility of local medical practitioners. Physicians who banded together in a recently organized Clinton County Medical Society (1857) sought to shore up their professional authority by denying membership to practitioners who lacked "standard" qualifications.[47] The "regular" doctors cast a shadow of suspicion on the use of cold water as a form of treatment; however, several factors enabled Juliet Stillman's water-cure practice to grow despite their efforts: a scarcity of physicians beyond the county's Mississippi River towns, a constant turnover in early practitioners, and the county's rapidly growing population. Her practice also flourished because she made medical services available to previously underserved populations—women and African Americans.[48]

In addition to treating such ailments as burns, poison ivy, earaches, and fevers, water-cure practitioners like Stillman competed successfully with male physicians for obstetric and gynecological patients. A colleague, located in Ypsilanti, Michigan, described her obstetric practice as most "annoying" to "regulars": the seventy-three obstetric cases she had cared for in 1858 included some of the town's most prominent women. Using sitzbaths, injections, and wet bandages, hydropaths treated prolapsed uteri, painful menstruation, and vaginal inflammations and delivered babies. Emphasizing to their patients the necessity of exercise and a healthful diet through "presence, touch, communication, arousing hope and expectancy of cure, and the reinforcement of ties with the social group," hydropaths reduced "the sense of isolation that so often accompanies sickness."[49]

Stillman's treatment of "withered and blighted" wives, combined with her own experiences, informed her critique of marriage as a form of women's sexual enslavement.[50] Relying on a young servant to help care for two sons and a daughter, the latter born in 1861, a zealous Juliet Stillman enthusiastically pursued her medical practice, traveled regionally to give health lectures, and aided with the work of the Clinton County Underground Railroad.[51] In 1862, however, Juliet and John Dwight Stillman decided to relocate to the bustling farming community of Whitewater, Wisconsin. He traveled ahead, presumedly to make arrangements, but when Juliet and the children followed two weeks later he was nowhere to be found. Surfacing in Whitewater eight months later, he remained several weeks before abandoning them again, this time permanently. When Juliet filed for divorce in 1866 on grounds of desertion, Stillman countered by accusing her of being an unfit mother. With her medical practice and lecturing trips, Juliet Stillman did not fit the customary image of middle-class motherhood at mid-century. Nonetheless, the Walworth County judge who heard the case granted the divorce, awarding her the "care, custody, and education" of the couple's three children.[52]

Unlike hydropathic physicians who treated middle-class patients in water-cure resorts, Stillman traveled to patients' homes and consulted with them in leased rooms (where she and the children also resided) on Whitewater's main street. The community of approximately thirty-five hundred residents offered several advantages. On the one hand, Spiritualism had "struck" some southern Wisconsin residents "with considerable force" in 1861. The city also contained a number of like-minded residents who endorsed dress and dietary reform, magnetic healing, and clairvoyant powers. Furthermore, excellent railroad connections enabled Stillman simultaneously to pursue her medical practice and to continue her career as a lecturer. On the other hand, Stillman would have been at odds with much of Whitewater's religious community for two major reasons: first, mainstream denominations would have been disturbed by her Spiritualism and infidelism, and second, local Catholics would have joined most Protestants in opposing her dissemination of information about reproduction, contraceptives, and abortion. Like her mentor, the hydropathist Russell Trall, she believed that such information must be made available so long as women had to bear unwanted children. Additionally, as an abolitionist, she would have offended residents of Whitewater disturbed by the "dark invaders" who arrived in the community via the Underground Railroad.[53]

As a Spiritualist and water-cure physician, Juliet Stillman had access to many venues through which she could promote and refine her ideas about the relationship between women's freedom and health. An uncompromising reformer, she thrived on challenging orthodox views. Active as both a health and Spiritualist lecturer, she began speaking out on the subject of "social freedom" shortly after her husband's desertion. Joining Lois Waisbrooker, she had by the mid-1860s become a well-known presence on the platform of Spiritualist meetings throughout the Midwest. In 1865, Russell Trall established the Minnesota Hygeio-Therapeutic College in Minneapolis. Traveling there, Stillman not only conferred with him and local Spiritualists but also attended a meeting of the Minnesota state medical association. Never content to participate passively, she chaired the committee that introduced a controversial resolution endorsing magnetism as a curative agent.[54]

Confident in herself and her ideas, Stillman challenged people's perceptions of women's capabilities by serving as a model for the many causes she embraced: she eschewed the tight lacing of corsets, attired herself in the bloomer costume, maintained a vegetarian diet, improved her body through physical exercise, cultivated her mind through reading and debates, and sat as the lone woman among men on public platforms. Despite her husband's desertion, the water-cure physician also remained a confirmed believer in the ideal of love. Health and happiness, she expounded, would result from one's partnership with a spiritual affinity. "Let not the heart-strings," declared Stillman, "become rusted by bitter tears shed over disappointed hopes. Shared with one we love, how labor is lightened! . . . Oh! who can picture the beauty, the glory, the strength, that comes from the union of two congenial souls."[55] She spoke from experience, having met her future husband, Anson B. Severance, a well-known Spiritualist, health reformer, and musician who also resided in Whitewater.

In A. B. Severance, Juliet Stillman had found a partner in reform. Gregarious, with long locks of hair and a striking beard, he shared her beliefs about temperance, physical culture, and Spiritualism. Born in Vermont, he had moved with his reform-minded parents and siblings to southwestern Wauke-sha County, Wisconsin, in 1837. A popular local musician and dancing mas-ter, he had well-developed social and Spiritualist connections throughout the state.[56] Married at the time he first met Juliet Stillman in late 1862, A. B. Sev-erance ceased living with Mary Malcomson Severance "as man and wife" shortly thereafter. As Spiritualists who had married in 1849, A. B. and Mary Severance, a Scotch-Irish immigrant, may have regarded the loss of one of their six children in infancy and the birth of two others with epilepsy as confirmation that they were "not congenial one to the other." Legally end-ing their partnership on what appears to have been an amicable note in late April 1869, Mary Severance's clairvoyant gift provided her with a means to support herself and her children. In addition to providing psychometric read-ings through the mail and in person well into the 1880s, she developed and sold "Mrs. Severance's Good Health Tablets."[57]

Marriage to Anson B. Severance on 12 May 1869, less than two weeks after his divorce became final, led critics to pronounce Juliet Stillman Severance a "practical" as well as a "theoretical" free lover. This was not the first time she had risked—and received—criticism due to her convictions: as a Seventh Day Baptist convert, dress reformer, abolitionist, Spiritualist, and female physician she had become accustomed to defending minority viewpoints. Standing proud, she placed a prominent advertisement in the *Whitewater Register* announcing the relocation of her practice to Milwaukee and her willingness to visit patients wherever there was a railway stop. With the move to a much larger and more diverse city, Juliet for a time used Stillman Sever-ance as her surname and modified her appearance, exchanging the bloomer attire she had worn since the late 1840s for a knee-length dress and trousers.[58]

With the demise of *Woodhull and Claflin's Weekly* in 1876 and *Hull's Cru-cible* in 1877, reform-minded Spiritualists like Juliet Severance lost one means of reaching and influencing women and men. The Spiritualist lecture circuit, however, remained an important venue for circulating her alternative per-spective of women's rights. Branded the "Woodhull of Wisconsin," the skilled lecturer and parliamentarian soon emerged as a leading voice among Spiri-tualist reformers.[59] Notices of lectures she gave in Massachusetts, Iowa, In-diana, and Minnesota describe a "handsome, well-proportioned, dark-haired woman" who spoke with a "bold and frank terseness." Her talk, a reporter for the *Dubuque (Iowa) Herald* noted, "was perfect in arrangement and she indulged in no circuitous methods of whipping the devil round the stump."[60]

Offering her services through the Chicago-based Slayton's Lyceum Bureau, Severance also used the lecture circuit to tackle economic and industrial matters in spellbinding and well-reasoned talks bearing such titles as "Strikes and the Commune" and "Industrial Problems." She also continued speaking at Spiritualist and reform camp meetings, but a combination of her frank language, eagerness to discuss the labor question, and denunciation of marriage as a form of slavery occasionally led to her ejection from the platform. When denied her allotted time at the Lake Pleasant, Massachusetts, Spiritualist camp meeting in September 1877, for instance, she adjourned to a nearby pine grove and spoke to the hundreds of women and men who had followed her to the alternate site. Necessity prompted several men to improvise a rostrum, "a large express wagon," which Severance mounted "without making so much as a punctuation mark in her discourse."[61]

As monopolism became the "dominant feature of American capitalism" in the 1870s, wage earners and farmers experienced a "radical alteration of their status."[62] Wages spiraled downward and unemployment spread as a result of an influx of immigration and an economic depression in the mid-1870s, returning again in the early 1880s. With fathers unable to support their families adequately, the incidence of women's and children's wage work increased. Severance, driven by a desire to alleviate the suffering of working women, offered her services to them, as well as to "unfortunate girls," free of charge.[63] Sensitized from having treated working women, she rejected the Social Darwinist tendency to blame poor laboring families for their condition by considering them weak or indolent. Instead, she charged the ruling powers—powers excluding her, as a woman, from the ballot box and state medical associations—with having created an oppressive environment in which few outside the privileged could thrive.

Consistent with their opposition to the monopolistic practices in business so prevalent during the second half of the nineteenth century, sex radicals like Severance, Waisbrooker, and Francis Barry (of the Berlin Heights Free Lovers) also attacked church, state, and medical monopolies. Believing that imbalances of power in church-sanctioned or state-licensed marriage and the suppression of discussion about sexual topics stood in the way of women's equality, such sex radicals gravitated to the National Liberal League, organized in 1876 to work for the total separation of church and state. Severance, like many of her colleagues, expected the league to take a strong stand on behalf of women's social and economic rights but soon discovered that many self-proclaimed "liberal" reformers remained intolerant when it came to discussions of sexuality. When "extremists" in attendance at the league's 1880 Chicago Congress called for a repeal of the Comstock Law, the meeting chair and noted infidel Robert Ingersoll left in protest. Filling the void, Severance seized the gavel and conducted the remainder of the meeting. When she called the league's sixth annual convention to order in Saint Louis two years later, only thirty delegates, including her husband A. B. Severance, answered the roll call. The free love controversy, she recognized, had rendered the league ineffectual to battle monopolies of any kind. It was not easy, she concluded, to accomplish reform from within an organization.[64] Nonetheless, she and her husband hosted and financed the league's seventh annual meeting in Milwaukee.

Muting but not abandoning her sex radicalism, Severance continued to campaign for women's economic, political, and social equality. Like Elizabeth Cady Stanton and Susan B. Anthony, she believed that intelligent women who possessed the right to vote could achieve much-needed reforms. Traveling from spring to fall each year, Severance gave addresses on woman suffrage at meetings of the National Liberal League, the Iowa State Spiritual Association, and the Iowa Woman's Suffrage Association during the 1880s. She supported "equal political rights," Severance explained in 1883, because they guaranteed "equal personal protection and opportunity, that is all." Although she expressed no overt political aspirations, her success as a political speaker led members of Milwaukee's Greenback Labor party to consider nominating Severance as a mayoral candidate in the mid-1880s.[65]

Severance's earlier association with Victoria Woodhull, opposition to organized religion, diminished status as a divorced woman who defied gendered expectations of women, and midwestern residence combined to prevent her from playing a central role within the woman suffrage movement nationally. Nonetheless, she carried feminist thought to countless women, also outside the mainstream, when she appeared on Spiritualist, liberal club, agricultural, and reform political movement platforms. In addition to suffrage, she stressed the need for women's economic self-sufficiency, the flaws of the marriage system, and how civilization could not advance unless women did.[66]

During the 1880s, Severance immersed herself in labor and political organizations: the Greenback Labor party, Knights of Labor, Union Labor party, and People's party. She believed that the economic restructuring they advocated not only would provide relief to the victims of business and government monopolies but also would hasten the advent of women's equality. After the resumption of Specie payment in 1879 deflated the Greenback party's primary argument, party members adopted a broader platform, one that included woman suffrage and social welfare legislation. Reform-minded Spiritualist men active in those movements, aware of Severance's experience as a parliamentarian and reform speaker, welcomed her to their ranks. Consequently, she often played an active role at meetings numerically dominated by men. In addition to chairing committees, she delivered political speeches in a variety of venues, and in May 1884 she served as an alternate delegate to an upcoming national Greenback Labor convention.[67]

One of the few, if not the only, Milwaukee women elected as a delegate to Knights of Labor conventions, Severance served for three years as a Master Workman. The Knights' emphasis on "education, cooperation, collective moral suasion of employers and legislators, and mediation of industrial disputes by national leadership" and the fact that the movement sought "a radical change in the existing industrial system" appealed to the inveterate reformer. Severance's Knights of Labor participation easily led to her subsequent involvement in the Union Labor party; by 1887 she often was sharing the platform with the Milwaukee labor leader and her Spiritualist colleague and friend Robert Schilling. True to her feminist convictions, she attempted to introduce a woman suffrage plank at the 1887 Union Labor party's Cincinnati convention.[68]

Severance's views about the evils of marriage informed the political phase of her career as a reformer. Speaking with the confidence of her convictions, she broadened her outlook by focusing on the right of individuals—be they workers or wives—to own and control the products of their labor. Envisioning a society in which such principles would render wives no longer husbands' legal property, she sarcastically denounced capitalists and described their acquisition of property (be it human or material) as theft: "It's because the beggars and thieves have got so much," she stated vehemently, "that the laborers have so little."[69]

Severance's increasing identification with the oppressed is evident in the support she lent to the defendants in legal actions in 1886–87: the prosecution of the Milwaukee socialist Paul Grottkau and a Kansas couple who challenged that state's law by marrying without the benefit of license or clerical blessing. Grottkau was arrested after allegedly agitating in worker actions that led to Milwaukee's "Bay View Massacre" (on 5 May 1886, one day after Chicago's Haymarket Massacre). In an unusual yet telling demonstration of support, Severance faithfully attended the trial proceedings, often seated at the defense table. "Her tall and somewhat angular form and decisive manners," wrote a reporter for the *Milwaukee Sentinel*, "show Mrs. Severance to be a woman of strong will, that does not always subject itself to the popular idea of right and wrong."[70] At the same time, she also lent moral and financial support to two Kansas sex radicals, Lillian Harman and Edwin Walker. "Comrades," she wrote to them in November 1886, "We are in the midst of a most vital conflict . . . shall the liberty of the individual in his own domain be sustained or shall the domination of church and state and their impudent meddlesome policy be the controller of all individual life and liberty. I, for one, will not tolerate such interference."[71]

After spending much of the 1880s involved with politically oriented agitation and activity, Severance returned her focus to the destruction of marital slavery. Marriage, she informed a meeting of liberals gathered in Milwaukee in 1889, "is simply a cloak under which men outrage the persons of their wives without fear of having to answer for it." Like Lois Waisbrooker, she cited John Stuart Mill when she pronounced the marriage contract "the only form of serfdom left."[72] Even an economically self-sufficient woman such as herself, she had to admit when questioned, remained the legal property of her husband. In 1891, having labored together for twenty years in behalf of health reforms and other liberal causes, the fifty-eight-year-old physician moved her practice to Chicago while Anson B. Severance remained in Milwaukee and continued to offer dancing lessons. Having returned permanently to the fold of radical reformers, Juliet H. Severance announced her new residence to readers of several anarchist and freethought periodicals, indicating her availability for medical consulting, lecturing, and officiating at funerals.[73]

Over the span of a decade spent in Chicago, Severance practiced medicine, participated in liberal causes, and continued to critique marriage. Her uncompromising views of marriage and sexuality surfaced full force in 1893 when she joined several other sex radical women on the platform at a "Woman's Day" held in conjunction with the International Congress of Freethinkers in Chicago. The *Truth Seeker* reporter who covered the meeting, held at the same time as the World's Columbian Exposition, commended female speakers for wearing dresses when they mounted the platform but lamented their focus on men's "depravity." "Mrs. Severance," he noted, "talked about marriage, to the grief of many, who objected to her plain words."[74] After the Kansas sex radical Moses Harman moved his publishing offices to Chicago in 1897, Severance interacted with other sex radicals at Harman's residence as she became intimately involved in the production of *Lucifer*'s "Light-Bearer Library" of pamphlets.

During the winter of 1908, the active septuagenarian suffered a physical collapse that necessitated relocation to her daughter's home in New York City. Activist to the end, she spent her remaining years volunteering her medical services, attending and speaking at meetings of the city's liberal clubs, and writing for the *Truth Seeker*. Unlike Victoria Woodhull, who abandoned the sex radical cause after less than a decade, an indomitable Juliet H. Severance remained committed until her death in 1919.[75]

The Road to Freedom

"Dear Friends," wrote Mary E. Preston in June 1887 after she finished reading *Irene; or, The Road to Freedom,* "It is a remarkable book. . . . I wish everybody—old and young—could read it." Sada Bailey Fowler's feminist novel, which some praised while others blasted as "a vulgar trashy mess that no right-minded woman would be guilty of writing," describes the roads that several young women had taken on the way to realizing their social and economic freedom.[76] A Spiritualist reformer who sat on podiums with Waisbrooker and Severance, Fowler memorialized aspects of their lives in the novel, written a decade after the Beecher-Tilton scandal. In *Irene,* idealistic and optimistic young women travel long and obstacle-filled roads to social and economic freedom. The novel's colorful characters include cunning clergymen, Spiritualists, itinerant lecturers, ethical infidels, health and dress reformers, "fallen women," strong-minded spinsters, ex-slaves, honest prostitutes, and a water-cure physician named Mrs. Dr. Raymond. The latter, a holistic healer who practices water cure, mesmerism, and vegetarianism, encourages Irene and her friends to shed their corsets and cumbersome dresses, to engage in physical exercise, and to stimulate their minds through reading and debate. Uniting their labor and property in an agricultural cooperative, which hostile neighbors dub the "Free Love farm," Irene and her friends remain committed to the principle of equal rights, thrive materially, and ultimately gain the community's admiration for their honesty and integrity.

As in the novel, the real-life roads traveled by Waisbrooker and Severance are marked by similarities as well as differences. Both had rural roots, abolitionist sympathies, and personal experiences that left them disillusioned with marriage. Spiritualism played an important role in helping each woman find her voice, understand her marital failure, achieve a measure of economic independence, and cultivate a network of supportive and radical friends receptive to her ideas. It also made each woman a confirmed believer in progress—the idea that imperfect beings have the potential to advance to a higher plane of development. To move forward, both believed, it first was necessary to demystify the subject of sexuality, which had been shrouded in secrecy by the church and state. Identifying with oppressed groups against the monopolies of business, church, and state, the two agitated on behalf of currency reform, shed their religious affiliations for infidelism, and joined protest political movements.

Despite the similarities in their convictions, the two women's efforts to achieve social and economic freedom diverged in several significant ways. A less political Lois Waisbrooker contributed to the cultural dimension of the sex radical movement. A competent if not charismatic speaker, she preferred to reach out to women through the printed word. As Waisbrooker achieved higher levels of understanding—of sexual politics and economics—she grew disenchanted with Spiritualism's cautious tendencies and with the federal government's efforts to legislate moral reform. Nonetheless, she remained affiliated with the Spiritualist-based communication network that had for so long transmitted her reformist visions throughout the nation. Poor and less well-educated than Severance, Waisbrooker wrote both to inform others and to support herself. Influenced by personal circumstances to focus on the economic roots of sexual inequality, she regarded many of the struggles sex radicals faced as class-based, a fact that resulted in her ultimate alignment with impoverished individualist anarchists and experimental cooperatives. Carefully choosing the battles in which she wished to engage, Waisbrooker eschewed wearing the reform dress because she believed it would deflect attention from her primary cause. Instead, she joined the ranks of sex radicals who tested the limits of government tolerance by publishing material deemed obscene by Anthony Comstock and his army of postal inspectors. Regarding herself as a martyr for the cause, Waisbrooker remained single, plowed the proceeds of her lecturing and publications back into her crusade, and encouraged others to follow her example of uncompromising ideals and personal sacrifice.

An inveterate reformer who enjoyed greater educational opportunities and material comfort than did Lois Waisbrooker, Juliet H. Severance initially sought the scientific reform of the individual—through diet, dress, exercise, and water-cure treatments—rather than the abolishment of a government that reinforced women's inequality. Even during those years she spent fighting the evils of monopoly and industrialization through political protest parties, she pragmatically remained focused on the goal of women's full independence. Able to support herself and her family with resources accrued from her medical practice and lectures, Severance enjoyed greater independence than did Waisbrooker. Operating from a position of strength, she played an active role in a variety of reform causes. Much like Mary Gove Nichols, Severance challenged society's customary expectations of women by proudly wearing the reform dress and finding happiness in remarrying soon after her divorce.

As both women discovered, the parameters of freedom can only be pushed so far at any given time. Waisbrooker and Severance's encounters with such patriarchal institutions as the church, the medical profession, and the law illustrate the powerful cultural forces late nineteenth-century women had to contest before they could travel the road to sexual equality. Others shared the two women's views, but their stories have been—and are—for a variety of reasons obscured by the media's preference for sensationalistic accounts of such provocateurs as Victoria Woodhull and, later, Emma Goldman. Wais-brooker and Severance also found themselves overshadowed by the con-sciously self-promotional efforts of two Kansas sex radicals associated with *Lucifer*. Nonetheless, their experiences as sex radical women have survived because they regarded printed and spoken words as tools for women's eman-cipation. Whether they turned to anarchism, third-party politics, or didac-tic literature for solutions, the intent of each remained the same: to overthrow the people and institutions preventing women from achieving equality. The hostility their activism engendered confirms the highly contested nature of the power they claimed for themselves and for their sex.

6. The Lucifer Match

I feel far more free and self-reliant than ever before in my life.
—Lillian Harman, 1886

ON 19 SEPTEMBER 1886, sixteen-year-old Lillian Harman and thirty-seven-year-old Edwin C. Walker put their abstract ideas about freedom and women's rights to the test when they stood in the parlor of Lillian's home in Valley Falls, Kansas, and entered into a nonstate, nonchurch marriage referred to by social radicals as the "free marriage" or the "Lucifer match." Exchanging vows without the benefit of clergy or a wedding license, Walker promised that Lillian would "be free to repulse any and all advances of mine. . . . She remains sovereign of herself." Lillian, claiming that actions spoke louder than words, asserted that she entered into this union of her own free will and that she retained her maiden name and "the right to act, always, as my conscience and best judgment shall dictate."[1]

Harman and Walker chose to protest church- and state-sanctioned marriage because of the power it gave a husband to control his wife's property, identity, and body. A woman could never, they argued, achieve equality until *she* was free to determine if, when, and with whom she had children. The couple was not the first to marry without the benefit of church blessing or state license: Quakers had adopted modified marriage vows earlier in the century, as had Spiritualists beginning in the 1850s.[2]

Lillian's stepbrother, W. F. Hiser, a guest at the wedding, waited until the following morning and then reported his sister's action to the authorities. Arrested, convicted of violating the Kansas Marriage Act (requiring men and women to obtain a license from the state before marrying), and sentenced to serve forty-five and seventy-five days, respectively, in Topeka's Shawnee County jail, Harman and Walker purposely prolonged their stay behind bars by refusing to pay court costs. Four months later their case reached the Kansas State Supreme Court. The contradictory ruling, which affirmed that even a common-law marriage must be in compliance with state marriage statutes, nonetheless represented a partial victory for the Valley Falls sex radicals. Justice Horton ruled that a wife could legally keep her maiden name and that she did not have to "merge her individuality as a legal person in that of her husband."[3]

In February 1887, the couple still incarcerated, a U.S. marshal traveled to Valley Falls to arrest Moses Harman (Lillian's father) and members of the *Lucifer* editorial team for mailing printed matter that government officials pronounced obscene. The previous summer Harman had adopted an uncompromising stance on the freedom of the press. Indicted on 270 counts of obscenity, the *Lucifer* editorial team had attracted the postal inspector's attention by publishing, verbatim, a letter from the Tennessee anarchist W. G. Markland containing a graphic description of a husband's sexual abuse of his wife immediately after childbirth. Several other unedited letters considered such prohibited (by Anthony Comstock) subjects as the use of sexual organs and contraceptives.[4]

Lillian and Edwin, aware that *Lucifer* would cease publication with all of its staff behind bars, immediately paid their court costs, returned to Valley Falls, and resumed work on the paper. Publicity surrounding the Harman/ Walker marriage and the government's prosecution of Moses Harman for his uncompromising stand on the freedom of the press helped swell *Lucifer*'s subscription list and transformed the struggling regional weekly into the nation's leading voice for sex radicalism. In their eagerness to learn the latest news of the family's prosecution, readers sent contributions to the Harman/ Walker defense fund, renewed subscriptions, and enlisted dozens of new subscribers. Thus, by February 1887, *Lucifer*'s editorial staff distributed approximately two thousand copies of each issue of a paper that only five months earlier had circulated to no more than seven hundred readers.[5]

The actions of the Harman family and Edwin Walker have several levels of significance. First, the free marriage transformed Lillian Harman into a national icon for women's sexual emancipation and prompted sex radical women and others to debate such feminist issues as age-of-consent legislation and marital rape and to challenge authorities denying them access to sexual information. Second, reactions to the case reveal striking fault lines among anarchists, freethinkers, and sex radicals when forced to confront a key issue related to women's quest for equality: sexual freedom. Finally, the Harman family's legal battles for the free marriage and the right to discuss sexual topics in print prompted hundreds of late nineteenth-century rural

Americans—marginalized because of their gender or social, political, and economic status—to question the validity of suffrage.

The Woman's View of It

When Susan Scheuck wed Moses Harman in the mid-1860s, she deviated from customary marriage practices by signing a prenuptial contract stipulating certain standards of conduct based on love rather than duty. Her death in childbirth less than a decade later left seven-year-old Lillian and her brother George motherless and fueled her husband's commitment to marriage reform. Moving from their Missouri home to Valley Falls, Kansas, in 1879, Harman and his children immersed themselves in liberal circles. Within a year, he had begun his career as a freethought editor and publisher, work that would consume the remainder of his life. In 1883, as thirteen-year-old Lillian set type for issues of her father's newly christened weekly, *Lucifer, the Light-Bearer,* she learned about such causes as women's sexual emancipation and the freedom of the press to address sexual topics. Editing the paper, she recognized, had become part of her father's larger campaign against monopolistic practices.

Lillian Harman's initial reticence to speak after her arrest in 1886 led some critics to charge that the sixteen-year-old girl had not acted of her own accord when she participated in the free marriage. "[R]aised under the advice of a brute" and with "brothers in the swine pens," they suggested, the motherless child could not know better than to join them in challenging the state's authority to regulate marriage.[6] Even sympathetic observers like the Massachusetts sex radical Angela Heywood, who defended the young woman's right to choose, questioned Lillian's choice of a divorced man more than twice her age.

Several months' imprisonment transformed young Harman and marked the advent of her long career as a sex radical activist. Despite curiosity seekers—men and boys who came "to stare through the bars at me"—she declared: "I feel far more free and self-reliant than ever before in my life. I know now . . . just how much I am willing and ready to do and sacrifice for what I believe to be right."[7] In letters written from her cell in the Oskaloosa County jail, Lillian reiterated her commitment to the sex radical principles embodied in her free marriage. Responding to puzzled female readers who asked why Walker had not legally married her, she patiently explained: "It takes two to make a bargain . . . and I should not have consented to such a surrender of my individuality." Too many readers, she further remonstrated, seemed surprised that a young woman "should have the will-power sufficient to decide such important matters for herself."[8] Such criticism reinforced her conviction that women must demonstrate their individuality and capability through similar actions.

After her release, Lillian assumed a more active role in the publication of *Lucifer* until she and Walker in 1888 decided to establish an anarchist publication entitled *Fair Play* (published intermittently until its demise in 1908). In the 1890s and 1900s Harman again joined her father in the publication of the short-lived *Our New Humanity* and *American Journal of Eugenics* (which ceased after her father's death in 1910). Sustaining her commitment to the cause of free marriage and free motherhood, in 1893 she chose to have a child with Walker (despite the fact that they lived separately for much of their married life).[9] Before becoming a "free mother," Harman required Walker to sign a document stipulating that he would provide his share of support for the child, whom she named Virna Winifred Walker. Lillian Harman's sex radical activism and lifestyle earned her international recognition in 1897 when she became president of the British Legitimation League (established in England in 1893 to advocate the legitimacy of nonmarital sexual relations and to ensure that partners and their offspring would have the same rights of property and inheritance). Harman wrote numerous articles for the league's journal, *Adult* (1897–99). One correspondent, acknowledging Lillian Harman's role in ensuring *Lucifer*'s regular appearance for so many years, declared it "a lasting monument . . . of what a woman in freedom can do."[10]

Like Lillian Harman, WCTU members and social purity reformers yearned for social (sexual) purity, but they differed in their understanding of what this term meant for women's lives. To the former, sexual purity "meant confining sex within marriage and moderating its indulgence even there."[11] This conviction led them to seek the prosecution of the clientele of prostitutes, to attempt to end the practice of abortion and infanticide, to support the censorship of material they deemed obscene, and to campaign for age-of-consent laws. At a time when state-mandated age-of-consent laws varied from ten to eighteen years, they believed that a uniform law could protect young single women from men's sexual advances. While male social purity reformers focused almost exclusively on legislative measures, many of their female counterparts embraced an empowering strategy known as voluntary motherhood—the idea that married women would become pregnant only when they chose. But in choosing this path, they reinforced the idea of female sexuality as synonymous with reproduction.

Harman, however, actively campaigned against age-of-consent legislation because she opposed the limits it placed on women's freedom. First, she challenged social purity reformers' efforts to establish "a hard and fast line" controlling the age at which a woman could express herself sexually. Noting different rates of physical and emotional maturation, she observed that some young women are more advanced at fifteen than others at twenty, "or even when older." Elaborating, she wrote: "To say that the right of choice and determination should be withheld from all young women until they are eighteen is to utter an absurdity." What kind of law, she demanded, established that women under eighteen could not be trusted with "the guardianship of their own bodies" yet allowed them to secure responsible positions teaching in the state's school system and working "in industry, business, and journalism"?[12]

Harman also believed that the reforms Frances Willard and WCTU members advocated, if successful, would "necessarily weaken the sense of responsibility of womankind."[13] Such well-intentioned women, she explained, reinforced the image of women as sexually vulnerable, potential victims needing protection offered by male-enacted laws. Determined to empower women by giving them opportunities to choose, Harman thus found herself at odds with social purity reformers and, at times, with her father. His commitment to airing married women's sexual grievances also reinforced an image of woman as victim and man as oppressor. A *Firebrand* reader who also subscribed to *Lucifer* observed a tendency among the latter's writers to present women as "nearly all angels, although without wings," and men as "brutes and rascals."[14] Indeed, a number of *Lucifer*'s most vocal female authors did foster this impression. In 1894, for instance, one regular contributor, Lillie D. White, published a tract entitled "The Coming Woman," in which she pronounced virtually all of women's sufferings as "man-inflicted." Even the many readers who admired Lillian Harman as a "noble and brave" martyr could not free themselves from the deeply ingrained image of her as a victim and piece of sexual property.[15]

Outraged by many sex radicals' tendency to dwell on women's victimization, the anarchist Lucy Parsons countered that progress could not occur so long as women continued to wrong themselves. Mothers, she stated, helped perpetuate women's problems by raising their daughters with one goal in mind: marriage. Unless this changed, she predicted, generation after generation of women would remain content with wage slavery because they expected that condition to be temporary. Pointing to the thousands of women who never married, she demanded: "Is sex slavery the only slavery from which women suffer?"[16]

Despite a difference of opinion over women's portrayal in print, most sex radical women whose letters appeared in *Lucifer* concurred with Lillian Harman's position on protective legislation. External efforts to legislate morality, they reasoned, inevitably failed because man-made laws could not alter human nature. One who campaigned against all age-of-consent laws, an indignant Minnesotan named Flora Fox, protested statutes that put "a premium upon commission of crime" rather than on reforming an individual's behavior. Indeed, concurred a *Lucifer* subscriber, Emma Best, in 1905, what women needed was protection *from* marriage laws and customs, seduction, and illegitimacy—not laws dictating the age at which women could legally express their sexual feelings.[17]

Social purity, explained sex radical women, stemmed from self-governance, not arbitrarily constructed and externally imposed moral regulations. Moreover, they asserted, social purity did not depend on an absence of sexual feelings. As had their predecessors in the 1850s, late nineteenth-century sex radicals believed that mutually loving sexual intercourse would enhance a woman's physical and emotional well-being, and in so elevating her would raise a man to her level. "When sex is rightly understood and properly honored," Lois Waisbrooker wrote, "it will be a builder in more than that of offspring."[18]

Waisbrooker and other correspondents who accepted sexual desire as a positive and valid part of their lives nonetheless recognized that years of living under the rule of domineering and sexually demanding husbands had rendered women passionless. Accusing men of sexual intemperance, Angela Heywood blamed their "invasive Heism" for destroying "woman's personality and welfare." In agreement, a contributor named Eudora declared: "If a man cannot call out a response, he has no right to any woman and I would teach all women to rebel." Others, trying to make their demands more attractive to men, stressed that a woman would make a far more responsive sexual partner "if man did not insist on consummation."[19]

Lucifer's female correspondents couched their comments about sexuality in the language of spirituality or nature for several reasons. First, they portrayed sexual desire as a spiritual or "soul attraction" and believed that it elevated animalistic passion to a form of spiritual communion. Second, they proposed that a pregnant woman's sexual desire represented the fetus calling for "more life force." Finally, sex radical women saw sexual desire as nature's way of providing both women and men with the life force they needed to thrive and survive in their daily lives.[20] Infused with such ideas, some female contributors to *Lucifer* admitted their desire for meaningful sexual intercourse with a soul mate, which they expected to be the capstone of their existence.

Radical Fault Lines

Reactions to the Harman/Walker marriage published in such sex radical, anarchist, and freethought periodicals as *The Word, Liberty,* and *Truth Seeker* reveal fault lines within late nineteenth-century social radicalism. Initially, editors of other sex radical publications gave the jailed couple their unconditional support. The Iowan Jay Chaapel, acting editor of *Foundation Principles,* encouraged liberty-loving readers to send Walker and Harman "words of cheer & pecuniary aid." Likewise, *Foote's Health Monthly* supported Lillian Harman's assertion of a woman's right to control her body, even after marriage. In *The Word,* the sex radicals Ezra and Angela Tilton Heywood praised Lillian's exercise of her "right of personal, private judgment" but took a more critical stance toward Walker. He was, they accused, degrading "self & mate in vain effort to prove the match 'legal,' whereas it can be right and chaste only as it is superior to 'law.'"[21]

Eastern individualist anarchists who gravitated to Benjamin R. Tucker's *Liberty* denied the state's authority to regulate an individual's private life. Tucker at first portrayed the couple's action as "a brave defiance of the State" and encouraged readers to contribute to their defense fund. Before a month had passed, however, he retracted his support and adopted a caustic tone whenever writing about the free marriage. It had become evident, he informed readers, that the couple wanted "to establish in the courts that a man and woman who agreed to live together thereby put themselves legally in the same position as those who are married by a minister or magistrate."[22] As an individualist anarchist who rejected all efforts of the political ruling class to regulate any aspect of an individual's life, Tucker denounced Harman and Walker's effort to force state recognition of their nonstate, nonchurch marriage as an act of conformity. If the couple emerged victorious from their trial, Tucker warned, their case would set a dangerous precedent: people in common-law marriages would be bound together for life.

The Valley Falls couple, however, argued that legal recognition of the free marriage would establish a precedent for free divorce. It would ease the way, they explained, for women and men "to unmarry themselves when they discover that their happiness is no longer served by their union." According to Walker, the couple hoped to accomplish two additional goals. First, they sought to reclaim individual rights unjustly usurped by the state. A legal victory, he reasoned, would affirm rather than weaken individualist anarchism. Second, the couple wanted to establish a woman's right "to control all matters pertaining to sex" or, in other words, to control her body.[23]

Initially, Samuel P. Putnam, the secretary of the American Secular Union and editor of the freethought weekly *Truth Seeker,* had professed indifference to the couple's action and treated it as a side issue. When it became apparent that Harman and Walker sought legal recognition for a nonreligious marriage ceremony, however, Putnam lent his "emphatic support and endorsement." *Truth Seeker* readers who supported the couple's challenge to church-sanctioned marriage included reform-minded Spiritualists and those who believed in the separation of church and state. In contrast to individualist anarchists who supported Harman and Walker's action, freethinking liberals wished to reform rather than to abolish the federal government, which, they believed, had erred in allowing "the Christian morality of Comstockism" to turn the post office into "a criminal detective bureau."[24]

Unlike Tucker and Putnam, the Milwaukee-based social reformer Juliet H. Severance attempted to place the Harman/Walker marriage in the broadest possible context. A contributor to *Liberty, Lucifer,* and *Truth Seeker,* she likened the Kansas couple's protest to Chicago's Haymarket Massacre and Milwaukee's Bay View Riot. In each instance, she explained, the state had interfered with the rights of the people, keeping them enslaved by "the yoke that capitalism has fastened about their necks." "Give woman sex liberty," Severance proclaimed, "and a race of freemen would be born that no ecclesiastical yokes could bind, and no august laws fetter."[25]

Despite their differing interpretations of the Harman/Walker free marriage, neither eastern individualist anarchists nor liberal readers of the *Truth Seeker* felt comfortable with Moses Harman's strident print-based advocacy of women's emancipation. Early on, *Liberty* had adopted a hostile tone whenever the subject arose. "Probably many people think us very severe and unjust to women," explained Tucker in 1883, but "we oppose their efforts to get possession of the ballot, that modern instrument of tyranny." He often took a caustic tone when responding to sex radical women. When the veteran free lover Hannah J. Hunt (the mother of Lillie White and Lizzie Holmes) challenged that "Tucker & Co." did not "have a monopoly on everything logical or scientific," he retorted: "My good correspondent should have employed a man to defend her position. Perhaps he would have made out a case that I should have thought worth answering." While eastern individualist anarchists adopted a misogynistic attitude toward sex radical women, freethinking liberals opposed censorship yet became increasingly hesitant to discuss such subjects as female sexuality and free love. Their reluctance to engage in such conversations led Edwin Walker to pronounce them on the "high road to respectability, i.e., *death.*" Juliet H. Severance, at one time vice president of the National Liberal League, expressed her disgust with "professed Liberals who justify the law" by labeling them "very stupid or exceedingly vicious."[26]

Readers Respond

Women and men from twenty-three states and territories supported the free marriage with contributions ranging from twenty-five cents to ten dollars. Cornelia Boecklin, a fifty-one-year-old dress reformer living in Burlington, Iowa, sent regular contributions. A former reader of *Woodhull and Claflin's Weekly*, she also supported such other radical papers as *Fair Play* and *Liberty*. The radical pamphleteers Dr. E. B. Foote Jr., Juliet H. Severance, and Elmina Slenker donated dozens of copies of their works to be sold in support of the couple's defense. Others expressed their support in print. The Florida radical J. William Lloyd, inspired by Lillian's stand, composed a poem entitled "Heroine of Valley Falls."[27] Hundreds of other women and men sent words of encouragement and endorsement, ranging from such well-known individuals as the California social reformer Caroline Severance to dozens of small-town radicals and farmer's wives.

On one level, readers' praise for the "noble and brave" Lillian and her father can be read as a form of heroine or hero worship.[28] But readers' letters—many of them from agricultural communities in the Midwest and Great Plains states—published in *Lucifer* during the 1880s and 1890s represent far more than fan mail: their content sheds light on rural women's critiques of the economic and political system in which they lived and of the gender system that governed their lives. Until the Harman/Walker marriage, confided one reader, a great many "like myself, have not had the courage to come out" on the subjects of marriage and sexuality.[29]

A majority of *Lucifer's* correspondents resided in the Midwest, an area hard hit by drought and economic depression during the 1880s and 1890s. A rising number of farm tenancies, increased railroad rates, and rising levels of indebtedness made farmers all the more vulnerable to crop failures and collapsed land values. In Kansas alone, banks foreclosed on approximately eleven thousand farm mortgages during the early 1890s. Such conditions heightened men's and women's receptiveness to radical critiques of government.[30] Calling for land reform, the redistribution of wealth, and the abolition of marriage, the rural anarchists and freethinkers who read *Lucifer* sought to overturn a system in which property—in the form of both land and people—empowered some as rulers and relegated most to the ranks of the enslaved.[31] Thus, as fluctuating economic conditions in the 1870s, 1880s, and 1890s rendered rural men increasingly powerless to support their families, marriage remained one of the few places where they could exert authority. Sanctioned by state and church, husbands could repeatedly subject their wives to sexual demands and physical abuse.[32]

From her Missouri farmstead, the regular *Lucifer* contributor Kate Austin reflected on the difficult existence of farm wives in her community: "The womenfolk have nothing but cares, drudgery, and frequent child-bearing. . . . You have no idea what the sexual practices of these farmers are. But it is the result mostly of their dreary existence . . . no other outlet, no distraction, no colour of any sort in their lives. . . . Sex is all they have."[33] In this context, the Harman/Walker "free marriage" assumed great significance to *Lucifer* readers who viewed it as an attempt to establish the married woman's right to protect her person from sex abuse on the part of her husband. "Every woman in the land," wrote Lydia E. Blackstone from Chester, New Hampshire, in 1887, "should realize that this is emphatically woman's battle that you are fighting and should feel it a privilege to help you as far as she can."[34]

To many of *Lucifer*'s female correspondents, the Harman/Walker marriage represented the epitome of liberty because it stood for a married woman's freedom to govern the use of her body. Inspired by Lillian Harman's example and grounded in the conviction that exposing the extent of female sexual slavery represented the only way "whereby we can be saved," hundreds of women shared their stories in letters written to *Lucifer*.[35]

Like their predecessors in the 1850s, the sex radical women who shared their experiences in *Lucifer* equated unwanted sexual intercourse in marriage with rape. Few accused their husbands of sexual abuse but instead relayed examples they had witnessed and confidences shared with them by abused women.[36] Many expressed concern about the deleterious consequences of frequent pregnancies, botched abortions, and sexually induced gynecological ailments for married women's health. Some of the most graphic and moving accounts of marital sexual abuse—both mental and physical—came from female physicians.[37] Dagmar Mariager, from Santa Barbara, California, told of a woman in her care who suffered from numerous bodily ailments, "deranged nerves," and want of courage. Each year she spent four months "at the insane asylum." Her husband, whom Mariager blamed for his wife's illness, "is duly praised for being *faithful* to her, and condoled, when she is sent away. Who cares for the cause? Who dares even hint at it?"[38] Sex radicals underscored the pervasiveness of marital sexual abuse by pointing to examples appearing in mainstream newspapers. In 1888, for example, *Lucifer* excerpted an account from the *Kansas Democrat* of thirty-six year-old Belle S. Dickinson, declared insane and committed to the state asylum. "'The evidence,'" this Topeka newspaper had reported, "'showed that her husband abused her body worse than a

Satyr could be capable of, resulting in the loss of her mind.'"[39] Citing the example of a man whose two wives had died after bearing a total of eighteen children, a correspondent named J. Hacker concluded: "Every year thousands of wives go to untimely graves by the sexual abuse of their husbands."[40]

Aware that legal statutes did not recognize the existence of marital rape, W. G. Markland asked: "Can there be legal rape? Did this man [referring to a newspaper article he had read] rape his wife? Would it have been rape had he not been married to her?" Continuing this line of logic, Markland observed that a man who stabbed his wife to death with a knife would be held accountable for murder, but "if he stabs her to death with his penis, what does the law do?"[41] The hypocrisy of such conditions prompted Edwin Walker to declare that men should be subject to conviction for rape whether or not the victim is his wife.[42] Walker and the other male sex radicals who called for the prosecution of men who forced their wives to have sexual intercourse believed that they possessed greater sexual self-control and therefore had nothing to fear from such a law.

Sex radical women recognized that despite some male correspondents' verbal support for a woman's right to protect herself from sex abuse on the part of her husband, many others found women's assertion of equality in all things threatening to their patriarchal privilege and masculine prowess. Rather than equate masculinity with a man's ability to command a woman's sexual submission, *Lucifer*'s female correspondents defined manhood as a husband's ability to exercise sexual self-control. When passion overcame Mr. Cawley, wrote his wife in 1894, he "lost his manhood and became a brute." She did not consider herself a prude but instead believed with many other sex radical women that sexual relations should occur only when the couple experiences mutual desire.[43] Her testimony, along with that of others like her, confirms sex radical women's belief that expression of female sexuality could coexist with purity.

Expression, Not Suppression

Female readers of *Lucifer* welcomed the opportunity to communicate openly with each other about sexual topics because they believed that uncensored investigation rather than legislation represented the key to eliminating "sex evils from society."[44] Male readers also acknowledged that most wives knew little about "the uses of sexualism except for reproduction" because law and custom denied them access to information on sexual topics.[45] In an effort to remedy this condition, *Lucifer*'s editor dedicated himself to the twin platform of free speech and women's emancipation from sex slavery. Women could play a role in their liberation, he believed, by speaking out. To further this goal, he risked prosecution under the Comstock Law, an action that earned him the confidence and devotion of his female readership.[46]

Like women who had written to the *Social Revolutionist* and the Nicholses' publications in the 1850s, *Lucifer* contributors in the 1880s and 1890s routinely filled their letters with references to "sexual slavery," "marital bondage," and husbands who, like slaveholders, fought to preserve their status.[47] Many who viewed marriage as a form of slavery likened Harman and Walker to abolitionists. Were not they, asked G. C. Jones of Pierce City, Missouri, "the John Browns of this great progress?"[48] Female contributors, who often compared themselves to slaves struggling to be free, believed that free discussion of sexuality would empower women to throw off their chains. After reading several issues of *Lucifer,* a correspondent named Virginia declared: "Slowly, I am removing the shackles that bind me."[49]

As they assessed the situation, sex radical women concluded that "sex slavery" constituted the root cause of their social and economic oppression. Necessity compelled women to exchange sexual favors for money, a home, or status, and the gendered imbalance of power embedded in marriage reinforced their subordinate status: for centuries the Christian church had taught men to regard wives and children as property while at the same time instructing women to be submissive. Reflecting on this injustice, Caroline Severance denounced marriage as "the damnedest force that exists today," "cussed [the] selfishness which a feeling of ownership instills," and reasoned that "true love needs no civil law behind it." After years of socialization as dutiful and submissive wives, she and other correspondents reflected, the victims of marital sexual abuse had been rendered unable to help themselves.[50] Why else, they demanded, would a woman say after receiving a beating: "I needed it, and I got it, and it did me good"?[51] One woman, deeply embittered by her recognition of this fact, declared: "I do sometimes feel like saying God damn such a religion; one that makes people either insane or hypocrites."[52]

Many *Lucifer* correspondents who championed the idea of free marriage did so because of their belief in individual freedom. "Shall the liberty of the individual in his own domain be sustained," demanded Juliet H. Severance from Milwaukee, "or shall the domination of church and state and their impudent meddlesome policy be the controller of all individual life and liberty?"[53] Moreover, Severance and others argued, children born in the context of officially sanctioned patriarchal families learned key lessons of gender—paternal power and female submissiveness—at an early age. By observing their parents, male children learned that they could expect to command not only women but also anyone they deemed economically or socially inferior. This cycle could not be broken, they contended, until the time when all women gave birth to children in freedom.[54]

As they looked about them, however, sex radical women and men recognized several factors that impeded the advent of a much-desired egalitarian world order. One of the most powerful, wrote the sex radical pamphleteer Dora Forster in 1903, was women's inability to escape the wish on one side to enslave, a long history of passive submission on the other side, and the "seal of society" on both.[55] Others believed that it would remain impossible to reach the root of women's inequality so long as people depended on externally imposed laws and moral codes to regulate their behavior. Moreover, they protested, the "old Mosaic law" taught men to blame women for "the fall" and to believe that children were "conceived in inequity."[56] Finally, many more writers shared Lois Waisbrooker's conviction that men and women could never improve their condition "as long as sex desire in a woman is looked upon as degrading" and people equated purity with the absence of sexual feelings.[57]

Continence and Contraception in the Comstock Era

As they searched for the path to equality, women who wrote to *Lucifer, The Word, Foundation Principles,* and *Free Society* struggled to assert control over their reproductive functions and to restore their sexuality to its natural condition. "The *pivotal* question of today," Angela T. Heywood wrote in 1883, "is what proportion of motion (or Liberty, the ethical name of motion), of vibration hav [*sic*] the Penis & Womb a right to without creating babies, faces; what degree of association is justifiable this side of impregnation."[58] No single theory prevailed, yet all shared a common thread—the idea of male continence.

One of the more exacting forms of male self-control, continence involved "prolonged coition with no emission of semen and with gradual loss of the erection while the penis is still in the vagina." According to the historian Janet Brodie, few couples actually practiced male continence outside the Oneida Community. In that environment, male continence promised women opportunities to experience sexual pleasure with less fear of pregnancy, but it nonetheless required them to surrender the right to determine when and with whom they had sexual relations and when they could become pregnant. Those decisions resided in the hands of community elders.[59] The former Berlin Heights Free Lover Francis Barry considered this system "worse than monogamy" because participants never learned to "sustain a true relationship."[60]

In the late 1870s, some sex radicals looked with interest to a small work entitled *Cupid's Yokes*. Written by Ezra Heywood, editor of *The Word*, the controversial pamphlet served two purposes: it attacked the institution of marriage, and it reprinted information about Noyes's then out-of-print explanation of male continence. Attempting to "bring sexuality within the domain of reason and moral obligation," Heywood argued that once reason governed passion and altruistic "bonds of affection" had replaced marriage, such selfish and destructive behaviors as animalism, brutality, and greed would yield to the spiritualized expression of sexuality so longed for by women.[61] The publicity surrounding Heywood's arrest and conviction for publishing this work, however, overshadowed its feminist message.

In the 1880s and 1890s, several sex radical women explored additional theories, most of which entailed a modified version of male continence. Only the most conservative endorsed Aphaism, a restrictive theory that required women and men to refrain from all sexual contact except for times when they mutually decided to conceive children. Promoted by the lapsed Quaker and temperance reformer Elmina Drake Slenker, this theory presented carnal desire as degrading and encouraged women and men to govern strictly their every interaction with members of the opposite sex, even if husbands and wives found it necessary to maintain separate bedrooms.[62] So rigid was Alphaism that the former *Vanguard* editor Alfred Cridge compared it to "St. Simeon Stylites and the Hindoo enthusiasts" who took pleasure in their suffering.[63] Few in their current imperfect state of development, he informed *Lucifer* readers, could hope to adhere to such a rigid code of behavior.[64]

A modified version of Alphaism known as Dianaism had greater resonance with *Lucifer*'s female readers because it advocated the exchange of affectionate yet chaste contact between the sexes. The sociologist Henry M. Parkhurst later explained that he had written *Diana* (published anonymously in 1882) because theories that tried to control sex through the practice of mental repression had failed. Named for the goddess of chastity, this contraceptive technique permitted such interactions as conversation, hand holding, embracing, and even nudity. The latter was premised on the assumption that familiarity with another's body would diminish desire. Like Alphaism, Dianaism stipulated that intercourse to the point of orgasm should only occur when a couple desired to have children. Drawing heavily on the ideas of John Humphrey Noyes, he posited that there would be little danger of "sexual excess" if men and women could only learn "to enjoy . . . caresses disassociated from passional feelings."[65]

In general, sex radical women praised Dianaism because of its female-centeredness.[66] Persuaded by its logic, Slenker abandoned Alphaism and embraced Dianaism as a form of "sexual temperance," a more realistic alternative to total abstinence.[67] Others concurred. In 1894 an Iowa farm wife named Mary Clark informed *Lucifer* readers that under this system her husband never initiated sexual intercourse without her consent. If men exchanged their old habits for the ways of Diana, she predicted, they would have better sexual partners—and healthier children—in return. Citing herself as an example, Clark informed readers that she now enjoyed "sex communion as fully as does my companion."[68]

Francis Barry criticized Dianaism, arguing that "no manly man can be a Dianist." Remaining idealistic, he equated manliness with self-control, explaining: "If he loves a woman he will have no desire for any manifestation that will not make her happy." Indeed, he informed readers, during their years together he had not once approached Cordelia Barry without her full consent. Physicians had other reasons for denouncing Dianaism. Dependent on pregnant women and ill children for part of their income, they proclaimed it "nonsense." In response, Slenker dismissed regular doctors as poor judges, reminding *Lucifer* readers that bloodletting once had been universal practice among their profession. The male physicians who objected to this female-empowering contraceptive technique, she asserted, were more concerned about the sexually demoralized male patient than they were about "thousands of wives with ruined constitutions from sexual abuse."[69]

Sex radicals who feared that Dianaism might encourage promiscuity (in part because the technique of male continence was so widely associated with the Oneida Community's practice of complex marriage) could turn to Alice B. Stockham's *Karezza: Ethics of Marriage* (1896). Stockham's ideas appealed to Christian sex radicals because she situated sex within the context of monogamous marriage, presented it as a gift from God, and taught that when rightly used it could lead to "spiritual exaltation" and even "visions of a transcendent life." Stockham pinpointed a key difference between herself and social purity reformers even as she made plans to attend their national conference in 1906: "I think most of the people connected with this conference believe rather in suppression than expression."[70]

In her work, Stockham criticized the "ordinary hasty spasmodic method of cohabitation . . . in which the wife is a passive party," and she stressed that husband and wife—by exercising control—could learn to have a "pleasurable exchange" that satisfied both "without emission or crisis by either party." At that point, she suggested, the couple might wish to participate in "some devotional exercises."[71] Women responded enthusiastically. A correspondent writing from Durant, Indian Territory, declared: "Karezza is truly worth its weight in gold." Another, writing from Ohio, proclaimed: "If only all people could and would live according to its teachings how much happier every one would be."[72] While not explicitly stated, Stockham expected the loving behavior she described to carry over into other aspects of a couple's married life.

Suffrage: A Lower Priority

As sex radical women contemplated the meaning of freedom in their lives, they focused their attention not on access to the ballot box but rather on social and economic applications. Woman suffrage never became a high priority for them. A few sex radical women referred to their limited participation in state woman suffrage organizations, but their interactions with suffragists and members of the WCTU often left them disenchanted. Albina Washburn, an inveterate reformer, devoted many hours to the campaign for woman suffrage in Colorado, but when leaders of the state organization learned of her fondness for *Lucifer* and her support of Moses Harman, they asked her to resign her membership. Disillusioned, she announced: "I no longer use the ballot. . . . We imagined it meant self-government, but such are the tricks of politicians who constitute the vast army of engineers for the monied interests of our country."[73] Also eschewing woman suffrage, Mrs. Maria Ingraham, of Lake Mills, Wisconsin, declared in 1887 that there was "enough ignorance to do the voting, already." Concurring with this sentiment, Lois Waisbrooker added: "I see in woman's suffrage only an extension of the rule of force."[74] A similar conviction prompted the longtime sex radical Lillie D. White to dismiss suffragists and church women who demanded the ballot as hypocritical and to criticize them for "asking for their rights" while at the same time "sustaining the oppressor who denies them."[75] Woman suffrage would, many of *Lucifer*'s female correspondents agreed, address only symptoms and never would truly alleviate the injustices so prevalent in their daily lives.

Like most anarchists, sex radical men saw little value in the ballot box for themselves, let alone women. Casting a vote, Edwin Walker reminded readers, had not brought laboring men any greater peace or prosperity or happiness. Certainly, he argued, readers could find more effective ways to promote change than to work in a political arena ruled by "the ignorant and prejudiced."[76] In general, the economically struggling sex radicals who professed freethought believed that wealthy Christian men controlled the ballot box and therefore saw little prospect for impoverished liberals to overturn their majority decision. "What on earth can dropping a bit of paper into a ballot box do for anybody?" asked William Gilmore in 1897. "All it can do . . . [is] for one section of the people to enforce *their* desires and whims on another section . . . creating more enmity between those who are already the slaves of government officials."[77]

In the end, sex radical women and men mutually agreed to downplay the subject of voting, yet female correspondents nonetheless recognized that their male counterparts, by virtue of their gender, enjoyed economic, legal, and social freedom that they did not. Gender differences among sex radicals became even more pronounced in the 1890s and early 1900s when sex radical discourse shifted from the desirability of women's emancipation from sex slavery to their responsibility for the "right" reproduction of children.

Sex radicals argued that women's emancipation from marital slavery would have numerous benefits for society. Under the present system of "slave marriage," contended Edwin Walker, his "brothers" could not attain their manhood because they were given "playthings and tools by courtesy called wives" rather than "free, large, abundant women."[78] Moreover, other contributors added, the children of enslaved women inherited negative traits stemming from their mothers' status. In accord with this sentiment, D. C. S. of Miltonvale, Kansas, pondered: "Why can't the masses see that this continued slave marriage . . . is filling our prisons to overflowing, our hospitals and asylums, our poor houses and homes for the friendless, full to repletion?"[79] Only the emancipation of women, sex radicals asserted in unison, would lead to the birth of an improved race, and until that time children would continue to inherit their mothers' enslaved status. But in the coming "Mother Age," predicted one correspondent, women would "give to the earth a race of Gods."[80] The divergent views of sex radical men and women became even more pronounced when eugenics emerged as a means to retain patriarchal privilege.

7. Motherhood in Freedom

The sex fountain is the source of power and consenting to tamper
with it to please man diverts that power to man's law.
—Lois Waisbrooker, *Lucifer, the Light-Bearer*, 21 April 1897

Woman must rescue herself and consciously assume all
responsibilities of maternity on behalf of the children.
—Moses Harman, *Motherhood in Freedom*

THE EPIGRAPHS opening this chapter—voices of two leading turn-of-the-
century sex radicals—illustrate distinctive differences in their visions for
women's emancipation and capture the gendered and generational tensions
that characterized nineteenth-century sex radicalism by century's end. Lois
Waisbrooker regarded sexual intercourse as a source of women's pleasure and
fulfillment, an almost mystical experience. But, she contended, centuries of
living with the imbalance of power embedded in the patriarchal institution
of marriage had stifled women's natural desire and led men to develop an
unnatural sexual appetite. The solution, she stressed, was for women to determine if and when sexual relations occurred. Only then could both sexes
experience pleasure and advance to a much-desired higher level of existence.
Only then could women—conceiving wanted children presumedly free of
hereditary defects and disease—begin the work of regenerating a severely
troubled world.[1]

Moses Harman, like Waisbrooker, devoted several decades of his life to the
emancipation of women from sexual slavery and made women's freedom a
high priority. Over time, however, his beliefs underwent a subtle but significant change as he moved from emphasizing women's emancipation from
sexual slavery to stressing the right of children to be born well. Pronouncing the newly emerging field of eugenics as a promising remedy for many of
the nation's social problems, he urged sex radical women to put aside their
fight for individual freedom and instead to assume the mantle of motherhood and responsibility for the scientific reproduction of the race.[2]

From the 1850s until the turn of the twentieth century, female sex radicals across a spectrum ranging from utopians and Spiritualists to water-cure physicians and anarchists envisioned a future in which autonomous women entered into mutually governed relationships with men who respected their minds and bodies. They looked to a day when women no longer would be worn down by demanding husbands, the burden of household work, and the care of innumerable children. Moreover, they adopted a positive view of sexuality as a means by which both sexes could attain physical and spiritual fulfillment. By the close of the nineteenth century, however, it had become evident that the sex radical men who endorsed free marriage and free motherhood generally anticipated no major change in existing domestic arrangements. Two of their assumptions—that women would continue to need men's protection and that women should subordinate their desire for personal fulfillment to a higher goal (the birth of eugenically superior children)—stood in stark contrast to the goal of veteran sex radical women. Nowhere are those gendered and generational tensions more evident than in turn-of-the-century sex radical discussions about the meaning of motherhood.

A Woman's Rebellion

In constructing their vision of a newly ordered gender system, sex radical women looked to a variety of print sources for insight and inspiration. In addition to reading each other's letters in *Foundation Principles, Lucifer, the Light-Bearer,* and other anarchist and freethought publications, women explored such subjects as female sexuality and marriage reform in novels and serialized fiction. Such widely read authors as Charles Bellamy, Thomas Hardy, Henry Olerich, Mrs. M. A. (Weeks) Pittock, and Olive Schreiner offered readers fictional critiques of marriage and explored the possibilities of free love in several popular novels. Spiritualist, socialist, and anarchist authors like Lizzie Doten, Sada Bailey Fowler, Marie Stevens Howland, Florence Finch Kelly, Elmina D. Slenker, Alice B. Stockham, and Lois Waisbrooker offered additional fictionalized portrayals of women and men who put their free love principles to practice. And in a highly unusual work for the era, an African American clergyman named Theophilis G. Steward addressed the subject of free love in his novel, *A Charleston Love Story; or, Hortense Vanross.*[3]

But one story, *Hagar Lyndon; or, A Woman's Rebellion,* is especially noteworthy because it exemplifies and encapsulates the recurring issues with which late nineteenth-century sex radical women struggled. Beginning in March 1893 and continuing until September, *Lucifer's* female subscribers eagerly consumed this serialized novel written by the anarchist Lizzie Hunt

Swank Holmes. The author, writing under the pseudonym May Huntley, came from a nationally active family of freethinkers and feminists. Her mother, Hannah J. Hunt, had lived at Berlin Heights among the Free Lovers at mid-century. Her brother, C. F. Hunt, and sister, Lillie D. White, regularly contributed letters for publication in anarchist and freethought periodicals; White also had acted as interim editor of *Lucifer* during one of Moses Harman's four prison terms.[4]

Widowed in 1850 at the age of twenty-two, the author of *Hagar Lyndon* supported herself and two small children by teaching in rural Ohio schools before moving to Chicago in 1877. In Chicago she became involved in organizing sewing women to agitate for better working conditions. Initially a member of the Socialist Labor party, by 1883 Lizzie Hunt had shifted her allegiance to the International Working People's Association and had become friends with the Haymarket anarchists Albert and Lucy Parsons and William Holmes, whom she married in 1885. On 4 May 1886, the day before the Haymarket Massacre, she led a parade of several hundred women through Chicago streets demanding the eight-hour day. After spending seven more years in that city, Holmes moved with her family to Colorado, where she continued to advocate radical causes in the pages of the anarchist and freethought press.[5]

In *Hagar Lyndon*, Holmes explores the question of whether or not a woman can live freely in an unfree environment. Her narrative critiques existing social customs and economic realities governing women's lives and illustrates her vision of an ideal world and the impediments that stood in the way of its lasting achievement. After watching her mother die an early death from years of "enforced" childbearing, Hagar Lyndon rejects the possibility of ever marrying. Yet she cannot resist a powerful desire from within for motherhood after she becomes economically self-sufficient. Recognizing that health, independence, and intelligence qualify her to be a good mother, she solicits the assistance of her longtime and liberal-minded friend, Paul Deane, in becoming pregnant. The result, a "truly 'well-born'" son whom she names Paul, is pronounced an "aristocrat among babies" by a neighboring physician who admires Hagar's scientific approach to motherhood. As much as she loves being a free mother, however, Hagar Lyndon is deeply troubled by the responses of those around her. The society women with whom she formerly associated snub her because she has "fallen," and the madam of a house of prostitution assumes that she, as a "ruined" woman, will welcome the opportunity to work for her. Additionally, Hagar Lyndon must fend off the sexual advances of a landlord who considers her legitimate prey because she has no protector, and she must deal with a well-meaning clergyman who wants to bring her "betrayer to justice."[6]

Despite these difficulties, Hagar Lyndon determinedly persists in living as an independent woman because she is convinced that "a pioneer" must force people to rethink their ideas about motherhood. But then young Paul falls ill. Hagar summons Paul Deane—who to this point in the story has played no role in his son's upbringing or support—not because she needs his assistance but because she believes a father has a right to see his child. Deane, however, interprets her action as a sign of feminine weakness, announces that her actions are harming both *his* child and herself, and proposes marriage as the solution. The times, he informs her, are not yet right for a woman to live without a protector. The story ends on an ambiguous note, with Hagar attempting to negotiate a relationship with Deane that would preserve both her identity and her ability to act freely. Reminding readers that women have an opportunity to be the mothers of a new world order, Holmes concludes: "All of society is heaving, struggling, feeling the throes of pain for the birth of a new idea."[7]

Female readers of *Lucifer* responded enthusiastically to *Hagar Lyndon,* pronouncing it the best serial they had ever read, while men remained uncharacteristically silent. Writing from San Andreas, California, Thirza Rathbun praised May Huntley's narrative for portraying a woman who followed "the dictates of her nature irrespective of man-made laws." "Such tales *are needed,*" agreed a correspondent living in Tennessee. Hinting that she had herself "lived what the writer of Hagar Lyndon represents her heroine as doing," Lois Waisbrooker predicted that the novel would inspire others to model themselves after its heroine and that "the seed being sown will bear fruit in the future, and then we shall have intelligent and honored motherhood."[8] Though fictional, Hagar Lyndon's life underscores a belief—shared by sex radical women and men—that wanted children, born to loving, healthy, and economically independent parents, would inherit superior mental and physical traits from their parents and no longer could be branded illegitimate.

In Hagar Lyndon, female readers found a woman they could admire, someone who possessed the means and the courage to practice the principles they endorsed. Hagar exercises her right to determine if, when, and with whom to have a child. Because she does not become a mother until she has attained economic self-sufficiency, she does not have to rely on her child's father for support. Nor does he possess a right to make any claims of her. This, speculated Elmina Slenker, explained men's silence: they were uncomfortable with the story's denial of paternal love. Reflecting on *Hagar Lyndon* and the comments of others, L. E. H. of Milpitas, California, wistfully declared: "I would like to live my life over as a mother in freedom."[9] As the story illustrates, however, several factors prevented women from becoming mothers in freedom: sexually demanding husbands who did not respect their wives' right to say no to unwanted sexual intercourse, women's attitudes toward the use of contraceptives, the pervasiveness of a moral double standard, conflict over the subject of variety, the question of who would care for children born to free love unions, and the emergence of eugenic beliefs.

The Meaning of Freedom

In *The Story of American Freedom,* the historian Eric Foner argues that the Reconstruction era marked a turning point in which the dominant understanding of freedom shifted from economic autonomy to political equality. In a parallel development, he contends, advocates of women's rights shifted from a broadly defined platform that included social and economic planks to a more focused campaign for woman suffrage. Exchanging their "equal rights feminism" (grounded in the abolitionist ideal of all citizens as equal) for a "feminism of difference" (which emphasized "the moral contribution their special nature enabled them to make to American society"), suffragists channeled their energies into such causes as social purity and temperance.[10] Consequently, the laws governing marriage and the conventions moderating gender relations survived the Civil War era largely intact. Yet older understandings of freedom—grounded in a long tradition of American individualism and libertarianism—persisted. According to Foner, such groups as "labor radicals, populists, socialists, and the like" derived their alternative understanding of freedom from "the older idea of economic autonomy" as its essence.[11]

Like suffragists, sex radical women emphasized their inherent moral superiority to men and the potential it offered to reform the world. Keenly aware of their relative economic powerlessness, they nonetheless disdained political solutions and stood apart from other nineteenth-century advocates of women's rights because they chose to make a *woman's* right to personal freedom their highest priority. "Every human being has one inheritance," wrote a *Lucifer* correspondent from New Jersey in 1887, "and that is the power of choice—which is in itself freedom." At present, this correspondent observed, choice was seen as "the privilege of the male, acceptance as the option of the female."[12] To claim the freedom of choice, female sex radicals recognized, they must first overcome persistent social and cultural forces, including customary discomfort with acknowledging their own sexuality. Even *Hagar Lyndon* had not succeeded there, portraying sexual intercourse solely for the purpose of reproduction.

Coming to Terms with Sexual Desire

Late nineteenth-century women who read and corresponded to *Lucifer, the Light-Bearer* used the publication as an opportunity to communicate openly to editor Moses Harman and with each other about sexual topics. After a personal encounter with Harman, a fifty-six-year-old Colorado farmwife informed other readers that he was "a man whom women need not fear to approach or confide in on the plane of their own personality." She praised him for his willingness to risk prosecution to tackle subjects that few other editors would. Lois Waisbrooker concurred. Only uncensored investigation, not legislation, would eliminate "sex evils from society." Had not law and custom, other readers demanded, routinely denied woman access to information on sexual topics and left wives knowing little about "the uses of sexualism except for reproduction"?[13]

Both sex radicals and the more conservative advocates of women's rights yearned for social (sexual) purity, but they differed significantly in their vision of how it could be attained. The latter defined sexual purity as the containment of male and female sexual expression within marriage.[14] Accepting the premise of male sexuality as uncontrolled and the idea of females as sexual victims, advocates of social purity reform began promoting the concept of voluntary motherhood because they believed it would empower women. In keeping with their beliefs, social purity reformers also campaigned for measures intended to protect women: age-of-consent laws, prosecution of prostitutes' clientele, criminalization of abortion, and censorship of material deemed obscene. Their efforts not only promoted an image of women as passionless but also reinforced the notion that sexuality should be reserved for the purposes of reproduction.

Sex radical women viewed the free expression of a woman's sexuality as a necessary prerequisite for individual fulfillment and therefore did not desire to limit sexual expression to reproduction. As had their predecessors in the 1850s, late nineteenth-century sex radicals believed that mutually loving sexual intercourse could enhance a woman's physical and emotional well-being. One attributed her feeling of "vague unrest, a thirst unquenched, in fact a longing for something I know not what" to never having experienced "grand passion." Others viewed the primary purpose of sex as twofold: for reproduction and "renewal of the already created bodies and minds of the participants." Lois Waisbrooker elaborated further: "When sex is rightly understood and properly honored, it will be a builder in more than that of offspring."[15] But this could only occur after removing the imbalance of power seen in most heterosexual relationships.

Some sex radical women preferred to ground their discussion of sexuality in familiar scientific, Spiritualistic, or naturalistic rhetoric. Women, they wrote, should enter into sexual relationships when "soul attraction" dictated or when they had "spiritual and intellectual needs that are calling for more life force." Intense desire, such women reasoned, was "nature's call," speaking through a human body as it sought the elements necessary for its completion. Still others compared sexual intercourse to such biological necessities as eating and drinking, arguing that adult women and men required all three activities to sustain themselves.[16]

Freedom from a Moral Double Standard

While *Hagar Lyndon* does not consider the subject of contraception, the novel does address another concern of great interest to sex radical women: the moral double standard that prescribed one code of sexual behavior for women and another for men. Women, *Lucifer* correspondents well knew, must remain chaste until marriage and then monogamous until death if they wished to retain community approval. Married men, observed one correspondent, Josephine Croff, often practiced free love without adverse consequence while thinking nothing of inflicting terrible punishment "upon their helpless wives for the slightest infringement of their marriage vows." Moreover, a single woman who engaged in sexual activity prior to marriage risked becoming a "fallen" woman, a stigma virtually impossible to overcome. "No matter how great was the love of that woman for the father of her child," wrote Cornelia Forward of Manton, California, "she will wear the brand of shame and be forever lost." How ironic, wrote an indignant female correspondent in 1893, that the male-dominated institutions of church and state "compel us women who have striven so hard to retain our honor in single life to yield our precious treasures to the males" who did not hold themselves to the same standard.[17] Once a single standard prevailed, they believed, women would be free to express their sexuality without fear of the consequences—loss of reputation and children who bore the stigma of illegitimacy.

Sex radical women who corresponded to *Lucifer* could not avoid observing that both wives and prostitutes exchanged sexual favors for pragmatic reasons. Mattie Hursen, a Michigan resident who previously had worked as a dressmaker for prostitutes, urged readers to avoid judging those women:

they—like wives—had taken up this line of work out of economic need. Although she objected to the socioeconomic conditions that forced women into prostitution, one *Liberty* contributor, Sarah M. Chipman, concurred that women possessed the right "to make terms for their 'sexual favors.'" But when the day of economic equality arrives, predicted the Chicago anarchist Lucy Parsons, "sex slavery will be a lost art."[18] Because that time had yet to arrive, however, sex radicals joined many other Americans in debating the need for protective measures.

Sex radicals agreed in theory that a woman should have the right to freely express her sexuality, but in practice they could not even agree on a woman's right to correspond with a man. Tensions surfaced in 1894 when the veteran reformer and Spiritualist Elmina Slenker proposed the establishment of a correspondence bureau for sex radicals. Several decades earlier, she had placed her own advertisement in the *Water-Cure Journal*: it yielded messages from over sixty respondents, one of whom eventually became her husband. Slenker, recognizing that many sex radical men and women hungered for the companionship of like-minded individuals, offered to collect names from men and women and to pair them for the purpose of meaningful communication. Offering women greater assurance of confidentiality than they had when placing an advertisement in a liberal paper, Slenker promised to screen out any obviously insincere writers. Idealistically, Slenker envisioned her plan as an opportunity for women and men "to write freely on religion, sexology, heredity, and equality."[19] Her critics, however, accused her of creating an organized means for men to find sexual partners. The vigorous and lengthy debate Slenker's proposal prompted among female contributors to *Lucifer* and *Foundation Principles* reveals a key tension among sex radical women: despite their bold declarations, they remained reluctant to trust each other with freedom.

Lois Waisbrooker, foremost among the opponents of Slenker's proposal, vehemently opposed the notion of a correspondence bureau because she saw young or naive women as incapable of dealing with "unclean letters." The only men who would participate in such a scheme, she argued, would be "lascivious hunters after excitement." The anarchist Volteraine de Cleyre and the *Lucifer* reader Mary W. Conway lent support to Waisbrooker's contention by sharing accounts of the "undesirable correspondence" they had received from men who saw women's names in radical papers and assumed that any woman who wrote publicly about sex freedom must practice it privately.[20] In addition to the risk in exposing oneself to unnecessary lewdness, Waisbrooker warned, a woman who corresponded with unhappily married men encouraged their tendency toward adultery and coarse behavior. Implicit in her criticism of Slenker's plan was the notion that anyone who chose to participate in the bureau lacked good moral judgment.

Eager to protect young, impressionable minds from vulgar ideas, Waisbrooker—like men who adopted a protectionist attitude toward women—ignored the possibility that a woman could find written exchanges with a man enjoyable and educational. Attempting to counter her objections, women provided first-person testimonials of the many ways in which Slenker had aided them. Writing from Washington, Elsie Wilcox reported that she had formed some of her "most pleasant acquaintances" with Mrs. Slenker's assistance. Another regular contributor expressed satisfaction in knowing that "men were inquiring of women, as students on matters of sexology," because previously "man's word has been the ultimatum." Flora Fox praised the plan because it gave women an equal opportunity to exercise judgment in the choice of correspondents and to determine how long they communicated and upon which subjects. Others commended Slenker for matching people with similar values and priorities. A North Dakota farmwife, for instance, reported in 1904 that having met her husband through *Lucifer* made it possible for her to live a "normal, natural life and still be mistress of myself."[21]

Many of the *Lucifer* contributors who defended Elmina Slenker's proposal viewed the exchange of letters between the sexes as an opportunity for women to reform and uplift men. John Heritage, writing from Washington, attributed his "first good clean ideas on sex" to the radical women with whom he corresponded. And while Elsie Wilcox advised female readers to terminate exchanges if a man proved incorrigibly licentious, she expressed no reservations about the risk of being exposed to such ideas. Instead, she believed that "true women should know how to deal with coarse men" because they have a "duty" to "educate him kindly."[22] Such communications affirm that both male and female sex radicals continued to accept the idea of women as inherently responsible for the moral governance of both sexes.

Sex radical women struggled to reconcile their ideas about female erotic desire with those affirming women's reproductive role. Their concerns are best illustrated in debates about sexual intercourse during pregnancy. Some correspondents, evoking Sylvester Graham's theories about the conservation of energy, took an uncompromising stand against any and all sexual excitement during pregnancy. It would, they asserted, drain the fetus of vital energy. Writing from her farmstead near Caplinger Mills, Missouri, Kate Austin supported that position by pointing to nature. Male farm animals, she observed, wisely left females alone after having impregnated them. Arguing that sexual relations during pregnancy would result in higher incidences of hereditary defects and infant mortality, Austin concluded that women had no choice in the matter: the rights of the unborn must take precedence over men's selfish desires for sexual gratification.[23]

Yet those who differed with Austin countered that sexual desire during pregnancy was both normal and utilitarian. Writing from California in 1894, a woman named Alma Vail informed readers that women could expect to feel sexual desire even in periods during which they experienced morning sickness. Attributing such desire to nature, she advised women to listen to the wisdom of their bodies. Lois Waisbrooker shared Vail's belief that sexual relations at such times served a functional purpose. Desire, she reasoned, was nature's way of helping a woman extract from a man any missing elements needed for fetal growth and development. "It is a well-known fact," she wrote, "that if a pregnant woman *strongly* desires a particular kind of food and does not get it the child will have an inordinate desire for the same." Moreover, she continued, "if there ever was a time when a woman needs loving attention it is when she is gestating a new being."[24]

Still others, often the sex radical women who had come of age in the 1890s, more readily acknowledged sexuality as an important component of a healthy and fulfilling life. Acknowledging that she felt sexual desire even when she did not wish to become pregnant, Laura H. Earle in 1903 asked *Lucifer* readers if a woman could legitimately justify "a sex attraction that is exclusively physical." Arguing in the affirmative, Dora Forster blamed "the Church" for teaching people "that all sexing except for propagation is low and vulgar." Over time, other youthful sex radical women openly acknowledged sexual pleasure as an important dimension in their lives. "The primary use of sex," wrote Sara Crist Campbell from Illinois in 1903, "is for renewal of the already created bodies and minds of the participants." Few women, however, described sexual intercourse as rapturously as had Angela Heywood in the 1880s, when she unabashedly embraced "coition" (her term for sexual intercourse) as a source of both pleasure and propagation. "Sexuality," she wrote in 1881, "is a divine ordinance, elegantly natural from an eye-glance to the vital action of penis and womb [her word for vagina], in personal exhilaration or for reproductive uses." Even Lois Waisbrooker, with her mind often focused on the spiritual, concurred that when a woman spontaneously sought sexual intercourse, "it is proof to me that she has spiritual and intellectual needs that are calling for more life force." This was why, she argued, women continued to experience sexual desire even during and after the "change of life."[25]

The story of *Hagar Lyndon* does not address the subject of contraception because its author sought to portray an ideal world peopled with economically independent women and sexually self-controlled men. An assumption visible throughout much of sex radical women's discourse on this subject of contraception was that men's interactions in a corrupt public sphere had diminished their capacity for self-restraint in any and all human relationships. A Clinton, Iowa, woman explained in 1887 that men had become "abnormal sexual monsters" because they focused on the material rather than the spiritual world. Emphasizing the female's inherently superior moral character, sex radical women declared that men's redemption could occur only if they allowed women to help them advance to a higher plane. This explained why men sought women "so persistently," explained Lois Waisbrooker in 1894. They recognized that women possessed something they "must receive."[26]

Whether they opposed or endorsed the use of contraceptive devices, sex radical women considered this decision a feminist issue. Women grounded in antebellum perfectionism, for instance, stated that lasting improvement would occur only after women and men reformed their behavior. In their opinion, contraceptive devices like the syringe or sponge merely alleviated the symptoms rather than the root cause of women's oppression. Also, readers who shared Lois Waisbrooker's view of female sexuality as the source of women's power agreed that "consenting to tamper with it to please man diverts that power to man's law."[27] In their eyes, self-control represented the only viable solution.

Those who advocated the use of contraception viewed the syringe and other such devices as legitimate weapons in women's fight for their rights and regarded it as an interim measure, necessary until women and men together advanced to a higher, presumably more spiritual, plane of development. Until men ceased using their "penis-power" as "a matter of commerce" that "freights woman with child and sends her down the stream of prostituting disaster," Angela Heywood declared, the syringe must remain a necessity.[28] A smaller subset of sex radical women—often those in their twenties and thirties—endorsed the use of contraceptive devices as a means to reduce fear of pregnancy and thus increase the likelihood of experiencing sexual pleasure and fulfillment. "Many of our younger radical women," wrote one in her twenties, "are among those who are not ashamed to avow the deliciousness of their sex, as Walt Whitman puts it." In response to those who argued that such devices served men's purpose more than they did women's, she asserted: "The free woman does not 'consent to unnatural sex relations' (Mrs. Waisbrooker's expression for the use of contracepts) 'in order to please' her lover, but in order to please herself."[29]

Sexual Variety

The question of sexual variety—the right to love more than one person either simultaneously or sequentially, chastely or sexually—divided sex radicals for over five decades. Such idealistic-minded free lovers as Francis and Cordelia Barry regarded variety as the ultimate manifestation of women's freedom. They believed that it represented the only way to eliminate force from heterosexual relations: if self-sufficient women could have fulfilling sexual relations with men they loved, they no longer would enter into unloving relationships. Moreover, a man's or woman's willingness to let a partner go when love between them had faded represented an act of true selflessness.[30]

Women who accepted variety generally viewed it as a lower level of development, one they ultimately expected to yield to an exalted state of monogamic love. By monogamy, they meant lifelong, exclusive, heterosexual love, whether or not it was sanctioned by the state or blessed by the church. But while some saw monogamy as their goal, others dismissed it as a form of "possession, and possession means slavery, either of law, social restraint, or of habit." "Nature," wrote one advocate of variety, Carrie A., "never intended our lesser attractions to be permanent." Imperfect human beings, she reasoned in 1901, might err in selecting mates and therefore would need to continue making adjustments until they found their ideal complement in the opposite sex. Sex radical women who embraced this logic did not interpret variety as a form of promiscuity but rather a process by which they could achieve God's will or their natural destiny. An avowed varietist named Lena Belfort, for instance, in 1903 declared that a woman must follow her instincts and must practice "whatever her own nature demands and her own mind approves."[31]

Many sex radical women remained strict monogamists in practice yet asserted their right to be varietists if they so desired. Variety could include something so simple as the right to interact with men without the assumption that their association would lead to sexual intercourse. "Variety in love does not necessarily mean variety in cohabiting," wrote Elmina Drake Slenker in 1887. "We need a variety of friends . . . we seek and love each one, for something pertaining to that one alone, and in variety find completeness." Few endorsed perpetual change, but those who defended variety regarded it as the epitome of freedom. To Flora M. of Missouri, a woman's right to choose variety meant that she truly was free to "live my life my own way."[32]

Some women who viewed variety as the essence of freedom nonetheless feared its consequences in a society that did not provide adequate economic opportunities to women. Summing up her objections to variety, Lucy Parsons of Chicago in 1896 announced that it was destructive in a world that refused to make provisions for husbandless mothers and their children. Mothers in particular saw variety as merely another way men could victimize women. "Are we to feel miserably insecure about the homes we have labored so hard to make?" inquired an anonymous woman in 1887. After digesting years of debate on the subject of variety, the longtime *Lucifer* contributor Lucinda B. Chandler concluded that variety, like marriage, represented a code of behavior constructed by men to suit their sexual desires. Even men like Moses Harman and Edwin Walker who championed women's emancipation from sex slavery, she reasoned, did so from a gendered perspective and had failed to incorporate into their system women's vision of a new social order. Had Harman and Walker, she demanded, ever inquired of women if these ideas were acceptable?[33]

More male than female sex radicals endorsed the idea of sexual variety in theory and practice. Some shared women's belief that variety represented a stage of development on the path to perfection, one that would yield to monogamy upon the discovery of one's true life partner. "I expect to be so enraptured by the charms of the one, select, and precious above all others," a correspondent named A. Warren informed *Lucifer* readers, "as to forget the existence of my side lover, altogether." Others, however, viewed variety more pragmatically. The longtime sex radical J. William Lloyd, for instance, contended that the children of variety free lovers would benefit from having multiple fathers (for economic support) and mothers (for care and nurture).[34] Justifying variety on the grounds of evolution, male *Lucifer* readers declared that those who practiced it would give birth to superior children. "The whole process of evolution," explained James Thierry in 1893, "is based on free variety." Thus, he reasoned, any institution—including legal marriage—that inhibited men's and women's natural inclination to variety hindered "race progress."[35]

Unlike women, however, men generally regarded variety—not monogamy—as a higher level of development. "It may take many individuals of the opposite sex," Edwin Walker observed in 1897, "to fully complement the finely organized woman or man . . . therefore, [it] must be that monogamy represents a comparatively undeveloped physical, emotional, intellectual, and social state." While a few men embraced variety for the physical pleasure they believed it entailed, many others viewed it through a lens of utopian idealism. Variety, elaborated Lloyd, helped break down the "narrow, selfish, exclusive feeling" that caused so many social problems.[36]

What about the Children?

Sex radicals, like many other Americans during the economically depressed 1880s and 1890s, were haunted by the specter of dependent citizens. Thus, they struggled to address concerns about fathers who shirked parental responsibility, women worn out by caring for children whom they could not adequately support, and overburdened relief rolls in communities throughout the nation. But try as they might, one of the social ills that *Lucifer* contributors could not resolve was the question of responsibility for children when their parents decided to separate. The most idealistic of sex radicals argued that only love between parents could ensure the care of children. Opponents of variety free love assumed that men would impregnate women only to abandon them and the children they had fathered. Even the many sex radicals who held monogamy as their ideal struggled over an acknowledgment that men and women might become parents several times before they found their ideal partners. "Love unions," wrote an anonymous woman in 1887, "result in responsibilities which demand homes."[37]

The stereotype of sex radicals as irresponsible parents troubled turn-of-the-century *Lucifer* correspondents. In reality, protested J. B. Elliott of Pennsylvania in 1903, sex radicals generally refrained from the conception of children except for those times when a man and woman mutually desired to become parents and possessed the financial and emotional resources to support a child. Moreover, stated Kate Austin in 1897, paternal love was every bit as strong as maternal love: the fathers "who do not strain every nerve to provide for their children are the exception." Thus, she reasoned, the few who abandoned or killed their children took such abominable actions "for the same reason that illegitimate mothers desert and often murder them—because Respectable People consider them a disgrace."[38]

In addition to believing optimistically that free lovers would limit the number of children they conceived, most *Lucifer* correspondents believed that "love children"—like Hagar Lyndon's son—would be superior to those born within a contentious and flawed marriage. By "superior" they meant healthier, purer, and happier offspring, untainted by their parents' anger and selfishness. Children born under such circumstances, reasoned one correspondent, Julia C. Franklin, in 1891, "need very little control to keep them on the straight and narrow path of true principle."[39] As this example shows, sex radicals who believed in the hereditary transmission of such traits as hatred, jealousy, and violence assumed that children conceived in love would be spared such behavioral consequences.

Despite such idealistic pronouncements, late nineteenth-century sex radicals recognized that the issue of responsibility for children could not be resolved satisfactorily so long as women remained economically dependent on men for their support. But they could not agree on an interim solution to this problem. Committed anarchists staunchly advocated individual responsibility, while others, harkening back to free love's utopian roots, endorsed communal solutions. The concept of the unitary household—endorsed by Stephen Pearl Andrews in the 1850s—continued to resonate with late nineteenth-century *Lucifer* readers, including those who lived in rural settings. By "unitary" they meant a living arrangement in which people had private quarters yet shared responsibility for such gendered chores as cooking, laundry, and child care. Others, however, eschewed such proposals and instead argued that the state should erase the distinction between legitimate and illegitimate children by assuming responsibility for all of them.[40]

More Than a Mere Procreating Machine

In virtually all of the theories that female sex radicals embraced during the final quarter of the nineteenth century, conception must be a woman's choice, not her fate. The success of those plans, however, depended on men's cooperation—and especially their willingness to exercise sexual self-control. Despite the many benefits women cited—their personal fulfillment and improved health and reduced infant mortality, birth defects, and childhood diseases—some men within the movement became increasingly insistent that women subordinate their quest for personal freedom to a higher cause: they must dutifully assume responsibility for the creation of an improved race of children. Gendered and generational conflict ensued as angry sex radical women who had devoted years to the movement resisted the notion that conception had become not their *choice* but their principal life's purpose.

Several factors contributed to the evolution of nineteenth-century hereditarian ideas into twentieth-century eugenic thought. The 1859 publication of Charles Darwin's *Origin of Species* lent scientific support to the idea that the flawed or weak propagate their kind, an idea also reinforced by Christian theology. With the occurrence of each nineteenth-century economic depression, people perceived as hereditary "losers" became all the more visible. Moreover, a steady influx of new immigrants exacerbated concern about the declining birthrate of middle-class white women and prompted Theodore Roosevelt to sound the alarm of "race suicide" (a fear that their birthrate was dropping far below that of immigrants and the working class).[41] Sex radical men, along with many others, feared that women's insistence on regulating their maternal function would subvert the existing social order and, along with it, men's hierarchical privilege. Interest in scientific breeding also became increasingly institutionalized between the publication of Mendel's pathbreaking genetic research in 1866 and its rediscovery in 1900. Congressional passage of the Hatch Act, which established national government support for the establishment of agricultural experiment stations, further encouraged rural people's interest in scientific breeding. In that context, the existing practice of displaying crops and livestock at agricultural fairs advanced to another level: an appearance of better-baby contests at those same fairs, which clearly confirms that American interest in genetics had gained wider popular acceptance.[42]

Like many Americans, Moses Harman became infected by the eugenic fever that swept the nation. Citing Galton's *Hereditary Genius* and the example of the Jukes family (which, according to Richard L. Dugdale's research, included over 128 prostitutes and more than 76 criminals), he praised Theodore Roosevelt for giving "an impetus to the discussion of the marriage and population questions that has not been imparted by any other force for a long time."[43] While Harman continued to confirm a commitment to the emancipation of women from sex slavery, his interest in the study of scientific breeding nonetheless began to take precedence.

Eager for his publication to appear more scientific, Harman pursued several courses. First, through editorials, he discouraged women from submitting contributions detailing their sexual trials and tribulations—something they had done since the mid-1880s. In addition to knowing how to write powerful and succinct arguments, Harman further suggested, male contributors were far more likely than women to enclose money to subsidize the publication of their thoughts. A frequent female contributor from Iowa, angered by Harman's new vision for *Lucifer,* complained that he wanted women "pruned down and polished up." "O, dear!" she concluded in a tongue-in-cheek tone, "Makes us most 'a-feared' to write." Harman began to replace lengthy reader correspondence with such articles as "The Science of Stirpiculture" and "Our Drift toward Imperialism." Longtime female readers dismissed men's theoretical essays about economics and politics as boring, irrelevant, and verbose. "I read a half column from the pen of some earnest mother," the Iowa woman declared, "with more interest than I can possibly bring to the lengthy articles from him [a regular male contributor] and many other men."[44] Finally, in an attempt to exploit *Lucifer*'s long history of advocating hereditarian ideas, Harman in 1907 shed what many readers by then regarded as an onerous name by changing the masthead to *American Journal of Eugenics.* By the time it ceased publication in 1910, only brief excerpts of a few readers' letters appeared in a column entitled "Various Voices," and men's voices dominated even there.

Prior to that change, contributions from an articulate, well-read Canadian sex radical named R. B. Kerr triggered rancorous debate among *Lucifer* readers, their words demonstrating wide differences about the matter of eugenics. Favoring nature over nurture, Kerr argued that only careful breeding would enable men and women to improve "the mental and moral, as well as the physical" makeup of their offspring. He further argued that this laudable end could not be achieved unless women devoted their energies and focused their attention on the production of human beings and deferred their fight for personal liberty to a later day. But what most infuriated longtime sex radical women was his condemnation of monogamy as "the absolute negation of all scientific breeding." "No breeder of dogs, horses, cattle, sheep or any other kind," Kerr asserted, "would ever dream of breeding on monogamous principles." Thus justifying sexual variety on scientific grounds, he suggested that only unenlightened women would be "so unfortunately constituted as to feel a repugnance to intercourse with every man capable of making a good father."[45]

Male correspondents praised Kerr as one of *Lucifer*'s "wisest, most logical and clearest-headed" writers. Enthusiastically endorsing Kerr's ideas, Moses Harman put himself "on record" as "an advocate of breeding prize animals . . . whether quadrupeds or bipeds." It was well and good "to make each woman free to do what she pleases with her own person," he conceded, but a man had a responsibility "to educate her in the wise choice of a father for her child." Many other men commended Kerr's position on variety. In a response to Lizzie Holmes, who denounced variety as a disease afflicting men, Alex E. Wright accused women of "concealing their practice of variety more effectually and persistently than do men." It was not their fault, he conceded, but rather an "outcome of commercialism and the resulting dependence of woman upon man for support." Other male correspondents shared Kerr's assessment of women's emphasis on intuition and emotion as unscientific, asserting that women could not develop to their full potential until they learned to think like men.[46]

But female contributors who for decades had advocated the sexual emancipation of women responded in *Lucifer*'s pages with numerous objections to Kerr's ideas. Firm believers that children born of true love matches would be superior to all others, such women were in closer accord with Social Darwinists (who believed that natural processes inherent in men and women would render eugenic involvement in human reproduction unnecessary) than with the sex radical men who embraced Kerr's eugenicism. Many typically dismissed Kerr's ideas as "cold and heartless." Addressing a male assertion that women would choose "sick or weak men as fathers because they love them," Lizzie B. Holmes countered that a woman's desire to have a healthy child with the man she loved would triumph over heredity. Moreover, she asked *Lucifer*'s freedom-loving readership, who decides to deny a woman this right? "Surely not any lover of liberty." Other sex radical women objected to the notion that men would set the standard of what represented desirable traits. While men might know best about the breeding of animals, female correspondents conceded, physical science "had its limits." With a child, Rebecca Goodheart argued, "you can have no such definite idea of what you want to produce. Is it to be a Shakespeare, a Pascal, a Plato, or a martyr?" Reminding their less-developed "dear brothers" that enforced maternity smothered a woman's soul and deprived her children of the full benefit of her "creative power," sex radical feminists further emphasized that free women could make a unique contribution to the improvement of the race: they could create souls as well as bodies.[47]

In addition to opposing men's eugenic theories, veteran sex radical women resented the idea of "old men grannies" telling them what to do, essentially treating women in a condescending manner. Moses Harman had begun addressing female correspondents—even those his own age—as "daughter" in a high-handed manner that reeked of patriarchal authority. At this, Lillie White considered herself "'read out' by our good Father Harman." Reminding readers of her long record of support for his right to free speech, White charged that Harman had begun to impose restraints on ideas that he now found unsuitable. Other women, especially those active in sex radicalism for as many years as Harman, if not longer, protested the demeaning message he now conveyed through *Lucifer*'s pages. "I do want to have it understood," declared Celia B. Whitehead, "that a woman is something more than a procreating machine" and that motherhood involves more than an act of conception. Exasperated with male *Lucifer* subscribers who shared Harman's views, *Hagar Lyndon*'s author declared: "You have no right to ask a mother to make sacrifices for unborn children—that is, personal sacrifices of her feelings, rights, tastes, and inclinations."[48]

Increasingly distanced from male contributors, veteran female sex radicals also discovered their opinions diverging from those of younger sex radical women. Their letters reveal a contest between emotion and reason. One, Adeline Champney, summed up the latter position: "There are women today who know that love alone will not insure superior children." Another, Amy Linnett, wrote "to show that some women at least support" Kerr's ideas and to dismantle other women's objections. Why not consider a man's physical traits when selecting the father of your child? she asked. "[W]e can at least try to give a good physique to our children, and environments will do a great deal for their mentality." Citing examples of personal acquaintances who systematically had chosen prospective fathers on the basis of their physical traits, Linnett urged others to step forward with examples.[49] Few did. Yet those who came of age in the 1890s and who consumed such novels as Grant Allen's *The Woman Who Did* and *Hagar Lyndon,* the historian George Robb writes, were "products of a post-Darwinian world, and their arguments for free love were couched in the language of biology and evolution rather than the vocabulary of the Enlightenment." For decades female advocates of sex radicalism had been motivated by their "indigenous faith in womanhood," but among those born after 1870, few espoused "the old values or aspirations."[50]

In 1907 the octogenarian sex radical Lois Waisbrooker cautioned members of the Social Science League of Chicago to beware of the eugenic fever infecting the nation. At first glance, such concern may seem contradictory, coming as it did from a woman who since the Civil War era had relied on hereditarian ideas to support her campaign for women's rights.[51] In her twilight years, however, Waisbrooker recognized that the cause for which she had devoted so much of her life had been consumed by another movement—eugenics. For nearly half a century, a shared sense of oppression had sustained male and female sex radicals as they fought first and foremost for women's emancipation from sexual slavery, with the freedom of speech and the regeneration of the race as highly desirable by-products. At the turn of the century a deepening fissure within sex radicalism saw most men and a few younger women turn to science to establish a new priority—the creation of sound minds and bodies—while veteran sex radical women remained steadfast in their conviction that only motherhood in freedom held the key to women's full equality.

Earlier periods of economic depression had reinforced sex radicals' resolve, but ironically that very resolution had masked differences of opinion among females and males, young and old. By century's end, with an improved economy, theirs had become a fragile coalition of aging individualist anarchists, free lovers, freethinkers, Spiritualists, and assorted radicals whose center failed to hold. As debates over eugenics dominated the pages of *Lucifer* and its successor the *American Journal of Eugenics* after the turn of the century, it became evident that nineteenth-century sex radicals no longer fought for social and sexual equality. Instead, they were engaged in a highly gendered contest for power.

Veteran women in the movement continued to advance maternalist arguments in support of their right to freedom and equality, even as sex radical men attempted to solidify their hegemony by transforming conception into a science and affirming themselves as the regulators of reproduction. Reform-minded women had a responsibility, they argued, to subordinate themselves (and their quest for personal and sexual fulfillment) for the greater good of society. Yet scores of women, introduced to feminist ideas through five decades of sex radical agitation, remained committed to one basic concept: that a woman's "*right to choose for herself* be generally recognized."[52]

Appendix:
Methodological Note

THE CHALLENGE OF STUDYING nineteenth-century sex radicals is to move beyond the editors' personae to the lives of the women and men who read their periodicals. It is important to determine whether real people wrote the letters appearing on the pages of sex radical periodicals or if editors fabricated them. To do this, I took decade-by-decade samples of 3,439 letters. As the table below indicates, sample size varies for several reasons. First, editors published fewer letters in the 1850s than they did in later decades (for example, *Nichols' Journal* and *Nichols' Monthly* published infrequent excerpts from letters in the 1850s, whereas reader contributions dominated the pages of *Lucifer, the Light-Bearer* in the 1890s). Second, sex radical periodicals all but disappeared in the 1860s, yet correspondence boomed in the 1870s, 1880s, and 1890s before diminishing in the early 1900s when Moses Harman adopted a more scholarly publication format. Finally, sample size also depends on the availability of complete and consecutive runs of periodicals.

For each of the letters examined, I recorded the correspondent's name, sex, place of residence, age (if available), and the topic discussed. With the assistance of Dominican University graduate assistant Holly Burt, I constructed two databases: the first contains entries for the 1,751 women and men who during my sample periods sent letters to sex radical periodicals; the second categorizes the content of the 3,439 letters they wrote. The two databases include biographical data extracted from my reading of sex radical periodicals as well as information retrieved from federal manuscript census records, city directories, and county histories. Geographical mobility, correspondents' use of pseudonyms, and changes in women's names presented a methodological challenge, yet overall we found census data for approximately 15 percent of the correspondents (many of them ordinary women and men). Based on this data, I am confident that most of the letters appearing in sex radical periodicals are authentic. Such data enhance our understanding of demographic change and continuity within the sex radical movement over time. These data are presented and discussed in chapter 3.

Sex Radical Periodicals, 1853–1910

Title	Place of Publication	Frequency and Dates Published	Editor(s)	Number of Letters for Years Sampled
Nichols' Journal of Health, Water-Cure, and Human Progress	Port Chester, N.Y.	Weekly 1853–54	Thomas L. and Mary Gove Nichols	17 (1853–54)
Nichols' Monthly	New York; Cincinnati	Monthly 1855–57	Thomas L. and Mary Gove Nichols	9 (1855–56)
Social Revolutionist	Greenville and Berlin Heights, Ohio	Monthly 1856–57	John Patterson	345 (1856–57)
Vanguard	Dayton, Ohio; Richmond, Ind.	Weekly 1857–58?	Anne Denton Cridge, Albert Cridge	5 (1859)
Age of Freedom	Berlin Heights, Ohio	Weekly 1858	John Patterson, Francis Barry, Cordelia Barry,	6 (1858)
Good Time Coming	Berlin Heights, Ohio	Weekly 1859	C. M. Overton	11 (1859)
Kingdom of Heaven	Anderson, Ind.; Huntsville, Ind.; Berlin Heights, Ohio	Monthly 1864–68	Thomas Cook	23 (1865 and 1867)
New Campaign	Berlin Heights, Ohio			—[a]
Woodhull and Claflin's Weekly	New York	Weekly 1870–76	Victoria Woodhull, Tennessee Claflin	585 (1873–74)
Hull's Crucible	Boston	Weekly 1871–77	Moses Hull, D. W. Hull, Mattie Sawyer	—[a]
The Word	Princeton, Mass.	Monthly 1872–93	Ezra Heywood	42 (1878 and 1887)
Lucifer, the Light-Bearer	Valley Falls and Topeka, Kans.; Chicago	Weekly 1883–1907	Moses Harman	1520 (1883–84, 1886–87, 1893–94, 1897–1900, 1903, 1905, and 1907)
Foundation Principles	Clinton, Iowa; Topeka, Kans.; Antioch, Calif.	Irregular Mid-1880s–1893–94	Lois Waisbrooker	87 (1893–94)
Fair Play	Valley Falls, Kans.; Sioux City, Iowa	1888–1908	Edwin C. Walker, Lillian Harman	15

(cont.)

Title	Place of Publication	Frequency and Dates Published	Editor(s)	Number of Letters for Years Sampled
Our New Humanity	Chicago	1895–97	Moses Harman	—[a]
Firebrand	Portland, Ore.	Weekly 1895–97	Henry Addis, Abner J. Pope, Abe Isaak	—[a]
Free Society	San Francisco; Chicago	Weekly 1897–1905	Abe Isaak	513
Discontent	Lake Bay, Wash.	Weekly 1898–1902	Home Colony residents	159
Clothed with the Sun	San Francisco; Home, Wash.	Irregular 1900–1902	Lois Waisbrooker	Not sampled
American Journal of Eugenics	Chicago; Los Angeles	Monthly 1907–10	Moses Harman	102
				3,439

a. Letters read but not included in the sample.

Notes

Abbreviations

AoF	*Age of Freedom* (Berlin Heights, Ohio)
AJE	*American Journal of Eugenics* (Los Angeles)
BoL	*Banner of Light* (Boston)
FPl	*Fair Play* (Valley Falls, Kans.; Sioux City, Iowa)
FPr	*Foundation Principles* (Clinton, Iowa; Antioch, Calif.; Topeka, Kans.)
GA	*Golden Age* (New York)
GTC	*Good Time Coming* (Berlin Heights, Ohio)
HW	*Harper's Weekly* (New York)
HC	*Hull's Crucible* (Boston)
KoH	*Kingdom of Heaven* (Anderson and Huntsville, Ind.; Berlin Heights, Ohio)
LLB	*Lucifer, the Light-Bearer* (Valley Falls, Kans.; Chicago; Los Angeles)
MS	*Milwaukee Sentinel*
NYT	*New York Times*
NYTr	*New York Tribune*
NJ	*Nichols' Journal of Health, Water-Cure, and Human Progress* (New York)
NLG	*Norton's Literary Gazette* (New York)
NM	*Nichols' Monthly: A Magazine of Social Science and Progressive Literature* (Cincinnati, Ohio)
ONH	*Our New Humanity* (Topeka, Kans.)
RPJ	*Religio-Philosophical Journal* (Chicago)
SCR	*Sandusky Commercial Register* (Ohio)
SR	*Social Revolutionist* (Greenville and Berlin Heights, Ohio)
SpR	*Springfield Republican* (Mass.)
TS	*Truth Seeker* (New York)
VG	*Vanguard* (Dayton, Ohio; Richmond, Ind.)
WCJ	*Water-Cure Journal* (New York)

WR   *Whitewater Register* (Wis.)
WCW   *Woodhull and Claflin's Weekly* (New York)

Introduction

1. The term "free love," according to *Merriam Webster's Collegiate Dictionary*, tenth edition, originated in the early 1820s and connotes the practice of living with or engaging in sexual relations with a member of the opposite sex who is not one's husband or wife. By mainstream, I am referring to editors of such widely read or influential publications as the *Chicago Tribune*, the *New York Times*, and the *Springfield (Mass.) Republican*. Their editors routinely labeled adulterers, bigamists, and polygamists, as well as anyone who called for the abolition of marriage, "free lovers." See, for example, "The Concubinage of the Plains," *SpR*, 25 June 1858, 2; "Divorce and Free-Love," *SpR*, 3 Jan. 1860, 2.

2. The divorce reformer Robert Dale Owen served in the Indiana state legislature and helped transform that state into a haven for divorce-seeking women and men in the 1850s. For further insight into the legal history of nineteenth-century marriage and divorce, see Blake, *Road to Reno*; Cott, *Public Vows*; Griswold, *Family and Divorce in California*; Hartog, *Man and Wife in America*; Riley, *Divorce*.

3. For additional works on free love, see Battan, "Politics of 'Eros'"; Leach, *True Love and Perfect Union*; Ditzion, *Marriage, Morals, and Sex in America*. For a documentary history, see Stoehr, *Free Love in America*. Recent studies of sex radicals have focused on their free speech activism. See, for example, Beisel, *Imperiled Innocents*; Hovey, "Stamping Out Smut"; Rabban, *Free Speech in Its Forgotten Years*.

4. Spurlock, *Free Love*, 2.

5. Sears, *Sex Radicals*, 23.

6. Sex radicalism receives scant attention, if any, in histories of woman suffrage such as Flexner, *Century of Struggle*; DuBois, *Feminism and Suffrage*; DuBois, *Woman Suffrage and Women's Rights*; Hoffert, *When Hens Crow*; Kraditor, *Ideas of the Woman Suffrage Movement*. For other aspects of late nineteenth-century women's social activism, see Bordin, *Woman and Temperance*; Duster, *Crusade for Justice*.

7. Mary Gove Nichols makes brief appearances in several histories because of her role in Spiritualism and the water-cure movement. For examples, see Braude, *Radical Spirits*; Cayleff, *Wash and Be Healed*; D'Emilio and Freedman, *Intimate Matters*; Gordon, *Woman's Body, Woman's Right*; Hayden, *Grand Domestic Revolution*; Mintz, *Moralists and Modernizers*; Walters, *American Reformers*; Wunderlich, *Low Living and High Thinking at Modern Times*. Gove Nichols tends to receive lengthier treatments in popular, as opposed to scholarly, works. She is dismissed in one sentence in Flexner, *Century of Struggle*, but receives more extensive treatment in Rugoff, *Prudery and Passion*. For biographical studies, see Noever, "Passionate Rebel"; Silver-Isenstadt, *Shameless*.

8. Biographers have struggled to capture the complex and contradictory life of Victoria Woodhull with varying degrees of success. Although dated, one work that succeeds in depicting the whole woman rather than one aspect of her personality is Sachs, "*Terrible Siren.*" Other studies include Brough, *The Vixens*; Gabriel, *Notorious Victoria*; Goldsmith, *Other Powers*; Johnston, *Mrs. Satan*; Marberry, *Vicky*; Underhill, *Woman Who Ran for President*.

9. For other studies in which historians have examined rural readers' correspondence in periodicals, see Brady, "Populism and Feminism in a Newspaper by and for Women of the Kansas Farmers' Alliance"; Folkerts, "Functions of the Reform Press"; Barthelme, *Women in the Texas Populist Movement.*

10. For a helpful overview of rural conditions during this era, see Hahn and Prude, *Countryside in the Age of Capitalist Transformation.*

11. See Jensen, "Sexuality on a Northern Frontier"; Jensen, "Death of Rosa."

12. Works in which sex radicals are categorized as freethinkers include Gordon, *Woman's Body, Woman's Right,* 94; Sears, *Sex Radicals;* Whitehead, *Freethought on the American Frontier;* Kirkley, *Rational Mothers and Infidel Gentlemen.*

13. For a discussion of early national optimism, see Bestor, *Backwoods Utopias,* 240.

14. Sellers, *Market Revolution,* 5. For discussions of individualism and agrarian self-sufficiency, see Foner, "Radical Individualism in America"; Hahn and Prude, *Countryside in the Age of Capitalist Transformation.*

15. For more about antebellum revivalism, see Hatch, *Democratization of American Christianity;* Butler, *Awash in a Sea of Faith.* For insight into the life and work of Charles Grandison Finney, see McLoughlin, "Charles Grandison Finney."

16. Johnson and Wilentz, *Kingdom of Matthias,* 9. Postmillennialists believed that the Kingdom of God on earth could be achieved through human effort toward righteousness and holiness and that Christ would return after that condition had been achieved. Premillennialists foresaw increasing levels of wickedness and believed that only Christ's Second Coming could inaugurate the thousand-year reign of justice and peace. The Millerites are one example of a premillennialist group.

17. Pitzer, *America's Communal Utopias,* 9. For further discussion of the utopian impulse during times of economic panic, see Guarneri, *Utopian Alternative,* 41, 66–67. For discussion of the fluidity of antebellum reform, see Walters, *American Reformers,* 72.

18. Sellers argues that religion "has long appealed more strongly to women as their main defense against patriarchal abuse" (*Market Revolution,* 227).

19. For analysis of feminism and Quakers, see Bacon, *Mothers of Feminism;* on Spiritualism as a feminist movement, see Braude, *Radical Spirits,* 124–33.

20. For further insight into antebellum comparisons of chattel slavery with marriage, see Hersh, *Slavery of Sex;* Lerner, *Grimke Sisters from South Carolina;* Stewart, *Holy Warriors,* 83, 90–93; Clark, "Matrimonial Bonds." For additional insight into antebellum abolitionism, see Friedman, *Gregarious Saints;* Perry, *Radical Abolition.*

21. For an extended discussion of Graham's philosophy, see Nissenbaum, *Sex, Diet, and Debility in Jacksonian America,* esp. chaps. 2 and 7. For additional insight into sexual attitudes and bodily reforms of this era, see Cott, "Passionlessness."

22. For Swedenborg's ideas about love, see Swedenborg, *Conjugial Love and Its Chaste Delights.* According to Alfred Habegger, "well-educated Protestants who were engaged in slipping their orthodox tethers" also were drawn to Swedenborgianism (*The Father,* 229).

23. Jane K. Williams-Hogan, "Swedenborg," 16.

24. Johnson and Wilentz, *Kingdom of Matthias,* 173. For additional insight into groups that grappled with inequalities in marriage, see Gaustad, *Rise of Adventism;* Shipps, *Mormonism;* Brooke, *Refiner's Fire.*

25. For discussions of utopian critiques of marriage, see Muncy, *Sex and Marriage in Utopian Communities;* Mandelker, *Religion, Society, and Utopia in Nineteenth-Century America;* Kern, *An Ordered Love;* Foster, *Religion and Sexuality;* Foster, *Women, Family, and Utopia.* Muncy argues that only utopian communities practicing celibacy had lasting power, whereas those practicing polygyny and complex marriage suffered from societal hostility. For an in-depth treatment of the Shakers, see Stein, *Shaker Experience in America.*

26. Polygamy, as opposed to polygyny, is marriage in which either spouse may have more than one mate simultaneously. In complex marriage, as practiced at the Oneida Community, members were discouraged from forming exclusive emotional attachments by the frequent exchange of sexual partners.

27. Noyes also advocated a birth control technique called "coitus reservatus," which required the male to avoid ejaculation while remaining in his partner's vagina until detumescence occurred. He governed which Oneida Community couples could reproduce because he believed in a form of eugenic breeding known as stirpiculture. For a biography of Noyes, see Thomas, *Man Who Would Be Perfect;* for more on the impact of Noyes's beliefs on the men and women who resided at the Oneida Community, see Fogarty, *Special Love/Special Sex.*

28. For a useful overview of Fourier and his vision of utopian life, see Beecher and Bienvenu, *Utopian Vision of Charles Fourier,* 1–75.

29. *The Phalanx,* which Brisbane began in 1840 (not to be confused with a later title of the same name), was followed in 1841 by *The Future* (endorsed by Horace Greeley and written by Brisbane), which was in turn succeeded by a daily front-page column in the *New York Tribune,* appearing from Mar. 1842 to Sept. 1843. Brisbane founded the second incarnation of *The Phalanx,* which became the primary organ of Fourierism in America, in Oct. 1843.

30. For a discussion of the influence of Swedenborgianism on Fourierists, see Hoover, "Influence of Swedenborg on the Religious Ideas of Henry James, Senior."

31. Guarneri, *Utopian Alternative,* 94.

32. Untitled biographical essay by Marx Edgeworth Lazarus, Lazarus Folder, Labadie Papers, Labadie Collection, Special Collections Department, University of Michigan, Ann Arbor (hereafter cited as Labadie Collection).

33. For further elaboration, see Guarneri, *Utopian Alternative,* 37, 56–60.

34. Ibid., 357.

35. Warren quoted in Martin, *Men against the State,* 14.

36. Wunderlich, *Low Living and High Thinking at Modern Times,* 74–78.

37. In the 1840s the *New York Tribune* publicized Fourier's ideas about the social and economic restructuring of civilization in a regular column, from which newspapers throughout the country extracted. Stephen Pearl Andrews published the full text of his debate with Greeley and James, along with some letters rejected by Greeley, in Andrews, *Love, Marriage, and Divorce and the Sovereignty of the Individual.*

38. Gordon, *Woman's Body, Woman's Right,* xix–xxii. For another discussion of the stages through which social movements pass, see Goodwyn, *Populist Moment,* chap. 2. For additional discussion, see Wood and Jackson, *Social Movements,* who argue that social movements "can be defined as unconventional groups that have varying degrees of for-

mal organization and that attempt to produce or prevent radical or reformist type of change" (3). See also Berlin, Introduction, vii–xxx.

39. One example of a regional organization is the New England Free Love League, founded in 1873 by Ezra Heywood to provide a venue from which Victoria Woodhull could lecture. See "Free Love League," *The Word* 5 (May 1876): 1–2.

40. For additional discussion of the relationship between public and private spheres, see Habermas, *Structural Transformation of the Public Sphere*.

41. Foucault, *History of Sexuality*, 58. Foucault studied cultures in terms of relationships, and while he was influenced by Marxist and Annales schools, he was a disciple of neither. He refused to see power as a form of repression exercised by a dominant class over a subservient class or as a tool employed by one individual or institution over another, but instead he viewed it as a complex web of forces.

Chapter 1: Revelations from a Life

1. Nichols, *Mary Lyndon;* Henry B. Blackwell to Lucy Stone, 17 Sept. 1855, in Wheeler, *Loving Warriors*, 146–48.

2. "Notes and Reviews," *Norton's Literary Gazette* 2 (2 July 1855): 268.

3. Elizabeth Cady Stanton to Susan B. Anthony, 1 Mar. 1853, in Stanton, *Elizabeth Cady Stanton as Revealed in Her Letters, Diary, and Reminiscences*, 48. In 1858, leaders at a women's rights convention tabled the free lover Stephen Pearl Andrews's resolution that declared: "The very first right of woman . . . was the right to [determine] . . . the very best relations under which the human race can be sired and generated." See "Woman's Rights Convention," *NYT*, 14 May 1858, 5.

4. Mary Gove was born in Goffstown, N.H., to William Neal and his second wife, Rebecca R. Neal. She was the fifth of six children. The family's enumeration appears in the federal population census for Goffstown, Hillsboro County, N.H., in 1810, and for Craftsbury, Orleans County, Vt., in the 1820 census.

5. Bestor, *Backwoods Utopias*, 240.

6. For biographical accounts of Mary Gove Nichols's life, see Blake, "Mary Gove Nichols, Prophetess of Health"; Noever, "Passionate Rebel"; Perry, "Mary Gove Nichols." For works that consider the lives of both Thomas L. Nichols and Mary Gove Nichols, see Silver-Isenstadt, *Shameless;* Stearns, "Two Forgotten New England Reformers." For fictional accounts of her life, see Nichols, *Mary Lyndon;* Webber, *Yieger's Cabinet, Spiritual Vampirism.*

7. Nichols, *Mary Lyndon*, 111–12.

8. See Nichols, *Woman's Work in Water Cure and Sanitary Education*, 11, for more on her miscarriages and how awareness of high infant mortality in her community motivated her to search medical texts for a solution.

9. Mary Gove began writing stories and poems for the *Boston Traveller* (later known as the *American Traveller*) at eighteen, albeit anonymously. A list of her early published works appears in Nichols, *Nichols' Health Manual*, 425–27. During the early years of their marriage, Hiram Gove forbade her to write and limited her reading to the Bible and religious books. See Nichols and Nichols, *Marriage*, 194.

10. Hiram Gove's opposition to his wife's pursuit of knowledge fueled her "burning zeal to save women from the miseries she saw, and from some that she endured." See

Nichols, *Nichols' Health Manual,* 29. See also pp. 20–21 for a discussion of books that had a significant impact on her.

11. Nichols and Nichols, *Marriage,* 193.

12. Gove Nichols describes Graham and his lectures in Gove, *Lectures to Ladies on Anatomy and Physiology,* v. For insight into Graham and his health reform theories, see Nissenbaum, *Sex, Diet, and Debility in Jacksonian America.*

13. Dr. Harriot K. Hunt boarded with the Goves when she visited Lynn in 1838 and described the school as well as Mary Gove's interest in Grahamism in *Glances and Glimpses,* 139.

14. Walters, *American Reformers,* 154. For Gove Nichols's ideas about marriage, see Nichols and Nichols, *Marriage,* 201.

15. Nichols, *Woman's Work in Water Cure and Sanitary Education,* 13.

16. Kerr, *Lucy Stone,* 73, 93–94.

17. Richards, "Mary Gove Nichols and John Neal," 341; Hunt, *Glances and Glimpses,* 139. For additional details about Gove Nichols's lecturing activities and her sense of mission, see Richards, in which Gove Nichols addresses her mission: "I have a great work before me" ("Mary Gove Nichols and John Neal," 343). For the description of her speaking ability, see Hale, *Woman's Record,* 757. For reference to her youthful experiences with corsets, see Nichols, *Mary Lyndon,* 66. For an account of Gove demonstrating tight lacing, see Nichols, *Nichols' Health Manual,* 23–24.

18. A Friend, "Case of Mary S. Gove," *The Reformer* 1 (11th month 1839): 24.

19. Gove, *Solitary Vice.* The four articles, all published under the pseudonym A. B. and appearing in the *Boston Medical and Surgical Journal,* are "Critical Observations of Dr. Durkee's 'Remarks on Scrofula,'" 21 (18 Dec. 1839), 297–99; "Quotations and Remarks on the Blood, No. 1," 22 (19 Feb. 1840): 24–27; "Quotations and Remarks on the Blood, No. 2," 22 (26 Feb. 1840): 43–45; "Respiratory Apparatus—Mr. Bronson, &c." 22 (26 Aug. 1840): 49–51.

20. Richards, "Mary Gove Nichols and John Neal," 352–54. She sought Neal's advice about the circumstances under which her husband could remove Elma from her custody.

21. Brisbane, *Social Destiny of Man.* By 1843, Fuller, Stanton, and Gove were writing for the Fourierist publication *The Phalanx.* Such Fourier sexual theories as the value of variety in sexual partnerships were not revealed to American readers until the late 1840s; hence, they did not stand in the way of the trio's embrace of Fourierism. For an example of Mary Gove's contributions, see *The Phalanx* 1 (5 Feb. 1844): 64–65.

22. For a fuller account of her interactions with the Brook Farm community, see Guarneri, *Utopian Alternative,* 198.

23. Gove, *Lectures to Ladies on Anatomy and Physiology,* 273.

24. For more on her career as a water-cure physician, see Nichols, *Woman's Work in Water Cure and Sanitary Education.*

25. Cayleff, *Wash and Be Healed,* 32.

26. Marx Edgeworth Lazarus, born in 1822, was the son of a Jewish father and a Christian mother. According to his autobiography, he held "Jesus as the first historic anarchist, & R. W. Emerson as his philosophic disciple." His views, he wrote, were closely "akin to those of E. C. Walker." See Lazarus Folder, Labadie Papers, Labadie Collection.

27. For discussion of her treatment of working-class women, see Nichols, *Woman's Work in Water Cure and Sanitary Education,* 24, 44–48.

28. An explanation of how she came to blame marriage for gynecological illnesses may be found in Mrs. Mary S. Gove, "Case of Uterine Haemorrhage [*sic*]," *WCJ* 1 (15 Jan. 1846): 55; Nichols and Nichols, *Marriage*, 222.

29. Her early poems and short stories appeared anonymously, but beginning in the 1840s she used the pseudonym "Mary Orme." Edgar Allan Poe, whose wife was one of Mary Gove's patients, exposed Mary Orme's true identity in "The Literati of New York City, No. III," *Godey's Magazine and Lady's Book* 33 (July 1846): 16. Mary Gove's stories (written under the pseudonym Mary Orme) in *Godey's* include "Marrying a Genius," 32 (Sept. 1844): 104–7; "The Artist," 30 (Apr. 1845): 154–56; "The Evil and the Good," 31 (July 1845): 36–38; "Mary Pierson," 32 (Jan. 1846): 39–41; "Minna Harmon; or, The Ideal and the Practical," 37 (Dec. 1848): 335–38. Poems appeared in *The United States Magazine and Democratic Review* 18 (Feb. 1846): 141; 18 (May 1846): 388. She also published *Uncle John; or, "It Is Too Much Trouble"* (1846).

30. For a discussion of the literary salon in which Mary Gove participated, see Stern, "House of the Expanding Doors."

31. "Letter from Dr. T. L. Nichols," *American Vegetarian and Health Journal* 1 (Feb. 1851): 41–42.

32. Nichols, *Journal in Jail*, 11. Found guilty, he spent four months in the Erie County jail.

33. Ibid., 81.

34. Gove Nichols published two novels in 1849—*Agnes Morris; or, The Heroine of Domestic Life* and *The Two Loves; or, Eros and Anteros*—and *Experience in Water-Cure*, while Thomas L. Nichols published *Woman in All Ages and Nations*.

35. Mrs. R. B. Gleason, "A Visit to the American Water Establishments," *WCJ* 9 (Jan. 1850): 13.

36. Gove Nichols used her pregnancy as an occasion to prepare two instructive articles: "Water-Cure in Childbirth—Again," *WCJ* 9 (Apr. 1850): 117; "Maternity; and the Water-Cure of Infants," *WCJ* 11 (Mar. 1851): 57–59.

37. Letters between Gove Nichols and Stanton are reproduced in the Elizabeth Cady Stanton Papers, microfilm edition. See Gove Nichols to "My Dear Friend" [Elizabeth Cady Stanton], 21 Aug. [1851]; Stanton to Gove Nichols, 21 Aug. 1852; and Stanton to Gove Nichols, 31 Aug. 1852, reel 7, frames 103 and 161–63, and reel 14, frame 1020. In general, the letters reflect a cordial relationship; however, a letter from Gove Nichols to Gerrit Smith, with copy to Stanton, suggests that Stanton "was *shocked* at the *impropriety*" of Gove Nichols receiving Smith alone in her parlor. See reel 7, frame 162.

38. Lazarus, *Love vs. Marriage*.

39. Nichols discussed such topics as orgasm, contraceptive methods, masturbation, monogamy, and abortion and included drawings of male and female genitalia.

40. The letter, from "Villager," appeared in the *NYTr*, 21 July 1853, 5. One of the female students who left the school gave Trall information that Nichols believed was used to discredit his school. Nichols responded to the accusation in "American Hydropathic Institute," *NYTr*, 22 July 1853, 7.

41. Webber, *Yieger's Cabinet*. Mary Gove Nichols attempted to dismiss the work as the product of an insane mind made worse after she denied him permission to marry Elma.

42. The Nicholses provided readers of *NJ* 1 (Apr. 1853): 7 with a description of Modern Times. For one analysis of that utopian community, see Wunderlich, *Low Living and High Thinking at Modern Times*.

43. Wunderlich, *Low Living and High Thinking at Modern Times,* 208 n.58.

44. For Blackwell's assessment of Gove Nichols, see Wheeler, *Loving Warriors,* 146–47.

45. Baym, *Woman's Fiction,* 257. For further analysis of *Mary Lyndon,* see Danielson, "Healing Women's Wrongs"; Myerson, "Mary Gove Nichols's *Mary Lyndon.*"

46. Fern, *Ruth Hall.* This novel portrays an economically independent woman who attains happiness without a man's assistance. Child, *Fact and Fiction.* For further insight into Child's views of marriage, see Karcher, *First Woman in the Republic,* esp. chap. 14. Other examples of novels that explore the politics and trials of heterosexual marriage include: Fern, *Rose Clark;* Phelps, *Story of Avis;* Child, *Philothea, a Romance.* In *Rose Clark,* Fern explores the subject of male sexual demands in marriage, portraying a sexually liberated heroine who seeks freedom to refuse rather than to submit.

47. Mintz, *Moralists and Modernizers,* 6–7.

48. Gove, *Lectures to Ladies on Anatomy and Physiology,* 211–12. Gove did not "plead for the equality of the sexes" but instead sought to prove that "men are better adapted to some pursuits, and women to others." For more on her views of gender differences, see also Nichols and Nichols, *Nichols' Medical Miscellanies,* 42.

49. The quote is from *Mary Lyndon,* 384. Publicity for the book compared it to Harriet Beecher Stowe's novel, noting that like "all great original efforts of genius," it was being "admired and abused." See "The Predicted Run Verified," *NYT,* 30 July 1855, 1. For a week's earlier advertisement, see *NYT,* 25 July 1855, 1.

50. "A Bad Book Gibbeted," *NYT,* 17 Aug. 1855, 2. For discussion of women as weak-minded readers, see A. B., "The Marriage Institution," *The Lily* 7 (1 June 1855): 82.

51. "The Free Love System," *Littell's Living Age* 49 (29 Sept. 1855): 815–21.

52. For a review of *Mary Lyndon* in the *Chicago Daily Democratic Press,* see "Mary G. Nichols," 21 Nov. 1855, 3. For discussion of the spread of free love ideas from New York to the Midwest, see the following articles in the same title: "New York Agent Organizes Free Love Leagues in the West," 21 Nov. 1855, 2; "Free Love Association Organized in Columbus, Ohio," 31 Dec. 1855, 6.

53. "A Bad Book Gibbeted," 2.

54. "Free Love System," 820. For further discussion of unitary homes, see Hayden, *Grand Domestic Revolution,* esp. chap. 5.

55. "Notes and Reviews," *Norton's Literary Gazette,* new series, 2 (2 July 1855): 269; "New Publications," *New York Daily Tribune,* 4 Aug. 1855, 3.

56. "Critical Notices," *SR* 1 (Mar. 1856): 90.

57. "A Bad Book Gibbeted," 2.

58. "A Letter from Mrs. Gove Nichols," *NYT,* 11 Oct. 1858, 5. Other reviews appeared in *New York Commercial Advertiser,* the *Home Journal,* and the *Savannah (Ga.)Journal and Courier.*

59. "The Free Lovers: Practical Operation of the Free-Love League in the City of New York," *NYT,* 10 Oct. 1855, 1–2; "A Rich Development," *NYT,* 19 Oct. 1855, 4.

60. Anonymous Illinois correspondent, *NJ* 3 (2 Sept. 1854): 29.

61. According to this correspondent, her husband "laughs at my enthusiasm." See Anonymous, "Vital Correspondence," *NJ* 2 (13 May 1854): 2.

62. Anonymous Iowa correspondent, *NJ* 3 (2 Sept. 1854): 30.

63. Anonymous Illinois Correspondent, *NJ* 3 (2 Sept. 1854): 29.

64. "American Hydropathic Institute," *The Lily* 4 (Mar. 1852): 22; A. B., "The Marriage Institution," 82.

65. "A Letter from Mrs. Gove Nichols," 5.

66. Gove Nichols described being mobbed by men and women in New York City and Connecticut in "Letter from Mrs. Gove Nichols," *WCJ* 14 (Nov. 1852): 112.

67. For the reference to a "loving shield," see "From a Lady of the Empire State," *NM* 2 (Jan. 1856): 92; for the reference to the "timid reformer," see "Vital Correspondence," *NJ* 2 (18 Mar. 1854): 3.

68. Gove Nichols said that she would "gladly write to each individually" if her strength permitted. This quote is from "Letter from Mrs. Gove Nichols," *WCJ* 15 (Jan. 1853): 11. Her reference to the "mass of women" appears in Gove Nichols, "Water-Cure in Childbirth— Again," 117; the reference to spiritual kinship is from "Friendly Greetings," *NM* 3 (Dec. 1856): 332. For more instances of her relationship with readers, see *WCJ* 14 (Nov. 1852): 112–13; *NM* 3 (Dec. 1856): 327.

69. Her expulsion from the Society of Friends, her divorce from Hiram Gove, her long-standing advocacy of spiritual affinities, and her implicit portrayal of the latter as more sacred than legal spouses further reinforced this impression. The term "infidel," widely used in the nineteenth century, referred to people who opposed Christianity. For further information, see Marty, *The Infidel*. The quotation is from "Atheism," *NJ* 2 (25 Feb. 1854): 2. For more insight, see Mary Gove Nichols to Paulina Wright Davis, Sept. 1870, in the Elizabeth Cady Stanton Papers, microfilm edition, reel 14, frame 1020.

70. For examples of Gove Nichols's use of religious rhetoric, see "A Lecture on Woman's Dresses," *WCJ* 12 (Aug. 1851): 36; "Letter from Mrs. Gove Nichols," *WCJ* 14 (Nov. 1852): 112–13.

71. For the reference to "Divinity," see Gove Nichols, "Human Culture—No. 7," *NJ* 1 (1 Oct. 1853): 51; for the "we believe" quotation, see Gove Nichols, "City of Modern Times," *NJ* 1 (July 1853): 38.

72. Gove Nichols, "Human Culture—No. 4," *NJ* 1 (July 1853): 29.

73. Discussions of her patients are found in Nichols, *Woman's Work in Water Cure and Sanitary Education,* chaps. 4–7.

74. Nichols, *Nichols' Health Manual,* 94.

75. "The Progressive Union," *NM* (July 1855), 130. While the union did not solicit dues, it encouraged voluntary gifts of money or property. See also Nichols, *Work of Reform*.

76. *NM* (July 1855), 131.

77. The earlier influence of Robert Dale Owen's utopian vision in the 1820s had primed residents—especially those living in the southwestern portion of the state—for the reception of Fourierism in the 1840s. According to John Humphrey Noyes, fully one-third of the Fourierist phalanxes established during the 1840s were within Ohio's borders. For insight into social radicalism in nineteenth-century Ohio, see Noyes, *History of American Socialisms,* 18. Noyes attributes eight Fourieristic phalanxes to Ohio, in contrast to Guarneri, who claims the state had five (*Utopian Alternative,* 154).

78. Several radical reform conventions met in Ohio during the 1850s, among them the "Friends of Progress" at Yellow Springs in Sept. 1856; a meeting at Milan in Oct. 1856; a free meeting held at Ravenna in the summer of 1857; and a convention at Berlin Heights in the fall of 1857. Ravenna continued to be the site of social radicalism; a "national" free

love convention met there in Dec. 1873. For further information, see *LLB*, 5 Nov. 1898, 354; and Francis Barry, letter to the editor, *SR* 3 (Mar. 1857): 79.

79. Nichols, *Free Love;* Nichols, "Oration."

80. An ardent abolitionist and Spiritualist, Nicholson and his family had participated in the "Prairie Home" experiment, a communal farm near Urbana, Ohio.

81. As collateral, Mary Gove Nichols gave Nicholson the stereotyped plates to some earlier works. See Gove Nichols to Nicholson, [1855]; A. Brooke to Friend Jane [Nicholson], 22 June 1855; Aug. O. Moore to Valentine Nicholson, all from the Valentine Nicholson Papers, Indiana Historical Society, Indianapolis. Brooke noted the deaths of two treated by Nicholses methods.

82. For a discussion of Memnonia, see Stearns, "Memnonia."

83. Sophia Hawthorne to Mary Mann, 12 Aug. 1856, Mann Bibliography 3713-A, Antiochiana Collections, Antioch College Archives, Yellow Springs, Ohio (hereafter cited as Antiochiana Collections). Mann attributed a decline in the number of women in the entering class of 1856 to "the infernal Nichols." See Mann to Austin Craig, 20 Oct. 1856, Mann Bibliography 3752, Antiochiana Collections. Local residents met to determine how to "nip it [Memnonia] in the bud." See "Local and Miscellaneous," *Daily Springfield (Ohio) Nonpareil,* 7 Mar. 1856, 3.

84. Jared Gage, "Address to the Friends, Officers, and Students of Antioch College," [1856], Antiochiana Collections. Gage's mother had been one of Mary Gove Nichols's patients. See also "Minutes of the Adelphian Union Literary Society," Nov. 7, 1856, Mann Bibliography 3755.

85. "Law of Progression in Harmony," *NM* (July 1855), 109.

86. Gleason, "From Free-Love to Catholicism," 300.

87. Saphronia Powers, "Then and Now," *AoF* 1 (4 Mar. 1858): 2; and "Dr. and Mrs. Nichols," *VG* 1 (2 May 1857): 68. The Nicholses moved to England in 1861, where they continued to write, advocate health reforms, and practice water cure until their deaths, she in 1884, he in 1902. For discussion of their years in England, see Silver-Isenstadt, "Pure Pleasure."

Chapter 2: The Power of Print

1. Julia C. Coon, *AJE* 2 (Jan. 1908): 44.

2. "From a Friend in Boston," *SR* 2 (Dec. 1856): 192.

3. Gifts in kind included books and pamphlets, often written by the donor, which editors could advertise and sell.

4. The literacy rate for native-born whites was over 90 percent by 1860. For information on the spread of literacy in nineteenth-century America, see Soltow and Stevens, *Rise of Literacy and the Common School in the United States;* Kaestle, *Literacy in the United States;* Stevenson, *Victorian Homefront.*

5. The Post Office Act of 1852 eliminated the necessity for subscribers to pay postage upon delivery, shifted the burden to the publisher, and reduced rates. The cost to mail an average magazine decreased from 6½ cents in 1845 to 1½ cents in 1852. See Mott, *History of American Magazines, 1850–1865,* vol. 2, 18–19. For further information about the economics of early nineteenth-century publishing, see Zboray, *Fictive People.*

6. See Newton, *Learning to Behave;* Haller, "From Maidenhood to Menopause." According to R. Laurence Moore and Timothy L. Smith, a Protestant consensus continued to exert

a significant influence on American manners and morals even after separation of church and state. For further discussion, see Moore, *Selling God;* Smith, *Revivalism and Social Reform.* See Spurlock, *Free Love,* 21, for a discussion of books on marriage published in the 1840s and 1850s.

7. For discussion of the narrowing of acceptable female sexual behavior that occurred in the eighteenth and nineteenth centuries, see Cott, "Passionlessness," esp. 220. The HarpWeek electronic index to *Harper's Weekly* for 1857–65 contains 466 entries for marriage and 61 for divorce. For examples of articles on marriage in the *Liberator,* see "Marriage," 21 Apr. 1854, 61; "Free Love and Marriage," 26 Sept. 1856, 150. For articles in the *WCJ* see "Marriage," 4 (Aug. 1847): 251–52; "Discussion of Marriage," 14 (Dec. 1852): 42; "The Marriage Question" 15 (5 Jan. 1853), 58. *WCJ* also included book reviews on this topic. For examples, see 1 (1 Feb. 1846): 79; 4 (Aug. 1847): 242–44. See *The Lily* (temperance, published 1849–56), *The Sibyl* (dress reform, published 1856–64), and *Una* (women's rights, published 1853–55).

8. Davidson, *Revolution and the Word,* vii, 46.

9. Russo and Kramarae, *Radical Women's Press of the 1850s,* 5. For an additional work on nineteenth-century periodicals, see Price and Smith, *Periodical Literature in Nineteenth-Century America.*

10. Even some who opposed free love admitted that the book had set them to thinking "like no other work" (*SR* 1 [Jan. 1856]: 23). Sales figures are not available on a systematic basis, but an Ohio-based correspondent noted in *NJ* 3 (2 Sept. 1854): 30, that approximately seventeen thousand copies had circulated. The reference to "love children" is found in Nichols, *Esoteric Anthropology,* 142.

11. Patterson, a member of a Darke County utopian experiment known as the Rising Star Community, edited the *Social Revolutionist* in southwestern Ohio until the fall of 1857, at which time he moved north with his printing press to join the growing numbers of sex radicals settling in Berlin Heights. The Berlin Heights Free Lovers—Francis and Cordelia Barry and the veteran sex reformer C. M. Overton—published forty-eight issues of the weekly *Age of Freedom* in 1858. It was followed by thirty-four issues of a weekly, *Good Time Coming,* in 1859. In 1871, the Berlin Heights socialists published yet another periodical, *New Campaign,* but it only lasted a few issues.

12. For an account of this incident, see "To Our Readers," *SR* 4 (Dec. 1857): 189. Members of the community also threatened local sex radicals' lives and property.

13. Stoehr, *Free Love in America,* 39. For a discussion of efforts to restrict the press during the Civil War years, see Emery, *Press and America,* 296–97; Donald, *Lincoln,* 380; Harper, "Ohio Press in the Civil War;" Randall, "Newspaper Problem in Its Bearing upon Military Secrecy during the Civil War." With the exception of Francis Barry, who moved to Cleveland and began another reform publication entitled the *New Republic* (5 Apr. to 11 Oct. 1862), the free love editors of the 1850s stopped publishing.

14. Nichols, *Forty Years of American Life,* 7.

15. Ziegler, *Advocates of Peace in Antebellum America,* 178–79. According to Ziegler, nonresistants tended to struggle economically, whereas members of the American Peace Society generally came from more prosperous and socially privileged families.

16. Braude, *Radical Spirits,* 3–4, 84–90. For an example of a trance medium who delivered a message on free love, see Doten, *Free Love and Affinity.*

17. "The Free Love Question in the New York Spiritualist Convention," *KoH* 1 (July 1864): 3.

18. For Cook's definition of free love and his ideas about the love principle, see "Low Spirits," *KoH* 1 (June 1864): 2. For his ideas about monogamy, see "Psychometrical Delineation of Thomas Cook," *KoH* 1 (Sept. 1864): 1; "How Strange!" *KoH* 2 (May 1865): 2.

19. Cook fathered at least five children and possibly one born well after he proclaimed his marriage to Harriet Cook dissolved. For examples of women who felt attracted to Cook and his ideas, see "More Talk about the Kingdom of Heaven," *KoH* 2 (June 1865): 2, in which an anonymous woman wrote: "I feel very much drawn to you through your paper." For another example, see *KoH* 2 (July 1865): 1, in which a woman expressed agreement with Cook's "free love principle" and indicated that she had been an "independent woman" since her companion's death the previous January.

20. For Cook's ideas about the Golden Rule as applied to love, see *KoH* 2 (Apr. 1865): 2; for additional insight into his beliefs, see "Spiritualism and Institutionalism," *KoH* 2 (July 1865): 2; "The Social Question Again," *KoH* 2 (Aug. 1865): 2.

21. For examples of women's enthusiasm for Cook's ideas, see Mrs. Mary of Sherman's Hollow, N.Y., to Cook, *KoH* 1 (Oct. 1864): 4; Anonymous to Cook, *KoH* 2 (June 1865): 1. The comparison of free love to war is from "Free Love," *The Optimist and Kingdom of Heaven* 3 (Jan. 1867): 4.

22. *Woodhull and Claflin's Weekly* ceased publication in June 1872 due to inadequate financial resources but resumed in November of that year.

23. Sachs, *"Terrible Siren,"* 198, provides a discussion of the formation of clubs among Woodhull's readers. A. J. Stowe, San Jose, organized a club of ten readers, according to *WCW*, 22 Mar. 1873, 5. The quote is from *WCW*, 11 Oct. 1873, 8.

24. For an excellent biography of Ezra Heywood, see Blatt, *Free Love and Anarchism*. For a shorter treatment, see Blatt, "Ezra Hervey Heywood."

25. Angela Heywood, a diligent housekeeper with young children, differed from many other prominent female sex radicals in that she spent most of her life in one state, Massachusetts. According to Blatt, Comstock never arrested her because he "did not see women as significant actors in the world" (*Free Love and Anarchism*, 147). For a biographical sketch, see Battan, "Angela Fiducia Tilton Heywood."

26. "Yes, I am owned by Mr. C. C. B. Sawyer, he has a deed for me and if ever I take that deed out of his hands, it will not be to put into [*sic*] the hands of another." See Mattie E. B. Sawyer, "Wayside Pencillings," *HC* 5 (14 Oct. 1876).

27. For references to the ways by which the Hulls and Sawyer supported their publication, see *HC* 5 (17 June 1876): 7. Mattie Sawyer's breakdown is discussed in *HC* 7 (11 Aug. 1877): 8. The reference to subscribers is from *HC* 7 (28 July 1877): 8.

28. Sears, *Sex Radicals*, 49. Throughout this work, I convert Moses Harman's Era of Man dating system to standard practice. For instance, E.M. 286 is given as 1886.

29. Supplement, *LLB*, 2 Mar. 1894. As a Liberal League paper in Kansas, *Lucifer, the Light-Bearer* had sixty-five local subscribers in 1884, but this figure began to decline once the paper's focus shifted from liberalism to anarchism and sexual reform. See *LLB*, 11 July 1884. According to Sears, the *LLB* subscription list totaled from six to seven hundred in 1885 (only a few more than the number of subscribers that Benjamin Tucker had for his anarchist periodical, *Liberty*) and stabilized at fifteen hundred by 1890 (*Sex Radicals*, 64, 99).

30. Mrs. Susie P., Philadelphia, *LLB*, 25 May 1894, 4.

31. For a discussion of "venereal ulcers" resulting from oral sex, see Richard V. O'Neill, M.D., "A Physician's Testimony," *LLB*, 14 Feb. 1890, 3.

32. For further information about the Comstock Law, see Beisel, *Imperiled Innocents;* Brodie, *Contraception and Abortion in Nineteenth-Century America.* For further insight into Moses Harman's convictions, see Sears, *Sex Radicals,* 112–14, 263–64; *Summary of Prosecutions against Lucifer, the Light-Bearer, and Its Editor, Moses Harman; The Persecution and Appreciation.*

33. For Walker and Harman's editorial policy, see *FPl* 1 (19 May 1888): 2.

34. See *Firebrand* 1 (27 Jan. 1895).

35. Oliver O. Verity, "Something about *Discontent,*" *Discontent* 1 (11 May 1898); 1 (4 Jan. 1899); 3 (10 July 1901); Thomas Sheedy, *Discontent* 2 (14 June 1899): 1; E. J. Schellhous, *Discontent* 2 (12 July 1899): 4. For more on the publication history of *Discontent* and its successor, *Demonstrator,* see LeWarne, *Utopias on Puget Sound,* 174–85.

36. According to Sears, Moses and Lillian Harman reputedly modeled the *American Journal of Eugenics* after the *American Journal of Sociology* and the *North American Review* (*Sex Radicals,* 267). For more on Moses Harman, see Sears, *Sex Radicals,* esp. chap. 2; Kern, "Moses Harman."

37. Anonymous, *FPr* 4 (Oct. 1893): 6.

38. "From a friend in Iowa," *NM* 2 (Jan. 1856): 93; J. D., Elkhorn, Wis., *SR* 3 (June 1857): 189.

39. O. D. H., Worcester, Mass., *SR* 3 (Mar. 1857): 89.

40. William Denton, "Registration," *SR* 2 (Aug. 1856): 57.

41. *NM* served as the official organ of the Progressive Union. For its prospectus, see the end flyleaf of *NM* 4 (Dec. 1856). See *Circular* n.s. 7 (27 June 1870): 116, for the number of Progressive Union members on the various lists.

42. "List of Varietists," *SR* 3 (Mar. 1857): 157. According to "The Social Democracy-Registration," *SR* 4 (Nov. 1857): 135–36, the list contained nearly five hundred names, of which over one-fifth were from Ohio.

43. For insight into the life of an itinerant lecturer, see Chase, *Life-line of the Lone One,* 114. For a list of communities visited by Francis Barry, see "From Francis Barry," *SR* 1 (May 1856): 147. Another popular lecturer, William Denton, described his interactions with audiences in "Notes from the Lecturing Field," *VG* 1 (20 June 1857): 124.

44. Mrs. J. M. S., Bay City, Mich., *WCW,* 3 Jan. 1874, 7. Through her lectures, Woodhull found an effective way to extend her reach to middle-class women. An account from a St. Joseph, Mo., newspaper (excerpted in *WCW,* 31 Jan. 1874, 11) noted that Woodhull's audience was composed "of our most solid and sensible citizens."

45. For insight into how women gained access to sex radical works, see C. M. Overton, "How to Read the Bible," *New Republic* 1 (10 May 1862): 52–53.

46. Mrs. Malachi Ellis, Westmoreland, N.Y., *WCW,* 13 May 1876, 6.

47. For an example of a correspondent expressing appreciation for the role women played in publishing sex radical periodicals, see "Letter from G. A. H.," *SR* 3 (Mar. 1857): 88.

48. The reference to "Our Sister Contributors" is found in *SR* 3 (June 1857): 192. The references to women recruiting subscribers are from "The Mormons," *NM* 2 (Jan. 1856): 95; "An Agent Worth Having," *NJ* 1 (July 1853): 30. For information about free conven-

tions, especially those in which free lovers participated, see "Call for a Convention," *SR* 2 (Sept. 1856): flyleaf; and "Convention at Berlin," *SR* 4 (Sept. 1857): 89. Women comprised six of twelve individuals who signed the call in 1856 and ten of thirty-six in 1857.

49. *SR* editors announced that they had approximately four hundred paying subscribers in "A Talk about the Social Revolutionist," *SR* 2 (Nov. 1856): 189. For information about subscribers to *VG*, see "Subscriptions Received," *VG* 1 (14 Mar. 1857): 6; "Payments," *VG* 1 (4 Apr. 1857): 35; "Payments," *VG* 1 (2 May 1857): 70; "Agents for the *Vanguard* on the Reserve," *VG* 2 (18 Dec. 1858): 3. In "Our Position and Prospects," *VG* 1 (11 Apr. 1857): 44, the editors claimed to have 377 reliable subscribers. *The Lily* circulation statistics are from Mott, *History of American Magazines, 1850–1865*, 50. Mott states that only a few periodicals— *Harper's Weekly, Godey's Lady's Book,* and *Frank Leslie's Illustrated*—had a national circulation between 1850 and 1865 (103).

50. For an example of conflicting numbers of subscribers given in the same issue, see *NJ* 1 (Aug. 1853): 37. For a discussion of "clubbing," see *NJ* 2 (18 Feb. 1854): 3.

51. "A Call for Facts," *SR* 3 (Feb. 1857): 64.

52. "Letter from O. D. H.," *SR* 3 (Mar. 1857): 89.

53. Jane A. Simpson, N.Y., *WCW*, 3 Apr. 1875, 3.

54. "The Sibyl," *SR* 4 (July 1857): 30.

55. Albina Washburn, Loveland, Colo., *LLB*, 8 Dec. 1893. C. P. and S. A. Chambers of Ballston, Ore., advocated in 1893 that people read articles to prospective subscribers rather than giving them copies they might burn without reading. See *LLB*, 24 Nov. 1893, 4. For other discussions of *LLB* copies shared, see Mrs. P. Clark, Ionia, Mich., *LLB*, 26 Jan. 1894; Portia Gage, Vineland, N.J., *LLB*, 9 Feb. 1894; and Mrs. S. Van Arman, *LLB*, 29 June 1894.

56. Of the 1,135 correspondents for whom identity is known, 111 appear in more than one sample.

57. In Oct. 1873, for instance, Victoria Woodhull announced that the *Weekly* had adopted a policy of requiring correspondents to include names and addresses with their submissions. See editorial, *WCW*, 4 Oct. 1873, 7.

58. Without names, readers might assume that a publication consisted primarily of an editor's opinion. *Nichols' Journal, Nichols' Monthly,* and *Foundation Principles,* for instance, consisted largely of excerpts from the Nicholses' own writings. In contrast, the *Social Revolutionist* and *Lucifer* published lengthy essays from a variety of contributors. Although published lists of subscribers are not comprehensive and sometimes contain incomplete information or errors, they remain the best source for identifying the names of women and men who sympathized with the sex radical cause.

59. G. P., Vineland, N.J., *LLB*, 2 Mar. 1894; Lois Waisbrooker, *FPr*, 1 Oct. 1894, 4.

60. Mary W. Conway, *LLB*, 18 Jan. 1895, 4, in reference to Anthony Comstock, who led a national campaign to eliminate the distribution of obscene material through the mail.

61. I have not attempted to compile an aggregate geographical distribution of readership between 1853 and 1908 because of correspondents' geographic mobility. Instead, I chose to take readership snapshots at intervals to examine change over time.

62. In 1853–54, *NJ* also had few subscribers in the South. A South Carolina correspondent informed Mary Gove Nichols that "a few starved souls here are feasting on your words." See S. C. to Mrs. Nichols, *NJ* 2 (18 Feb. 1854): 3.

63. For further discussion of geographic mobility in Ohio, see Vartorella, "The Other 'Peculiar Institution,'" 189.

64. See Mattie Sawyer, "Home Pencillings," *HC* 6 (16 June 1877), for references to the Boston and Maine Railway. When the lecturer Juliet H. Severance traveled from Wisconsin to New England in 1877, she relied on *Hull's Crucible* to announce her availability for lecturing engagements en route.

65. Goldman, *Living My Life*, 249–53. Historians of nineteenth-century rural women have documented their material and economic circumstances but have devoted little attention to their intellectual lives. See, for example, Faragher, "History from the Inside-Out;" Fink, *Agrarian Women;* Fink, *Open Country Iowa.* For explorations into farm women's social and political lives, see Marti, *Women of the Grange;* Osterud, "Gender and the Transition to Capitalism in Rural America"; Barthelme, *Women in the Texas Populist Movement;* Goldberg, *An Army of Women.*

66. Mrs. Eliza Cooper, Eureka, Calif., *WCW,* 24 July 1875, 3; Abbie C. Culver, Madrid, Iowa, *FPr* 5 (1 Sept. 1894): 1; N. M. M., Junction City, Wash., *FPr* 5 (15 July 1894): 1.

67. A. W., Iowa, *LLB,* 17 June 1903, 182; E. F. Curtis, Farmington, Ohio, *LLB,* 15 June 1894; Jesse S. Perkins, Gaines Station, Mich., *LLB,* 9 Feb. 1894. For examples of letters from octogenarians, see O. Child, Moline, Ill., *LLB,* 9 Feb. 1894; J. Hacker, Berlin, N.J., *LLB,* 25 Nov. 1887; H. A. Richardson, Santa Barbara, Calif., *LLB,* 15 June 1894.

68. James Jefferson, Providence, R.I., *WCW,* 29 Mar. 1873, 5.

69. This is in contrast to Spurlock's findings in *Free Love,* in which he portrays antebellum sex radicalism as an intellectual avant garde. Focusing on such individuals as Stephen Pearl Andrews and Marx Edgeworth Lazarus and the urban women and men who participated in the New York Free Love Club, he downplays the existence and significance of grassroots free lovers.

70. According to Jennie Austin, her mother preferred to spend money on subscriptions to *LLB* and *Free Society,* not material comforts. See Jennie Austin, undated manuscript circa 1934, Kate Austin Papers, Labadie Collection.

71. For the reference to "impecunious," see S. G. Dodge, Memphis, Tenn., *The Word* 1 (July 1873): 3. For the reference to "bread and butter," see Thomas Lee, Cleveland, Ohio, *LLB,* 17 Aug. 1894, 3.

72. For examples of impoverished subscribers, see Rosa Rhea Parkhurst, Ballwin, Mo., *LLB,* 13 Apr. 1894, 3; Mrs. Elizabeth Hughes, San Francisco, Calif., *The Word* 3 (Mar. 1875): 3. For a discussion about Harmon's willingness to keep subscribers on his list even when they failed to pay, see Mrs. Gail Barnes, Loveland, Colo., *LLB,* 15 June 1894, who hoped that *Lucifer* did "not have *all* poor subscribers." For the Waisbrooker quote, see "A Prostitute," *FP* 4 (15 Dec. 1893): 3.

73. For the reference to "Monster, Monopoly," see Henry Baird, *LLB,* 1 June 1894; for Coxey's Army, see Lydia Blackstone, *LLB,* 27 Apr. 1894. Coxey's Army marched from Massillon, Ohio, to Washington, D.C., in the spring of 1894.

74. Martin discusses the differences between American and European anarchism (*Men against the State*, 5–8). For other classic studies of American anarchism, see Nelson, *Beyond the Martyrs;* Reichert, *Partisans of Freedom.*

75. See F. E. K., "The Sexual Freedom of Women," *Liberty* 5 (31 Mar. 1888), 5.

76. Marsh, *Anarchist Women,* 20–21. For other work on anarchist women, see Avrich, *An American Anarchist;* Falk, *Love, Anarchy, and Emma Goldman.* Although his focus is the life of Ezra Heywood, Blatt's *Free Love and Anarchism* provides important insights into the lives of several anarchist women.

77. Women's involvement in freethought merits further research. Existing studies include Underwood, *Heroines of Freethought;* Miller, "Kate Austin"; Whitehead and Muhrer, *Freethought on the American Frontier.* Most histories of freethought have focused on men and their ideas. Classic monographs include Porter, *400 Years of Freethought;* Warren, *American Freethought;* MacDonald, *Fifty Years of Freethought;* Post, *Popular Freethought in America.* More recent scholarship includes Marty, *The Infidel;* Kirkley, *Rational Mothers and Infidel Gentlemen.*

78. Readers who criticized organized religion for subordinating women include Charlotte Barber, Clyde, Ohio, *WCW,* 15 Nov. 1873, 4; W. Chamberlain, *FPr,* 15 Sept. 1894, 5. For examples of postbellum correspondents who wrote about their belief in a divine being and the "Good Time Coming," see Eliza D. Burns, *WCW,* 22 Oct. 1870, 3; Nellie L. Davis, Louisville, Kent., *WCW,* 5 Dec. 1874, 5; Anonymous, *WCW,* 11 Mar. 1876, 3.

79. Alliances, writes Goldberg, appealed to Anglo farm families whose "sense of community on the Plains was transient and fractured" (*An Army of Women,* 128). Jeffrey Ostler argues that in the case of Populism, its absence in states east of the Missouri River "does not obviate the hardship and discontent prevalent throughout the Midwest; it only suggests that in many states unrest was channeled in a different direction" (*Prairie Populism,* 36). For more on Bellamy Nationalism, see Lipow, *Authoritarian Socialism in America.*

80. "To the Working Women," *HC* 5 (29 July 1876): 5.

81. Myra Pepper, *LLB,* 4 June 1903, 163; Anonymous, Mo., *LLB,* 10 Aug. 1901, 238.

82. Moses Harman, "Free Motherhood and the Economic Reconstruction," *LLB,* 15 Dec. 1897, 397.

83. Albina Washburn, *LLB,* 8 Dec. 1893, 2. For the quote about "good moral character," see Jeffrey, "Women in the Southern Farmers' Alliance," 75. For more on women's participation in alliances, see Watkins, "Political Activism and Community-Building among Alliance and Grange Women in Western Washington."

84. Goldberg, *An Army of Women,* 32.

Chapter 3: The Good Time Coming

1. Patterson, *Charles Hopewell,* 275. For an assessment of the novel, see Spurlock, *Free Love,* 89–90, 148.

2. Patterson, *Charles Hopewell,* 281.

3. For more about the Rising Star Community, situated seven miles from Greenville, Ohio, see "Rising Star Community," *SR* 1 (Jan. 1856): 6–7; "Reform Communities," *VG* 1 (7 Mar. 1857): 7. Its residents farmed 110 acres, operated a saw mill, and owned four town lots in nearby Stelvideo.

4. See Spurlock, *Free Love;* Vartorella, "The Other 'Peculiar Institution'"; McKinley, "Guide to the Communistic Communities of Ohio."

5. For insight into the comparison of chattel slavery with marriage, see Hersh, *Slavery of*

Sex; Lerner, *Grimke Sisters from South Carolina;* Stewart, *Holy Warriors,* 83, 90–93; Elizabeth Clark, "Matrimonial Bonds." For additional insight into antebellum abolitionism, see Friedman, *Gregarious Saints;* Perry, *Radical Abolition.* For a discussion of Lucy Stone's attempt to agitate the twin causes of women's rights and abolitionism, see Kerr, *Lucy Stone,* 63.

6. Noyes, *Slavery and Marriage.* The participants in Noyes's debate included Judge North, who criticized slavery and defended marriage; Major South, who defended slavery; and Mr. Free Church, who challenged both. For another example of a work that compared marriage to slavery, see Chase, *Fugitive Wife.* David S. Reynolds regards the phenomenon known as free love as "a direct response to what was seen as the enslaving marriage institution" (*Walt Whitman's America,* 224). The *Augusta Chronicle and Sentinel* is cited in Whites, *Civil War as a Crisis in Gender,* 18. Men enhanced their patriarchal power through the acquisition of property in the form of goods, land, and people. For the reference to Massachusetts, see S. E. W., "Woman's Legal Rights," *Liberator* 25 (20 Apr. 1855): 62.

7. Pleck, *Domestic Tyranny,* 53. Pleck argues that the antebellum temperance movement provided an outlet for women to vent suppressed rage at a time when a strong belief in the family and privacy concealed much of women's suffering.

8. For more on Stanton's ideas about temperance, see Griffith, "Elizabeth Cady Stanton on Marriage and Divorce," 233. Stanton served as president of the New York Women's Temperance Society. Other advocates of women's rights, among them Ernestine Rose and Lucy Stone, also reinforced the image of marriage as a form of women's slavery when they argued that existing laws rendered married women a form of property. See "Address by Ernestine Rose"; The Concise History of Woman Suffrage, Lucy Stone, "Marriage," *Liberator* 24 (21 Apr. 1854): 61.

9. For additional insight into the antebellum dress reform movement, see Fischer, "Who Wears the Pants?"; Kriebl, "From Bloomers to Flappers." The "doll-baby" quote is found in Lucine Pool, "Woman's Position and Rights," *The Sibyl* 7 (July 1862): 1057. For the argument linking dress reform to women's rights, see John Patterson, "The Entire Front of Reform, Chapter VI: Woman's Rights and the Dress Reform," *SR* 3 (June 1857): 161.

10. For further discussion of the rhetoric of slavery and the politics of the body, see Sanchez-Eppler, *Touching Liberty.* The references to ultraism are found in Hamm, *God's Government Begun,* xvi, xxi, xxiii, 57. Nancy Hewitt's study of Rochester, N.Y., also locates ultraist reformers on "the bottom rungs" of that city's emerging middle class. See Hewitt, *Women's Activism and Social Change,* 6, 41.

11. Braude, *Radical Spirits,* 3. That sentiment is evident in the comments of Mrs. Hannah F. M. Brown, who in "Gags vs. Free Speech," *VG* 1 (8 Aug. 1857): 180, declared that if Spiritualism "was not calculated to elevate woman, improve her condition, and exalt her to the enjoyment of her God-given rights," she wanted "nothing to do with it." For the quote about mediumship, see Braude, *Radical Spirits,* 82. For an example of a trance medium who spoke on free love, see Doten, *Free Love and Affinity.* The quote about "mental bondage" is from Anonymous, Portage, Ohio, *Agitator* 1 (1 July 1858): 6.

12. G. W. S., Maquon, Ill., "Divorce," *Agitator* 2 (15 Oct. 1858): 14. For definitions of "true love" and "true marriage," see Jennie G. Adams, "What Love Is Not," *SR* 4 (July 1857): 3; Mrs. H. M. F. Brown, "Marriage—the Reason and Results," *Agitator* 2 (1 Mar. 1859): 84.

13. Mrs. H. M. F. Brown, "The True Marriage," *Agitator* 2 (1 Apr. 1859): 100. "How long

will a true marriage last?" wrote a divorced Mrs. Brown. "Just so long as love lasts and no longer."

14. For the reference to "false marriages," see "Letter from Geauga County, Ohio," *VG* 1 (4 July 1857): 142; for the comments about "love children," see Milo A. Townsend, "Religion and Generation," *Agitator* 1 (1 Sept. 1858): 1.

15. Cayleff, *Wash and Be Healed,* 143, discusses women's sharing of sexual and medical information at water-cure resorts. For the information on Bush, see "A Dear One Departed," *SR* 4 (Dec. 1857): 181–82. According to J. H. Cook, water-cure resorts served as "important preparatory schools of social freedom" ("The Love Cure," *SR* 4 [Sept. 1857]: 110). The Oneida Community's John Humphrey Noyes also praised "hydropathic socialism" in *Oneida Circular* 4 (13 Sept. 1855): 134.

16. Francis Barry, "What Is Marriage," *SR* 3 (Feb. 1857): 42–43. For additional discussion, see Examiner to the editor, *Agitator* 1 (1 July 1858): 6. Readers would have been aware of urban prostitution because of Dr. William Sanger's highly publicized report on that subject. See "Rev. H. R. Nye and the Marriage Question," *Agitator* 2 (15 Feb. 1859): 76. For Joseph Treat's views, see Treat, "Free Love, Fairly Stated," *SR* 3 (Feb. 1857).

17. Minerva Putnam, "Glimpses of Life," *SR* 3 (Jan. 1857): 29. Minerva Putnam was a pseudonym for Damaris Colburn Bush. See "A Dear One Departed," *SR* 4 (Dec. 1857): 181–82.

18. Information about grounds for divorce is from Pleck, *Domestic Tyranny,* 55. For a discussion of cases in which men were charged with sexual abuse, see Griswold, *Family and Divorce in California,* esp. 56–59, 72–73, 116–17, and 120–24; for a statistical analysis of divorce complaints, see pp. 78–79. Many of the cases Griswold discusses illustrate instances in which husbands demeaned their wives by treating them as servants and slaves, but they also document marriages in which husbands refused to practice sexual self-restraint. For insight into the relationship between moral reform movement and sexuality, see Smith-Rosenberg, *Disorderly Conduct,* 109–28. For discussion of women's participation in moral reform societies, see Cott, *Bonds of Womanhood,* esp. 149–54.

19. For more on the context in which these women wrote, see Basch, "Women's Rights and Wrongs of Marriage in Mid-Nineteenth-Century America," 26–48. Textual clues suggest that many correspondents, especially those who resided in Ohio, knew each other but wanted to protect their identities from their families, neighbors, and the strangers who read *SR* as it circulated far and wide. For discussion of the letters, see "A Call for Facts," *SR* 3 (Feb. 1857): 64; "Mean Husbands—Enslaved Wives," *SR* 4 (Oct. 1857): 117.

20. Lily White, "Sexual Abuse in Marriage," *SR* 3 (Mar. 1857): 85; for the quote from a dress reformer, see B., "Progressive Movements," *SR* 3 (Apr. 1857): 123; for the "I have bought you" quote, see Justicia, "What Is," *SR* (Apr. 1857): 115.

21. Minerva Putnam, "Glimpses of Life," *SR* 3 (Jan. 1857): 29. For the "holocaust of death" quote, see Justicia, "What Is," 115.

22. Louisa, "Another Nut for Peter," *SR* 3 (Feb. 1857): 50; Justicia, "What Is," 115; Vivian Grey, "Sexual Slavery," *SR* 2 (Nov. 1856): 138. For the sleeping alone quote, see Lily White, "More Facts," *SR* 3 (Apr. 1857): 139. Louisa described the use of Dr. Nichols's methods. There is no indication of the type of medicine Vivian Grey practiced.

23. White, "More Facts," 139. For more discussion of the brute/slave analogy, see "Spiritualism—Free Love," *SR* 3 (Apr. 1857): 121.

24. *SR* correspondents did not seek absolute freedom in social relationships but rather "a higher freedom." For further elaboration, see "A Question as to Free Journalism," *SR* 4 (Sept. 1857): 120. The quote about marital slavery is from B[arry], "Progressive Movements," *SR* 3 (Apr. 1857): 124.

25. For the reference to dreary slavery, see "Mean Husbands—Enslaved Wives," 117. Grey, "Sexual Slavery," 137. For the reference to "animalistic" sexuality, see "To T. L. N.," *SR* 3 (Feb. 1857): 48.

26. For the reference to the "finger-touch of God," see C. M. Overton, "Horrors of Slavery," *SR* 4 (Dec. 1857): 163; for the reference to "holiness," see Justicia, "What Is," 115. For related examples, see Louisa, *SR* 3 (Feb. 1857): 50; Minerva Putnam, *SR* 3 (Jan. 1857): 29. Such awareness led Putnam to reject Christianity.

27. For the reference to "juggernut," see Cordelia Barry, *SR* 1 (May 1856): 158. For another who shared her view, see Carrie, "Questionings," *AoF* 1 (4 Feb. 1858), 3. For the reference to "cooking stoves," see Cora Corning, "The Other Side of the Picture," *SR* 4 (July 1857): 25. Corning was a pseudonym for *Vanguard* editor Anne Denton Cridge. For the quote from Bush, see Damaris Colburn Bush, "The Need of Association," *SR* 3 (June 1856): 182. The discussion of cooperative housekeeping is found in "The Economy of Co-Operation," *SR* 4 (July 1857): 31; "The Entire Front of Reform, Chapter VI," 165. For more on an effort by free lovers to establish a unitary household in New York City, see "Practical Socialism in New York," *NYT*, 22 June 1858, 5. For an assessment of such ventures, see Hayden, *Grand Domestic Revolution*, 95–96.

28. See Foucault, *History of Sexuality*, 92–102.

29. Jennie in Bonds, "A Page of Life History," *SR* 4 (Sept. 1857): 104.

30. "Noble Utterances," *SR* 4 (Sept. 1857): 94. For more on her speech and the reactions it provoked, see Carrie S. Lewis, "Letter to G. W. S.," *AoF* 1 (18 Mar. 1858), 1–2; "Gags vs. Free Speech," *VG* 1 (8 Aug. 1857): 180; "Carrie Lewis and the Ravenna Convention," *SR* 4 (Sept. 1857): 115.

31. Laura Jones, "Helps and Hindrances," *VG* 1 (28 Mar. 1857): 27. Jones spoke in the Quaker community of Richmond, Ind.

32. For the Branch quote, see *BoL* 3 (3 July 1858): 3. For the editorial criticism of Branch, see "Our Ishmaelites," *SpR*, 30 June 1858, 2. For the description of and editorial commentary about Branch, see *SpR*, 6 July 1858, 2. For the quote about modesty, see "Letter from G. B. Pond, Marion, Ohio," *Agitator* 1 (1 Aug. 1858): 2. Pond denied that married women had any rights in determining the father of their children: "No matter if the husband is actuated by the basest sensualism in thus determining her course," he wrote, "she is his— soul and spirit." The full text of her speech is found in *Proceedings of the Free Convention Held at Rutland, Vermont, June 25th, 26th, 27th, 1858*. Additional discussion of the Free Convention is found in Stoehr, *Free Love in America*, 24–26; Braude, *Radical Spirits*, 69–73, 133.

33. For the reference to "property and political rights," see D'Emilio and Freedman, *Intimate Matters*, 57; for the reference to "good investment," see Boydston, *Home and Work*, 140; for the reference to "sexual politics," see Sellers, *Market Revolution*, 242. The construction of woman as passionless, Sellers contends, occurred because those women deprived of autonomy in household production "claimed hegemony" over their homes and children. For further discussion, see Cott, "Passionlessness"; Sellers, *Market Revolution*, 242.

For more on the market's encroachment on domestic morals and shifts in antebellum women's moral responsibilities, see Coontz, *Social Origins of Private Life,* 211–20.

34. For discussion of gender and antebellum politics, see Edwards, *Angels in the Machinery,* 16–17. For an annotated bibliography of conduct manuals, see Newton, *Learning to Behave.*

35. Cora Corning, *SR* 4 (July 1857): 24; Mary A. Chilton, *SR* 4 (July 1857): 5. Corning attributes women's lack of sexual desire to fashion, lack of exercise, poor diet, isolation in the home, and force and rape in "the marriage bed."

36. For a discussion of sexual desire during pregnancy, see Anonymous from Buffalo, N.Y., *SR* 2 (Nov. 1856): 187. For the quote about being half-satisfied, see Anne Denton Cridge, "The Other Side," *SR* 4 (Oct. 1857): 122. For the quote on growing more amorous in marriage, see Lily White, *SR* 4 (Aug. 1857): 44–45. For the reference to electricity, see Mary A. Chilton, "Sexual Purity," *SR* 4 (July 1857): 5. For the reference to an angel visitation, see "Reply to A. Hunter," *SR* 4 (Aug. 1857): 50.

37. Denton attributed disease and the "sin-stamped" condition of children to variety. See William Denton, "Marriage," *VG* 1 (9 Dec. 1857): 300. For critiques of Denton's ideas, see J. W. Towner, "Marriage, Reply to W. Denton," *VG* 1 (9 Jan. 1858): 330–31; "Another Reply to Wm. Denton," *VG* 1 (30 Jan. 1858): 355; "Cook's Reply to Denton," *VG* 1 (20 Feb. 1858): 382.

38. Charlotte H. Bowen, "Exclusiveness in Love," *SR* 4 (July 1857): 7–8; Cordelia Barry, "Laying Down the Law," *SR* 4 (Aug. 1857): 55–56.

39. Minerva Putnam, "A Woman's Experience in Freedom," *SR* 3 (Mar. 1857): 71; J. W. Towner, "Marriage, Reply to W. Denton," *VG* 1 (9 Jan. 1858): 330.

40. Stewart, *Holy Warriors,* 78–81, 113. For a discussion of northerners' fear of a slave-power conspiracy, see Sellers, *Market Revolution,* 405–6. The 1846 annexation of Texas proved to some that the federal government could be corrupted easily by a slaveholding power. The Panic of 1857 lasted two years, bottoming out during the summer of 1858. For further discussion, see Schapsmeier and Schapsmeier, *Encyclopedia of American Agricultural History,* 261; Huston, *Panic of 1857 and the Coming of the Civil War;* Stampp, *America in 1857.*

41. For the reference to the Western Reserve, see Francis Barry, "Practical Socialism," *SR* 3 (Mar. 1857): 83. For the estimate of Denton's audience, see Denton, "Field Notes," *SR* 2 (Aug. 1856): 58–59. Francis Barry's travels as an itinerant lecturer are described in "From Francis Barry," *SR* 1 (May 1856): 147. Additional information about the settlement of the Western Reserve is found in Peacefull, *Geography of Ohio.* The federal government awarded tracts of land to veterans of the Revolutionary War, but where those soldiers and their heirs refused to take up their claims the land was sold to speculators. See Hamm, *God's Government Begun,* for discussion of radicalism in southern Ohio.

42. Readers included survivors of Fourieristic-inspired Ceresco, Wis.; James W. Towner's communal experiment in West Union, Iowa; members of the Rising Star Community in Darke County, Ohio; and participants in Memnonia, the harmonial experiment headed by Thomas and Mary Gove Nichols, near Yellow Springs, Ohio.

43. For the reference to "habits, tastes, opinions," see "From Francis Barry to J. K. Ingalls," *The Optimist, and Kingdom of Heaven* 3 (June 1867), 3. For the reference to organi-

zation, see Francis Barry, "Practical Socialism," *SR* 2 (Sept. 1856): 73. For insight into Barry's ideas about communal living, see Barry, "Berlin Movement," *SR* 3 (Jan. 1857): 15; Barry, "Letter to T. L. Nichols," *SR* 3 (Mar. 1857): 79; Barry, "To James W. Towner," *SR* 4 (July 1857): 22.

44. Barry offered resolutions at the National Abolitionist Convention in 1848 in which he advocated an armed invasion of the South to liberate the slaves by force. For accounts of the 1856 convention, see *SR* 2 (Oct. 1856): flyleaf; Joseph Treat, "Berlin Movement," *SR* 3 (Jan. 1857): 15; Alvin Warren, "Reminiscences of Berlin Heights," *ONH* 1 (June 1896): 4–34. Participants attended from Memnonia, the Rising Star Community, Ceresco, Wis., and West Union, Iowa. Descriptions of convention participants are from Francis Barry, "The Berlin Convention," *SR* 2 (Nov. 1856): 157–58.

45. *SR* 1 (Apr. 1856): 100–101. For comments by socialists who opposed southern locations, see "From Alfred Cridge," *SR* 1 (June 1856): 189–92. Socialists ruled out Memnonia as a potential site because of its location in a region known for southern sympathizers.

46. Barry, "Practical Socialism," *SR* 2 (Sept. 1856): 73–74. For another description of Berlin Heights, see *Combination Atlas Map of Erie County, Ohio,* xvii. In the early 1870s, the community had three stores, three churches (Methodist, Congregational, Baptist), a town hall, a school house, and a hotel.

47. For Cordelia Barry's ideas about marriage and homes, see "Correspondence," *SR* 1 (May 1856): 157. According to the 1860 federal manuscript population census, Berlin Township, Erie County, Ohio, sixty-three-year-old Daniel Benschoter owned $6,000 of real property and $2,500 of personal property. Barry corresponded to the *Liberator* from Berlin Heights in 1854, and a Barry-Benschoter marriage, dated 1 Jan. 1857, is registered at the Probate Division, Erie County Common Pleas Court, Erie County, Ohio.

48. "Berlin vs. Free Love," *SCR,* 25 Aug. 1857, 2. According to "The Free Love Iniquity," *NYT,* 22 July 1858, 2, Saphronia Powers leased the hotel in June 1857. An announcement in *NM* 3 (Dec. 1856), 337, describes the Free Love farm as being able to accommodate twenty people.

49. The quoted material is from Francis Barry, "Practical Socialism," *SR* 3 (Mar. 1857): 81. For further insight into the comparison of chattel slavery with marriage, see Hersh, *Slavery of Sex;* Lerner, *Grimke Sisters from South Carolina;* Clark, "Matrimonial Bonds."

50. Ward, "Among the Free Lovers," 86–90. The quote is taken from Peeke, *Centennial History of Erie County, Ohio,* 650–51. Some accounts indicate that Ward never actually visited Berlin Heights. The Hannah Brown quote is from "Extracts from Letters," *Agitator* 2 (1 Nov. 1858): 23. The Fish quote is from John Fish to Job Fish, 5 June 1864, Fish Family Papers, Ohio Historical Society, Columbus. According to Job Fish, the Free Lovers were avid readers and willingly lent their books to others in the community ("Free Love Community," 322–23).

51. "From J. A. Clay, Maine," *SR* 1 (June 1856): 187.

52. Alvin Warren, "Reminiscences of Berlin Heights," *ONH* 1 (June 1896): 34. While the first two identifiers are surnames, the latter may refer to the group's place of residence. For details about the community's composition, see the federal manuscript population census for Berlin Township, Erie County, Ohio, 1860.

53. According to Warren, Hall did not allow prayers or hymns in her school. Alvin

Warren, "Reminiscences of Berlin Heights," *ONH* 1 (June 1896): 32. The 1860 federal manuscript population census for Berlin Township, Erie County, indicates that she was thirty-eight, had a two-year-old daughter, and lived with the Samuel Patterson family.

54. For an account of Mary Lewis [married to Harlow Lewis], see "Wanted! Wanted!" *Agitator* 1 (1 Sept. 1858): 5. An account of the Lewis episode, reprinted from the *Detroit Free Press*, appeared in "Melancholy Case of Free Love Folly" *SpR*, 28 June 1858, 2. The Ward quote is from "Among the Free Lovers," 90.

55. The Barry quote is from "Practical Socialism," *SR* 3 (Mar. 1857): 82. For discussion of women and Fourieristic communities, see Savagian, "Women at Ceresco"; Tomasek, "Pivot of the Mechanism"; Guarneri, *Utopian Alternative*.

56. Sixteen of twenty-nine adult female Free Lovers gave "domestic" as their occupation. For an example of a Free Lover who attempted to divide property with his wife, see J. W. Towner, "Something Practical," *SR* 3 (Jan. 1857): 31–32. Free Lovers believed in women's right to hold property, yet only one did in 1860, a thirty-six-year-old domestic living in the Overton household.

57. For the reference to dancing, see *Portage (Ohio) Sentinel*, 15 Aug. 1858. Aldrich claims that only one local person (presumably Cordelia Benschoter) joined the Free Lovers yet admits that "the atmosphere of their restless ideas seemed to affect many who never became identified with it, and there is no doubt that Berlin was more or less injured by the contact" (*History of Erie County, Ohio*, 447).

58. Anne Hunter, "The Miseries of Free Love," *SpR*, 15 July 1858, 2. The same article appeared a day earlier as "The Berlin Free-Lovers, Letter from a Deserted Wife," *NYT*, 14 July 1858, 2. For details of the Kline divorce suit, see *Rosetta Kline v. Barnhart Kline*, Divorce Petitions, Sandusky County (Ohio) Chancery Records, vol. 9 (Dec. 1857), 100–16, Rutherford B. Hayes Presidential Library, Fremont, Ohio.

59. "Berlin vs. Free Love," *SCR*, 25 Aug. 1857, 2. In the 1860 federal manuscript population census for Berlin Township, Erie County, Zenophin Philips is listed as a farmer, forty-six, who owned $2,500 in real property, and Hudson Tuttle, twenty-four, owned $5,000 in real property. Reports of the indignation meeting were sent to Ohio newspapers in Milan, Sandusky, and Cleveland.

60. Job Fish, "The Free Love War," Fish Family Papers, Ohio Historical Society, Columbus; "Florence, Berlin, and Free Lovers," *SCR*, 8 Sept. 1857, 2.

61. "The Berlin Convention," *SR* 4 (Oct. 1857): 123–24. The convention was held 25–27 Sept. 1857.

62. According to "The End of the Free Love Cases," *SCR*, 21 Nov. 1857, 3, those charged included the Free Love farm residents Mary Dame and others bearing the surnames Woodhull, Smith, Wright, Horner, and Tyler. For details, see *Henry Hammond v. Joseph Treat*, Erie County Court of Common Pleas, Erie County, Ohio (17 Oct. 1857).

63. According to the *NYT*, men named Hill, Hopkins, Kellogg, and Fowler sold the Free Lovers land, extended them credit, and provided bail. As the 1860 census for Erie County reveals, the men who aided the Free Lovers were financially secure. B. I. Hill, a forty-three-year-old physician, owned $4,000 real property, and Isaac Fowler, a fifty-five-year-old mechanic, owned $2,500 real property and $600 personal property. For accounts of the Free Lovers during this period, see "The Free-Love Settlement of Berlin Heights, Ohio," *NYT*, 21 July 1858, 3; "The Berlin Free-Lovers Redivivus," *NYT*, 25 June 1858, 2.

64. "The Free Lovers Again—A Bonfire," *SCR*, 4 Dec. 1857, 3.

65. "To Our Readers," *SR* 4 (Dec. 1857): 189.

66. C. M. Overton, "The Berlin Free Lovers' Confession of Faith," *AoF* 1 (18 Mar. 1858), 2–3. Not all of the Free Lovers approved of Overton's use of religious rhetoric. See Charles Latcher, "A Protest," *AoF* 1 (18 Mar. 1858): 3.

67. For discussion of the election, see Fish, "Free Love War"; "Berlin Hights [*sic*] Revived," *SpR*, 20 Apr. 1858, 2.

68. For discussion of the nude bathing incident, see "The Berlin Free-Lovers Redivivus," *NYT*, 25 June 1858, 2. The "aid and comfort" quote is from "The Free-Love Settlement of Berlin Heights, Ohio," *NYT*, 21 July 1858, 3. For references to the threats of mob violence, see *SpR*, 28 July 1858, 2.

69. The reference to the mob is from "The Free-Lovers Ready for Action," *SpR*, 11 Sept. 1858, 4; the "justice" quote is from Fish, "The Free Love War"; and the reference to Alton, Ill., where a mob had killed the Reverend Elijah P. Lovejoy in Nov. 1837, is from "To the Cotton Mather of Berlin Hights [*sic*]," *SR* 4 (Dec. 1857): 186.

70. "From the Cleveland *Spiritualist,* Correction," *AoF* 1 (28 Jan. 1858), 2.

71. For information about the Bishop Hill community, see Tyler, *Freedom's Ferment*, 132–38. For information about the Western Woman's Emancipation Convention, see *The Word* 2 (Jan. 1874): 3; 2 (Aug. 1874): 4.

72. McKinley, "Guide to the Communistic Communities of Ohio," notes the existence of twenty men and women living communally in Berlin Heights, Ohio, in 1860 under the name Point Hope Community. There is a reference to them in *SCR*, 14 Mar. 1870. Aldrich notes the existence of a second twenty-member community, the Industrial Fraternity, also in 1860 (*History of Erie County, Ohio*, 447). According to this source, those who still lived there communally in 1865 called themselves the Christian Republic. For maps and illustrations of their homes, orchards, and factory, see Nunan, *Map of Erie and Part of Ottawa Counties; Combination Atlas Map of Erie County, Ohio.* For accounts of Berlin Heights residents who visited the Oneida Community in the hopes of becoming members, see the *Daily Journal of Oneida Community,* 26 Mar. 1863; "A. W. C.," *Daily Journal of Oneida Community,* 20 Aug. 1863, 97. Those who sought membership included Mrs. H. J. Scott, Mr. John P. Lasley [*sic*], Miss Clara Waite, Mr. A. F. Page, Mrs. James A. Clay, and W. A. Hunter.

73. "Remarks," *The Optimist, and Kingdom of Heaven* 3 (June 1867), 3. A report in *The Sibyl* 5 (1 Sept. 1860): 805, noted that the Berlin Heights reformers had never prospered so well as they did during the summer of 1860. In 1925, Job Fish remembered the Free Lovers as "dreamers," "conspicuous for intelligence, industry, and good citizenship." See Fish, "Free Love Community," 322–23.

74. "The Social Question," *KoH* 1 (June 1864): 2. Living intermittently with his estranged wife Harriet in Huntsville, Ind., Cook ultimately settled in Berlin Heights, Ohio. See "Affinities," *KoH* 2 (Apr. 1865): 3. For Cook's definition of free love and his ideas about the love principle, see "Low Spirits," *KoH* 1 (June 1864): 2. For Cook's ideas about monogamy, see "Psychometrical Delineation of Thomas Cook," *KoH* 1 (Sept. 1864): 1; "How Strange!" *KoH* 2 (May 1865): 2.

75. L. H. Bettes, Ravenna, Ohio, *KoH* 2 (May 1865): 1; Anonymous woman, *KoH* 2 (July 1865): 1. For other examples of women's interpretation of Cook's ideas as the epitome of purity, see four letters by anonymous women, *KoH* 2 (June 1865): 1. Cook argued that

"souls redeemed from all selfish exclusiveness, lust and desire to have, to hold . . . will have no fears or misgivings about promiscuity; but will see its divine use." See "Promiscuity," *True Union* 2 (Nov. 1865): 3 (formerly *Kingdom of Heaven;* Cook's paper changed names several times).

76. For the "food and soul" quote, and for insight into Cook's ideas about male continence, see Cook, "The Social Question Again," *KoH* 2 (Aug. 1865): 2, 4.

Chapter 4: We Are Cowards and She Is Not

1. Emphasis in the original. Woodhull, *Speech on the Principles of Social Freedom*, 23. According to "Social Freedom," *WCW*, 2 Dec. 1871, 12, "the [Steinway Hall] audience was about as equally divided between the sexes."

2. Because historians often treat the Civil War as a watershed, the persistence of antebellum ideologies in the postbellum period sometimes is obscured. See Unger, *Greenback Era*, for further discussion.

3. For additional insight into the conditions that prevailed during the years 1873–77, see Sharkey, *Money, Class, and Party;* Goodwyn, *Populist Moment,* esp. 16–17; Nugent, *Money and American Society.*

4. Nineteenth-century woman suffrage organizations, the historian Ellen DuBois asserts, pursued multiple goals; yet the campaign for political rights remained the highest priority among the women whose ideas dominated the national agenda. Fearful of jeopardizing their cause by addressing topics sometimes associated with free love, leaders of the American Woman Suffrage Association and the National Woman Suffrage Association preferred to defer discussions of such topics as divorce and female sexuality until after women's enfranchisement. For additional information, see DuBois, *Woman Suffrage and Women's Rights*, 9.

5. Degler, *At Odds*, 168. For divorce statistics, see *Marriage and Divorce*, 41. For additional insight into nineteenth-century divorce, see Carlier, *Marriage in the United States*, 114–15; Blake, *Road to Reno;* Cott, *Public Vows,* esp. 47–53; Griswold, *Family and Divorce in California;* Griswold, "Sexual Cruelty and the Case for Divorce in Victorian America"; Griswold, "Law, Sex, Cruelty, and Divorce in Victorian America"; Grossberg, *Governing the Hearth;* Hartog, *Man and Wife in America;* May, *Great Expectations;* O'Neill, *Divorce in the Progressive Era;* Riley, *Divorce.*

6. Barry quotes a contemporary account of the Hester Vaughn case (*Susan B. Anthony*, 217).

7. For a probing analysis of the McFarland-Richardson case, see Ganz, "Wicked Women and Veiled Ladies." For additional insight into reactions to the murder and trial, consult DuBois, *Woman Suffrage and Women's Rights*, 76–77; Cooper, *Lost Love;* Cott, *Public Vows,* 107–9; Ireland, "Death to the Libertine." Indiana became the "divorce capital" of the nation after 1860, following passage of legislation championed by the reformer and state legislator Robert Dale Owen. Henry Ward Beecher "fancied himself as the vanguard of a new revolution of love, one which brought partners together through their spiritual affinity and elevated the feelings they shared to paramount importance." For more on his ideas about romantic love, see Barry, *Susan B. Anthony*, 226–27.

8. For Stanton's assessment of the McFarland-Richardson case, see *NYT*, 18 May 1870. For Henry Blackwell's observations, see "Woman Suffrage and the McFarland Case,"

Woman's Journal 1 (4 June 1870): 169. Additional comments by Blackwell on the case's negative impact on the woman suffrage movement are found in "Woman Suffrage and Divorce," *Woman's Journal* 1 (4 June 1870): 173.

9. DuBois with Gordon, "Seeking Ecstasy on the Battlefield," 145. For historians' discussions of the meaning of social purity, see Gordon, *Woman's Body, Woman's Right,* 114. For additional insight into social purity reform, see Boyer, *Purity in Print;* Pivar, *Purity Crusade.*

10. DuBois with Gordon, "Seeking Ecstasy on the Battlefield," 146.

11. For further details about the Comstock Law and subsequent state legislation, see Brodie, *Contraception and Abortion in Nineteenth-Century America,* 255–58. The legal historian Elizabeth Hovey argues that Comstock even drove a few women to suicide. See Hovey, "Stamping Out Smut."

12. For Pivar's assessment of the relationship between the WCTU and the social purity movement, see Pivar, *Purity Crusade,* 85. For the historian Ruth Bordin's reading of Pivar, see *Woman and Temperance,* 111. WCTU membership information is found on pp. 3–4. For background on liberal feminism, see Marilley, *Woman Suffrage and the Origins of Liberal Feminism in the United States,* 100–123.

13. For a classic biography of Comstock, see Broun and Leech, *Anthony Comstock.* The discussion of his early involvement in the New York City YMCA is on p. 73. For further information about the increased power of the federal government resulting from the Civil War, see Frederickson, *Inner Civil War.* For feminist assessments of Comstock, see Beisel, *Imperiled Innocents;* Brodie, *Contraception and Abortion in Nineteenth-Century America.* Brodie argues that Comstock's marriage to a woman ten years his senior and the death of his only child in infancy, along with other psychological factors, motivated him to resent women who could prevent pregnancy and in part explains the aggressive campaign he mounted to curtail the dissemination of reproductive information (272–73).

14. Boyer, *Urban Masses and Moral Order in America,* 120.

15. Although dated, one work that captures the whole woman rather than one aspect of her personality is Sachs, *"Terrible Siren."* Other older studies include Brough, *The Vixens;* Johnston, *Mrs. Satan;* Marberry, *Vicky.* More recent accounts have focused on her presidential candidacy and her Spiritualism, among them a well-crafted and sensitive interpretation by Mary Gabriel, *Notorious Victoria;* Goldsmith, *Other Powers;* Underhill, *Woman Who Ran for President.* For biased accounts of Woodhull written during her lifetime, see Tilton, *Victoria C. Woodhull;* Treat, *Beecher, Tilton, Woodhull.* Both documents exaggerate aspects of Woodhull's career but nonetheless contain elements of truth.

16. It is difficult to give precise dates for events in Woodhull's life because biographical accounts contain conflicting information. Theodore Tilton reports that she married at fourteen and divorced after eleven years. According to Stern, Woodhull and Blood signed an "intention" rather than an actual "return" for marriage in Montgomery County, Ohio, on 14 July 1866, and may not have been legally married (*Victoria Woodhull Reader,* 2).

17. Woodhull and Claflin opened the brokerage on 4 Feb. 1870, reportedly the first women stockbrokers on Wall Street. *Liberty* editor Benjamin R. Tucker, however, claimed that the office was merely window dressing and that the sisters did not actually function as brokers. See Sachs, *"Terrible Siren,"* 236–66.

18. Paulina Wright Davis also supported Woodhull's interpretation of the Fourteenth

Amendment. While the Judiciary Committee denied her petition, General Benjamin F. Butler of Massachusetts did issue a favorable minority report.

19. For a description of the NWSA meeting at which Woodhull sat on the platform, see Sachs, *"Terrible Siren,"* 87. For Woodhull's quote, see *Speech on the Principles of Social Freedom,* 23. For a discussion of Stanton's perception of Woodhull, see Barry, *Susan B. Anthony,* 244–45. For Isabella Beecher Hooker's views of Woodhull, see Boydston, Kelley, and Margolis, *Limits of Sisterhood,* 188, 295.

20. *Daily Iowa State Register,* 4 Oct. 1871, 2. For a detailed examination of Woodhull's influence on the Iowa suffrage campaign, see Pounds, "Suffragists, Free Love, and the Woman Question."

21. See Goldsmith, *Other Powers,* 314–23, for one account of the May 1872 NWSA convention and Woodhull's formation of the Equal Rights party.

22. Reporters accused Woodhull of bigamy, implying that she had never divorced Canning Woodhull, who continued to reside with her and second husband Colonel Blood. For a discussion of Harriet Beecher Stowe's portrayal of Woodhull in *My Wife and I,* see Hedrick, *Harriet Beecher Stowe,* 373–74. The Thomas Nast cartoon of "Mrs. Satan" appeared in *Harper's Weekly,* Feb. 1872. The comparison of Woodhull to Satan backfired on at least one occasion. After seeing the Nast cartoon, an unmarried woman concluded that "marriage is there depicted as a risk sufficiently horrible to make even an old maid thankful for her loneliness." See "An Old Maid's Protest," *Golden Age* 2 (24 Feb. 1872): 3.

23. For details and further analysis of the Beecher-Tilton scandal, see Underhill, *Woman Who Ran for President,* 228–46; Fox, "Intimacy on Trial"; Waller, *Reverend Beecher and Mrs. Tilton.*

24. Goldsmith, *Other Powers,* 255.

25. For a discussion of Woodhull's efforts to lecture on political topics, see Sachs, *"Terrible Siren,"* 248–49, 254. The formation of the New England Free Love League is described in "The Beginning of the End," *WCW,* 5 Apr. 1873, 3. For insight into the formation of local leagues, see a letter from San Francisco entitled "Spirit of '76," *WCW,* 19 Apr. 1873, 4; M. C. Dwight, Elkader, Iowa, *WCW,* 30 Aug. 1873: 7.

26. For a discussion of the spread of Spiritualism, see Braude, *Radical Spirits,* esp. 25–31. Trance speakers, writes Braude, could challenge patriarchal authority because they were thought to be passive instruments expressing the words and ideas of others (pp. 2–3). For a discussion of Spiritualist beliefs about progression, see pp. 40, 44. The size of the audience when Woodhull delivered "The Scare-crows of Sexual Slavery" at a Spiritualist camp meeting at Silver Lake, Mass., in 1871 is one indicator; according to Sachs, over fifteen thousand men and women reportedly attended (*"Terrible Siren,"* 166).

27. Lois Waisbrooker, Battle Creek, Mich., *The Word* 1 (Dec. 1872): 3. For additional praise of Woodhull, see "Proceedings of the Tenth Annual Convention," *WCW,* 11 Oct. 1893, 12. Spiritualists did not believe in formal organizations but nonetheless formed two loosely structured national associations: the American Association of Spiritualists (organized in 1866) and the National Association of Spiritualists (founded in 1893), as well as dozens of regional and local associations. For a list of delegates to the Chicago meeting, see *WCW,* 4 Oct. 1873, 12. The list includes only those who could afford to pay the one-dollar fee entitling them to voting rights. Of the 172 named as being in attendance, fifty-four were women. The largest number hailed from the Midwest—Indiana, Illinois, Iowa,

Michigan, and Wisconsin—and the fifteen states with female delegates included California, Connecticut, Illinois, Indiana, Iowa, Kentucky, Massachusetts, Michigan, Missouri, New Jersey, New York, Ohio, Pennsylvania, Rhode Island, and Wisconsin.

28. Woodhull refuted those rumors in "Personal," *WCW*, 11 July 1874, 8, but nonetheless admitted that the West Coast offered one of the best localities for her work.

29. For the reference to "virtuous mothers," see Selah, Buffalo, N.Y., "To Editors," *WCW*, 23 Dec. 1871, 6. For the "elephant" reference, see Mrs. M. E. French, Greenville, Mich., "Dear Mrs. Woodhull," *WCW*, 24 Apr. 1875, 3. The expression "seeing the elephant" often is associated with the California gold rush of 1849, although it predates that era. To gold rushers, it symbolized an unequaled experience. For the "orang-outing" comments, see "From the *Cedar Springs* (Mich.) *Clipper*," *WCW*, 20 Dec. 1873, 7. The Ohio quote is from D. M. Allen, South Newbury, Ohio, "Dear Weekly," *WCW*, 14 Mar. 1874, 13. For insight into husbands and wives who discussed Woodhull's ideas after they encountered them, see Adelbert Ames to Blanche Butler Ames, 27 Sept. 1872, in Ames, *Chronicles from the Nineteenth Century*, 384. Their exchange about the Beecher-Tilton scandal is on pp. 380–81.

30. "Naked Truth," *MS*, 24 Mar. 1873; the reference to "crazy harridan" is in "Victoria C. Woodhull," *MS*, 16 Feb. 1874; the "Opera House" quote is from "The Woodhull," *MS*, 26 Mar. 1873; the Chicago quote is from "Opera House," *MS*, 20 Mar. 1873.

31. The "eloquence" quote is from *MS*, 16 Feb. 1874. For articles about Woodhull's Wisconsin lecture tour, see "Victoria C. Woodhull," *Oconto County (Wis.) Register*, 9 Oct. 1875; "Sheboygan Gossip," *MS*, 1 Oct. 1875; [Berlin], *MS*, 23 Apr. 1874; [Janesville], *MS*, 6 Feb. 1874; [La Crosse], *MS*, 11 Feb. 1874; [Menasha], *MS*, 20 Sept. 1875; [Portage], *MS*, 4 May 1874.

32. "Victoria C. Woodhull," *Oconto County (Wis.) Register*, 9 Oct. 1875.

33. According to a report from the *Lincoln (Neb.) State Journal:* "The first portion of her speech was read from printed copy, but when she took up the social question she spoke entirely extempore." This account was reprinted in *WCW*, 7 Feb. 1874, 11. For a study arguing that Woodhull in fact constructed a feminist theology, see Miles, "Sex in Context."

34. A. C. Stowe, San Jose, Calif., *WCW*, 18 July 1874, 4. For another impression of her speaking ability, see "Mrs. Woodhull in Western Michigan," *WCW*, 13 Dec. 1873, 11. For the correspondent who found herself unable to sleep after hearing Woodhull lecture, see *WCW*, 3 Jan. 1874, 7. For Hooker's assessment, see Hooker to Susan B. Anthony, 11 Mar. 1871, in Boydston, Kelley, and Margolis, *Limits of Sisterhood*, 206.

35. See Woodhull, *WCW*, 4 Oct. 1873, 14; *WCW*, 25 Oct. 1873, 6.

36. For the reference to "nails," see Anthony Higgins, *WCW*, 11 Oct. 1873, 6; for the "cross," see Cephas R. Lynn, *WCW*, 25 Oct. 1873, 7; for "bread of life," see Mrs. Fannie E. Reece, Farmington, Minn., *WCW*, 31 Jan. 1874, 7; for "savior of spiritualism," see Addie M. Ballou, *WCW*, 11 Oct. 1873, 7; for "last victim sacrificed," see Elizabeth Cady Stanton, *WCW*, 15 July 1871, 9. For the reference to "noble woman," see Mary M. D. Sherman, *WCW*, 29 Nov. 1873, 12. For additional examples, see Mrs. Dr. Barnes, Chicago *WCW*, 18 Oct. 1873, 5; Mrs. Sarah J. Penoyer, Saginaw, Mich. *WCW*, 18 Oct. 1873, 13; Lucy Swain, Forest Home, *WCW*, 29 Nov. 1873, 13; Elvira Wheelock Ruggles, *WCW*, 25 Dec. 1875, 2.

37. James Heddon, Dowagiac, Mich., *WCW*, 14 June 1873, 4.

38. For details about "clubbing," see Sachs, *"Terrible Siren,"* 198. The Fremont, Ind., quote is by Mrs. M. F. Hopkins, *WCW*, 22 Feb. 1873, 4. For the reference to cowards, see Eliza Brad-

ford, *WCW*, 28 Dec. 1872, 15. For the discussion of unchaste themes, see Helen Nash, *WCW*, 2 Aug. 1873, 3. For Nash, such themes included prostitution, which she attributed to the flawed structure of marriage, rather than to an individual's moral deficiencies.

39. Biographical information about correspondents is taken from the federal manuscript population census records and from city directories. For Jennie Tibbot, see Halstead Township, Harvey County, Kans., 1880; for Nancy A. Adams, see Fitchburg, Worcester County, Mass., 1870; for the farm machinery dealer John M. Follett, see Cambridge City, Henry County, Ill., 1880; for Milwaukee baker James Ormsby, see the Milwaukee, Wis., City Directory, 1873; for attorney and Chief Justice of the Kansas Supreme Court (in 1900), see Frank Doster, Marion Center, Marion County, Kans., 1880 and 1900; for the broom maker William Gould, also a *SR* correspondent, see New Berlin, Sangamon County, Ill., 1870.

40. Woodhull referred to herself as "poor, weak, and unlettered" in her address to the American Association of Spiritualists in 1873. See "Proceedings of the American Association of Spiritualists," *WCW*, 4 Oct. 1873, 14. For examples of correspondents who recognized Woodhull's appeal to "the masses," see H. F. J., Chicago, *WCW*, 24 July 1875, 3; D. M. Allen, South Newbury, Ohio, *WCW*, 14 Mar. 1874, 13; A. J. Boyer, "Circular Letter," *WCW*, 26 Aug. 1871, 5; Lois Waisbrooker, "Proceedings," *WCW*, 11 Oct. 1873, 13.

41. For examples of letters in which readers describe themselves as "downtrodden," "poor," and oppressed, see *WCW*, 24 July 1875, 3; 24 Apr. 1875, 3; 25 Dec. 1875, 2. The Nellie L. Davis quote is from *WCW*, 5 Dec. 1874, 5.

42. For the "free from barbarous control" quote, see "Social Freedom," *The Word* 3 (Apr. 1875): 4. Laura Cuppy Smith condemned the double standard in *WCW*, 18 Oct. 1873, 7, as did Grace Nettleton in "A Woman's Thoughts on 'a Man's View of Free Love,'" *Golden Age* 1 (9 Sept. 1871): 2; Angela Heywood, "Correspondence," *The Word* 1 (Jan. 1873), 3. For the Mrs. Dr. Barnes quote, see *WCW*, 18 Oct. 1873, 5.

43. Sarah F. Norton, "Marriage vs. Freedom," *WCW*, 5 Nov. 1870, 6; Mrs. L. M. R. Pool, Vermillion, Ohio, "What Women Owe to Men," *WCW*, 15 Apr. 1871, 11; Sada Bailey, Waukegan, Ill., *WCW*, 31 May 1873, 4–5; Anonymous Michigan woman on Christianity, *WCW*, 26 Dec. 1874, 3; Elvira Wheelock Ruggles cites the example of a Catholic woman in *WCW*, 26 June 1875, 1. For a reference to religion losing its power to influence people's behavior, see an untitled article, *WCW*, 13 Mar. 1875, 1.

44. This analogy comes from Unger, *Greenback Era*.

45. C. L. James, *WCW*, 1 Jan. 1872, 6; Nellie Davis, *WCW*, 6 Dec. 1873, 4. For similar assessments, see Elvira Wheelock Ruggles, *WCW*, 13 Nov. 1875, 2; Lucinda B. Chandler, *Golden Age* 2 (8 June 1872), 2. For the Maine correspondent's quote, see Maddox, *WCW*, 30 Jan. 1875, 6.

46. Victoria C. Woodhull, *WCW*, 18 June 1870, 5; Woodhull, "Slavery Redivivus," *WCW*, 16 July 1870, 9.

47. Laura Cuppy Smith, *WCW*, 11 Oct. 1873, 3. For the quote about prostitution as transitional, see *WCW*, 23 July 1870, 11. For Austin Kent's ideas, see *WCW*, 13 Dec. 1873, 11. And for the Angela Heywood quotation, see "Correspondence," *The Word* 2 (Feb. 1874): 3.

48. Frances Rose Mackinley, *WCW*, 22 July 1871, 12. For other examples, see G., Salem, Ohio, *WCW*, 5 Aug. 1871, 8; Juliet H. Severancem "Woodhullism-Promiscuity," *WCW*, 11 Apr. 1874, 11.

49. A physician, Mrs. Witchener, St. Louis, in *WCW*, 18 Oct. 1873, 2, discusses the number of abortions sought by married churchgoing women.

50. For the Corry, Pa., woman, see Mrs. Stearns, *WCW*, 18 Oct. 1873, 4; for discussion of the Toledo, Ohio, woman, see P. B. Randolph, *WCW*, 11 Oct. 1873, 5.

51. Helen Nash, *WCW*, 8 May 1875, 2.

52. Mrs. H. A. Richardson, *WCW*, 28 Nov. 1874, 12. For another example, see H., Iowa, *WCW*, 3 Apr. 1875, 3.

53. Emily Bryant, West Brookfield, Vt., commented on stages in *WCW*, 13 Mar. 1875, 3. Laura Cuppy Smith argued that "between souls that love each other it [sexual intercourse] is the very eucharist of the affections, a holy sacrament of love in which shame has no part." See *WCW*, 18 Oct. 1873, 7.

54. Sarah J. Penoyer, Saginaw, Mich., *WCW*, 24 Jan. 1874, 12.

55. "The Emancipation Convention," *The Word* 2 (Jan. 1874): 3.

56. J. H. Cook, *LLB*, 30 May 1884, 3.

Chapter 5: Roads to Freedom

1. *Proceedings of the Tenth Annual Convention of the American Association of Spiritualists.*

2. In the early nineteenth century, the utopian visionary Frances Wright, the abolitionist sisters Sarah and Angelina Grimke, and the authors Lydia Maria Child and Margaret Fuller articulated a broad understanding of women's rights that included the principles of self-ownership and equality under the law. Building on this foundation, women and men who gathered at Seneca Falls, N.Y., in 1848 and those who held numerous national, regional, and local women's rights meetings throughout the 1850s agitated for women's economic, political, and social rights.

3. Waisbrooker, *Mayweed Blossoms*, 137.

4. Waisbrooker, *Alice Vale*, 243.

5. Waisbrooker, *Mayweed Blossoms*, 84.

6. "Social Reform Convention, Feb. 28–Mar. 1, 1875," *HC* [Mar. 1875], Ginzburg Papers, box 3, folder 19, Wisconsin Historical Society Archives, Madison (hereafter cited as Ginzburg Papers). According to Waisbrooker's descendent James B. Hardin, she married George Fuller on 12 Apr. 1843 in Cuyahoga County, Ohio. Fuller died on 21 Feb. 1846 (James B. Hardin, e-mail to the author, 25 Jan. 2000). For additional biographical information, see Malin, *Concern about Humanity*, 117.

7. Waisbrooker, *Mayweed Blossoms*, 87.

8. "Social Reform Convention," *HC* clipping [Apr. 1875], Ginzburg Papers. For information about her teaching career, see *To-Morrow Magazine* (Oct. 1906): 6. According to James B. Hardin, Waisbrooker married Isaac Snell on 9 Aug. 1856 in Morrow County, Ohio. Census records locate him in Morrow County in 1860. She used the name Waisbrooker as early as 1865, when she served as secretary for a meeting of Spiritualists held in Chicago. Family legend, however, records that she changed her name because relatives disapproved of the controversial ideas she espoused, one of which was Spiritualism. "It was more than a 'pen name,'" Hardin states. "Her granddaughter never mentioned her in her 'diary' as other than 'grandmother Waisbrooker.'"

9. For coverage of Julia Branch's speech, see "Convention in Rutland," *BoL* 3 (10 July

1858): 3. For an account of Lizzie Doten's speech, see "Lizzie Doten at the Melodeon," *BoL* 5 (2 Apr. 1859): 5. The quote is from "Marriage, Individual and National," *BoL* 9 (29 June 1861): 8.

10. Braude, *Radical Spirits*, 201.

11. "Minnesota Quarterly Convention of Spiritualists," *RPJ*, 10 Apr. 1869, 6. According to this report, she was a trance speaker. For a description of her speaking style, see *BoL* 24 (6 Feb. 1869): 4: "Mrs. Waisbrooker's lectures on Sunday were not largely attended, but her audiences were made up of people who are not afraid of new ideas—people who desire further light on the new and startling facts pertaining to the living issues of the present age. Though speaking without notes, her discourses were distinguished for good logic, progressive ideas, conciseness in arrangement, and were forcibly delivered."

12. One of the first steps toward perfect motherhood, she wrote in 1893, "is to secure to woman freedom from intrusion upon her person, even by a husband." See "The First Step," *FP* 4 (Aug. 1893): 4.

13. "These are documents which should be scattered broadcast over the land. They do lasting credit to the *head* as well to the heart of woman." See E. Hovey, Buffalo, Mo., "Illness of Lois Waisbrooker," *BoL* 24 (30 Jan. 1869): 8. She left nearly two thousand of the tracts with C. C. Colby of Carthage, Missouri. See "Mrs. Waisbrooker's Tracts in Southwestern Missouri," *BoL* 24 (20 Mar. 1869): 8.

14. For a full listing of Waisbrooker's books and pamphlets, see the bibliography. For discussion of her book's themes, see Braude, *Radical Spirits*, 137. In *Helen Harlow's Vow*, for instance, she tells the story of a young woman, seduced and deserted, scorned by society, and left alone to raise a son. Waisbrooker's descendants claim that *Mayweed Blossoms* is an autobiographical novel. She edited *Foundation Principles* (Clinton, Iowa, and Antioch, Calif., 1885–86; Topeka, Kans., 1893–94), served as acting editor of *Lucifer* (Topeka, Kans., 1892–93), and edited *Clothed With the Sun* (San Francisco, Calif., and Home, Wash., ca. 1900–1902). Waisbrooker is interred in an Antioch, Calif., grave with her son, Abner Fuller.

15. *Helen Harlow's Vow* was reprinted as late as 1890 by the Murray Hill Publishing Company, N.Y.

16. *BoL* 3 (27 Jan. 1872): 2; H. W. T., Laona, N.Y., *BoL* 30 (6 Jan. 1872).

17. No issues of *Our Age* appear to be extant today. In 1873 Waisbrooker reprinted *The Sex Question* with two other pamphlets as *The Occult Forces of Sex*.

18. *WCW*, 16 Oct. 1875.

19. *HC* 7 (29 Sept. 1877): 2.

20. Prompted by Heywood's conviction in 1878 for publishing and distributing a free love treatise entitled *Cupid's Yokes*, Waisbrooker wrote *From Generation to Regeneration* (1879), a tract in which she articulated her belief that sexuality would provide the human race with the key to immortality.

21. Quoted in Sears, *Sex Radicals*, 232.

22. Waisbrooker, "Wanted—Correspondents," *HC* 5 (17 June 1876): 1.

23. During this time Waisbrooker published *Facts and Figures for Working Men* (1886) as well as new editions of her novels.

24. For discussion of the horse penis episode, see Sears, *Sex Radicals*, 229–31. Moses

Harman provided her with his mailing list. The quote is from Mary E. Lease, *FPr* 4 (July 1893): 1.

25. "Not a Nickel," *FPr* 5 (15 July 1894): 6.

26. Anonymous [alone in her study], *FPr* 4 (Oct. 1893): 6; N. M. M., Junction City, Wash., *FPr* 5 (15 July 1894): 1; Ellen H. Taylor, *FPr* (14 Aug. 1894).

27. B. Childs, Council Bluffs, Iowa, *FPr* 4 (Aug. 1893): 3; Sylvina L. Woodard, Golden Eagle, Ill., *FPr* 4 (Aug. 1893): 3; George McNinch, New Basil, Kans., *FPr* 5 (15 July 1894): 6. For examples of those who distributed copies, see Mrs. Rose C. Dunham, Mammoth Springs, Ark., *FPr* 4 (Apr. 1894): 5; D. S. Hall, Riverside, Calif., *FPr* 5 (1 Aug. 1894): 6.

28. Waisbrooker, *FPr* 5 (15 Aug. 1894): 4; E. B. Foote to the U.S. attorney general, undated, Ginzburg Papers, box 6, folder 2. Waisbrooker discusses the arrest in a letter to E. B. Foote, 1 Aug. 1894, Ginzburg Papers, box 6, folder 2. The case was dismissed 30 June 1896. While waiting for its resolution, Waisbrooker published *Anything More My Lord* (1895).

29. Stephen T. Byington, "Anarchist Letter-Writing Corps," *Liberty* 13 (Aug. 1897): 5.

30. Federal manuscript population census, San Francisco, Calif., 1900; and "Signs of Progress," *FS*, 17 Dec. 1897.

31. Issues of *Clothed with the Sun* are available in the Library of the Kansas State Historical Society, Topeka, Kans., and in the Labadie Collection. The "Oh, woman" quote is from *CWTS* (Jan. 1902); the "Remember!!!" quote is from *FPr* 3 (20 Oct. 1886): 8.

32. For a fuller account of the Home Colony, see LeWarne, *Utopias on Puget Sound*.

33. X. X., Des Moines, Iowa, *LLB*, 10 Sept. 1898.

34. The well-known abolitionist Gerrit Smith also came from Madison County, N.Y. For further details, see Hammond, *History of Madison County,* 254.

35. Severance, "Farmer's Wives," 275.

36. Ibid., 274–75.

37. For information about the DeRuyter Seminary, see Hammond, *History of Madison County,* 266–67. For insight into Juliet Worth's formative years, see "A Dress Reform Basket Picnic," *Universe,* 28 Aug. 1869.

38. Although few institutions admitted women to study medicine, some studied privately with liberal physicians. For additional information on this practice, see Bacon, *Mothers of Feminism,* 152; Cross, *Burned-Over District,* 241, 329, 351. It is likely that Juliet Worth studied with Dr. Ira Spencer, who completed his medical studies and settled in DeRuyter in 1830. A self-made man, he pursued his studies while teaching school and went on to have a forty-year medical career. For more about the Madison County medical society, see Smith, *Our Country and Its People,* 532–33.

39. Cayleff, *Wash and Be Healed,* 16. Eager to shore up their professional authority, members of the Madison County Medical society ridiculed the lecturers on mesmerism and clairvoyance who in the 1840s and 1850s circulated throughout the county speaking to responsive audiences.

40. Juliet Stillman described her practice as a water-cure physician in *WCJ* 29 (May 1860): 70. Trall opened the New York Hydropathic School in 1853, shortly after Thomas L. and Mary Gove Nichols discontinued their American Hydropathic Institute, and in 1857 he changed its name to the New York Hygeio-Therapeutic College.

41. Trall, *Sexual Physiology*, 214. For more on Trall's views of female sexuality, see Cayleff, *Wash and Be Healed*, 56–57.

42. Cayleff, *Wash and Be Healed*, 17, 18. For a resolution prepared by the 1858 graduating class stipulating, "we rejoice in the gradual emancipation of woman's mind from the narrow sphere which is commonly assigned her," see *WCJ* 25 (Apr. 1858): 74.

43. "A Wedding on Hydropathic Principles," *WCJ* 24 (Nov. 1857): 107. Elizabeth Blackwell, the first American woman trained as a regular physician, applied to numerous medical schools without success before being admitted—as an exception—to New York's Geneva College in 1847. The Medical College of Pennsylvania, influenced by Quakers, admitted women beginning in 1850. For further information, see Bacon, *Mothers of Feminism*, 152.

44. Willard and Livermore, *Woman of the Century*, 643.

45. Severance, *Lecture on the Evolution of Life in Earth and Spirit Conditions*, 12; "Famous Woman Once Whitewater Resident," *WR*, 16 Oct. 1919.

46. *Gazetteer and Directory of Clinton County, Iowa*, 250. For the population of Clinton County in 1850, which was 2,822, see *History of Clinton County, Iowa* (1976), 39. The population in 1856 was about a thousand.

47. For a discussion of water-cure graduates and their degrees, see Cayleff, *Wash and Be Healed*, 99.

48. *History of Clinton County, Iowa* (1978), 53; *History of Clinton County, Iowa* (1879), 425.

49. "The Regulars and Our Grads," *WCJ* 25 (Nov. 1858): 89. The "presence" quote is from Cayleff, *Wash and Be Healed*, 53. For discussion of ailments treated, see pp. 15, 145.

50. For "withered and blighted," see Severance, *Lecture on the Evolution of Life in Earth and Spirit Conditions*, 23.

51. Information about the Clinton County Underground Railroad is found in *History of Clinton County, Iowa* (1976), 55; *History of Clinton County, Iowa* (1879), 414–16. Some county residents shared Juliet Stillman's opposition to slavery and gave money and supplies to support the cause, while others threatened to tar and feather the "damned" abolitionists in their midst. Stillman handled fundraising and correspondence for the local Underground Railroad and at times provided agents.

52. *Juliet H. Stillman v. J. Dwight Stillman*, case no. 3863, 18 June 1866, Circuit Court, Walworth County, Wis.

53. Announcements of Juliet H. Stillman's water-cure practice are found in *WR*, 14 Nov. 1862 and 28 Nov. 1862. The *WR* contained ads for clairvoyants and magnetists. Whitewater is described in Cravath, *Early Annals*. Local dress reformers and vegetarians included Mary Severance, wife of Anson B. Severance. For more on reform in Whitewater, see Hampsten, *Read This Only to Yourself*, 107. The reference to "dark invaders" is from *WR*, 22 May 1863.

54. Stillman spoke throughout Illinois, Minnesota, and Wisconsin. See "Sixth Annual Festival of the Religio-Philosophical Society," *RPJ*, 26 Aug. 1865, 1; "Grove Meeeting at Belvidere, Boone County, Illinois," *RPJ*, 14 Oct. 1865, 8; Willard and Livermore, *Woman of the Century*.

55. Severance, *Lecture on the Evolution of Life in Earth and Spirit Conditions*, 22.

56. Anson B. Severance, a fiddler, performed at inaugural balls, weddings, barn raisings, quilting bees, and other events as he traveled throughout the state with members of

the Severance and Williams Band, at one time composed entirely of Spiritualist musicians. With his brother, he also embarked on a successful career as a dancing master and encouraged hundreds of Wisconsin citizens to take up this form of exercise, which would improve circulation, develop "muscular activity and nerve power," and improve one's performance in social situations. For more, see his obituary, *Waukesha (Wis.) Freeman,* 4 Oct. 1897.

57. Anson B. Severance/Mary Severance divorce, 28 Apr. 1869, Circuit Court for Milwaukee (Equity), Record Book 32, p. 151, case no. 9671, Milwaukee County Historical Society, Milwaukee, Wis. For the Mary Severance psychometric reading of Lyman Draper, see Mrs. A. B. Severance to Lyman Draper, 25 Sept. 1888, Lyman C. Draper scrapbook, Wisconsin Historical Society Rare Book Collection, Madison. The "Good Health Tablets" are advertised in *AJE* 1 (1907): 168. The tablets remained available even after her death, sold by Truman M. Watson, the man with whom she had lived after her divorce from A. B. Severance.

58. Severance/Stillman, Marriages, 1868–85, vol. 4, p. 13, Walworth County Courthouse, Office of County Clerk, Elkhorn, Wis. For sarcastic comments about Juliet Stillman Severance following her marriage, see "Frontier Department," *RPJ,* 10 July 1869, 8. Severence wore the reform dress throughout the 1870s.

59. Juliet Severance was elected president of Wisconsin's Spiritualists in 1878 and also served as president of state associations of Spiritualists in Illinois and Minnesota.

60. The quote from the *Dubuque Herald* is reprinted in "Juliet H. Severance, M.D.," *Circular of Slayton's Lyceum Bureau,* 1878–79, Chicago Historical Society, Chicago, Ill.

61. "Our Lake Pleasant Battle," *HC* 7 (Sept. 1877), 4.

62. Foner, *Story of American Freedom,* 13–14.

63. "Famous Woman Once Whitewater Resident," *WR,* 16 Oct. 1919.

64. Commenting on factionalism within the Liberal League, Severance's hometown paper editorialized: "The difficulty with which the better class of Liberals have to contend is with the faction of free lovers." See "A New Liberal League," *MS,* 22 Sept. 1880, 8.

65. Juliet H. Severance, "Woman Suffrage in Wyoming," *MS,* 26 Nov. 1883, 7. Discussion of her possible mayoral candidacy appears in *TS* 15 (13 Oct. 1888): 652.

66. See *Transactions of the Wisconsin State Agricultural Society* (1885), 253–56; "Mrs. Severance on Spiritualism," *MS,* 16 Feb. 1885, 3.

67. *MS,* 25 May 1884, 3.

68. In 1885, the Knights of Labor in Milwaukee formed two women's assemblies. A diverse national organization, the Knights of Labor at its peak in 1886 included approximately thirty to thirty-five thousand female members—a scattering of suffragettes, temperance workers, and farm women, with the remainder engaged in the textile and shoe trades. For more information, see Sanders, *Roots of Reform,* 38–41. According to Sanders, the Union Labor party in 1887 represented a coalition of members from the Farmers' Alliance, Agricultural Wheel, Greenbackers, Grangers, and an unofficial delegation of Knights (*Roots of Reform,* 44). For an account of Severance at Union Labor party conventions, see *MS,* 19 Mar. 1887, 3; *MS,* 21 Mar. 1888, 1–2.

69. *MS,* 21 Mar. 1888, 2.

70. For information about Grottkau, see Fink, *Workingmen's Democracy,* 189; for the description of Severance, see "As Seen in Court," *MS,* 6 Dec. 1886, 2.

71. Juliet H. Severance, *LLB*, 12 Nov. 1886.

72. "Is It a Failure? Mrs. Severance's Opinion of Marriage," *MS*, 27 May 1889, 3.

73. For examples of announcements, see *LLB*, 22 May 1902, 149; *Liberty* 8 (12 Sept. 1891).

74. The description of Severance's "Woman's Day Speech" is from *TS* 20 (21 Oct. 1893): 649.

75. Juliet H. Severance, *AJE* 1 (1907): 231–32.

76. Mary E. Preston, "Dear Friends," *LLB*, 17 June 1887, 4; Mrs. Lizzie Putnam, *LLB*, 24 June 1887.

Chapter 6: The Lucifer Match

1. For accounts of the marriage and ensuing events, see especially *LLB*, 24 Sept. 1886, 1 Oct. 1886, 15 Oct. 1886, 22 Oct. 1886. For additional discussion, see Sears, *Sex Radicals*, 81–96. According to Sears (*Sex Radicals*, 91), Moses Harman orchestrated the "free marriage" as a challenge to the state's marriage statutes (the couple was charged with violating *Sec. 12, Chap. 61, Comp. Laws, 1879*). See *LLB*, 31 Aug. 1901, 266, for additional biographical information about Lillian Harman and Edwin C. Walker.

2. Examples of other "reform ceremonies," in which couples challenged marriage laws, include Robert Dale Owen and Mary Robinson (1832), Henry B. Blackwell and Lucy Stone (1855), and Moses Hull and Mattie Sawyer (1874). Many other nineteenth-century Americans lived together in common-law marriages.

3. The quote is from Sears, *Sex Radicals*, 95. The stepbrother's name was W. F. Hiser. For Moses Harman's view of Horton's ruling, see "Horton's Opinion," *LLB*, 1 Apr. 1887, 4. For additional details about the marriage, arrest, trial, and sentencing, see *LLB*, 31 Aug. 1901, 267.

4. A Mr. Thompson of Topeka arrested Moses Harman on 16 Feb. 1887. For an account of his arrest, prolonged legal battle, and prison sentence, see *LLB*, 31 Aug. 1901, 267. For the challenged letters, see *LLB*, 18 June 1886, 25 June 1886, 23 July 1886, 14 Jan. 1887. Malin argues that Harman published those letters to provoke prosecution (*Concern about Humanity*, 109).

5. According to Sears, Harman's growing commitment to free speech stemmed in part from the "suppression of free speech in the Chicago Haymarket case" (*Sex Radicals*, 76). Harman, however, grounded his beliefs about the freedom of expression in natural law, not the First Amendment. Seeking to act on his principles, Harman announced his intent to publish contributors' communications verbatim. See *LLB*, 28 May 1886, 4 June 1886, 11 June 1886. See *LLB*, 24 Sept. 1886 and 24 Feb. 1887, for information about numbers of subscribers. According to J. A. Huffman, Elma, Iowa, readership there doubled after Lillian and Edwin's arrest and quadrupled after Moses Harman's arrest (*LLB*, 19 Aug. 1887, 4).

6. Seward Mitchell, Newport, Maine, quoting Benjamin R. Tucker, editor of *Liberty*, "Can You Afford to Pay the Costs?" *LLB*, 31 Dec. 1886, 3.

7. *LLB*, 22 Nov. 1886, 2.

8. *LLB*, 12 Nov. 1886, 2.

9. After years of living separately from Walker, Harman quietly and legally married George O'Brien.

10. For examples of Lillian Harman's role in sustaining *LLB*, especially during her fa-

ther's imprisonment, see Jo Labadie Papers, folder Fm-Hi, and the Henry Bool Papers, Labadie Collection. Her publications included *Problems of Social Freedom* (1898), *Marriage and Morality* (1900), and *The Regeneration of Society* (1900). For the quote about a woman in freedom, see Mary M. Clark, Albia, Iowa, *LLB*, 13 July 1901, 204.

11. Gordon, *Woman's Body, Woman's Right*, 6; for more on social purity reform, see chap. 6. Boyer, *Purity in Print;* Pivar, *Purity Crusade*. For a more detailed explanation of voluntary motherhood, see Gordon, *Woman's Body, Woman's Right*, chap. 5.

12. Lillian Harman, "An 'Age-of-Consent' Symposium," *LLB*, 1 Mar. 1895, 2–3.

13. Lillian Harman, "An Age-of-Consent Symposium," *Liberty* 10 (9 Feb. 1895): 2–5.

14. A. I., response to "To Free Lovers by P.A.S.," *Firebrand* 3 (2 May 1897).

15. Lillie D. White, "The Coming Woman," *LLB*, 2 Dec. 1893, 3. Other correspondents who helped reinforce the idea of women as victims include Lois Waisbrooker, "A Prostitute," *LLB*, 2 Dec. 1893, 3; Susan A. Catton, Franhurst, Del., *LLB*, 3 Nov. 1893, 4; W. G. Markland, Sale Creek, Tenn., *LLB*, 15 July 1887, 4. Had not, asked Mell Peirce of readers, Edwin Walker secured "a prize" for his companion when he entered into the "free marriage" with Lillian Harman? See Peirce, *LLB*, 24 Dec. 1886, 4.

16. Lucy Parsons, *LLB*, 27 Apr. 1894.

17. Flora Fox, Minn., *LLB*, 3 Nov. 1893, 1; Emma Best, *LLB*, 27 Apr. 1905, 294.

18. Lois Waisbrooker, *LLB*, 23 Mar. 1894, 3.

19. Angela T. Heywood, "Ethics of Sexuality," *The Word* 9 (Apr. 1881): 3; Eudora, *LLB*, 9 Feb. 1894, 3. On numerous occasions, Lois Waisbrooker argued that women's sexual passion could be increased if men delayed or deferred orgasms. See, for example, *FPr* 5 (5 June 1894): 5, in which Waisbrooker writes that "many women would like to caress their husbands if they then didn't press on to consummate their animal desire." For additional insight into her ideas about sexual desire, see Waisbrooker, "Which Is Best?" *FPr* 5 (1 Oct. 1894): 4.

20. For the reference to soul attraction, see Mattie E. Hurson, Clinton, Iowa, *LLB*, 25 Mar. 1887, 1; for the reference to "spiritual and intellectual needs," see Lois Waisbrooker, *LLB*, 16 Feb. 1894, 3; for the reference to "nature's call," see Waisbrooker, *LLB*, 23 Mar. 1894, 3. See also Allie Lindsay Lynch, *LLB*, 26 Jan. 1894.

21. All references are from *The Word* 15 (Oct. 1886): 1–3.

22. "Not Compromise, but Surrender," *Liberty* 4 (30 Oct. 1886): 4. For more commentary on Tucker's position, see also "The Kansas Victims of Law," *TS* 13 (6 Nov. 1886): 713.

23. The reference to "unmarry themselves" is from *Liberty* 4 (30 Oct. 1886): 4. Walker's position is described in Sears, *Sex Radicals*, 103.

24. For Putnam's endorsement, see *Liberty* 4 (20 Nov. 1886): 4. For the reference to "Comstockism," see *TS* 6 (13 Sept. 1879): 585.

25. Juliet H. Severance, "The Kansas Arrests," *TS* 13 (30 Oct. 1886): 694–95. See also Severance, "The Truth Seeker's Editor Misled," *TS* 13 (29 May 1886), 343.

26. "On Picket Duty," *Liberty* 2 (14 Apr. 1883): 1; Hannah J. Hunt, "A Woman's Defense of Women," and editor's response, *Liberty* 8 (19 Sept. 1891): 1; E. C. Walker, Valley Falls, Kans., *The Word* 14 (13 Dec. 1885): 3; Juliet H. Severance, *TS* 21 (10 Nov. 1894).

27. According to *LLB*, 12 Nov. 1886, 3, contributors to the defense fund sent money from Alabama, Arkansas, California, Colorado, Connecticut, Dakota Territory, Delaware, Florida, Illinois, Iowa, Kansas, Massachusetts, Michigan, Minnesota, Missouri, Montana, New

Jersey, Nebraska, New York, Pennsylvania, Texas, Virginia, and Wisconsin. The same issue contains acknowledgements of the gift of pamphlets.

28. For examples of women's admiration for Lillian Harman and requests for her photo, see Mell Pierce, New Hartford, Iowa; Miss M. E. Gleason, Geneva, Ohio; and Milda Thorne, Philadelphia, Pa., all in *LLB*, 24 Dec. 1886, 4. Men also expressed their admiration of young Harman. John Stoll, for example, compared her to the martyrs of old in *LLB*, 24 Dec. 1886, 4; Seward Mitchell, Newport, Maine, likened her to "the world's saviors" in *LLB*, 31 Dec. 1886, 3; Francis Barry of Ohio expressed similar sentiments in the same issue.

29. Anonymous, *LLB*, 29 Oct. 1886, 6. Caroline Severance made a similar observation in the same issue (p. 3). Writing fifteen years later, Mrs. L. J., *LLB*, 14 Sept. 1901, 286, described her own coming out as the time when she became "ashamed to write anonymously" and thereafter wrote her views "over my own name."

30. Ostler, *Prairie Populism*, esp. chap. 2. For another perspective on economic conditions in late nineteenth-century rural Kansas, see Whitehead, *History of Radical Politics in America*.

31. An Illinois contributor, J. C. Barnes, argued, "All protests against laws are Anarchistic in degree." See "Free Land and Free Motherhood," *LLB*, 2 Apr. 1903, 91.

32. As proof, correspondents made frequent comments about "pale and sunken features of the wives and mothers, telling but too plainly of lust run rampant." See D. C. S., Miltonvale, Kans., *LLB*, 26 Nov. 1886, 4. For other examples, see Maud Abbey, "A Sketch from Real Life," *LLB*, 27 July 1901, 222; Annie E. Higby, *LLB*, 6 May 1887, 3.

33. Quoted in Goldman, *Living My Life*, 240–43.

34. Lydia E. Blackstone, Chester, N.H., *LLB*, 14 Oct. 1887, 4.

35. Elmina Slenker believed that free and open communication represented the only way women could be saved. See *LLB*, 29 July 1887, 4.

36. See, for example, Maud Abbey, *LLB*, 27 July 1901, 22.

37. For examples, see Elsie H. Clark, Kipton, Ohio, *LLB*, 14 July 1893, 3; Lucille Meredith, Stockton, Calif., *LLB*, 9 Mar. 1894, 2. For a nurse's insights, see N. E. P., Oklahoma City, Okla. *LLB*, 29 Nov. 1893, 4.

38. Dagmar Mariager, "Another Open Letter," 30–31.

39. Quoted in *LLB*, 22 June 1888. For examples of wife abuse excerpted from newspapers, see "Two Recent Divorces," *LLB*, 8 Dec. 1893, 1; "Another 'Markland Letter' Case," *LLB*, 17 Aug. 1901, 244.

40. J. Hacker, Vineland, N.J., *LLB*, 9 Nov. 1894, 1.

41. W. G. Markland, letter to *LLB*, reprinted in *Kansas Fight for Free Press*, 4–5. For another examples, see J. H. Cook, "Sexual Rapacity, Rape, Legal and Illegal," *LLB*, 18 Mar. 1887, 1.

42. Edwin C. Walker, "The Protection of Woman," *LLB*, 2 Dec. 1887, 2.

43. W. Cawley, *LLB*, 23 Mar. 1894, 3. Using the same logic, correspondents viewed Edwin C. Walker as the embodiment of manhood because he promised, in his "free marriage" vows, that Lillian could "repulse any and all advances of mine." See Virginia, *LLB*, 10 Oct. 1886, 3.

44. Lois Waisbrooker, "The Difference," *FPr* 5 (15 Sept. 1894), 5.

45. A. B. Severance, *LLB*, 9 Feb. 1894, 3.

46. A. L. Washburn, Loveland, Colo., *LLB*, 22 Sept. 1893, 3.

47. For examples in which correspondents make references to shackles, see J. F. Macomber, Minneapolis, *LLB*, 26 Nov. 1886, 4; to chains and bondage, see Miss E. M. Gleason, Geneva, Ohio, *LLB*, 4 Dec. 1886, 4. Lucinda B. Chandler charged in 1886 that husbands, like slaveholders, "covered up" the "inhumanities" inherent in marriage "lest the 'sacred institution' itself be called to account." She is quoted in *Kansas Fight for Free Press*, 5. Numerous sex radicals also made reference to their earlier involvement in abolitionism. See, for example, Jesse S. Perkins, Gaines Station, *LLB*, 9 Feb. 1894, 3–4; Abner J. Pope, *LLB*, 6 Apr. 1894, 2; R. M. Stanton, Chadron, Neb., *LLB*, 1 Feb. 1895, 3; Sarah M. Chase, *LLB*, 15 Mar. 1895, 4. At times they called themselves abolitionists. For one example, see Moses Harman, "Are We Abolitionists?" *LLB*, 18 Feb. 1887, 2.

48. G. C. Jones, Pierce City, Mo., *LLB*, 24 Dec. 1886, 4.

49. Virginia, *LLB*, 29 Oct. 1886, 3.

50. Caroline Severance, *LLB*, 29 Oct. 1886, 3. For other examples of women finding fault with Christian teachings about marriage, see Lois Waisbrooker, "An Opportunity," *FP* (Mar. 1894), 5; Annie E. Higby, *LLB*, 6 May 1887, 3; Caroline Severance, *LLB*, 11 Feb. 1887, 3.

51. S. W. Prescott, *LLB*, 23 Mar. 1894, 4. Many expressed sentiments similar to Virginia's Elmina Slenker, who in "Superior," *LLB*, 25 May 1894, 3, concluded that "slaves are not expected to free themselves." See *LLB*, 19 Oct. 1894, 2. Some women, however, had little sympathy for "a willing slave." For this example, see Alice M. P., Keokuk, Iowa, *LLB*, 25 Aug. 1893, 3.

52. Anonymous, "Not a Nickel," *FPr* 5 (15 July 1894): 6.

53. *LLB*, 12 Nov. 1886, 4.

54. See Moses Harman's response to Alice M. P., *LLB*, 25 Aug. 1893, 3, in which he reasons, "Like begats like."

55. Dora Foster, *LLB*, 10 Oct. 1903, 310.

56. For the reference to Mosaic law, see Thorne, *LLB*, 24 Dec. 1886, 4. The discussion about women's responsibility for the fall is found in *FPr* 4 (Aug. 1893): 4. The quote about motherhood is from W. Chamberlain, *FPr* 5 (15 Sept. 1894): 5.

57. Lois Waisbrooker, *LLB*, 23 Mar. 1894, 3. For more of her views, see *FPr* 5 (15 July 1894): 4.

58. Angela T. Heywood, "The Woman's View of It—No. 4," *The Word* 11 (Apr. 1883): 2. "Womb" is her word for vagina.

59. Brodie, *Contraception and Abortion in Nineteenth-Century America*, 66. For more about the theory of male continence, see Noyes, *Male Continence*. For insight into its practice at Oneida, see Fogarty, *Special Love/Special Sex*. An ancient technique, coitus reservatus (or, as Noyes called it, male continence) was not widely used in the United States until after he described it in *The Bible Argument.*

60. Francis Barry, "Crudities Criticized—No. 4," *LLB*, 18 June 1898, 190.

61. Heywood, *Cupid's Yokes*, 19, 23. Heywood triggered his prosecution by Anthony Comstock with this pamphlet by providing information about a version of male continence. Convicted in 1878 and sentenced to a two-year federal prison sentence, Heywood later received a pardon from Rutherford B. Hayes. For more on those events and their politicizing affect on Heywood's life, see Blatt, *Free Love and Anarchism*, esp. chap. 5.

62. Contrary to popular perception, sex radicals did not endorse licentious behavior but instead encouraged women and men to impose rigid restrictions on their sexuality.

Thus, it was not so incongruous that Elmina Slenker promoted the *Alpha* (a periodical published by Christian social purity reformers) in the pages of *Lucifer*.

63. Alfred Cridge, *LLB*, 17 Dec. 1886, 1. The logical outcome, Cridge noted as he reminded readers of Thomas and Mary Gove Nichols, was conversion to Catholicism.

64. For further discussion of Alphaism, see Sears, *Sex Radicals*, 207–9.

65. Parkhurst, *Diana*, 20–22, 39. The author explained his motivation for writing Diana in *LLB*, 29 July 1887, 1.

66. This female-centeredness is evident in the serialized story "Hagar Lyndon." Near the close of the story, Hagar's brother-in-law Dan, a selfish and demanding husband, informs her that he has left his wife Lucy and their children. He loves her, but the two fight constantly and he becomes "a brute." Hagar instructs him to make a comfortable room for himself over the stables and to "leave the house, except at meal-times and when invited." Advising Dan to treat Lucy "as though she were a lady . . . whom you wish to please and attract," Hagar emphasizes that, above all, he must not "obtrude" himself upon her. See "Hagar Lyndon," *LLB*, 8 Sept. 1893, 1, 4

67. Elmina Slenker, *LLB*, 23 Mar. 1894, 3, wrote: "Under present hereditary conditions and present teaching all cannot be Dianites . . . but all can grow towards it."

68. Mrs. Mary M. Clark, "My Testimony," *LLB*, 25 May 1894, 3–4. She credited Dianaism with the birth of her three healthy children

69. Francis Barry, "Crudities Criticized—No. 4," *LLB*, 18 June 1898, 190; Elmina Dranke Slenker, "Nonsense," *LLB* [1894], undated clipping in Ginzburg Papers, box 5, folder 10.

70. Alice B. Stockham to Theodore Schroeder, 27 Aug. 1906, Ginzburg Papers, box 5, folder 17.

71. Stockham, *Karezza*, 19, 23–25. The author defined her system as "no more male than female continence" and defined Karezza as "to express affection in both words and actions." Sears, *Sex Radicals*, 210, notes that Stockham, like Heywood before her, reprinted portions of Noyes' *Male Continence*, no longer in print in 1897. Stockham also published *Tokology*, which, according to the research of the Stanford University physician Clelia Duel Mosher, served as a key text from which late nineteenth-century women learned about sexual physiology. For more details, see Brodie, *Contraception and Abortion in Nineteenth-Century America*, 202–3.

72. J. V. Carter, Durant, I. T. [Indian Territory], *LLB*, 22 Jan. 1903, 14; Mrs. G. L., Canton, Ohio, *LLB*, 12 June 1902, 173.

73. Albina Washburn, *LLB*, 24 Nov. 1897, 374. For other examples of her interactions with WCTU members, see *LLB*, 8 Dec. 1893, 2; Washburn, *LLB*, 23 Mar. 1894, 4. For additional letters on the subject of woman suffrage, see Zoa Topsis, *LLB*, 5 Aug. 1887, 1; J. G. Truman, *LLB*, 29 June 1894.

74. Mrs. Maria Ingraham, Lake Mills, Wis., *LLB*, 6 May 1887, 4; Lois Waisbrooker, *LLB*, 22 Dec. 1897, 407.

75. Lillie D. White, *LLB*, 2 Dec. 1893, 3.

76. Edwin C. Walker, "A Fundamental Error," *LLB*, 15 Apr. 1887, 3.

77. William Gilmore, *LLB*, 10 Nov. 1897, 354.

78. Edwin C. Walker, *LLB*, 29 Oct. 1886, 3.

79. D. C. S., *LLB*, 26 Nov. 1886, 4. Others who believed that mothers must be free in order

to give birth to free children include Frank Harman, *LLB,* 15 Apr. 1887, 4; Lois Waisbrooker, *FPr* 4 (July 1893), 2.

80. Milda Thorne, "Mrs. Lillian Harman," *LLB,* 24 Dec. 1886, 4.

Chapter 7: Motherhood in Freedom

1. For insight into Lois Waisbrooker's understanding of female sexuality, see her publications, esp. *The Fountain of Life; The Occult Forces of Sex; A Sex Revolution.*

2. For more on Harman's hereditarian theories and eugenic beliefs, see Sears, *Sex Radicals,* 78, 121–22, 125–26.

3. See Bellamy, *Experiment with Marriage;* Hardy, *Jude, the Obscure;* Olerich, *Cityless and Countryless World;* Pittock, *God of Civilization;* Schreiner, *Story of an African Farm.* For a discussion of why *Jude, the Obscure* was seen as part of a crusade against marriage, see Heilman, "Hardy's *Sue Bridehead.*" For examples of Spiritualist, socialist, and anarchist works, see Doten, *My Affinity and Other Stories;* Fowler, *Irene;* Howland, *The Familistere;* Kelly, *Frances* and *On the Inside;* Slenker, *The Darwins;* Stockham and Hood-Talbot, *Koradine;* Waisbrooker, *Alice Vale, Helen Harlow's Vow, Maywood Blossoms, Perfect Motherhood.* See Steward, *Charleston Love Story* for a fictional critique of free love.

4. A former resident of Berlin Heights, Ohio, Lillie D. White represents a link between antebellum and postbellum sex radicals.

5. For further biographical information about Holmes, see Tax, *Rising of the Women,* chap. 2.

6. "Hagar Lyndon," *LLB,* 28 July 1893, 1, 4; 18 Aug. 1893. Readers familiar with the Bible would have recognized Hagar as the name of Abraham's concubine who was driven into the desert with her son Ishmael because of his wife Sarah's jealousy. Some also would have noted the connection suggested by Hagar Lyndon's last name with the title character of Mary Gove Nichols' earlier novel, *Mary Lyndon.*

7. "Hagar Lyndon," *LLB,* 8 Sept. 1893, 4.

8. Thirza Rathbun, San Andreas, Calif., *LLB,* 8 Sept. 1893, 3; Allie Lindsay Lynch, Memphis, Tenn., *LLB,* 24 Nov. 1893, 3; Lois Waisbrooker, "Hagar Lyndon," *LLB,* 28 July 1893, 3.

9. L. E. H., Milpitas, Calif., *LLB,* 11 Aug. 1893, 1. For examples of women's praise of *Hagar Lyndon,* see Allie Lindsay Lynch, Tenn., *LLB,* 24 Nov. 1893, 3; Mrs. P. Clark, Ionia, Mich., *LLB,* 26 Jan. 1894; Elmina Slenker, "Paternal Love," *LLB,* 15 Sept. 1893, 1. Readers of *Foundation Principles* also discussed *Hagar Lyndon* and used it as a point of reference, comparing themselves and their friends to the novel's heroine. Sylvana L. Woodard, Golden Eagle, Ill., writing in *FPr* 4 (Aug. 1893): 3, complimented a friend by comparing her with the title character of Holmes's novel: "She was born and brought up in hell at home . . . but somehow being a sensible girl she has like Hagar Lyndon grown into a thinker."

10. Foner, *Story of American Freedom,* 112. For additional insight into Reconstruction-era women's rights, see DuBois, *Woman Suffrage and Women's Rights;* Flexner, *Century of Struggle;* Gordon with Collier-Thomas, *African American Women and the Vote.*

11. Foner, *Story of American Freedom,* 113. The sex radical feminists who are the subject of this study also belong in this grouping because they derived their alternative understanding of freedom from "powerful currents of American individualism and libertarianism." See Hirshman and Larsen, *Hard Bargains,* 138.

12. I. E. R., N.J., *LLB,* 29 July 1887, 4.

13. A. L. Washburn, Loveland, Colo., *LLB,* 22 Sept. 1893, 3; Lois Waisbrooker, "The Difference," *FPr* 5 (15 Sept. 1894), 5; A. B. Severance, *LLB,* 9 Feb. 1894, 3.

14. Gordon, *Woman's Body, Woman's Right,* 6. For more on social-purity reform, see Gordon, chap. 6; Boyer, *Purity in Print;* Pivar, *Purity Crusade.* For a more detailed explanation of voluntary motherhood, see Gordon, chap. 5.

15. Mattie Hursen, Mich., *LLB,* 7 Apr. 1897, 111; Sara Crist Campbell, *LLB,* 3 Dec. 1903, 37; Lois Waisbrooker, *LLB,* 23 Mar. 1894, 3.

16. For the reference to "soul attraction," see Mattie E. Hurson, Clinton, Iowa, *LLB,* 25 Mar. 1887, 1; to "spiritual and intellectual needs," see Lois Waisbrooker, *LLB,* 16 Feb. 1894, 3; to "nature's call," see Waisbrooker, *LLB,* 23 Mar. 1894, 3.

17. Josephine Croff, *LLB,* 7 Oct. 1887, 1; Cornelia Forward, Manton, Calif., *LLB,* 20 Mar. 1902, 78; S. P., *LLB,* 1 Sept. 1893, 4.

18. Mattie Hursen, *LLB,* 7 Apr. 1897, 112; Sarah M. Chipman, "Natural Rights," *Liberty* 5 (12 May 1888): 1; Lucy Parsons, *LLB,* 27 Apr. 1894.

19. For more on Slenker's motives, see *LLB,* 15 June 1894, 3; *LLB,* 7 Sept. 1894, 2; *LLB,* 19 Oct. 1894, 3. The quote is from Slenker, *LLB,* 15 June 1894, 3.

20. Lois Waisbrooker, *LLB,* 5 Oct. 1894, 4; Volteraine deCleyre, *LLB,* 5 Oct. 1894, 3; Mary W. Conway, *LLB,* 18 Jan. 1895, 4.

21. Elsie Wilcox, *LLB,* 28 Dec. 1894, 3; Lucinda B. Chandler, *LLB,* 22 Feb. 1895, 3; Flora Fox, *LLB,* 11 Jan. 1895, 3; Mrs. M., N.D., *LLB,* 18 Feb. 1904, 55.

22. John Heritage, *LLB,* 25 Jan. 1895; Elsie Wilcox, Wash., *LLB,* 28 Dec. 1894, 3. Lucinda Chandler, *LLB,* 22 Feb. 1898, 3, countered that it was easy to drop onerous correspondence.

23. For the discussion of "vital energy," see Celia B. Whitehead, *LLB,* 17 Dec. 1886, 1. For Kate Austin's observation about nature, see "Is Such Desire Normal?" *LLB,* 9 Feb. 1894, 1; for her assertion that sex during pregnancy would have negative consequences for the fetus, see *LLB,* 9 Mar. 1894, 2. She drew support for her position from the writings of Alice B. Stockham, especially *Tokology.*

24. Alma Vail, Calif., *LLB,* 13 Apr. 1894, 3; Lois Waisbrooker, *LLB,* 23 Mar. 1894, 3; Lois Waisbrooker, "Loving Attentions," *LLB,* 16 Feb. 1894, 3. Vail relayed the story of a pregnant soldier's wife who suppressed her sexual urges during his extended absence only to give birth to a child who became a "sex maniac." Waisbrooker defined sexual relations broadly and argued that they did not always have to culminate in penetration and ejaculation. She offered a similar observation in *FP* 5 (15 Sept. 1894): 1.

25. Laura H. Earle, Redford, N.Y., *LLB,* 12 Nov. 1903, 350; Dora Forster, "Sex Morality, Bond and Free," *LLB,* 3 Dec. 1903, 369; Sarah Crist Campbell, "Perpetuity and Happiness of Humanity," *LLB,* 3 Dec. 1903, 373; Angela T. Heywood, "The Ethics of Sexuality," *The Word* 9 (Apr. 1881): 3; Lois Waisbrooker, *LLB,* 16 Feb. 1894, 3, and *LLB,* 23 Mar. 1894, 3. Heywood's descriptions in *The Word* led the free lover Marx Edgeworth Lazarus to call the journal "phallic and angelically voluptuous, while *Lucifer* is rather ascetic and Malthusian." See [Marx] Edgeworth [Lazarus], Guntersville, Ala., *The Word* 18 (Sept. 1889): 3.

26. According to Dora Forster, *LLB,* 3 Dec. 1903, "men more easily lose their self-control." The quotes are from Mattie Hursen, Clinton, Iowa, *LLB,* 25 Mar. 1887, 1; Lois Waisbrooker, *LLB,* 2 Mar. 1894, 2. For another explanation of how a woman "first reaches the

plane from which she can give of the spirit to her companion," see "The Key Note," *LLB*, 2 Mar. 1894, 2.

27. Lois Waisbrooker, "Woman's Power," *LLB*, 21 Apr. 1897, 126. Ida Craddock expressed similar reservations about "preventatives" in *LLB*, 10 Aug. 1901, 239. Waisbrooker's objection to the use of contraceptives was so strong that she endorsed the practice of "self-relief" over "a sex relation with a man and scientific appliances between."

28. During his trial, Ezra Heywood quoted sixteen women, one of whom was Elizabeth M. F. Denton, to show their support of his efforts to disseminate information about contraception. Denton declared "the syringe" a "war measure" that women could employ to "assert their right to exercise discretion in maternity." See Denton, *The Word* 12 (June 1883): 3. The daughter of the sex reformer Dr. E. B. Foote and the wife of *SR* corresponding editor William Denton, Denton contributed regularly to *The Word*, *LLB*, and other sex radical periodicals. The quote is from Angela T. Heywood, "Men, Women, and Things," *The Word* 12 (Oct. 1883): 3. For further examples of Heywood's defense of the syringe as a contraceptive measure, see "The Woman's View of It—No. 2," *The Word* 11 (Feb. 1883): 2; "Men, Women, and Things," *The Word* 12 (June 1883): 3.

29. Amy Linnett, "Continence and Contracepts," *LLB*, 5 May 1897, 139.

30. For one definition of variety, see Robert C. Adams, "A Definition," *LLB*, 3 Aug. 1901, 229. Adams emphasized that it was as wrong to assume a free lover was a varietist as it was to assume a freethinker was an atheist.

31. Edwin C. Walker, "Variety vs. Monogamy," 4; Carrie A., "Why Should Love Die?" *LLB*, 24 Aug. 1901, 250; Lena Belfort, *LLB*, 13 Aug. 1903, 241.

32. Elmina Slenker, *LLB*, 29 July 1887, 4; Flora M., *LLB*, 1 Oct. 1903, 302.

33. Lucy Parsons, "Objections to Variety," *Firebrand* 2 (27 Sept. 1896): 3. A. D., "Another Woman's Views," *LLB*, 25 Nov. 1887, 4, advised establishing cooperative homes before tearing down existing structures. Lucinda B. Chandler, *LLB*, 29 Sept. 1897, 307.

34. J. William Lloyd, *LLB*, 11 Aug. 1897, 250.

35. A. Warren, *LLB*, 8 Sept. 1897, 283; James Thierry, *LLB*, 6 Oct. 1893, 3. J. William Lloyd, *LLB*, 13 Jan. 1897, 2, also wrote of variety as a demand instilled in man by nature.

36. Walker, "Variety vs. Monogamy," 3; J. William Lloyd, *LLB*, 11 Aug. 1897, 250.

37. Anonymous woman, *LLB*, 25 Nov. 1887, 4. For an example of the idealistic perspective, see A. Warren, Wichita Falls, Tex., *LLB*, 11 Mar. 1887, 3.

38. J. B. Elliott, *LLB*, 9 Apr. 1903, 102; Kate Austin, "A Woman's View of It," *Firebrand* 3 (25 Apr. 1897): 6–7. Mrs. M. Beckwith of New York also lamented the disgrace attached to illegitimate children and longed for a time when they would "be considered pure and virtuous under any and all circumstances." See Mrs. M. Beckwith, N.Y., *LLB*, 24 Aug. 1901, 254. For additional insight into sex radical women's views of paternal and maternal love, see Elmina Slenker, *LLB*, 15 Sept. 1893, 1.

39. Franklin, "Freedom for Woman," 9. For further discussion of love children, see Caroline Severance, "Legitimacy," *LLB*, 29 Oct. 1886, 3; Josephine Croff, *LLB*, 7 Oct. 1887, 1. Croff argued that the children of unhappy marriages "are not the kind of children our country needs."

40. For one example of someone who urged individual responsibility, see David Andrade, *LLB*, 30 Sept. 1887, 1. For sex radical women's discussions of unitary, cooperative,

and industrial homes, see Mrs. H. C. Garner, "No Going Backward," *LLB*, 24 Aug. 1901, 251; Lois Waisbrooker, *LLB*, 9 Mar. 1894, 1; Sada Bailey to A. Warren, *LLB*, 8 Apr. 1887, 3. For more on more on unitary households, see Hayden, *Grand Domestic Revolution*, 38, 95, 112, 173. For an example of someone who believed the state should guarantee the care of children, see D. D. Chidester, *LLB*, 10 June 1887, 4. The subject also surfaced at an 1875 meeting of a Social Freedom convention held in Boston, where attendees resolved that a tax should be levied for the care of all children, whether born in or out of wedlock. For further elaboration, see "Social Freedom Convention Resolutions," *The Word* 3 (Apr. 1875): 4. For yet another plan, see Moses Hull, *The Word* 3 (Apr. 1875): 2.

41. For examples from Christian theology of the sins of the fathers being visited on their children, see Exodus 20:5; Leviticus 26:39; Numbers 14:18; 1 Kings 21:29; Isaiah 65:6–7; and Jeremiah 2:9. For more on the idea of race suicide, see Kline, "'Building a Better Race.'" Harbingers of doom attributed the steady decline in white women's birthrate to the advent of the "New Woman," a recurring trope in American history coined in response to changes in women's behavior during the last quarter of the nineteenth century. The historian Carroll Smith-Rosenberg traces the phrase to Henry James, who used it to refer to affluent, single, and urban American women who defied social conventions, while others attributed it to the novelist Ouida. For discussions of the term's origins and applications, see Ardis, *New Women, New Novels;* Caine, *English Feminism,* 134; Smith-Rosenberg, *Disorderly Conduct,* esp. 176–77, 245–96. For more on the ways in which antifeminists employed the idea of voluntary motherhood to support their arguments, see Koven and Michel, *Mothers of a New World;* Gordon, *Woman's Body, Woman's Right,* 128.

42. Johann Gregor Mendel (1822–84) is best known as the Augustinian monastic who in the mid-nineteenth century began genetic research on plants, which led to his explanation of the basic laws governing the transfer of traits from one generation to another. "The rediscovery of Mendelian genetics in 1900," writes George Robb, "galvanized the eugenics movement by providing a mechanism that seemed likely to explain heredity with mathematical precision." See Robb, "Way of All Flesh." For more information, see Cowan, *Sir Francis Galton and the Study of Heredity in the Nineteenth Century.* The Hatch Act became law on 2 Mar. 1887. For a discussion of the better-baby movement, see Holt, *Linoleum, Better Babies, and the Modern Farm Woman,* 109, 111–19, 121, 123.

43. For Harman's ideas, see "Thoughts on Race Suicide," *LLB*, 9 Apr. 1903, 194. For more on the development of eugenic thought, see Galton, *Hereditary Genius;* Dugdale, *The Jukes;* Haller, *Eugenics.*

44. Moses Harman, "Ideals-Ascending and Descending," *LLB*, 27 Aug. 1903, 260; Mary M. Clark, Albia, Iowa, *LLB*, 25 May 1894, 4.

45. R. B. Kerr, "Monogamy and Heredity," *LLB*, 9 Apr. 1903, 99. Kerr wrote to *LLB* from his home in Phoenix, B.C. For additional insight into Kerr's ideas, see "Shall Nature Take Her Course?" *LLB*, 26 Feb. 1903, 49; "Justice to the Unborn," *LLB*, 11 June 1903, 169–70.

46. Philip G. Peabody, *LLB*, 17 June 1903, 179, praised Kerr. Moses Harman, "Ideals—Ascending and Descending," *LLB*, 27 Aug. 1903, 260; *LLB*, 9 Apr. 1903, 99; Lizzie B. Holmes, *LLB*, 14 May 1903, 138; Alex E. Wright, Mass., "The Fatherhood Question," *LLB*, 28 May 1903, 153. For examples of other men who supported Kerr, see M. Trueman, *LLB*, 9 July 1903, 205; C. L. James, *LLB*, 11 June 1903, 170; J. William Lloyd, *LLB*, 16 Mar. 1905, 270. Pointing to the writings of the British sex radical Dora Forster (who later married Kerr) as a

model for American sex radical women, C. L. James noted: "She recognizes the value of studying social science." Carrie Austin argued in *LLB*, 2 July 1903, 193, that women's superior spirituality did not preclude "the possibility of establishing the relation of the sexes on a rational future basis."

47. "I venture to say," wrote Carrie Austin, "that among all the women readers of *Lucifer*'s columns, not more than two or three, or a half-dozen at most, will be found harmonizing with Mr. Kerr." See *LLB*, 20 Aug. 1903, 250. For the quote about "sick or weak men," see Lizzie B. Holmes, *LLB*, 14 May 1903, 138; for the "limits" of science, see Carrie Austin, *LLB*, 20 Aug. 1903, 250; for "Shakespeare," see Rebecca Goodheart, "The Problem of Future Generations," *LLB*, 20 Aug. 1903, 251; for "creative power," see Lillie D. White, *LLB*, 16 Aug. 1903, 234.

48. Lillie White, Lake Charles, La., "Who Shall Say Who Are Radicals?" *LLB*, 12 Nov. 1903, 349. For "old men grannies," see Lillie White, *LLB*, 16 Aug. 1903, 234; for Harman using the term "daughter," see *LLB*, 13 Aug. 1903, 246, and *LLB*, 27 Aug. 1903, 260; for the Whitehead quote, see Celia B. Whitehead, *LLB*, 12 Mar. 1903, 67; for the sacrifice quote, see Lizzie M. Holmes, "A Free Woman's Duties," *LLB*, 14 May 1903, 138. Cornelia Boecklin, of Iowa, concurred in "Woman's Duties," *LLB*, 4 June 1903, 163.

49. Adeline Champney, *LLB*, 27 Aug. 1903, 258; Amy Linnett, "Breeding Prize Animals," *LLB*, 3 Sept. 1903, 266. Linnett lamented the fact that Lillian Harman did not appear to be taking sides in the debate, as did J. C., in *LLB*, 31 Dec. 1903, 399.

50. Robb, "Way of All Flesh," 594.

51. For an account of Waisbrooker's talk, see "Eugenics of Human Culture," *LLB*, 9 May 1907. Sears states that she abandoned many of her earlier hereditarian ideas during the final months of her life in reaction to other sex radicals' enthusiasm for Progressive-era eugenics (*Sex Radicals*, 244).

52. Lizzie M. Holmes quoted in Francis Barry, "Who Were the Pioneers?" *LLB*, 5 Nov. 1898, 355.

Bibliography

Newspapers and Periodicals

Adult, the Journal of Sex (London)
Age of Freedom (Berlin Heights, Ohio)
Agitator: A Semi-Monthly Journal of Reform (Cleveland; Chicago)
American Journal of Eugenics (Los Angeles)
American Vegetarian and Health Journal (Philadelphia)
American Socialist (Oneida, N.Y.)
Banner of Light (Boston)
Boston Medical and Surgical Journal
Burlington Hawk Eye (Iowa)
Chicago Daily Democratic Press
Chicago Tribune
Circular (Oneida, N.Y.)
Clothed with the Sun (Home, Wash.)
Daily Dayton Journal (Ohio)
Daily Journal of Oneida Community (Oneida, N.Y.)
Daily Springfield Nonpareil (Ohio)
Daily Iowa State Register (Des Moines, Iowa)
Demonstrator (Home, Wash.)
Discontent (Home, Wash.)
Dr. Foote's Health Monthly (New York)
Dubuque Herald (Iowa)
Fair Play (Valley Falls, Kans.; Sioux City, Iowa)
Firebrand (Portland, Ore.)
Foundation Principles (Clinton, Iowa; Antioch, Calif.; Topeka, Kans.)
Free Society (San Francisco)
Godey's Magazine and Lady's Book (Philadelphia)

Golden Age (New York)
Good Time Coming (Berlin Heights, Ohio)
Harper's Weekly (New York)
Hull's Crucible (Boston)
Kansas Liberal (Valley Falls)
Kingdom of Heaven (Anderson and Huntsville, Ind.; Berlin Heights, Ohio; Boston)
Liberator (Boston)
Liberty (Boston)
The Lily (Seneca Falls, N.Y.)
Littell's Living Age (Boston)
Lucifer, the Light-Bearer (Valley Falls, Kans.; Chicago; Los Angeles)
Milwaukee Sentinel
National Advance (Milwaukee)
National Police Gazette (New York)
New Campaign (Berlin Heights, Ohio)
New Republic (Cleveland)
New York Times
New York Tribune
Nichols' Journal of Health, Water-Cure, and Human Progress (New York)
Nichols' Monthly: A Magazine of Social Science and Progressive Literature (Cincinnati, Ohio)
Norton's Literary Gazette (New York)
Oconto County Register (Wis.)
The Optimist and Kingdom of Heaven (Anderson and Huntsville, Ind.; Berlin Heights, Ohio)
Our New Humanity (Topeka, Kans.)
The Phalanx (New York)
Portage County Democrat (Ravenna, Ohio)
Practical Christian (Hopedale, Mass.)
The Reformer (Worcester, Mass.)
Religio-Philosophical Journal (Chicago)
Revolution (New York)
Sandusky Commercial Register (Ohio)
The Sibyl (Middletown, N.Y.)
Social Revolutionist (Greenville and Berlin Heights, Ohio)
Springfield Republican (Mass.)
Springfield Union (Mass.)
To-Morrow Magazine
Truth Seeker (New York)
Una (Providence, R.I.)
United States Magazine and Democratic Review (Washington, D.C.)
Universe (Chicago)
Valley Falls Liberal (Kans.)
Vanguard (Dayton, Ohio; Richmond, Ind.)
Water-Cure Journal (New York)
Waukesha Freeman (Wis.)

Whitewater Register (Wis.)
Woman's Journal (Boston)
Woodhull and Claflin's Weekly (New York)
The Word (Princeton, Mass.)
Xenia Torchlight (Ohio)

Manuscript Collections

Stephen Pearl Andrews Papers. Archives Division. State Historical Society of Wisconsin, Madison.
Antiochiana Collections. Antioch College. Yellow Springs, Ohio.
Henry Bool Papers. Labadie Collection. Department of Rare Books and Special Collections. University Library. University of Michigan at Ann Arbor.
Chaapel Papers. Labadie Collection. Department of Rare Books and Special Collections. University Library. University of Michigan at Ann Arbor.
Warren Chase Papers, microfilm edition. Archives Division. State Historical Society of Wisconsin, Madison.
Cassius V. Cook Papers. Labadie Collection. Department of Rare Books and Special Collections. University Library. University of Michigan at Ann Arbor.
Denton Family Papers. Labadie Collection. Department of Rare Books and Special Collections. University Library. University of Michigan at Ann Arbor.
Samuel Warren Dike Papers. Manuscript Division. Library of Congress, Washington, D.C.
Abby Kelley Foster Papers. Manuscripts Department. American Antiquarian Society. Worcester, Massachusetts.
Ralph Ginzburg Papers. Wisconsin Historical Society Archives. Madison, Wisconsin.
Lillian Harman Papers. Labadie Collection. Department of Rare Books and Special Collections. University Library. University of Michigan at Ann Arbor.
Moses Harman Papers. Labadie Collection. Department of Rare Books and Special Collections. University Library. University of Michigan at Ann Arbor.
Ezra and Angela Heywood Papers. Labadie Collection. Department of Rare Books and Special Collections. University Library. University of Michigan at Ann Arbor.
Jo Labadie Papers. Labadie Collection. Department of Rare Books and Special Collections. University Library. University of Michigan at Ann Arbor.
Marx Edgeworth Lazarus Folder. Labadie Collection. Department of Rare Books and Special Collections. University Library. University of Michigan at Ann Arbor.
Mann Bibliography. Antiochiana Collections, Antioch College Archives. Yellow Springs, Ohio.
Valentine Nicholson Papers. Collection no. M641B1F1. Indiana Historical Society, Indianapolis.
North American Woman Suffrage Association, microfilm edition. Manuscripts Division. Library of Congress, Washington, D.C.
George Schumm Papers. Labadie Collection. Department of Rare Books and Special Collections. University Library. University of Michigan at Ann Arbor.
Achsa W. Sprague Papers. Vermont Historical Society, Montpelier.
Elizabeth Cady Stanton Papers, microfilm edition. Manuscripts Division. Library of Congress, Washington, D.C.

Josephine Tilton Papers. Labadie Collection. Department of Rare Books and Special Collections. University Library. University of Michigan at Ann Arbor.

Edwin C. Walker Papers. Labadie Collection. Department of Rare Books and Special Collections. University Library. University of Michigan at Ann Arbor.

Josiah Warren Papers. Labadie Collection. Department of Rare Books and Special Collections. University Library. University of Michigan at Ann Arbor.

John S. Williams Papers. State Historical Society of Wisconsin, Madison.

Elizur Wright Papers. Manuscripts Division. Library of Congress, Washington, D.C.

Books, Articles, Chapters, Pamphlets, Dissertations, and Other Unpublished Material

Adams, Grace, and Edward Hutter. *The Mad Forties.* New York: Harper and Brothers, 1942.

"Address by Ernestine Rose." Second National Women's Rights Convention, Worcester, Mass., 1851. In *The Concise History of Woman Suffrage.* Ed. Mary Jo Buhle and Paul Buhle. Urbana: University of Illinois Press, 1978. 106–11.

Adler, Felix. *Marriage and Divorce.* New York: McClure, Phillips, and Co., 1905.

Aldrich, Lewis Cass, ed. *History of Erie County, Ohio.* Syracuse, N.Y.: D. Mason and Co., 1889.

Allen, Grant. *Plain Words on the Woman Question.* Chicago: M. Harman, 1900.

Ames, Blanche Butler, comp. *Chronicles from the Nineteenth Century: Family Letters of Blanche Butler and Adelbert Ames, Volume I.* [Clinton? Mass.]: Privately issued, 1957.

Anderson, Patricia. "Free Love and Free thought: *The Adult,* 1897–1899." In *Studies in Newspaper and Periodical History* (Westport Conn.: Greenwood Press, 1993): 179–81.

Andrews, Stephen Pearl. *Love, Marriage, and Divorce and the Sovereignty of the Individual.* New York: Stringer and Townsend, 1853.

———. *The Science of Society.* New York: Fowler and Wells, 1853.

Andrews, William L. "Liberal Religion and Free Love: An Undiscovered Afro-American Novel of the 1890s." *MELUS: the Journal of the Society for the Study of the Multi-Ethnic Literature of the United States* 9 (1982): 23–36.

Ardis, Ann. *New Women, New Novels: Feminism and Early Modernism.* New Brunswick, N.J.: Rutgers University Press, 1990.

Aspinwall, Bernard. "Social Catholicism and Health: Dr. and Mrs. Thomas Low Nichols in Britain." In *The Church and Healing: Papers Read at the Twentieth Summer Meeting and the Twenty-First Winter Meeting of the Ecclesiastical History Society.* Ed. W. J. Sheils. Oxford: Basil Blackwell, 1982. 249–70.

Avrich, Paul. *An American Anarchist: The Life of Voltairine de Cleyre.* Princeton, N.J.: Princeton University Press, 1978.

Bacon, Margaret, *Mothers of Feminism: The Story of Quaker Women in America.* New York: Harper and Row, 1986.

Badcock, John, Jr. *When Love Is Liberty and Nature Law.* London: W. Reeves, [1893].

Baker, Paula. *The Moral Frameworks of Public Life: Gender, Politics, and the State in Rural New York, 1870–1930.* New York: Oxford University Press, 1991.

Ball, John. *The Baptism of Fire: An Autobiographical Sketch.* Boston: The Author, 1877.

Ballou, Adin. *History of the Hopedale Community.* Lowell, Mass.: Thompson and Hill, 1897.

————. *True Love vs. Free Love: Testimony of a True-hearted Woman.* Hopedale, Mich.: Hopedale Press, 1985.

Bardaglio, Peter W. *Reconstructing the Household: Families, Sex, and the Law in the Nineteenth-Century South.* Chapel Hill: University of North Carolina Press, 1995.

Barker-Benfield, G. J. *The Horrors of the Half-Known Life: Male Attitudes toward Women and Sexuality in Nineteenth-Century America.* New York: Harper and Row, 1976.

Barkun, Michael. *Crucible of the Millennium: The Burned-Over District of New York in the 1840s.* Syracuse, N.Y.: Syracuse University Press, 1986.

Barry, Kathleen. *Susan B. Anthony: A Biography.* New York: New York University Press, 1988.

Barthelme, Marion K., ed. *Women in the Texas Populist Movement: Letters to the Southern Mercury.* College Station: Texas A&M University Press, 1997.

Barrett, Joseph O. *Social Freedom. Marriage: As It Is and As It Should Be.* Boston: Colby and Rich, 1873.

Basch, Francoise. "Women's Rights and the Wrongs of Marriage in Mid-Nineteenth-Century America." In *History of Women in the United States: Feminist Struggles for Sex Equality.* Ed. Nancy Cott. New Providence, N.J.: K. G. Saur, 1994. 26–48.

Basch, Norma. *In the Eyes of the Law: Women, Marriage, and Property in Nineteenth-Century New York.* Ithaca, N.Y.: Cornell University Press, 1982.

Bates, Anna Louise. "Protective Custody: A Feminist Interpretation of Anthony Comstock's Life and Laws." Ph.D. dissertation, State University of New York at Binghamton, 1991.

Battan, Jesse Frank. "Angela Fiducia Tilton Heywood." In *American National Biography.* Vol. 10. Ed. John A. Garraty and Mark C. Carnes. New York: Oxford University Press, 1999. 724–26.

————. "The Politics of 'Eros': Sexual Radicalism and Social Reform in Nineteenth-Century America." Ph.D. dissertation, University of California at Los Angeles, 1988.

————. "The Word Made Flesh." In *American Sexual Politics: Sex, Gender, and Race since the Civil War.* Ed. John C. Fout and Maura Shaw Tantillo. Chicago: University of Chicago Press, 1990. 101–22.

Baym, Nina. *Woman's Fiction: A Guide to Novels by and about Women in America, 1820–70.* 2d ed. Urbana: University of Illinois Press, 1993.

Beecher, Jonathan, and Richard Bienvenu, eds. *The Utopian Vision of Charles Fourier: Selected Texts on Work, Love, and Passionate Attraction.* Columbia: University of Missouri Press, 1971.

Beisel, Nicola. *Imperiled Innocents: Anthony Comstock and Family Reproduction in Victorian America.* Princeton, N.J.: Princeton University Press, 1997.

Bellamy, Charles. *An Experiment with Marriage, a Romance.* Albany, N.Y.: Albany Book Co., 1889.

Bender, Thomas. *New York Intellect: A History of Intellectual Life in New York City.* Baltimore: Johns Hopkins University Press, 1988.

Benedict, Murray. *Farm Policies of the United States, 1790–1950: A Study in Their Origins and Development.* New York: Twentieth Century Fund, 1953.

Bennett, Paula Bernat, ed. *Nineteenth-Century American Women Poets: An Anthology.* Malden, Mass.: Blackwell Publishers, 1998.

Berlin, Isaiah. Introduction to *Roots of Revolution: A History of the Populist and Socialist*

Movements in Nineteenth-Century Russia, by Franco Venturi. Trans. Francis Haskell. New York: Knopf, 1960. vii–xxx.

Besant, Annie. *Marriage As It Was, As It Is, and As It Should Be: A Plea for Reform.* 2d ed. London: Freethought Publishing Co., 1882.

Bestor, Arthur. *Backwoods Utopias: The Sectarian and Owenite Phase of Communitarian Socialism in America, 1663–1829.* 2d ed. Philadelphia: University of Pennsylvania Press, 1970.

Birkin, Lawrence. *Consuming Desire: Sexual Science and the Emergence of a Culture of Abundance, 1871–1914.* Ithaca, N.Y.: Cornell University Press, 1988.

Bisland, Elizabeth. "Modern Woman and Marriage." *North American* 160 (June 1895): 753–55.

Blake, John R. "Mary Gove Nichols, Prophetess of Health." *Proceedings of the American Philosophical Society* 106 (29 June 1962): 219–34.

Blake, Nelson Manfred. *The Road to Reno: A History of Divorce in the United States.* New York: Macmillan, 1962.

Bland, Lucy. *Banishing the Beast: Sexuality and the Early Feminists.* New York: New Press, 1995.

Blatt, Martin. "The Anarchism of Ezra Heywood (1829–1893): Abolition, Labor Reform, and Free Love." Ph.D. dissertation, Boston University, 1983.

———. "Ezra Hervey Heywood." In *American National Biography.* Vol. 10. Ed. John A. Garraty and Mark C. Carnes. New York: Oxford University Press, 1999. 727–29.

———. *Free Love and Anarchism: The Biography of Ezra Heywood.* Urbana: University of Illinois Press, 1989.

Blee, Kathleen M. *No Middle Ground: Women and Radical Protest.* New York: New York University Press, 1998.

Boozer, H. W. *Stubborn Facts Concerning True Sexual Relations.* Worcester, Mass.: Independent Tract Society, 1876.

Bordin, Ruth. *Woman and Temperance: The Quest for Power and Liberty, 1873–1900.* New Brunswick, N.J.: Rutgers University Press, 1990.

Bowler, Peter J. *The Mendelian Revolution: The Emergence of Hereditarian Concepts in Modern Science and Society.* Baltimore: Johns Hopkins University Press, 1989.

Boydston, Jeanne. *Home and Work: Housework: Wages, and the Ideology of Labor in the Early Republic.* New York: Oxford University Press, 1990.

Boydston, Jeanne, Mary Kelley, and Ann Margolis. *The Limits of Sisterhood: The Beecher Sisters on Women's Rights and Woman's Sphere.* Chapel Hill: University of North Carolina Press, 1988.

Boyer, Paul S. *Purity in Print: The Vice-Society Movement and Book Censorship in America.* New York: Charles Scribner's Sons, 1968.

———. *Urban Masses and Moral Order in America, 1820–1920.* Cambridge, Mass.: Harvard University Press, 1978.

Brady, Marilyn Dell. "Populism and Feminism in a Newspaper by and for Women of the Kansas Farmers' Alliance, 1891–1894." *Kansas History* 7 (1984–85): 280–90.

Braude, Ann. "News from the Spirit World: A Checklist of American Spiritualist Periodicals, 1847–1900." *Proceedings of the American Antiquarian Society* 99 (1990): 399–462.

————. *Radical Spirits: Spiritualism and Women's Rights in Nineteenth-Century America.* Boston: Beacon Press, 1989.

Brisbane, Albert. *Social Destiny of Man; or, Association and Reorganization of Industry.* Philadelphia: C. F. Stollmeyer, 1840.

Brock, Erland J. et al., eds. *Swedenborg and His Influence.* Bryn Athyn, Pa.: The Academy of the New Church, 1988.

Brodie, Janet Farrell. *Contraception and Abortion in Nineteenth-Century America.* Ithaca, N.Y.: Cornell University Press, 1994.

Brooke, John L. *The Refiner's Fire: The Making of Mormon Cosmology, 1644–1844.* New York: Cambridge University Press, 1994.

Brooks, Frank H., ed. *The Individualist Anarchists: An Anthology of Liberty (1881–1908).* New Brunswick, N.J.: Transaction Publishers, 1994.

Brough, James. *The Vixens: A Biography of Victoria and Tennessee Claflin.* New York: Simon and Schuster, 1980.

Broun, Heywood, and Margaret Leech. *Anthony Comstock, Roundsman of the Lord.* New York: A. and C. Boni, 1927.

Brown, Burton Gates, Jr. "Spiritualism in Nineteenth-Century America." Ph.D. dissertation, Boston University, 1973.

Brown, Hannah F. M. *The False and True Marriage.* Cleveland: Viets and Savage, 1861.

Brown, Richard D. *Knowledge Is Power: The Diffusion of Information in Early America, 1700–1865.* New York: Oxford University Press, 1989.

Bryan, John. *Fables and Essay, Volume 1.* New York: Arts and Letters Co., 1895.

Buhle, Mari Jo, and Paul Buhle, eds. *The Concise History of Woman Suffrage.* Urbana: University of Illinois Press, 1978.

Burnham, John C. "The Progressive Era Revolution in American Attitudes toward Sex." *Journal of American History* 59 (March 1973): 885–908.

Burrows, Edwin G., and Mike Wallace. *Gotham: A History of New York City to 1898.* New York: Oxford University Press, 1999.

Butler, Jon. *Awash in a Sea of Faith: Christianizing the American People.* Cambridge, Mass.: Harvard University Press, 1990.

Bynum, Victoria E. *Unruly Women: The Politics of Social and Sexual Control in the Old South.* Chapel Hill: University of North Carolina Press, 1992.

Caine, Barbara. *English Feminism, 1780–1980.* New York: Oxford University Press, 1997.

Campbell, Karlyn Kohrs. *Man Cannot Speak for Her: A Critical Study of Early Feminist Rhetoric.* New York: Praeger, 1989.

Campbell, Rachel. *The Prodigal Daughter; or, The Price of Virtue.* Valley Falls, Kans.: Lucifer, 1888.

Capron, Elias Wilkinson. *Modern Spiritualism: Its Facts and Fanaticisms.* Boston: B. Marsh, 1855.

Carlier, Auguste. *Marriage in the United States.* Trans. B. Joy Jeffries. New York: Leypoldt and Holt, 1867.

Carpenter, Edward. *Marriage in Free Society.* Chicago: Stockholm Pub. Co., n.d.

Carroll, Bret E. *Spiritualism in Antebellum America.* Bloomington: Indiana University Press, 1997.

Carter, Paul A. *The Spiritual Crisis of the Gilded Age*. DeKalb: Northern Illinois University Press, 1971.

Cayleff, Susan E. *Wash and Be Healed: The Water-Cure Movement and Women's Health*. Philadelphia: Temple University Press, 1987.

Cetti, Luisa. "Feminism and Free Love in Mid-Nineteenth Century America." *Storia Nordamericana* 5 (1988): 9–22.

Chapman, R. D. *Freelove a Law of Nature: A Plea for the Liberation of the Sexes*. New York: The Author, 1881.

Chase, Warren. *The Gist of Spiritualism*. Boston: W. White and Co., 1865.

———. *The Fugitive Wife: A Criticism of Marriage, Adultery and Divorce*. Boston: B. Marsh, 1861.

———. *The Life-line of the Lone One; or, Autobiography of the World's Child*. 3d ed. Boston: Bela Marsh, 1865.

———. *Three Lectures on the Harmonial Philosophy*. Cleveland: L. E. Barnard and Co, 1856.

Chauncey, George, Jr. "From Sexual Inversion to Homosexuality: Medicine and the Changing Conceptualization of Female Deviance." *Salmagundi* 58–59 (Fall 1982–Winter 1983): 114–46.

Child, Lydia Maria. *Fact and Fiction: A Collection of Stories*. New York: C. S. Francis and Co., 1846.

———. *Philothea, a Romance*. Boston: Otis Brothers, 1836.

Chused, Richard H. *Private Acts in Public Places: A Social History of Divorce in the Formative Era of American Family Law*. Philadelphia: University of Pennsylvania Press, 1994.

Clark, Elizabeth. "Matrimonial Bonds: Slavery, Contract, and the Law of Divorce in Nineteenth-Century America." Legal History Program Working Papers. Madison: Institute for Legal Studies, University of Wisconsin at Madison Law School, 1987.

Clay, James. *A Voice from the Prison*. Boston: Bela Marsh, 1856.

Cogan, Jacob Katz, and Lori Ginzberg. "1846 Petition for Woman's Suffrage." *SIGNS* 22 (1997): 427–39.

Combination Atlas Map of Erie County, Ohio. Philadelphia: Stewart and Page, 1874.

Comstock, Anthony. "Free Love Traps." In *Traps for the Young*. New York: Funk and Wagnalls, 1883.

Conrad, Susan Phinney. *Perish the Thought: Intellectual Women in Romantic America, 1830–1860*. New York: Oxford University Press, 1976.

Cook, Tennessee C. *Essays on Social Topics*. Westminster: Roxburghe Press, 1898.

———. *The Ethics of Sexuality Equality: A Lecture*. New York: Woodhull and Claflin, 1873.

Cooke, Nicholas Francis. *Satan in Society*. St. John, N.B.: R. A. H. Morrow, 1869.

Coontz, Stephanie. *The Social Origins of Private Life*. London: Verso, 1988.

Cooper, George. *Lost Love: A True Story of Passion, Murder, and Justice in Old New York*. New York: Pantheon Books, 1994.

Coryell, John Russell. *Love and Passion: An Address Made at Lyric Hall . . . before the Liberty Congregation*. New York: Corwill Publishing Co., [1907].

Cott, Nancy F. *The Bonds of Womanhood: Woman's Sphere in New England, 1780–1835*. New Haven, Conn.: Yale University Press, 1977.

———. "Marriage and Women's Citizenship in the United States, 1830–1934." *American Historical Review* 103 (1998): 1440–74.

————. "Passionlessness: An Interpretation of Victorian Sexual Ideology, 1790–1850." *SIGNS* 4 (1978): 162–181.

————. *Public Vows: A History of Marriage and the Nation.* Cambridge: Harvard University Press, 2000.

————, ed. *History of Women in the United States: Feminist Struggles for Sex Equality.* New Providence, N.J.: K. G. Saur, 1994.

Cowan, Ruth Schwartz. *Sir Francis Galton and the Study of Heredity in the Nineteenth Century.* New York: Garland, 1985.

Craddock, Ida C. *Right Marital Living.* Chicago: The Author, 1899.

————. *The Wedding Night.* 3d ed. New York: The Author, 1900.

Crane, John Mayo. *The Evolution of the Family.* Chicago: Moses Harman Publishing Co., 1900.

Cravath, Prosper. *Early Annals of Whitewater, 1837–1867.* [Whitewater, Wis.]: The Whitewater Federation of Women's Clubs, 1906.

Creshkoff, Maggie. "Hydropathy as a Physiological Religion: 'Wash and Be Healed.'" Senior project, Antioch College, 1976.

Cridge, Alfred. *Epitome of Spirit Intercourse.* Boston: Bela Marsh, 1854.

————. *Utopia; or, The History of an Extinct Planet.* Oakland: Winchester and Pew, 1884.

Cridge, Anne Denton. *The Crumb Basket.* Boston: William White and Co., 1868.

————. *Man's Rights; or, How Would You Like It?* Boston: W. Denton, 1870.

Cross, Whitney R. *The Burned-Over District: The Social and Intellectual History of Enthusiastic Religion in Western New York, 1800–1850.* Ithaca, N.Y.: Cornell University Press, 1950.

Cunningham, Edward. "The Culture That was Vineland," *The Vineland Historical Magazine* 26 (Apr. 1941): 197–200.

Curry, Jane, ed. *Samantha Rastles the Woman Question.* Urbana: University of Illinois Press, 1983.

Curtis, Susan. *A Consuming Faith: The Social Gospel and Modern American Culture.* Baltimore: Johns Hopkins University Press, 1991.

Dancis, Bruce. "Socialism and Women in the United States, 1900–1917." *Socialist Revolution* 6 (Jan.–Mar. 1976): 81–144.

Danielson, Susan Steinberg. "Healing Women's Wrongs: Water-Cure as (Fictional) Autobiography." *Studies in the American Renaissance* (1992): 247–60.

Darwin, Charles. *Origin of Species.* New York: Modern Library, 1859.

Davidson, Cathy N. *Revolution and the Word: The Rise of the Novel in America.* New York: Oxford University Press, 1986.

Davis, Andrew Jackson. *Appetites and Passions.* New York: A. J. Davis and Co., [1863].

————. *Free Thoughts Concerning Religion.* 2d ed. Boston: Bela Marsh, 1854.

————. *The Great Harmonia.* 5 vols. Rochester, N.Y.: Austin Publishing, 1863–1910.

————. *The Harmonial Philosophy: A Compendium and Digest of the Works of Andrew Jackson Davis.* Chicago: Marlowe Co., n.d.

————. *The Magic Staff: An Autobiography.* New York: A. J. Davis and Co., 1876.

————. *The Reformer.* Boston: Sanborn, Carter, and Bazin, 1856.

Davis, David Brion, ed. *Ante-Bellum Reform.* New York: Harper and Row, 1967.

Davis, Mary F. *Danger Signals: An Address on the Uses and Abuses of Modern Spiritualism.* New York: A. J. Davis, 1875.

Davis, Paulina Wright. *A History of the National Women's Rights Movement.* New York: Journeymen Printers' Cooperative Association, 1871.

de Cleyre, Voltairine. *Selected works of Voltairine de Cleyre.* Ed. Alexander Berkman. New York: Mother Earth Publishing Association, 1914.

———. *Sex Slavery: A Lecture Delivered before Unity Congregation, Philadelphia.* Valley Falls, Kans.: Lucifer Publishing Co., n.d.

Degler, Carl. *At Odds: Women and the Family in America from the Revolution to the Present.* New York: Oxford University Press, 1980.

———. "What Ought to Be and What Was: Women's Sexuality in the Nineteenth Century." In *The American Family in Social-Historical Perspective.* Ed. Michael Gordon. New York: St. Martin's Press, 1978. 1467–90.

D'Emilio, John, and Estelle B. Freedman. *Intimate Matters: A History of Sexuality in America.* New York: Harper and Row, 1988.

Denton, William. *Is Spiritualism True?* Boston: William Denton, 1871.

———. *Orthodoxy False, Since Spiritualism Is True.* Boston: William Denton, 1874.

Destler, Chester M. *American Radicalism, 1865–1901.* Chicago: Quadrangle Books, 1966.

Dickey, J. J. M. *An Examination and Explanation of Modern Spiritualism . . . also a Brief Review of 'Free Love,' Its Origin, Progress, and Influence on the World.* Malta, Ohio: E. Ballou, 1856.

Dike, Samuel W. *The Condition and Needs of Statistics of Marriage and Divorce.* N.p.: National Divorce Reform League, [1893].

———. "Some Aspects of the Divorce Question." *Princeton Review* 13 (Mar. 1884): 169–90.

———. *The Theory of the Marriage Tie.* Boston: National Divorce Reform League, 1893.

Ditzion, Sidney. *Marriage, Morals, and Sex in America: A History of Ideas.* New York: Bookman Associates, 1953.

Dixon, Christopher. "'An Equal and Permanent Relationship': Abolitionism, Gender, and Family Reform in the Nineteenth Century United States." Ph.D. dissertation, University of New South Wales, 1992.

Dixon, William Hepworth. *Spiritual Wives.* 2d ed. London: Hurst and Blackett, 1868.

Donald, David Herbert. *Lincoln.* London: Jonathan Cape, 1995.

Donegan, Jane B. *"Hydropathic Highway to Health": Women and the Water-Cure in Antebellum America.* Westport, Conn.: Greenwood Press, 1986.

Doten, Lizzie. *Free Love and Affinity: A Discourse Delivered under Spirit Influence.* Boston: Bela Marsh, 1867.

———. *My Affinity, and Other Stories.* Boston: W. White, 1870.

Drinnon, Richard. *Rebel in Paradise: A Biography of Emma Goldman.* Chicago: University of Chicago Press, 1961.

DuBois, Ellen C. *Feminism and Suffrage: The Emergence of an Independent Women's Movement in America, 1848–1869.* Ithaca, N.Y.: Cornell University Press, 1978.

———. "The Radicalism of the Woman Suffrage Movement: Notes toward the Reconstruction of Nineteenth-Century Feminism." *Feminist Studies* 3 (Fall 1975): 63–71.

———. *Woman Suffrage and Women's Rights.* New York: New York University Press, 1998.

———, ed. "On Labor and Free Love: Two Unpublished Speeches of Elizabeth Cady Stanton." *SIGNS* 1 (1975): 257–68.

DuBois, Ellen C., with Linda Gordon. "Seeking Ecstasy on the Battlefield." In *Woman*

Suffrage and Women's Rights. Ed. Ellen C. DuBois. New York: New York University Press, 1998. 139–59.

Dugdale, Richard L. *The Jukes: A Study in Crime, Pauperism, Disease, and Heredity.* 4th ed. New York: Putnam, 1902.

Duster, Alfreda M., ed. *Crusade for Justice: The Autobiography of Ida B. Wells.* Chicago: University of Chicago Press, 1970.

Eckhardt, Celia Morris. *Fanny Wright: Rebel in America.* Cambridge, Mass.: Harvard University Press, 1984.

Edwards, Rebecca. *Angels in the Machinery: Gender in American Party Politics from the Civil War to the Progressive Era.* New York: Oxford University Press, 1997.

Ellis, Havelock. *Sex in Relation to Society.* Philadelphia: F. A. Davis Co., 1910.

Ellis, John B. *Free Love and Its Votaries; or, American Socialism Unmasked.* New York: United States Publishing Co., 1870.

Emery, Edwin. *The Press and America: An Interpretative History of Journalism.* 2d ed. Englewood Cliffs, N.J.: Prentice-Hall, 1962.

Epstein, Barbara. "Family, Sexual Morality, and Popular Movements in Turn-of-the-Century America." In *Powers of Desire: The Politics of Sexuality.* Ed. Ann Snitow, Christine Stansell, and Sharon Thompson. New York: Monthly Review Press, 1983. 117–30.

Facher, Betsy Jean. "What 'Constitutes' Liberty? Ezra Heywood, Anthony Comstock, and the Meaning of the Free Love Debate." B.A. honors thesis, Harvard University, 1993.

Falk, Candace. *Love, Anarchy, and Emma Goldman.* New York: Holt Rinehart Winston, 1984.

Faragher, John Mack. "History from the Inside-Out: Writing the History of Women in Rural America." *American Quarterly* 33 (1981): 537–57.

Fellman, Anita Clair, and Michael Fellman. "The Rule of Moderation in Late-Nineteenth-Century American Sexual Ideology." *Journal of Sex Research* 17 (1981): 238–55.

Fern, Fanny. *Rose Clark.* Halifax: M. Iner and Saverby, 1860.

———. *Ruth Hall, a Domestic Tale of the Present Time.* New York: Mason Brothers, 1855.

Fernando, Lloyd. *"New Women" in the Late Victorian Novel.* University Park: Pennsylvania State University Press, 1977.

Ferris, Rev. William H. "Review of Modern Spiritualism." *The Ladies Repository* 16 (Jan.–June 1856): 46–52, 88–92, 139–44, 229–33, 297–300, 364–70.

Fields, Elizabeth. *Freedom in Marriage.* New York: Abbey Press, 1902.

Fink, Deborah. *Agrarian Women: Wives and Mothers in Rural Nebraska, 1880–1940.* Chapel Hill: University of North Carolina Press, 1992.

———. *Open Country Iowa: Rural Women, Tradition, and Change.* Albany: State University of New York Press, 1986.

Fink, Leon. *Workingmen's Democracy: The Knights of Labor and American Politics.* Urbana: University of Illinois Press, 1983.

Fischer, Gayle Veronica. "Who Wears the Pants? Women, Dress Reform, and Power in the Mid-Nineteenth-Century United States." Ph.D. dissertation, Indiana University, 1995.

Fish, Job. "The Free Love Community." *The Firelands Pioneer* n.s. 23 (April 1925): 322–23.

Flexner, Eleanor. *Century of Struggle: The Woman's Rights Movement in the United States.* New York: Atheneum, 1974.

Fogarty, Robert S., "Nineteenth Century Utopian." *Pacific Historian* 16 (Fall 1972): 70–76.

———, ed. *Dictionary of American Communal and Utopian History.* Westport, Conn.: Greenwood Press, 1980.

Fogarty, Robert S., and H. Roger Grant. "Free Love in Ohio: Jacob Beilhart and the Spirit Fruit Colony." *Ohio History* 89 (1980): 206–21.

Folkerts, Jean. "Functions of the Reform Press." *Journalism History* 12 (1985): 22–25.

Foner, Eric. "Radical Individualism in America: Revolution to Civil War." *Literature of Liberty* 1 (July–Sept. 1978): 5–31.

———. *The Story of American Freedom.* New York: W. W. Norton and Company, 1998.

Foote, Edward B. *Divorce: A Review of the Subject from a Scientific Standpoint.* New York: Murray Hill Publishing Co., 1884.

Forster, Dora. *Sex Radicalism as Seen by an Emancipated Woman of the New Time.* Chicago: M. Harman, 1905.

Foster, Lawrence. *Religion and Sexuality: The Shakers, the Mormons, and the Oneida Community.* Rev. ed. Urbana: University of Illinois Press, 1984.

———. *Women, Family, and Utopia: Communal Experiments of the Shakers, the Oneida Community, and the Mormons.* Syracuse, N.Y.: Syracuse University Press, 1991.

Foucault, Michel. *The History of Sexuality: An Introduction.* Vol. 1. Trans. Robert Hurley. New York: Vintage Books, 1978.

Fowler, Lorenzo Niles. *Marriage: Its History and Ceremonies.* New York: Fowler and Wells, 1847.

Fowler, Orson Squire. *Amativeness; or, Evils and Remedies of Excessive and Perverted Sexuality.* 13th ed. New York: Fowler and Wells, 1849.

———. *Love and Parentage.* 40th ed. New York: Fowler and Wells, 1844.

Fox, Richard Wightman. "Intimacy on Trial: Cultural Meanings of the Beecher-Tilton Affair." In *The Power of Culture: Critical Essays in American History.* Ed. Richard Wightman Fox and T. J. Jackson Lears. Chicago: University of Chicago Press, 1998. 103–32.

Fowler, Sada Bailey. *Irene; or, The Road to Freedom.* Philadelphia: H. N. Fowler and Company, 1886.

Franklin, Julia C. "Freedom for Woman." In *The Next Revolution, No. 1; or, Women's Emancipation from Sex Slavery.* Valley Falls, Kans.: Lucifer Publishing Co., 1890. 6–11.

Frederickson, George M. *The Inner Civil War: Northern Intellectuals and the Crisis of the Union.* New York: Harper and Row, 1965.

"The Free Love System: Origin, Progress, and Position of the Anti-Marriage Movement." *Littell's Living Age* 49 (29 Sept. 1855): 815–21.

Friedman, Lawrence J. *Gregarious Saints: Self and Community in American Abolitionism, 1830–1870.* New York: Cambridge University Press, 1982.

———. "Racism and Sexism in Ante-bellum America: The Prudence Crandall Episode Reconsidered." *Societas* 4 (1974): 211–27.

Frothingham, Octavious Brooks. *Elective Affinity: A Sermon Preached . . . in Lyric Hall . . . December 19, 1869.* New York: D. G. Francis, 1870.

Gabriel, Mary. *Notorious Victoria: The Life of Victoria Woodhull, Uncensored.* Chapel Hill, N.C.: Algonquin Books, 1998.

Gagel, Diane VanSkiver. "Ohio Women Unite: The Salem Convention of 1850." In *Women in Ohio History.* Ed. Marta Whitlock. Columbus: Ohio Historical Society, 1976. 4–8.

Galton, Sir Francis. *Hereditary Genius: An Inquiry into Its Laws and Consequences.* New York: St. Martin's Press, 1978.

Ganz, Melissa J. "Wicked Women and Veiled Ladies: Gendered Narratives of the McFarland-Richardson Tragedy." *Yale Journal of Law and Feminism* 9 (1997): 255–303.

Gardella, Peter. *Innocent Ecstasy: How Christianity Gave America an Ethic of Sexual Pleasure.* New York: Oxford University Press, 1985.

Garraty, John A., and Mark C. Carnes, eds. *American National Biography.* New York: Oxford University Press, 1999.

Gates, Paul W. *The Farmers' Age: Agriculture, 1815–1860.* New York: Holt, Rinehart, and Winston, 1960.

Gaustad, Edwin S., ed. *The Rise of Adventism: Religion and Society in the Mid-Nineteenth Century.* New York: Harper and Row, 1974.

Gazetteer and Directory of Clinton County, Iowa. Lyons, Iowa: J. C. Hopkins, 1876.

Gay, Peter. *Education of the Senses: Victoria to Freud.* New York: Oxford University Press, 1984.

Gifford, Carolyn DeSwarte, ed. *Writing Out My Heart: Selections from the Journal of Francis Willard, 1855–96.* Urbana: University of Illinois Press, 1995.

Ginzberg, Lori D. "'The Hearts of Your Readers Will Shudder': Fanny Wright, Infidelity, and American Freethought." *American Quarterly* 46 (June 1994): 195–226.

———. *Women and the Work of Benevolence: Morality, Politics, and Class in Nineteenth-Century United States.* New Haven, Conn.: Yale University Press, 1990.

Gleason, Philip. "From Free Love to Catholicism: Dr. and Mrs. Thomas L. Nichols at Yellow Springs." *Ohio Historical Quarterly* 70 (Oct. 1961): 283–307.

Godkin, E. L. "Another Delicate Subject." *The Nation* 11 (14 July 1870): 21–23.

———. "Society and Marriage." *The Nation* 10 (26 May 1870): 332–33.

Goldberg, Michael Lewis. *An Army of Women: Gender and Politics in Gilded Age Kansas.* Baltimore: Johns Hopkins University Press, 1997.

Goldman, Emma. *Living My Life.* New York: AMS Press, 1970.

———. *Marriage and Love.* 2d ed. New York: Mother Earth Publishing Association, 1916.

Goldsmith, Barbara. *Other Powers: The Age of Suffrage, Spiritualism, and the Scandalous Victoria Woodhull.* New York: Alfred A. Knopf, 1998.

Goodwyn, Lawrence. *The Populist Moment: A Short History of the Agrarian Revolt in America.* New York: Oxford University Press, 1978.

Gordon, Ann D., with Bettye Collier-Thomas et al., eds. *African American Women and the Vote, 1837–1965.* Amherst: University of Massachusetts Press, 1997.

Gordon, Linda. *Woman's Body, Woman's Right: Birth Control in America.* Rev. ed. New York: Penguin Books, 1990.

———. *The Moral Property of Women: A History of Birth Control Politics in America.* Urbana: University of Illinois Press, 2002.

Gove, Mary S. *Lectures to Ladies on Anatomy and Physiology.* Boston: Sax and Peirce, 1842.

———. *Solitary Vice: An Address to Parents and Those Who Have the Care of Children.* Portland, [Maine]: Journal Office, 1839.

———. *Uncle John; or, "It Is Too Much Trouble."* New York: Harper and Bros., 1846.

Grant, Miles. *Spiritualism Unveiled and Shown to be the Work of Demons.* Boston: The Crisis Office, [1866].

Griffith, Elisabeth. *In Her Own Right: The Life of Elizabeth Cady Stanton.* New York: Oxford University Press, 1984.

———. "Elizabeth Cady Stanton on Marriage and Divorce: Feminist Theory and Domestic Experience." In *Woman's Being, Woman's Place: Female Identity and Vocation in American History.* Ed. Mary Kelly. Boston: G. K. Hall, 1979. 233–51.

Griswold, Robert L. *Family and Divorce in California, 1850–1890: Victorian Illusions and Everyday Realities.* Albany: State University of New York Press, 1982.

———. "Law, Sex, Cruelty, and Divorce in Victorian America, 1840–1900." *American Quarterly* 38 (Winter 1986): 721–45.

———. "Sexual Cruelty and the Case for Divorce in Victorian America, 1840–1900." *SIGNS* 2 (Spring 1986): 529–41.

Grose, Janet Lynne. "The Sensation Novel and Social Reform: Revising Prescriptions of Gender, Marriage, and Domesticity." Ph.D. dissertation, University of South Carolina, 1995.

Grossberg, Michael. *Governing the Hearth: Law and the Family in Nineteenth-Century America.* Chapel Hill: University of North Carolina Press, 1985.

Guarneri, Carl J. *The Utopian Alternative: Fourierism in Nineteenth-Century America.* Ithaca, N.Y.: Cornell University Press, 1991.

Gurstein, Rochelle. *The Repeal of Reticence.* New York: Hill and Wang, 1996.

Habegger, Alfred. *The Father: A Life of Henry James, Sr.* New York: Farrar, Straus and Giroux, 1994.

Habermas, Jurgen. *The Structural Transformation of the Public Sphere.* Trans. Thomas Burger. Cambridge: Massachusetts Institute of Technology Press, 1989.

Hahn, Steven, and Jonathan Prude, eds. *The Countryside in the Age of Capitalist Transformation: Essays in the Social History of Rural America.* Chapel Hill: University of North Carolina Press, 1985.

Hale, Sarah Josepha. *Woman's Record; or, Sketches of All Distinguished Women from the Creation to a.d. 1854.* New York: Harper and Bros., 1855.

Halem, Lynne Carol. *Divorce Reform: Changing Legal and Social Perspectives.* New York: Free Press, 1980.

Haller, John S., Jr. "From Maidenhood to Menopause: Sex Education for Women in Victorian America." *Journal of Popular Culture* 6 (1972): 49–69.

Haller, John S., Jr., and Robin M. Haller. *The Physician and Sexuality in Victorian America.* New York: Norton, 1974.

Haller, Mark H. *Eugenics: Hereditarian Attitudes in American Thought.* New Brunswick, N.J.: Rutgers University Press, 1963.

Hamm, Thomas D. *God's Government Begun: The Society for Universal Inquiry and Reform, 1842–1846.* Bloomington: Indiana University Press, 1995.

Hammond, Luna. *History of Madison County, State of New York.* Syracuse, N.Y.: Truaer, Smith and Co., 1872.

Hampsten, *Read This Only to Yourself: The Private Writings of Midwestern Women, 1880–1910.* Bloomington: Indiana University Press, 1982.

Haney, Robert W. *Comstockery in America: Patterns of Censorship and Control.* Boston: Beacon Press, 1960.

Hardy, Thomas. *Jude, the Obscure.* New York: Harper and Brothers, 1895.

Harman, Lillian. *Marriage and Morality.* Chicago: M. Harman, 1900.

———. *Memorial of Moses Harman, October 12, 1830, January 30, 1910.* Chicago: L. Harman, 1910.

———. *Problems of Social Freedom.* London: The Adult, 1898.

———. *The Regeneration of Society.* Chicago: M. Harman, 1900.

Harman, Moses. *Digging for Bedrock: Camp-meeting Talks, Observations, and Experiences.* Valley Falls, Kans.: Lucifer Pub. Co., 1890.

———. *A Free Man's Creed: Discussion of Love in Freedom as Opposed to Institutional Marriage.* Los Angeles. The Journal of Eugenics, 1908.

———. *Institutional Marriage.* Chicago: M. Harman, 1901.

———. *Love in Freedom.* Chicago: M. Harman, 1900.

———. *Motherhood in Freedom.* Chicago: M. Harman, 1900.

Harper, Robert S. "The Ohio Press in the Civil War." *Civil War History* 3 (1957): 221–52.

Harrison, Fraser. *The Dark Angel: Aspects of Victorian Sexuality.* London: Sheldon Press, 1977.

Hartog, Hendrick. "Lawyering, Husbands' Rights, and 'The Unwritten Law' in Nineteenth-Century America." *Journal of American History* 84 (June 1997): 67–96.

———. *Man and Wife in America: A History.* Cambridge, Mass.: Harvard University Press, 2000.

Hatch, Nathan O. *The Democratization of American Christianity.* New Haven, Conn.: Yale University Press, 1989.

Hawley, Victor. *Special Love, Special Sex: An Oneida Community Diary.* Ed. Robert S. Fogarty. Syracuse, N.Y.: Syracuse University Press, 1994.

Hayden, Dolores. *The Grand Domestic Revolution: A History of Feminist Designs for American Homes, Neighborhoods, and Cities.* Cambridge, Mass.: Massachusetts Institute of Technology Press, 1981.

Haywood, Aaron S. *An Exposition of 'Social Freedom': Monogamic Marriage, the Highest Development of Sexual Equality.* Boston: The Author, 1875.

Hedrick, Joan D. *Harriet Beecher Stowe: A Life.* New York: Oxford University Press, 1994.

Heilman, Robert B. "Hardy's *Sue Bridehead.*" *Nineteenth Century Fiction* 20 (1966): 307–23.

Heinzen, Karl. *The Rights of Women and the Sexual Relations.* Boston: B. R. Tucker, 1891.

Hennequin, Victor. *Love in the Phalanstery.* Trans. Henry James Sr. New York: Dewitt and Davenport, 1849.

Hersh, Blanche Glassman. *The Slavery of Sex: Feminist-Abolitionists in America.* Urbana: University of Illinois Press, 1978.

Hewitt, Nancy. *Women's Activism and Social Change: Rochester, New York, 1822–1872.* Ithaca, N.Y.: Cornell University Press, 1984.

Heywood, Ezra. *Cupid's Yokes; or, The Binding Forces of Conjugal Love.* Princeton, Mass.: Co-operative Publishing Company, 1878.

———. *The Following Resolutions Were Presented to the Convention of the New England Free Love League; Held in Boston, May 20th and 21st, 1877.* Princeton, Mass.: E. Heywood, 1877.

———. *Uncivil Liberty: An Essay to Show the Injustice and Impolicy of Ruling Woman without Her Consent.* Princeton, Mass.: Co-operative Publishing Company, 1870.

Hirshman, Linda R., and Jane E. Larson. *Hard Bargains: The Politics of Sex.* New York: Oxford University Press, 1998.

The History of Clinton County, Iowa. Chicago: Western Historical Company, 1879.

History of Clinton County, Iowa. [Clinton, Iowa]: Clinton County American Revolution Bicentennial Commission, 1976.

Hobson, Barbara Meil. *Uneasy Virtue: The Politics of Prostitution and the American Reform Tradition.* New York: Basic Books, 1987.

Hoffert, Sylvia D. *When Hens Crow: The Woman's Rights Movement in Antebellum America.* Bloomington: Indiana University Press, 1995.

Hoganson, Kristin. "Garrisonian Abolitionists and the Rhetoric of Gender, 1850–1860." *American Quarterly* 45 (Dec. 1993): 558–95.

Holt, Marilyn Irvin. *Linoleum, Better Babies, and the Modern Farm Woman, 1890–1930.* Albuquerque: University of New Mexico Press, 1995.

Hoover, Dwight. "The Influence of Swedenborg on the Religious Ideas of Henry James, Senior." In *Swedenborg and His Influence.* Ed. Erland J. Brock et al. Bryn Athyn, Pa.: The Academy of the New Church, 1988. 263–76.

Hovey, Elizabeth. "Stamping Out Smut: The Enforcement of Obscenity Laws, 1872–1915." Ph.D. dissertation, Columbia University, 1998.

Howland, Marie Stevens. *The Familistere.* Boston: Christopher Publishing House, 1918.

Humphrey, Robert E. *The Children of Fantasy: The First Rebels of Greenwich Village.* New York: John Wiley and Sons, 1978.

Hunker, A. (pseud.) *Four Epistles on Free Love and Murder.* Troy, N.Y.: A. W. Scribner, 1870.

Hunt, Harriot K. *Glances and Glimpses; or, Fifty Years Social.* Boston: John P. Jewett and Co., 1856.

Hunt, Karen. "Equivocal Feminists: The Social Democratic Federation and the Woman Question, 1884–1911." Ph.D. dissertation, University of Manchester, 1988.

Huston, James L. *The Panic of 1857 and the Coming of the Civil War.* Baton Rouge: Louisiana State University Press, 1987.

Ireland, Robert M. "Death to the Libertine: The McFarland-Richardson Case Revisited." *New York History* 68 (1987): 191–217.

"Is Marriage a Failure?" *Cosmopolitan* 6 (1888): 93–96.

Isaacs, Ernest Jacob. "A History of Nineteenth Century American Spiritualism as a Religious and Social Movement." Ph.D. dissertation, University of Wisconsin, 1975.

Isenberg, Nancy. *Sex and Citizenship in Antebellum America.* Chapel Hill: University of North Carolina Press, 1998.

Iverson, Joan Smyth. "A Debate on the American Home: The Antipolygamy Controversy, 1880–1890." *Journal of the History of Sexuality* 1 (1991): 585–602.

Jackson, Margaret. *The Real Facts of Life: Feminism and the Politics of Sexuality, 1850–1940.* Bristol, Pa.: Taylor and Francis, 1994.

James, C. L. *The Future Relations of the Sexes.* St. Louis, Mo.: [The Author], 1872.

———. *The Law of Marriage: An Exposition of Its Uselessness and Injustice.* St. Louis: Times Printing House, 1871.

Jeffrey, Julie Roy. *Frontier Women: The Trans-Mississippi West, 1840–1880.* New York: Hill and Wang, 1979.

———. "Women in the Southern Farmers' Alliance: A Reconsideration of the Role and Status of Women in the Late Nineteenth-Century South." *Feminist Studies* 3 (Fall 1975): 72–91.

Jensen, Joan M. *Loosening the Bonds: Mid-Atlantic Farm Women, 1750–1850.* New Haven, Conn.: Yale University Press, 1986.

———. "The Death of Rosa: Sexuality in Rural America." *Agricultural History* 67 (Fall 1993): 1–12.

———. "Sexuality on a Northern Frontier: The Gendering and Disciplining of Rural Wisconsin Women, 1850–1920." *Agricultural History* 73 (Spring 1999): 136–67.

John, Richard R. *Spreading the News: The American Postal System from Franklin to Morse.* Cambridge, Mass.: Harvard University Press, 1995.

Johnson, Paul E., and Sean Wilentz. *The Kingdom of Matthias: A Story of Sex and Salvation in Nineteenth-Century America.* New York: Oxford University Press, 1994.

Johnston, Johanna. *Mrs. Satan: The Incredible Saga of Victoria C. Woodhull.* New York: Putnam, 1967.

Jones, Mary Somerville. *An Historical Geography of the Changing Divorce Law in the United States.* New York: Garland, 1987.

Kaestle, Carl F. *Literacy in the United States: Readers and Reading since 1880.* New Haven, Conn.: Yale University Press, 1991.

The Kansas Fight for Free Press: The Four Indicted Articles. Valley Falls, Kans.: Lucifer Publishing Co., 1889.

Karcher, Carolyn L. *The First Woman in the Republic: A Cultural Biography of Lydia Maria Child.* Durham, N.C.: Duke University Press, 1998.

Kelly, Florence Finch. *On the Inside.* New York: Sanfred and Co., 1890.

———. *Frances: A Story for Men and Women.* New York: Sanfred and Co., 1889.

Kelly, Mary, ed. *Woman's Being, Woman's Place: Female Identity and Vocation in American History.* Boston: G. K. Hall, 1979.

Kent, Austin. *Conjugal Love: The True and the False.* [Stockholm], N.Y.: S.N., 1872.

———. *Free Love; or, A Philosophical Demonstration of the Non-Exclusive Nature of Connubial Love.* Hopkinton, N.Y.: The Author, 1857.

———. *Mrs. Woodhull and Her 'Social Freedom.'* Clinton, Mass.: Independent Radical Tract Society, 1873.

Kern, Louis J. "Moses Harman." In *American National Biography.* Vol. 10. Ed. John A. Garraty and Mark C. Carnes. New York: Oxford University Press, 1999. 112–13.

———. *An Ordered Love: Sex Roles and Sexuality in Victorian Utopias: The Shakers, the Mormons, and the Oneida Community.* Chapel Hill: University of North Carolina Press, 1981.

———. "Sexuality and the Male Sexual Body in Victorian Free Love Literature." In *American Bodies: Cultural Histories of the Physique.* Ed. Tim Armstrong. New York: New York University Press, 1996. 46–72.

———. "Stamping Out the 'Brutality of the He': Sexual Ideology and the Masculine Ideal in the Literature of Victorian Sex Radicals." *American Transcendental Quarterly* 5 (Sept. 1991): 225–39.

Kerr, Andrea Moore. *Lucy Stone: Speaking Out for Equality.* New Brunswick, N.J.: Rutgers University Press, 1992.

Kerr, Howard. *Mediums and Spirit Rappers and Roaring Radicals: Spiritualism in American Literature, 1850–1900.* Urbana: University of Illinois Press, 1972.

Kerr, R. B. *A Tale of the Strassburg Geese: With Other Allegories.* Chicago: M. Harman, 1901.

————. *Up-to-Date Fables.* New York: Edwin C. Walker, 1905.

Kirkley, Evelyn A. *Rational Mothers and Infidel Gentlemen: Gender and Atheism, 1865–1915.* Syracuse, N.Y.: Syracuse University Press, 2000.

Kline, Wendy Anne. "'Building a Better Race': Eugenics and the Making of Modern Morality in America, 1900–1960." Ph.D. dissertation, University of California at Davis, 1998.

Kohl, Lawrence Frederick. *The Politics of Individualism: Parties and the American Character in the Jacksonian Era.* New York: Oxford University Press, 1989.

Kolmerton, Carol A. *Women in Utopia: The Ideology of Gender in the American Owenite Communities.* Bloomington: Indiana University Press, 1990.

Koven, Seth, and Sonya Michel, eds. *Mothers of a New World: Maternalist Politics and the Origins of Welfare States.* New York: Routledge, Chapman and Hall, 1993.

Kraditor, Aileen S. *The Ideas of the Woman Suffrage Movement, 1890–1920.* New York: Columbia University Press, 1965.

Kriebl, Karen Joyce. "From Bloomers to Flappers: The American Women's Dress Reform Movement, 1840–1920." Ph.D. dissertation, Ohio State University, 1998.

Lasch, Christopher. *The New Radicalism in America (1889–1963): The Intellectual as Social Type.* New York: Alfred A. Knopf, 1965.

Lazarus, Marx Edgeworth. *Love vs. Marriage, Pt. I.* New York: Fowlers and Wells, 1852.

Leach, William. *True Love and Perfect Union: The Feminist Reform of Sex and Society.* 2d ed. Middletown, Conn.: Wesleyan University Press, 1989.

Leland, Theron. "Letter from One of the 'Old Guard.'" *American Socialist* 1 (13 Apr. 1876): 18.

Lemons, Elizabeth Belknap. "Sex in Context: Toward a Contextual Feminist Theology of Heterosexual Relations in the Contemporary United States through an Analysis of Victoria Woodhull's Nineteenth-Century Free-Love Discourse." Ph.D. dissertation, Harvard University, 1997.

Lerner, Gerda. *The Grimke Sisters from South Carolina: Pioneers for Woman's Rights and Abolition.* New York: Schocken Books, 1967.

LeWarne, Charles Pierce. *Utopias on Puget Sound, 1885–1915.* Seattle: University of Washington Press, 1975.

Linton, E. Lynn. *The New Woman: In Haste and at Leisure.* New York: The Merriam Co., 1895.

————. "The Revolt against Matrimony." *Forum* 10 (Jan. 1891): 585–95.

————. "The Wild Women as Politicians." *Nineteenth Century* 30 (1891): 79–88.

————. "The Wild Women as Social Insurgents." *Eclectic Magazine* 117 (Nov. 1891): 667–73.

Lipow, Arthur. *Authoritarian Socialism in America: Edward Bellamy and the Nationalist Movement.* Berkeley: University of California Press, 1982.

Long, Kathryn Teresa. *The Revival of 1857–58: Interpreting an American Religious Awakening.* New York: Oxford University Press, 1998.

Luckock, Herbert Mortimer. *The History of Marriage, Jewish and Christian, in Relation to Divorce.* New York: Longmans, Green and Co., 1894.

Ludmerer, Kenneth M. *Genetics and American Society: A Historical Appraisal.* Baltimore: Johns Hopkins University Press, 1972.

Macdonald, George E. *Fifty Years of Free Thought*. Vol. 1, 1929; vol. 2, 1931. Reprint, New York: Arno Press, 1972.

Macdonald, W. Allan. *New Maids for Old: Free Women in Marriage and Out*. London: Questall Press, 1912.

McElroy, Wendy, ed. *Freedom, Feminism, and the State: An Overview of Individualist Feminism*. Washington, D.C.: Cato Institute, 1982.

Mahan, Asa. *Modern Mysteries Explained and Exposed*. Boston: J. P. Jewett and Co., 1855.

Mahoney, Timothy R. *Provincial Lives: Middle-Class Experience in the Antebellum Middle West*. New York: Cambridge University Press, 1999.

Malin, James C. *A Concern about Humanity: Notes on Reform, 1872–1912, at the National and Kansas Levels of Thought*. Lawrence, Kans.: The Author, 1964.

Mandelker, Ira L. *Religion, Society, and Utopia in Nineteenth-Century America*. Amherst: University of Massachusetts Press, 1984.

Marberry, M. Marion. *Vicky: A Biography of Victoria C. Woodhull*. New York: Funk and Wagnalls, 1967.

Margold, Charles William. *Sex Freedom and Social Control*. Chicago: University of Chicago Press, 1926.

Mariager, Dagmar. "Another Open Letter." In *The Next Revolution, No. 1; or, Women's Emancipation from Sex Slavery*. Valley Falls, Kans.: Lucifer Publishing Co., 1890. 30–33.

Marilley, Suzanne M. *Woman Suffrage and the Origins of Liberal Feminism in the United States, 1820–1920*. Cambridge, Mass.: Harvard University Press, 1996.

Marriage and Divorce, 1867–1906. Part 1. Washington, D.C.: U.S. Department of Commerce and Labor, Bureau of Census, 1909.

"Marriage and Free Thought." *Fortnightly Review* 56 (1891): 259–78.

Marsh, Margaret S. *Anarchist Women, 1870–1920*. Philadelphia: Temple University Press, 1981.

Marti, Donald B. *Women of the Grange: Mutuality and Sisterhood in Rural America, 1866–1920*. Westport, Conn.: Greenwood Press, 1991.

Martin, James J. *Men against the State: The Expositors of Individualist Anarchism in America, 1827–1908*. DeKalb, Ill.: Adrian Allen Associates, 1953.

Martin, Victoria Woodhull. *A Fragmentary Record of Public Work Done in America, 1871–77*. London: G. Norman and Son, 1877.

Marty, Martin E. *The Infidel: Freethought and American Religion*. Cleveland: Meredian Books, 1961.

Mason, Michael. *The Making of Victorian Sexual Attitudes*. New York: Oxford University Press, 1994.

Matthews, Jean V. *Women's Struggle for Equality: The Final Phase, 1828–1876*. Chicago: Ivan R. Dee, 1997.

May, Elaine Tyler. *Great Expectations: Marriage and Divorce in Post-Victorian America*. Chicago: University of Chicago Press, 1980.

Mayhew, William H. "Marriage and Chastity." *New Church Review* 4 (Jan. 1897): 79–88.

McKinley, Blaine. "Free Love and Domesticity: Lizzie M. Holmes, 'Hagar Lyndon' (1893), and the Anarchist-Feminist Imagination." *Journal of American Culture* 13 (Spring 1990): 55–62.

McKinley, Kenneth. "A Guide to the Communistic Communities of Ohio." *Ohio State Archaeological and Historical Quarterly* 46 (Jan. 1937): 1–15.

McLoughlin, William G. "Charles Grandison Finney." *Ante-Bellum Reform.* Ed. David Brion Davis. New York: Harper and Row, 1967. 97–107.

Melder, Keith E. *The Beginnings of Sisterhood: The American Women's Rights Movement, 1800–1850.* New York: Schocken, 1977.

Melosh, Barbara, ed. *Gender and American History since 1890.* New York: Routledge, 1993.

Merk, Frederick. *Economic History of Wisconsin during the Civil War Decade.* Madison: State Historical Society of Wisconsin, 1916.

Messer-Kruse, Timothy. "The Yankee International: Marxism and the American Reform Tradition, 1831–1876." Ph.D. dissertation, University of Wisconsin at Madison, 1994.

Miller, Howard S. "Kate Austin: A Feminist-Anarchist on the Farmer's Last Frontier." 1996. Unpublished manuscript in the author's possession.

Miller, Nina. "The Bonds of Free Love: Constructing the Female Bohemian Self." *Genders* 11 (1991): 37–57.

Mintz, Steven. *Moralists and Modernizers: America's Pre–Civil War Reformers.* Baltimore: Johns Hopkins University Press, 1995.

Minus, Paul M. *Walter Rauschenbausch: American Reformer.* New York: Macmillan, 1988.

"Monogamy and Free Love." *Open Court* 4 (12 Feb. 1891): 2699–2700.

Moore, R. Laurence. *In Search of White Crows: Spiritualism, Parapsychology, and American Culture.* New York: Oxford University Press, 1977.

———. *Selling God: American Religion in the Marketplace of Culture.* New York: Oxford University Press, 1994.

Morrison, Frances. *The Influence of the Present Marriage System upon the Character and Interests of Females Contrasted with That Proposed by Robert Owen.* Manchester: A. Heywood, [1838].

Mott, Frank Luther. *A History of American Magazines.* 5 vols. Cambridge, Mass.: The Belknap Press of Harvard University Press, 1957–68.

Muncy, Raymond. *Sex and Marriage in Utopian Communities: Nineteenth-Century America.* Bloomington: Indiana University Press, 1973.

Myerson, Joel. "Mary Gove Nichols' *Mary Lyndon:* A Forgotten Reform Novel." *American Literature* 58 (Dec. 1986): 523–39.

National League for the Protection of the Family. *Report of the National Divorce Reform League.* Montpelier: Vermont Watchman and State Journal Press, 1887.

Nelson, Bruce. *Beyond the Martyrs: A Social History of Chicago's Anarchists, 1870–1900.* New Brunswick, N.J.: Rutgers University Press, 1988.

Newton, Sarah E. *Learning to Behave: A Guide to American Conduct Books before 1900.* Westport, Conn.: Greenwood Press, 1994.

The Next Revolution, No. 1; or, Woman's Emancipation from Sex Slavery. Valley Falls, Kans.: Lucifer Publishing Co., 1890.

Nichols, Mary S. Gove. *Agnes Morris; or, The Heroine of Domestic Life.* New York: Harper and Bros., 1849.

———. *Experience in Water-Cure: A Familiar Exposition of the Principles and Results of Water Treatment.* New York: Fowlers and Wells, 1849.

————. *Mary Lyndon; or, Revelations of a Life, an Autobiography.* New York: Stringer and Townsend, 1855.

————. *The Two Loves; or, Eros and Anteros.* New York: Stringer and Townsend, 1849.

————. *A Woman's Work in Water Cure and Sanitary Education.* London: Nichols and Co., 1874.

Nichols, Thomas L. *Esoteric Anthropology.* Port Chester, N.Y.: The Author, 1853.

————. *Forty Years of American Life, 1821–1861.* 1864. Reprint, New York: Stackpole Sons, 1937.

————. *Free Love: A Doctrine of Spiritualism.* Cincinnati: F. Bly, 1856.

————. *Journal in Jail.* Buffalo, N.Y.: A. Dinsmore, 1840.

————. *Nichols' Health Manual: Being Also a Memorial of the Life and Work of Mrs. Mary S. Gove Nichols.* London: E. W. Allen, 1887.

————. "Oration." In *The Paine Festival.* Cincinnati: Valentine Nicholson and Co., 1856.

————. *Religions of the World.* Cincinnati: Valentine Nicholson and Co., 1855.

————. *Women In All Ages and Nations.* New York: Fowler and Wells, 1849.

————. *The Work of Reform.* Cincinnati: Watkin and Nicholson, 1856.

Nichols, Thomas L., and Mary S. Gove Nichols. *Marriage: Its History, Character, and Results.* Cincinnati: Valentine Nicholson and Co., [1854].

————. *Nichols' Medical Miscellanies: A Familiar Guide to the Preservation of Health and the Hydropathic Home Treatment of the Most Formidable Diseases.* Cincinnati: T. L. Nichols, 1856.

Nissenbaum, Stephen. *Sex, Diet, and Debility in Jacksonian America: Sylvester Graham and Health Reform.* Westport, Conn.: Greenwood Press, 1980.

Noever, Janet Hubly. "Passionate Rebel: The Life of Mary Gove Nichols, 1810–1884." Ph.D. dissertation, University of Oklahoma, 1983.

"Nordhoff's Communistic Societies." *The Nation* 20 (14 Jan. 1875): 26–28.

Northcote, Orford. *Ruled by the Tomb: A Discussion of Freethought and Free Love.* Chicago: Moses Harman, 1898.

Noyes, John Humphrey. *Bible Argument Defining the Relation of the Sexes in the Kingdom of Heaven.* Oneida Reserve: Leonard and Company Printers, 1849.

————. *Dixon and His Copyists.* 2d ed. Wallingford, Conn.: Oneida Community, 1874.

————. *History of American Socialisms.* Philadelphia: J. B. Lippincott and Company, 1870.

————. *Male Continence.* Oneida, N.Y.: Office of the American Socialist, 1872.

————. *Slavery and Marriage: A Dialogue Conversation between Judge North, Major South, and Mr. Free Church.* Oneida, N.Y.: Leonard and Co., 1850.

Nugent, Walter T. K. *Money and American Society, 1865–1880.* New York: Free Press, 1968.

Nunan, Philip. *Map of Erie and Part of Ottawa Counties, Ohio.* Sandusky, Ohio: Philip Nunan, 1863.

O'Callaghan, Jeremiah. *The Holy Bible Authenticated; Baptism and Matrimony; Free Lovers Abhorrent: Three Responses to Mr. Walker, a Presbyterian Minister.* New York: The Author, 1858.

Ocko, Stephanie. "Victoria Woodhull's Siege of New York." *American History Illustrated* 16 (1981): 32–37.

Olerich, Henry. *A Cityless and Countryless World.* Holstein, Iowa: Gilmore and Olerich, 1893.

Oliver, Leon. *The Great Sensation: A Full, Complete and Reliable History of the Beecher-Tilton-Woodhull Scandal . . . Also a Clear and Concise Statement of the Views of 'The Woodhull' upon Social Reform, Free Love.* Chicago: Beverly Co., 1873.

O'Neill, William L. *Divorce in the Progressive Era.* New Haven, Conn.: Yale University Press, 1967.

Osterud, Nancy. *Bonds of Community: The Lives of Farm Women in Nineteenth-Century New York.* Ithaca, N.Y.: Cornell University Press, 1991.

———. "Gender and the Transition to Capitalism in Rural America." *Agricultural History* 67 (1993): 14–29.

Ostler, Jeffrey. *Prairie Populism: The Fate of Agrarian Radicalism in Kansas, Nebraska, and Iowa, 1880–1892.* Lawrence: University Press of Kansas, 1993.

Outhwaite, R. B., ed. *Marriage and Society: Studies in the Social History of Marriage.* New York: St. Martin's Press, 1981.

Owen, Robert. *The Marriage System of the New Moral World.* Leeds: J. Hobson, 1838.

Owen, Robert Dale. *Footfalls on the Boundary of Another World.* Philadelphia: J. B. Lippincott, 1869.

Padgug, Robert A. "Sexual Matters: On Conceptualizing Sexuality in History." *Radical History Review* 20 (Spring–Summer 1979): 3–23.

Painter, Nell Irvin. *Sojourner Truth: A Life, a Symbol.* New York: W. W. Norton, 1996.

Parker, Alison M. *Purifying America: Women, Cultural Reform, and Pro-Censorship Activism, 1873–1933.* Urbana: University of Illinois Press, 1997.

Parkhurst, Henry M. *Diana: A Psycho-fyziological Essay on Sexual Relations for Married Men and Women.* 2d ed. New York: Burnz and Co., 1882.

Patterson, John. *Charles Hopewell; or, Society As It Is, and As It Should Be.* Cincinnati: Longley, 1853.

Patterson, John Stahl. *Reforms: Their Difficulties and Possibilities.* New York: D. Appleton and Co., 1884.

Paul, Diane B. *Controlling Human Heredity, 1865 to the Present.* Atlantic Highlands, N.J.: Humanities Press, 1995.

Peacefull, Leonard, ed. *A Geography of Ohio.* Kent, Ohio: Kent State University Press, 1996.

Peeke, H. L. *The Centennial History of Erie County, Ohio.* Cleveland: Penton Press, 1925.

Pence, Sandra Kay. "Victoria Claflin Woodhull: Victorian Advocate of Free Love." M.A. thesis, University of Georgia, 1974.

Pentecost, Hugh O. "A Good Man Sent to Prison." *Twentieth Century Library* 1 (31 May 1890): 1–10.

Perlberg, Marilyn. "Men and Women in Saint Simonianism: The Union of Politics and Morals." Ph.D. dissertation, University of Iowa, 1993.

Perry, Lewis. *Childhood, Marriage, and Reform: Henry Clarke Wright, 1797–1870.* Chicago: University of Chicago Press, 1979.

———. *Radical Abolition: Anarchy and the Government of God in Antislavery Thought.* Ithaca, N.Y.: Cornell University Press, 1973.

Perry, Marily Elizabeth. "Mary Gove Nichols." In *American National Biography.* Vol. 16. Ed. John A. Garraty and Mark C. Carnes. New York: Oxford University Press, 1999. 391–92.

The Persecution and the Appreciation: Brief Account of the Trials and Imprisonment of Moses Harman. Chicago: Lucifer Publishing Co., 1907.

Persons, Stow. *Free Religion: An American Faith.* New Haven, Conn.: Yale University Press, 1947.

Phelps, Elizabeth Stuart. *The Story of Avis.* Boston: J. P. Osgood, 1877.

Pike, J. W. *The Fallacies of the Free Love Theory; or, Love Considered as a Religion: A Lecture Delivered in Washington, D.C., April 25, 1875.* Boston: W. Denton, 1875.

Pittock, Mrs. M. A. Weeks. *The God of Civilization: A Romance.* Chicago: Eureka Publishing Co., 1890.

Pitzer, Donald E., ed. *America's Communal Utopias.* Chapel Hill: University of North Carolina Press, 1997.

Pivar, David J. *Purity Crusade: Sexual Morality and Social Control, 1868–1900.* Westport, Conn.: Greenwood Press, 1973.

Platt, William. *Judgment.* Chicago: M. Harman, 1900.

Pleck, Elizabeth. *Domestic Tyranny: The Making of Social Policy against Family Violence from Colonial Times to the Present.* New York: Oxford University Press, 1987.

Porter, Ray, and Mikulas Teich, eds. *Sexual Knowledge, Sexual Science: The History of Attitudes to Sexuality.* New York: Cambridge University Press, 1994.

Porter, Samuel. *400 Years of Freethought.* New York: Truth Seeker Company, 1894.

Post, Albert. *Popular Freethought in America, 1825–1850.* New York: Columbia University Press, 1943.

Potter-Loomis, Hulda L. *Social Freedom, the Most Important Factor in Human Evolution.* Chicago: M. Harman, [1890].

Pounds, Diana. "Suffragists, Free Love, and the Woman Question." *Palimpsest* 72 (1991): 2–15.

Price, Kenneth M. "Walt Whitman, Free Love, and *The Social Revolutionist.*" *American Periodicals* 1 (Fall 1991): 70–82.

Price, Kenneth M., and Susan Belasco Smith. *Periodical Literature in Nineteenth-Century America.* Charlottesville: University Press of Virginia, 1995.

Proceedings of the Free Convention, Rutland, Vermont, July 25th, 26th, 27th, 1858. Boston: J. B. Yerrington and Son, 1858.

Proceedings of the Tenth Annual Convention of the American Association of Spiritualists. Chicago: n.p, 1873.

Quale, G. Robina. *A History of Marriage Systems.* Westport, Conn.: Greenwood Press, 1988.

Quilter, Harry, ed. *Is Marriage a Failure? A Modern Symposium.* Chicago: Rand, McNally, 1889.

Rabban, David. *Free Speech in Its Forgotten Years, 1870–1920.* New York: Cambridge University Press, 1997.

Rakow, Lana, and Cheris Kramarae, eds. *The Revolution in Words: Righting Women, 1868–1871.* New York: Routledge, 1990.

Randall, J. G. "The Newspaper Problem in Its Bearing upon Military Secrecy during the Civil War." *American Historical Review* 23 (Jan. 1918): 303–23.

Randolph, Paschal Beverly. *The "Learned Pundit" and "Man with Two Souls," His Curious Life, Works, and Career: The Great Free-Love Trial.* Boston: Randolph Publishing House, [1872].

———. *Love and Its Hidden History.* 4th ed. Boston: W. White and Co., 1869.

Redfern, Bernice. "Victoria Woodhull: A Radical for Free Love." *San Jose Studies* 10 (1984): 40–48.

Reichert, William O. *Partisans of Freedom: A Study in American Anarchism.* Bowling Green, Ohio: Bowling Green State University Popular Press, 1976.

"The Revolt against Marriage." *Forum* 10 (Jan. 1891): 585–95.

Reynolds, David S. *Walt Whitman's America: A Cultural Biography.* New York: Alfred A. Knopf, 1995.

Richards, Irving T. "Mary Gove Nichols and John Neal." *New England Quarterly* 7 (June 1934): 335–55.

Riley, Glenda. *Divorce: An American Tradition.* New York: Oxford University Press, 1991.

Robb, George. "The Way of All Flesh: Degeneration, Eugenics, and the Gospel of Free Love." *Journal of the History of Sexuality* 6 (1996): 589–603.

Robertson, Stacey M. "'Aunt Nancy Men': Parker Pillsbury, Masculinity, and Women's Rights Activism in the Nineteenth-Century United States." *American Studies* 37 (Fall 1996): 33–60.

Root, Harmon Knox. *The Lover's Marriage Lighthouse: A Series of Sensible and Scientific Essays on the Subjects of Marriage and Free Divorce.* New York: By the Proprietor, 1858.

Rosenberg, Charles E. "Sexuality, Class and Role in Nineteenth-Century America." *American Quarterly* 25 (May 1973): 131–53.

Rosenberger, I. J. *An Exegesis on Marriage and Divorce: An Appeal for Reform.* Covington, Ohio: I. J. Rosenberger, 1899.

Ruedebusch, Emil F. *Freie Menschen in der Liebe und Ehe.* Mayville, Wis.: Selbstverlag des Verfassers, 1895.

———. *The Old and the New Ideal.* Mayville, Wis.: The Author, 1896.

Rugoff, Milton. *Prudery and Passion: Sexuality in Victorian America.* New York: G. P. Putnam's Sons, 1971.

Russo, Ann, and Cheris Kramarae, eds. *The Radical Women's Press of the 1850s.* New York: Routledge, 1991.

Ryan, Mary P. *The Empire of the Mother: American Writing about Domesticity, 1830 to 1860.* New York: Institute for Research in History and the Haworth Press, 1982.

Sachs, Emanie. *"The Terrible Siren": Victoria Woodhull, 1838–1927.* New York: Harper and Brothers, 1928.

The Salem, Ohio, 1850 Women's Rights Convention Proceedings. Comp. and ed. Robert W. Audretsch. Salem, Ohio: Salem Area Bicentennial Committee and Salem Public Library, 1976.

Sanchez-Eppler, Karen. *Touching Liberty: Abolition, Feminism, and the Politics of the Body.* Berkeley: University of California Press, 1993.

Sanders, Elizabeth. *Roots of Reform: Farmers, Workers, and the American State, 1877–1917.* Chicago: University of Chicago Press, 1999.

Sanders, Quincy A. "The Free-Love Movement in the United States in the Nineteenth Century." A.B. thesis, Harvard University, 1954.

Santley, Herbert. "Marriage." *Lippincott's Magazine* 8 (Oct. 1871): 395–403.

Savagian, John. "Women at Ceresco." *Wisconsin Magazine of History* 83 (Summer 2000): 258–80.

Schapsmeier, Edward L., and Frederick H. Schapsmeier. *Encyclopedia of American Agricultural History.* Westport, Conn.: Greenwood Press, 1975.

Schoeman, Ferdinand David. *Privacy and Social Freedom.* New York: Cambridge University Press, 1992.

Schreiner, Olive. *The Story of an African Farm.* New York: Merrill and Baker, 1883.

Schwantes, Carlos A. "Free Love and Free Speech on the Pacific Northwest Frontier." *Oregon Historical Quarterly* 82 (Fall 1981): 271–93.

Sears, Hal D. *The Sex Radicals: Free Love in High Victorian America.* Lawrence: Regents Press of Kansas, 1977.

Sellers, Charles. *The Market Revolution: Jacksonian America, 1815–1846.* New York: Oxford University Press, 1991.

Severance, Juliet. *A Discussion of the Social Question, between J. H. S., M.D., and David Jones, Editor of the "Olive Branch."* Milwaukee, Wis.: National Advance Print, 1891.

———. "Farmer's Wives." In *Transactions of the Wisconsin State Agricultural Society.* Madison, Wis.: Democrat Printing Company, 1886. 273–83.

———. *A Lecture on Religious, Political and Social Freedom.* Milwaukee, Wis.: Godfrey and Crandall, 1881.

———. *A Lecture on the Evolution of Life in Earth and Spirit Conditions.* Milwaukee: Godfrey and Crandall, 1882.

———. *Marriage.* Chicago: Moses Harman Publishing Co., 1901.

Shannon, Fred A. *American Farmers' Movements.* Princeton, N.J.: Van Nostrand, 1957.

———. *The Farmers' Last Frontier: Agriculture, 1860–1897.* New York: Farrar and Rinehart, 1945.

Shaplen, Robert. *Free Love and Heavenly Sinners: The Story of the Great Henry Ward Beecher Scandal.* New York: Knopf, 1954.

Sharkey, Robert P. *Money, Class, and Party: An Economic Study of the Civil War and Reconstruction.* Baltimore: Johns Hopkins University Press, 1959.

Shipps, Jan. *Mormonism: The Story of a New Religious Tradition.* Urbana: University of Illinois Press, 1985.

Silver-Isenstadt, Jean Lara. "Pure Pleasure: The Shared Life and Work of Mary Gove Nichols and Thomas Low Nichols in American Health Reform." Ph.D. dissertation, University of Pennsylvania, 1997.

———. *Shameless: The Visionary Life of Mary Gove Nichols.* Baltimore: Johns Hopkins University Press, 2002.

Simmons, Christina Clare. "Marriage in the Modern Manner: Sexual Radicalism and Reform in America, 1914–1941." Ph.D. dissertation, Brown University, 1982.

Sizer, Nelson. *Thoughts on Domestic Life; or, Marriage Vindicated and Free Love Exposed.* New York: Fowler and Wells, 1858.

Slenker, Elmina D. *The Darwins: A Domestic Radical Romance.* New York: D. M. Bennett, [1879].

Smith, Daniel Scott. "Recent Change and the Periodization of American Family History." *Journal of Family History* 20 (1995): 329–46.

Smith, Elizabeth Oakes. *Woman and Her Needs.* New York: Fowler and Wells, 1851.

Smith, John E. *Our Country and Its People—Madison County.* Boston: Boston History Co., 1899.

Smith, Timothy L. *Revivalism and Social Reform: American Protestantism on the Eve of the Civil War.* New York: Harper and Row, 1957.

Smith-Rosenberg, Carroll. *Disorderly Conduct: Visions of Gender in Victorian America.* New York: Oxford University Press, 1985.

Snitow, Ann, Christine Stansell, and Sharon Thompson, eds. *Powers of Desire: The Politics of Sexuality.* New York: Monthly Review Press, 1983.

Sochen, June. *The New Woman: Feminism in Greenwich Village, 1910–1920.* New York: Quadrangle Books, 1972.

Socialism vs. Legal Marriage. Chicago: Illinois Association Opposed to Woman Suffrage, 1910.

Solomon, Martha M., ed. *A Voice of Their Own: The Woman Suffrage Press, 1840–1910.* Tuscaloosa: University of Alabama Press, 1991.

Soltow, Lee, and Edward Stevens. *The Rise of Literacy and the Common School in the United States: A Socioeconomic Analysis to 1870.* Chicago: University of Chicago Press, 1981.

Soule, J. B. *Marriage As It Is, and Marriage As It Should Be.* Hamilton, Ohio: S. B. Smart, 1856.

Spurlock, John C. *Free Love: Marriage and Middle-Class Radicalism in America, 1825–1860.* New York: New York University Press, 1988.

———. "The Free Love Network in America, 1850 to 1860." *Journal of Social History* 21 (1988): 765–79.

———. "A Masculine View of Women's Freedom: Free Love in the Nineteenth Century." *International Social Science Review* 69 (1994): 34–44.

Srebnick, Amy Gilman. *The Mysterious Death of Mary Rogers: Sex and Culture in Nineteenth Century New York.* New York: Oxford University Press, 1995.

Stampp, Kenneth. *American in 1857: A Nation on the Brink.* New York: Oxford University Press, 1990.

Stansell, Christine. *City of Women: Sex and Class in New York, 1789–1860.* Urbana: University of Illinois Press, 1987.

Stanton, Theodore, and Harriot Stanton Blatch, eds. *Elizabeth Cady Stanton as Revealed in Her Letters, Diary, and Reminiscences.* Vol. 2. New York: Harper, 1922.

Stearns, Bertha-Monica. "Memnonia: The Launching of a Utopia." *New England Quarterly* 15 (June 1942): 280–95.

———. "Two Forgotten New England Reformers." *New England Quarterly* 6 (Mar. 1933): 59–84.

Stein, Stephen J. *The Shaker Experience in America.* New Haven, Conn.: Yale University Press, 1992.

Stemmen, Roy. *One Hundred Years of Spiritualism: The Story of the Spiritualist Association of Great Britain, 1872–1972.* London: Spiritualist Association of Great Britain, 1972.

Stern, Madeleine B. "The House of the Expanding Doors: Anne Lynch's Soirees, 1846." *New York History* 23 (Jan. 1942): 42–51.

———. *The Pantarch: A Biography of Stephen Pearl Andrews.* Austin: University of Texas Press, 1968.

———. "Stephen Pearl Andrews and Modern Times, Long Island." *Journal of Long Island History* 4 (1964): 1–15.

———, ed. *The Victoria Woodhull Reader.* Weston, Mass.: M and S Press, 1974.

Stevenson, Louise L. *The Victorian Homefront: American Thought and Culture, 1860–1880.* New York: Twayne Publishers, 1991.

Steward, Theophilus G. *A Charleston Love Story; or, Hortense Vanross.* New York: F. Tennyson Neely, 1899.

Stewart, James Brewer. *Holy Warriors: The Abolitionists and American Slavery.* New York: Hill and Wang, 1976.

Stiles, Joseph. "The Marriage Reform Movement in the United States." Ph.D. dissertation, Southern Baptist Theological Seminary, 1942.

Stock, Catherine McNicol, *Rural Radicals: Righteous Rage in the American Grain.* Ithaca, N.Y.: Cornell University Press, 1996.

Stockham, Alice B. *Karezza: Ethics of Marriage.* Chicago: Alice B. Stockham, 1897.

———. *Tokology, a Book for Every Woman.* Rev. ed. Chicago: Sanitary Publishing Co., 1886.

Stockham, Alice B., and Lida Hood-Talbot. *Koradine: A Prophetic Story.* Chicago: Alice B. Stockham and Co., 1893.

Stoehr, Taylor. *Free Love in America: A Documentary History.* New York: AMS Press, 1979.

Stowe, Harriet Beecher. *My Wife and I.* New York: V. B. Ford and Company, 1871.

Strauss, Sylvia. *Traitors to the Masculine Cause: The Men's Campaigns for Women's Rights.* Westport, Conn.: Greenwood Press, 1982.

Summary of Prosecutions against Lucifer, the Light-Bearer, and Its Editor, Moses Harman. Topeka, Kans.: M. Harman, 1893.

Swedenborg, Emanuel. *Conjugial Love and Its Chaste Delights.* London: Swedenborg Society, 1855.

Tax, Meredith. *The Rising of the Women: Feminist Solidarity and Class Conflict, 1880–1917.* New York: Monthly Review Press, 1980.

Taylor, M. F. "Marriage and Divorce." *Southern Magazine* 11 (Oct. 1872): 447–52.

Thierer, Joyce Mae. "The Country Life Movement and Rural Women, 1908–1931." Ph.D. dissertation, Kansas State University, 1994.

Thomas, Robert D. *The Man Who Would Be Perfect: John Humphrey Noyes and the Utopian Impulse.* Philadelphia: University of Pennsylvania Press, 1977.

———. "Sex, Religion and Reform." *Psychohistory Review* 11 (1983): 79–82.

Thompkins, Jane. *Sentimental Designs: The Cultural Work of American Fiction, 1790–1860.* New York: Oxford University Press, 1985.

Tilton, Theodore. *Victoria C. Woodhull, a Biographical Sketch.* New York: Golden Age Tract No. 3, 1871.

Tomasek, Kathryn Manson. "The Pivot of the Mechanism: Women, Gender, and Discourse in Fourierism and the Antebellum United States." Ph.D. dissertation, University of Wisconsin at Madison, 1995.

Trall, Russell. *Sexual Physiology: A Scientific and Popular Exposition of the Fundamental Problems in Sociology.* New York: Wood and Holbrook, 1866.

Transactions of the Wisconsin State Agricultural Society. Vol. 23. Madison: Democrat Printing Company, 1885.

Treat, Joseph. *Beecher, Tilton, Woodhull: The Creation of Society.* New York: The Author, 1874.

Tucher, Andie. *Froth and Scum: Truth, Beauty, Goodness, and the Axe Murder in America's First Mass Medium.* Chapel Hill: University of North Carolina Press, 1994.

Tyler, Alice Felt. *Freedom's Ferment.* New York: Harper and Row, 1944.

Underhill, Lois Beachy. *The Woman Who Ran for President: The Many Lives of Victoria Woodhull.* Bridgehampton, N.Y.: Bridge Works Publishing Co., 1995.

Underwood, Sarah A. *Heroines of Freethought.* New York: Charles P. Somerby, 1876.

Unger, Irwin. *The Greenback Era.* Princeton, N.J.: Princeton University Press, 1964.

Van Vleck, George W. *The Panic of 1857: An Analytical Study.* New York: Columbia University Press, 1943.

Varner, John Grier, Jr. "Sarah Helen Whitman: Seeress of Providence." Ph.D. dissertation, University of Virginia, 1941.

Vartorella, William F. "The Other 'Peculiar Institution': Free Thought and Free Love Reform Press in Ohio During Rebellion and Reconstruction, 1861–77." Ph.D. dissertation, Ohio University, 1977.

Veysey, Lawrence R. *The Communal Experience: Anarchist and Mystical Counter-Cultures in America.* New York: Harper and Row, 1973.

Waisbrooker, Lois. *Against Lucifer, the Light-Bearer, and Its Editor, Moses Harman.* Topeka, Kans.: N.p., 1893.

———. *Alice Vale: A Story for the Times.* New York: The American News Co., 1869.

———. *Anything More My Lord.* N.p., 1895.

———. *Bible Truth Bursting Its Shell That It May Express Its Larger Meaning.* N.p., n.d.

———. *Eugenics; or, Race Culture Lessons.* Chicago: n.p., 1907.

———. *Facts and Figures for Working Men: Usury and Land Monopoly Must Go or All Freedom Must Go.* Antioch, Calif.: The Author, 1886.

———. *The Fountain of Life; or, The Threefold Power of Sex.* Topeka, Kans.: Independent Publishing Co., 1893.

———. *From Generation to Regeneration; or, The Plain Guide to Naturalism.* Los Angeles: The Author, 1879.

———. *Helen Harlow's Vow; or, Self Justice.* Boston: W. White, 1870.

———. *Maywood Blossoms.* Boston: W. White, 1871.

———. *My Century Plant.* Topeka, Kans.: Independent Publishing Co., 1896.

———. *Nothing Like It; or, Steps to the Kingdom.* Boston: Colby and Rich, 1875.

———. *The Occult Forces of Sex: Three Pamphlets in One.* Chicago: Purdy Publishing Co., 1893.

———. *Perfect Motherhood; or, Mabel Raymond's Resolve.* New York: 1889.

———. *The Sex Question and the Money Power.* [Jackson, Mich.]: The Author, 1873.

———. *A Sex Revolution.* 2d ed. Topeka, Kans.: Independent Publishing Co., 1894.

———. *Suffrage for Woman: The Reasons Why.* St. Louis: Clayton and Babington, 1868.

———. *The Temperance Folly; or, Who's the Worst.* N.p., 1900.

———. *The Wherefore Investigating Company.* Topeka, Kans.: Independent Publishing Co., 1894.

Wakeman, Thaddeus Burr. *In Memory of Edward Bliss Foote, M.D., the Funeral Address.* New York: Edward Bond Foote, 1907.

Walker, Edwin C. *The Ethics of Freedom.* New York: E. C. Walker, 1913.

———. *Variety vs. Monogamy: An Address before the Ladies' Liberal League of Philadelphia.* Chicago: M. Harman, 1897.

———. *Who Is the Enemy? Anthony Comstock or You?* New York: E. C. Walker, 1903.

Walker, Edwin C., and William Josephus Robinson. *Sex Morality, Past, Present, and Future.* New York: Critic and Guide Co., 1912.

Waller, Altina L. *Reverend Beecher and Mrs. Tilton: Sex and Class in Victorian America.* Amherst: University of Massachusetts Press, 1982.

Walters, Ronald G. *American Reformers, 1815–1860.* New York: Hill and Wang, 1978.

Ward, Artemus. "Among the Free Lovers." In *Artemus Ward: His Book.* New York: Carleton, 1862. 86–90.

Warren, Josiah. *Practical Applications of the Elementary Principles of "True Civilization."* Princeton, Mass.: The Author, 1873.

Warren, Sidney. *American Freethought, 1860–1914.* New York: Columbia University Press, 1943.

Watkins, Marilyn P. "Political Activism and Community-Building among Alliance and Grange Women in Western Washington, 1892–1925." *Agricultural History* 67 (Spring 1993): 197–213.

Webber, Charles Wilkins. *Yieger's Cabinet, Spiritual Vampirism: The History of Etherial Softdown, and Her Friends of the "New Light."* Philadelphia: Lippincott, Grambo and Co., 1853.

West, William Lemore. "The Moses Harman Story." *Kansas Historical Quarterly* 37 (Spring 1971): 41–63.

Wheeler, Leslie, ed. *Loving Warriors: Selected Letters of Lucy Stone and Henry B. Blackwell, 1853–1893.* New York: Dial Press, 1981.

Whitehead, Fred. *The History of Radical Politics in America.* Chestertown, Md.: The Literary House Press, Washington College, 1995.

Whitehead, Fred, and Verle Muhrer, eds. *Freethought on the American Frontier.* Buffalo, N.Y.: Prometheus Books, 1992.

Whites, LeeAnn. *The Civil War as a Crisis in Gender: Augusta, Georgia, 1860–1890.* Athens: University of Georgia Press, 1995.

Willard, Elizabeth Osgood Goodrich. *Sexology as the Philosophy of Life.* 1867. Reprint, Buffalo, N.Y.: Heritage Press, 1974.

Willard, Frances E., and Mary Livermore. *A Woman of the Century.* Buffalo, N.Y.: Moulton, 1893.

Williams-Hogan, Jane K. "Swedenborg: A Biography." In *Swedenborg and His Influence.* Ed. Erland J. Brock et al. Bryn Athyn, Pa.: The Academy of the New Church, 1988. 3–27.

"The Woman's Fault." *Harper's Bazaar* 36 (Nov. 1902): 1021.

Wood, James L., and Maurice Jackson. *Social Movements: Development, Participation, and Dynanics.* Belmont, Calif.: Wadsworth Pub. Co., 1982.

Woodhull, Victoria C. *And the Truth Shall Make You Free: A Speech on the Principles of Social Freedom, Delivered in Steinway Hall, Monday, November 20, 1871.* New York: Woodhull, Claflin, and Co., 1871.

———. *Breaking the Seals; or, The Key to the Hidden Mystery, an Oration, Albany, New York, August 20, 1875.* New York: Woodhull and Claflin, 1875.

——— [Mrs. John Biddulph]. *Brief Sketches of the Life of Victoria Woodhull.* London: n.p., 1893.

———. *Carpenter and Cartter Reviewed: A Speech before the National Suffrage Associa-*

tion at Lincoln Hall, Washington, D.C., January 10, 1872. New York: Woodhull, Claflin, and Co., 1872.

———. *The Elixir of Life; or, Why Do We Die?* New York: Woodhull and Claflin, 1873.

———. *The Rapid Multiplication of the Unfit.* New York: The Women's Anthropological Society of America, 1891.

———. *Reformation or Revolution, Which? or, Behind the Political Scenes.* New York: Woodhull and Claflin, 1873.

———. *The Scarecrows of Sexual Slavery: An Oration Delivered at Silver Lake, Mass., Camp meeting, Aug. 17, 1873.* New York: Woodhull and Claflin, 1874.

———. *A Speech on the Garden of Eden; or, Paradise Lost and Found, Delivered at the Cooper Institute, New York City, December 30, 1875.* New York: Woodhull and Claflin, 1876.

———. *A Speech on the Great Social Problem of Labor and Capital, Delivered at Cooper Institute, NYC, 5/8/71, before Labor Reform League.* New York: Journeymen Printers' Co-Operative Assn., 1871.

———. *A Speech on the Impending Revolution.* New York: Woodhull and Claflin, 1872.

———. *A Speech on the Principles of Social Freedom.* New York: Woodhull, Claflin and Co., 1871.

———. *Tried as by Fire; or, The True and the False, Socially.* New York: Woodhull and Claflin, 1874.

Wright, Henry Clarke. *Marriage and Parentage; or, The Reproductive Element in Man.* Boston: Bela Marsh, 1854.

Wunderlich, Roger. *Low Living and High Thinking at Modern Times, New York.* Syracuse, N.Y.: Syracuse University Press, 1992.

Zaeske, Susan. "The 'Promiscuous Audience' Controversy and the Emergence of the Early Woman's Rights Movement." *Quarterly Journal of Speech* 81 (1995): 191–207.

Zboray, Ronald J. *A Fictive People: Antebellum Economic Development and the American Reading Public.* New York: Oxford University Press, 1993.

Ziegler, Valerie H. *The Advocates of Peace in Antebellum America.* Bloomington: Indiana University Press, 1992.

Index

Index

JOANNE E. PASSET is an assistant professor of history at Indiana University East. She is the author of *Cultural Crusaders: Women Librarians in the American West, 1900–1917* and coauthor, with Mary Niles Maack, of *Aspirations and Mentoring in an Academic Environment.*

Women in American History

The University of Illinois Press
is a founding member of the
Association of American University Presses.

Composed in 10.5/13 Adobe Minion
with Minion display
by Celia Shapland
for the University of Illinois Press
Designed by Dennis Roberts
Manufactured by Cushing-Malloy, Inc.

University of Illinois Press
1325 South Oak Street
Champaign, IL 61820-6903
www.press.uillinois.edu